DEBATES IN
INTERNATIONAL POLITICAL ECONOMY

Thomas Oatley
University of North Carolina at Chapel Hill

Longman

Boston   Columbus   Indianapolis   New York   San Francisco   Upper Saddle River
Amsterdam   Cape Town   Dubai   London   Madrid   Milan   Munich   Paris   Montreal   Toronto
Delhi   Mexico City   Sao Paulo   Sydney   Hong Kong   Seoul   Singapore   Taipei   Tokyo

Acquisitions Editor: Vikram Mukhija
Editorial Assistant: Toni Magyar
Marketing Manager: Lindsey Prudhomme
Production Coordinator: Scarlett Lindsay
Project Coordination, Text Design, and Electronic Page Makeup: GGS higher education
  resources, A division of PreMedia Global, Inc.
Cover Designer/Manager: John Callahan
Senior Manufacturing Buyer: Dennis J. Para
Printer and Binder: RR Donnelley & Sons Company/Harrisonburg
Cover Printer: RR Donnelley & Sons Company/Harrisonburg

For permission to use copyrighted material, grateful acknowledgment is made to the copyright
holders on pp. 371–372, which are hereby made part of this copyright page.

Library of Congress Cataloging-in-Publication Data

Oatley, Thomas H
  Debates in international political economy/Thomas Oatley.
    p. cm.
  ISBN-13: 978-0-205-74691-0
  ISBN-10: 0-205-74691-8
  1. International economic relations. 2. International finance. 3. Globalization.
4. Multinational corporations. I. Title.
  HF1359.O245 2010
  337—dc22   2009019117

Longman
is an imprint of

www.pearsonhighered.com

3 4 5 6 7 8 9 10—DOH—12 11 10 09

ISBN-13: 978-0-205-74691-0
ISBN-10:   0-205-74691-8

BRIEF CONTENTS

Preface ix

DETAILED CONTENTS

PREFACE

The American public was confronted by a bewildering array of complex and costly policy decisions in the fall of 2008. As the financial system buckled under the weight of the collapsing real estate market, the US government came under increasing pressure to develop an effective policy response to stem the crisis. Should the government bail out the financial industry? If so, should it bail out all lenders, or just some? Should the government help other large businesses, such as General Motors and Chrysler, which arguably were also hurt by the crisis? As the summer transitioned to fall it became clear that policymakers, and policy advisors, had different views about the appropriate government response. What is so evident in this crisis characterizes most important policy choices that governments confront. Rarely do important issues lend themselves to simple policy solutions that evoke unanimous agreement. Almost always policy questions are complex and associated with competing views about appropriate responses.

An undergraduate striving to understand the global economy must clear three hurdles. First, she must become familiar with a broad range of theories from both political science and economics that have been developed to study the global economy. Second, she must become familiar with the historical development of the global economic system. Third, she must become familiar with the issues and debates that are at the center of contemporary discussion among governments, international economic organizations, think tanks, and academics.

Existing textbooks and edited International Political Economy readers provide faculty with a wealth of options for material that promotes the development of core theoretical knowledge and historical background. Professors have fewer options when selecting a textbook that introduces students to contemporary issues and debates in the global economy. For this purpose, I suspect that most teachers rely on infrequently revised textbooks and a set of photocopied (or more commonly now, scanned or online) readings taken from some of the more policy-oriented journals. This book is intended to fill that niche by providing a set of articles that feature contemporary debates over enduring policy issues in the global economy.

FEATURES

This book's central pedagogical tool is reasoned debate between informed observers with distinct view points. Every chapter contains two articles that offer alternative and in most instances contending visions of policy solutions to pressing global economic problems. Each chapter contains a concise introduction that places the debate in a broader context and summarizes each article. Each introduction concludes with a few "Points to Ponder," questions that students can usefully keep in mind as they read through the chapter. The debate format encourages students to evaluate the quality of arguments and to see that most complex problems have more than one solution, and no single solution is obviously better than all others.

The chapters cover all of the major substantive areas of international political economy: the trade system, multinational corporations, developing countries, monetary and financial issues, and global governance. In addition, the book provides discussion of policy debates at the domestic and international levels. My selection of articles was governed by two concerns. I sought articles that focus on issues that are the subject of current debate and discussion, rather than focus on issues that are of largely historical interest. These current debates should be contemporary manifestations of enduring problems in the global economy. Consequently, most articles have been published recently, with few written and published prior to the year 2000.

NEW TO THIS EDITION

This second edition includes five brand new debates.

- Chapter 2 asks whether maintaining public support for trade liberalization requires expanded trade adjustment assistance or more ambitious redistribution.
- Chapter 3 examines the debate over migration.
- Chapter 8 examines the debate over Sovereign Wealth Funds.
- Chapter 10 explores the debate over Chinese exchange rate policy and the US trade deficit.
- Chapter 16 discusses the impact of the US financial crisis on global financial cooperation.

This edition also includes updated readings in chapter one's discussion of the impact of trade on manufacturing jobs, while chapter four's debate over preferential trade agreements as well as chapter nine's discussion of whether the euro will challenge the dollar, each contain two new readings. This edition thus updates fifteen of the thirty-two articles.

SUPPLEMENTS

Longman is pleased to offer several resources to qualified adopters of *Debates in International Political Economy* and their students that will make teaching and learning from this book even more effective and enjoyable.

For Instructors

MyPoliSciKit Video Case Studies Featuring video from major news sources and providing reporting and insight on recent world affairs, this DVD series helps instructors integrate current events into their courses by letting them use the clips as lecture launchers or discussion starters.

For Students

Longman Atlas of World Issues (0-321-22465-5) Introduced and selected by Robert J. Art of Brandeis University and excerpted from the acclaimed Penguin Atlas Series, the *Longman Atlas of World Issues* is designed to help students understand the geography and major issues facing the world today, such as terrorism, debt, and HIV/AIDS. These thematic, full-color maps examine forces shaping politics today at a global level. Explanatory information accompanies each map to help students better grasp the concepts being shown and how they affect our world today. Available at no additional charge when packaged with this book.

The Penguin Dictionary of International Relations (0-140-51397-3) This indispensable reference by Graham Evans and Jeffrey Newnham includes hundreds of cross-referenced entries on the enduring and emerging theories, concepts, and events that are shaping the academic discipline of international relations and today's world politics. Available at a discount when packaged with this book.

Research and Writing in International Relations (0-321-27766-X) Written by Laura Roselle and Sharon Spray of Elon University, this brief and affordable guide provides the basic step-by-step process and essential resources that are needed to write political science papers that go beyond simple description and into more systematic and sophisticated inquiry. This text focuses on the key areas in which students need the most help: finding a topic, developing a question, reviewing literature, designing research, analyzing findings, and last, actually writing the paper. Available at a discount when packaged with this book.

ACKNOWLEDGMENTS

This reader was strengthened by the very helpful comments I received from external reviewers, including

Gordon Bennett, *University of Texas*
Charles R. Boehmer, *University of Texas at El Paso*
John A. C. Conybeare, *University of Iowa*
Jonathon Crystal, *Fordham University*

Michelle Dion, *Georgia Institute of Technology*
William M. Downs, *Georgia State University*
Daniel Gibran, *Tennessee State University*
Peter B. Heller, *Manhattan College*
Ian Hurd, *Northwestern University*
Moonhawk Kim, *University of Colorado - Boulder*
Steven Livingston, *Middle Tennessee St. University*
Waltraud Queiser Morales, *University of Central Florida*
A. L. Morgan, *University of Tennessee*
Linda Petrou, *High Point University*
Strom Thacker, *Boston University*
Jaroslav Tir, *University of Georgia*

Finally, I owe my students a large debt for helping to convince me that sometimes one can grasp abstract theoretical concepts more easily by approaching them through the more familiar territory of contemporary issues and debates.

THOMAS OATLEY

PART I

INTERNATIONAL TRADE

International trade used to be obscure and uncontroversial. Governments would negotiate agreements in Geneva and nobody would pay them much attention. International trade has become substantially more controversial during the last fifteen years. The public and civil society now appear increasingly hostile toward trade and toward global trade institutions. Debates have emerged about whether trade and globalization more generally are good things for American workers. Debates have emerged about whether governments should liberalize trade exclusively through the World Trade Organization (WTO) or also through regional arrangements such as the North American Free Trade Agreement (NAFTA). Debates have emerged about whether global trade rules limit the ability of governments to achieve other desirable social objectives such as protecting the environment and safeguarding human and animal health. Part I examines these contemporary debates.

Chapter 1 explores the impact of international trade, and the U.S. trade deficit, on job destruction and job creation. Trade liberalization promotes specialization in production along the lines of comparative advantage. Societies that trade, therefore, should lose jobs in some sectors and create jobs in others. Robert Scott argues here that these labor market dynamics are compounded by the trade deficit the United States has run for more than twenty-five years. Focusing on the U.S.–China bilateral trade deficit, Scott argues that the excess of imports over exports results in net job reduction for the United States. Douglas Irwin challenges Scott's logic. He argues that the net job loss that may be attributed to the trade deficit is offset by net job creation attributable to foreign investment in the United States. For Irwin, therefore, trade, and even the trade deficit, does not affect how many jobs are available in the United States, but the kind of jobs available.

Chapter 2 examines how to maintain public support for trade given its impact on people employed in comparatively disadvantaged industries. Because trade eliminates jobs in some areas and creates jobs in others, some people must transition out of their current jobs to new work. In addition, the Stolper-Samuelson theorem tells us that trade also has some permanent redistributive consequences: It reduces the return to society's scarce factor. Hence, some people will earn less than they did previously. How can we best maintain public support for trade in the face of these labor market consequences? Howard Rosen argues that the best approach relies on a variety of instruments that retrain displaced workers and help them find new jobs in expanding sectors. Such "trade adjustment assistance" offers temporary support for people directly harmed by trade. Kenneth Scheve and Matthew Slaughter argue that trade adjustment assistance is inadequate. Instead of such exclusive reliance on short-term adjustment assistance, they call for permanent redistribution of income from those who clearly gain from trade to those who are made worse off.

Chapter 3 explores the debate over the free flow of people across borders. Whereas governments have greatly liberalized the cross-border flow of goods, services, technology, and capital, they continue to restrict the cross-border flow of people. Philippe LeGrain argues that governments should liberalize flows of people too. Migrants, he argues, may move to enhance their own position, but they end up providing substantial benefits to their host countries as well. The free flow of people, therefore, is a "win-win" situation. David Goodhart argues that governments should continue to restrict migration. Paying particular attention to the impact of migration to Great Britain from its former colonies, he argues that unfettered migration can weaken a society's cultural, linguistic, and political cohesion. He thereby highlights a tension between liberal commitment to social cohesion on the one hand and multicultural diversity on the other.

Chapter 4 considers the consequences of governments' current enthusiasm for preferential trade arrangements (PTAs). PTAs, which include free trade areas like the North American Free Trade Area and customs unions like the European Union, are trade-liberalizing affairs. Yet, debate exists about whether PTAs have a net positive or net negative impact on international trade. Dan Griswold argues that PTAs are a building block toward a world of global free trade. By this logic, governments will first eliminate all trade barriers within regional PTAs and then eliminate all trade barriers between regional PTAs. Jagdish Bhagwati argues that PTAs are a stumbling block to global free trade. He suggests that the preferential nature of PTAs introduces inefficiencies into the international trade system.

Chapter 5 discusses the impact of international trade and the international trade system on the environment. The central question under consideration is whether the rules that govern the international trade system undermine or constrain governments' efforts to protect the environment. Lori Wallach and Michelle Sforza assert that WTO rules force governments to dismantle existing environmental regulations, constrain their ability to implement new regulations, and vastly complicate efforts to create multilateral rules to protect the environment. Michael Weinstein and Steve Charnovitz argue that although the environmental movement may have lost many battles with the WTO, it has actually won the war. By this they mean that although in many very public cases the WTO favored trade over the environment, over time the WTO has become highly sensitive to the impact of trade and trade agreements on governments' environmental objectives.

CHAPTER 1

TRADE DEFICITS REDUCE TOTAL JOBS *v.* TRADE DEFICITS PRODUCE DIFFERENT JOBS

Trade Deficits Reduce Total Jobs

Advocate: Robert E. Scott

Source: The China Trade Toll, EPI Briefing Paper #219 (Washington, DC: Economic Policy Institute, 2008)

Trade Deficits Produce Different Jobs

Advocate: Douglas A. Irwin

Source: "The Employment Rationale for Trade Protection," in *Free Trade Under Fire* (Princeton, NJ: Princeton University Press, 2002), 70–90

The United States has run persistent trade and current account deficits since the early 1970s. These trade deficits mean that each year, residents of the United States purchase more goods and services from residents of other countries than they sell to residents of other countries. Between 1980 and 1999, the trade deficit averaged $94 billion per year. The deficit widened substantially to an average of $629 billion between 2001 and 2008.

Such persistent deficits raise a number of issues that have been at the center of policy debate during the last twenty years. What causes this trade imbalance? Does it reflect flaws or inequities in the international trade system, or does it instead reflect American domestic economic factors? What impact does the trade deficit have on the U.S. economy, especially on the jobs available to American workers? What policies might reduce the trade deficit?

TRADE DEFICITS REDUCE TOTAL JOBS

Some argue that the trade deficit is a consequence of multilateral and bilateral trade agreements that fail to limit unfair trade practices by the United States' trade partners. The World Trade Organization (WTO) does not prevent governments from implementing policies that enable their industries to prosper at America's expense. The resulting deficits eliminate jobs in the U.S. economy.

A commonly cited estimate suggests that between 1994 and 2000, the trade deficit eliminated close to 3 million jobs in the US.[1]

Robert E. Scott, an economist based at the Economic Policy Institute, embraces this framework to analyze the U.S. bilateral trade deficit with China. Scott attributes the bilateral trade deficit in large part to China's determination to keep its currency undervalued relative to the dollar and to the WTO's inability to prevent such policies. He estimates that the resulting bilateral trade deficit eliminated more than two million manufacturing jobs in the United States between 2001 and 2007.

TRADE DEFICITS PRODUCE DIFFERENT JOBS

Other analysts attribute the trade deficit to economic imbalances inside the United States. Americans have enjoyed a consumption boom during the last twenty-five years and have saved little. In addition, the U.S. government has run large budget deficits, which it must finance by borrowing. The trade deficit simply reflects these total expenditures relative to U.S. income. Moreover, the deficit does not eliminate jobs, as the foreign capital that finances the trade deficit creates new businesses that provide new jobs.

Douglas Irwin applies this lens to the U.S. multilateral deficit. He suggests that although a trade deficit does eliminate some jobs, the foreign investment that finances the deficit creates new jobs. Hence, the deficit merely changes the kind of jobs available. According to Irwin, the deficit is caused by an imbalance between U.S. savings and investment rates and has nothing to do with trade policy or tariffs. Irwin's analysis thus implies that the United States can engage in trade liberalization without concern that trade reduces the number of jobs available to American workers.

POINTS TO PONDER

1. What does Scott omit from his analysis that Irwin argues is a necessary component of a full accounting of the impact of the trade deficit on American jobs?

2. Irwin argues that the trade deficit has no net effect on the number of jobs in the U.S. economy. Does this mean that trade deficits have no impact on American jobs and American workers? Why or why not?

3. Suppose the Obama administration decided to enact policies to eliminate the trade deficit. What specific policy changes would Scott's analysis suggest? What specific policies would Irwin's analysis suggest? Which approach do you prefer, and why?

---

[1] Robert E. Scott, *Fast Track to Lost Jobs*, EPI Briefing Paper # 117 (Washington, DC: Economic Policy Institute, October 2001). Available at http://www.epi.org/content.cfm/bp117.

Robert E. Scott

The China Trade Toll

The growth of U.S. trade with China since China entered the World Trade Organization in 2001 has had a devastating effect on U.S. workers and the domestic economy. Between 2001 and 2007 2.3 million jobs were lost or displaced, including 366,000 in 2007 alone. New demographic research shows that, even when re-employed in non-traded industries, the 2.3 million workers displaced by the increase in China trade deficits in this period have lost an average $8,146 per worker/year. In 2007, these losses totaled $19.4 billion.[1]

The impacts of the China trade deficit are not limited to its direct effects on the jobs and wages of those displaced. It is also critical to recognize that the indirect impact of trade on other workers is significant as well. Trade with less-developed countries has reduced the bargaining power of all workers in the U.S. economy who resemble the import-displaced in terms of education, credentials, and skills. Annual earnings for all workers without a four-year college degree are roughly $1,400 lower today because of this competition, and this group constitutes a large majority of the entire U.S. workforce (roughly 100 million workers or about 70% of all workers, Bivens (2008)). China, with nearly 40% of our non-oil imports from less-developed countries, is a chief contributor to this wage pressure. . . .

A major cause of the rapidly growing U.S. trade deficit with China is currency manipulation. China has tightly pegged its currency to the dollar at a rate that encourages a large bilateral surplus with the United States. Maintaining this peg required the purchase of about $460 billion in U.S. treasury bills and other securities in 2007 alone.[2] This intervention makes the yuan artificially cheap and provides an effective subsidy on Chinese exports. The best estimates place this effective subsidy at roughly 30%, even after recent appreciation in the yuan (Cline and Williamson 2008).[3]

China also engages in extensive suppression of labor rights. An AFL-CIO study estimated that repression of labor rights by the Chinese government has lowered manufacturing wages by 47% to 86% (AFL-CIO 2006, 138). China has also been accused of massive direct subsidization of export production in many key industries (see, e.g., Haley 2008). Finally, it maintains strict, non-tariff barriers to imports. As a result, China's exports to the United States of $323 billion in 2007 were more than five times greater than U.S. exports to China, which totaled only $61 billion (Table 1.1). China's trade surplus was responsible for 52.3% of the U.S. total non-oil trade deficit

Table 1.1 U.S. China trade and job displacement, 2001–07

U.S. trade with China ($billions, nominal)

	2001	2006	2007	Changes in: ($billions) 2001–06	2006–07	2001–07	Percent change 2001–07
U.S. domestic exports[a]	$18.0	$51.6	$61.0	$33.7	$9.4	$43.1	240%
U.S. imports	102.1	287.1	323.1	185.0	36.0	221.0	217%
U.S. trade balance[b]	–84.1	–235.4	–262.1	–151.3	–26.6	–178.0	212%
Average annual change in the trade deficit				–30.0	–27.0	–30.0	21%

U.S. trade-related jobs supported and displaced (thousands of jobs)

	2001	2006	2007	Changes in: (thousands of jobs) 2001–06	2006–07	2001–07	Percent change 2001–07
U.S. domestic exports	166.7	425.7	482.3	259.1	56.5	315.6	189%
U.S. imports-jobs displaced	1,188.2	3,376.9	3,799.1	2,188.6	422.2	2,610.9	220%
U.S. trade balance–net jobs lost[b]	1,021.5	2,951.1	3,316.8	1,929.6	365.7	2,295.3	225%
Average annual job displacement				385.9	365.7	382.5	22%

[a]Domestic exports are goods produced in the United States. Total exports as reported by the Census Bureau include re-exports, i.e., goods produced in other countries and shipped through the U.S. Total exports were $12.8 billion in 1997, $19.2 billion in 2001, and 965.2 billion in 2007. U.S. re-exports to China rose from 2.1% of total exports in 1997 to 6.9% in 2007. The employment estimates shown here are based on domestic exports only.

[b]Domestic exports minus imports. This value is sometimes referred to as net exports, since re-exports are not included in this balance. Hence, the trade deficit reported here is slightly larger than the figure report by the Census Bureau.

SOURCE: EPI analysis of Census Bureau and BLS data.

in 2007, making the China trade relationship this country's most imbalanced by far. Unless China raises the real value of the yuan by an additional 30% and eliminates these other trade distortions, the U.S. trade deficit and job losses will continue to grow rapidly in the future.

While the overall U.S. trade deficit improved significantly in 2007, largely as a result of the 30% decline of the dollar against major currencies since 2002 (including a 44% fall against the euro), the U.S. deficit with China increased $26.6 billion, in large part because China allowed the dollar to fall only 12% against the yuan between 2002 and 2007. The annual increase in the U.S.-China trade deficit slowed from $31.6 billion in 2006 to $26.7 billion in 2007, reflecting both a decline in U.S. GDP growth (reducing import demand) and the initial effects of the stronger yuan. However, yuan appreciation was largely delayed until late 2007 and 2008—too little and too late to be of any help in slowing the current U.S.-China trade gap to date.[4] Furthermore, the appreciation of the yuan has had little effect on the prices of U.S. imports from China, which rose only 2.5% between July 2005 (when the yuan was first adjusted) and May 2008, much less than the 19% appreciation of the yuan in that period (Congressional Budget Office 2008, 2).

China's entry into the WTO was supposed to bring it into compliance with an enforceable, rules-based regime which would require that it open its markets to imports from the United States and other nations. The United States also negotiated a series of special safeguard measures designed to limit the disruptive effects of surging Chinese imports on domestic producers. However, the core of the agreement failed to include any protections to maintain or improve labor or environmental standards and, prior to 2007, the administration rejected all requests for special safeguards protection. As a result, China's entry into the WTO has further tilted the international economic playing field against domestic workers and firms and in favor of multinational companies from the United States and other countries as well as state- and privately owned exporters in China. This shift has increased the global "race to the bottom" in wages and environmental quality and closed thousands of U.S. factories, decimating employment in a wide range of communities, states, and entire regions of the United States. U.S. national interests have suffered while U.S. multinationals have enjoyed record profits on their foreign direct investments (Scott 2008).

False Promises

Proponents of China's entry into the WTO frequently claimed that it would create jobs in the United States, increase U.S. exports, and improve the trade deficit with China. President Clinton claimed that the agreement allowing China into the WTO, which was negotiated during his administration, "creates a win-win result for both countries" (Clinton 2000, 9). He argued that exports to China "now support hundreds of thousands of American jobs" and that "these figures can grow substantially with the new access to the Chinese market the WTO agreement creates" (Clinton 2000, 10). Others in the White House, such as Kenneth Liberthal, the special advisor to the president and senior director for Asia affairs at the National Security Council, echoed Clinton's assessment:

> Let's be clear as to why a trade deficit might decrease in the short term. China exports far more to the U.S. than it imports [from] the U.S. . . . It will not grow as much as it would have grown without this agreement and over time clearly it will shrink with this agreement.[5]

Promises about jobs and exports misrepresented the real effects of trade on the U.S. economy: trade both creates and destroys jobs. Increases in U.S. exports tend to create jobs in the United States, but increases in imports will lead to job loss—by destroying existing jobs and preventing new job creation—as imports displace goods that otherwise would have been made in the United States by domestic workers.

The impact of changes in trade on employment is estimated here by calculating the labor content of changes in the trade balance—the difference between exports and imports. Each $1 billion in computer exports to China from the United States supports American jobs. However, each $1 billion in computer imports from China displaces the American workers who would have been employed making them in the United States. On balance, the net employment effect of trade flows depends on the growth in the trade deficit, not just exports.

Another critically important promise made by the promoters of liberalized U.S.-China trade was that the United States would benefit because of increased exports to a large and growing consumer market in China. However, despite widespread reports of the rapid growth of the Chinese middle class, this growth has not resulted in a significant increase in U.S. consumer exports to China. The most rapidly growing exports to China are bulk commodities such as grains, scrap, and chemicals; intermediate products such as semiconductors; and producer durables such as aircraft. Furthermore, the increase in U.S. exports to China since 2001 has been overwhelmed by the growth of U.S. imports.

Growing Trade Deficits and Job Losses

The U.S. trade deficit with China has risen from $84 billion in 2001 to $262 billion in 2007, an increase of $178 billion, as shown in Table 1.1. Since China entered the WTO in 2001, this deficit has increased by $30 billion per year on average, or 21% per year.

While it is true that exports support jobs in the United States, it is equally true that imports displace them. The net effect of trade flows on employment is determined by changes in the trade balance.[6] The employment impacts of growing trade deficits are estimated in this paper using an input-output model that estimates the direct and indirect labor requirements of producing output in a given domestic industry. The model includes 201 U.S. industries, 84 of which are in the manufacturing sector.[7]

The model estimates the amount of labor (number of jobs) required to produce a given volume of exports and the labor displaced when a given volume of imports is substituted for domestic output.[8] The net of these two numbers is essentially the jobs lost due to growing trade deficits, holding all else equal.

Jobs displaced by the growing China trade deficit are a net drain on employment in trade-related industries, especially those in the manufacturing sector. Even if increases in demand in other sectors absorb all the workers displaced by trade (an unlikely event), it is likely that job-quality will suffer, as many non-traded industries such as retail trade and home health care pay lower wages and have less comprehensive benefits than traded goods industries.

U.S. exports to China in 2001 supported 166,700 jobs, but U.S. imports displaced production that would have supported 1,188,200 jobs, as shown in the bottom half of Table 1.1. Therefore, the $84 billion trade deficit in 2001 displaced 1,021,500 jobs in that year. Job displacement rose to 2,951,100 jobs in 2006 and 3,316,800 in 2007.

Since China's entry into the WTO in 2001 through 2007, the increase in U.S.-China trade deficits eliminated or displaced 2,295,300 U.S. jobs, as shown in the bottom half of Table 1.1. In the past year alone 365,700 jobs were lost, either through the destruction of existing jobs or by the prevention of new job creation. On average, 382,500 jobs per year have been lost/displaced since China's entry into the WTO.

Growth in trade deficits with China has reduced demand for goods produced in every region of the United States and has led to job displacement in all 50 states and the District of Columbia, as shown in Table 1.2. More than 200,000 jobs were lost in each of California and Texas and more than 100,000 each in New York, Illinois, Ohio, and Florida. Jobs displaced due to growing deficits with China exceeded 2.0% of total employment in 12 states including Idaho, New Hampshire, South Carolina, Oregon, California, Minnesota, Vermont, Texas, and Wisconsin as shown in Table 1.3. . . .

Growing trade deficits with China have clearly reduced domestic employment in traded goods industries, especially in the manufacturing sector, which has been hard hit by plant closings and job losses. Workers displaced by trade from the manufacturing sector have had particular difficulty in securing comparable employment elsewhere in the economy. More than one-third of workers displaced from manufacturing dropped out of the labor force (Kletzer 2001, 101, Table D2), and average wages of those who secured re-employment fell 11% to 13%.

Table 1.2 Net job loss due to growing trade deficits with China, ranked by number of job losses, 2001–07

State	Net job loss by state			State	Net job loss by state		
	2001–06	2006–07	2001–07		2001–06	2006–07	2001–07
California	270,400	55,400	325,800	Iowa	19,200	3,100	22,200
Texas	168,800	34,100	202,900	Arkansas	19,400	2,400	21,800
New York	105,700	21,300	127,000	Mississippi	19,100	2,700	21,700
Illinois	85,500	17,300	102,800	Utah	14,500	2,400	16,900
Ohio	85,800	17,000	102,700	Kansas	14,000	2,600	16,600
Florida	83,900	17,000	100,900	Louisiana	13,500	2,400	15,900
Pennsylvania	72,700	12,400	85,100	New Hampshire	13,400	2,300	15,700
North Carolina	67,400	12,400	79,800	Oklahoma	13,200	2,200	15,400
Michigan	67,300	12,300	79,500	Idaho	12,200	2,500	14,700
Georgia	62,000	11,500	73,600	Nebraska	10,200	1,700	12,000
New Jersey	56,400	11,400	67,800	Maine	10,300	1,400	11,700
Wisconsin	49,800	9,300	59,100	Nevada	9,100	1,600	10,700
Minnesota	49,300	9,400	58,700	Rhode Island	8,200	1,500	9,700
Massachusetts	48,800	9,600	58,400	New Mexico	8,000	1,500	9,400
Tennessee	45,900	8,800	54,700	West Virginia	6,300	900	7,200
Indiana	44,900	7,800	52,700	Vermont	5,500	1,000	6,500
Missouri	38,000	7,500	45,400	Delaware	3,900	700	4,600
Washington	38,000	6,900	44,900	South Dakota	3,800	600	4,400
Arizona	36,700	6,600	43,300	Hawaii	3,400	700	4,100
South Carolina	35,800	6,800	42,600	Montana	2,800	400	3,200
Virginia	33,200	6,300	39,500	North Dakota	2,300	400	2,700
Alabama	32,600	4,800	37,400	District of Columbia	2,000	400	2,400
Oregon	31,400	5,400	36,800	Alaska	2,000	300	2,300
Colorado	28,900	4,900	33,800	Wyoming	1,700	300	2,000
Kentucky	28,100	5,300	33,400				
Maryland	22,200	4,100	26,600	National total[a]	1,929,600	365,700	2,295,300
Connecticut	22,100	4,000	26,100				

[a] Totals vary slightly due to rounding errors.

SOURCE: EPI analysis of Census Bureau and BLS data.

Table 1.3 Net job loss due to growing trade deficits with China, ranked by share of state employment, 2001–07

	Net jobs lost	Share of total state employment in 2001 (%)		Net jobs lost	Share of total state employment in 2001 (%)
Idaho	14,700	2.59	Utah	16,900	1.56
New Hampshire	15,700	2.50	Connecticut	26,100	1.55
South Carolina	42,600	2.34	Colorado	33,800	1.52
Oregon	36,800	2.29	Iowa	22,200	1.51
California	325,800	2.23	Pennsylvania	85,100	1.50
Minnesota	58,700	2.18	New York	127,000	1.48
Vermont	6,500	2.15	Florida	100,900	1.41
Texas	202,900	2.13	Nebraska	12,000	1.30
Wisconsin	59,100	2.10	New Mexico	9,400	1.24
North Carolina	79,800	2.05	Kansas	16,600	1.23
Tennessee	54,700	2.03	South Dakota	4,400	1.16
Rhode Island	9,700	2.03	Virginia	39,500	1.12
Alabama	37,400	1.96	Delaware	4,600	1.10
Maine	11,700	1.92	Maryland	26,600	1.08
Mississippi	21,700	1.92	Oklahoma	15,400	1.03
Arizona	43,300	1.91	Nevada	10,700	1.02
Arkansas	21,800	1.89	West Virginia	7,200	0.98
Georgia	73,600	1.87	Louisiana	15,900	0.83
Ohio	102,700	1.85	North Dakota	2,700	0.82
Kentucky	33,400	1.85	Montana	3,200	0.82
Indiana	52,700	1.80	Wyoming	2,000	0.81
Massachusetts	58,400	1.75	Alaska	2,300	0.80
Michigan	79,500	1.74	Hawaii	4,100	0.74
Illinois	102,800	1.71	District of	2,400	0.37
New Jersey	67,800	1.70	Columbia		
Washington	44,900	1.66			
Missouri	45,400	1.66	National total[a] 2,295,300		

[a]Totals vary slightly due to rounding errors.
SOURCE: EPI analysis of Census Bureau and BLS data.

Some economists have argued that job loss numbers extrapolated from trade flows are uninformative because aggregate employment levels in the United States are set by a broad range of macroeconomic influences, not just by trade flows. However, while the trade balance is but one of many variables affecting aggregate job creation, the employment impacts of trade identified in this paper can be interpreted as the "all else equal" effect of trade on domestic employment. The Federal Reserve, for example, may decide to cut interest rates to make up for job loss stemming from deteriorating trade balances (or any other economic influence), leaving net employment unchanged. This, however, does not change the fact that trade deficits by themselves are a net drain on employment.

Further, even in the best-case scenario in which other jobs rise up one-for-one to replace those displaced by trade flows, the job numbers in this paper are a (conservative) measure of the involuntary job displacement caused by growing trade deficits and a potent indicator of imbalance in the U.S. labor market and wider economy. Economists may label it a wash when the loss of a hundred manufacturing jobs in Ohio or Pennsylvania is offset by the hiring of a hundred construction workers in Phoenix, but in the real world these displacements often result in large income losses and even permanent damage to workers' earning power (Bivens 2008). . . .

Conclusion

The growing U.S. trade deficit with China has displaced huge numbers of jobs in the United States and has been a prime contributor to the crisis in manufacturing employment over the past six years. Moreover, the United States is piling up foreign debt, losing export capacity, and facing a more fragile macroeconomic environment.

Is America's loss China's gain? The answer is most certainly no. China has become dependent on the U.S. consumer market for employment generation, has suppressed the purchasing power of its own middle class with a weak currency, and, most importantly, has held hundreds of billions of hard currency reserves in low-yielding, risky assets instead of investing them in public goods that could benefit Chinese households. Its vast purchases of foreign exchange reserves have stimulated the overheating of its domestic economy, and inflation in China has accelerated rapidly in the past year. Its repression of labor rights has suppressed wages, thereby artificially subsidizing exports.

The U.S-China trade relationship needs a fundamental change. Addressing the exchange rate policies and labor standards issues in the Chinese economy are important first steps.

The author thanks Lauren Marra and Emily Garr for research assistance and Josh Bivens for comments.

This research was made possible by support from the Alliance for American Manufacturing.

ENDNOTES

1. The $19.4 billion includes losses experienced by workers displaced by growing imports and net losses experienced by the movement of jobs from import-competing sectors to industries producing exports to China.

2. These purchases financed more than one-half of the U.S. $731 billion current account deficit (the broadest measure of all U.S. trade and income flows) in 2007. But for these purchases, the reduced demand would have put significant downward pressure on the U.S. dollar. A substantial depreciation in the dollar would begin to'improve the U.S. trade deficit within a few years.

3. The official name of the Chinese currency is the renminbi (RMB). The RMB is convertible for current account transactions but not for capital account flows. "Unlike the United States and many other countries, China uses a different word—yuan—for the unit in which product prices, exchange rates, and other such values are denominated from the word used for its currency" (Congressional Budget Office 2008, note 3). Hereinafter the word yuan will be used when referring to the Chinese exchange rate.

4. The trade balance usually responds to a fall in the dollar with a substantial lag of at least one to two years, due to "J-curve" effects. The major initial impact of a depreciation is usually to raise the price and total value of imports, and hence the trade deficit. In the medium- and long-term, the trade flows usually respond to the increase in the relative competitiveness of domestic products as the rate of growth of imports slows or imports decrease, and the rate of growth of exports accelerates, ultimately leading to an improvement in the trade balance for large currency adjustments. Most of the dollar adjustment against major currencies occurred between February 2002 and December 2004. For example, the dollar fell 36.4% against the euro in this period, and then fell only 4.0% between December 2004 and December 2007.

5. NewsHour With Jim Lehrer transcript. 1999. "Online NewsHour: Opening Trade - November 15, 1999." <http://www.pbs.org/newshour/bb/asia/july-dec99/wto_11-15. html>

6. Output (gross domestic product or GDP) is the sum of consumption, investment, government spending, and the trade balance. The trade balance is the sum of exports less imports. A declining trade balance lowers GDP. The growth of the U.S. trade deficit with China has therefore reduced U.S. GDP and the demand for labor. Holding all other sources of demand constant, growing trade deficits therefore reduce the demand for labor in the U.S.

7. See Scott (2006) for further details on the model and Ratner (2006) for a technical presentation and details on data sources used. This model has been completely updated for this study using new employment requirements tables for 2001 and related economic data from the Bureau of Labor Statistics (2008). Trade data collected by the U.S. Census Bureau was downloaded from the U.S. International Trade Commission (2008).

8. For the purposes of this report it is necessary to distinguish between exports produced domestically and re-exports—which are goods produced in other countries, imported into the United States, and then re-exported to other countries, in this case to China. Since re-exports are not produced domestically, their production does not support domestic employment and they are excluded from the model used here. See Table 1.1 for information about the levels of U.S. re-exports to China in this period.

REFERENCES

AFL-CIO, U.S. Representative Benjamin L. Cardin, and U.S. Representative Christopher H. Smith (AFL-CIO et al.). 2006. "Section 301 Petition [on China's repression of workers' rights]." June 8.

Bivens, L. Josh. 2008. Trade, Jobs, and Wages: Are the Public's Worries about Globalization Justified? Issue Brief No. 244. Washington, D.C.: Economic Policy Institute. http://www.epi.org.

Bureau of Labor Statistics, Office of Employment Projections. 2008a. Special Purpose Files—Industry Output and Employment. Washington, D.C.: U.S. Department of Labor. http://www.bls.gov/emp/empind2.htm.

Bureau of Labor Statistics, Office of Employment Projections. 2008b. Special Purpose Files—Employment Requirements. Washington, D.C.: U.S. Department of Labor. http://stats.bls.gov/emp/empind4.htm.

Cline, William R., and John Williamson. 2008. New Estimates of Fundamental Equilibrium Exchange Rates. Policy Brief #PB08–7. Washington, D.C.: Peterson Institute for International Economics.

Clinton, Bill. 2000. Expanding trade, protecting values: why I'll fight to make China's trade status permanent. New Democrat, Vol. 12, No. 1, pp. 9–11.

Congressional Budget Office. 2008. "How changes in the value of the Chinese currency affect U.S. imports." Washington, D.C.: Congress of the United States, Congressional Budget Office.

Faux, Jeff, Bruce Campbell, Carlos Salas, and Robert Scott. 2006. Revisiting NAFTA: Still not Working for North America's Workers. Briefing Paper. Washington, D.C.: Economic Policy Institute.

Haley, Usha C. V. 2008. Shedding light on energy subsidies in China: An analysis of China's steel industry from 2000–2007. Washington, D.C.: Alliance for American Manufacturing.

Kletzer, Lori G. 2001. Job Loss From Imports: Measuring the Costs. Washington, D.C.: Institute for International Economics.

Ratner, David. 2006. "Appendix: methodology and data sources." In Faux et al. 2006.

Scott, Robert E. 2006. "NAFTA's Legacy: Rising Trade Deficits Lead to Significant Job Displacement and Declining Job Quality for the United States." In Faux et al. 2006.

Scott, Robert E. 2008. Increase in Oil Prices, Fall in Investment Income Exacerbates Current Account Deficit Woes. Washington, D.C.: Economic Policy Institute. http://www.epi.org.

U.S. Census Bureau. 2008. "Basic Monthly Survey of the Current Population Survey (data for 2005–07)." Washington, D.C.: U.S. Department of Commerce.

U.S. International Trade Commission. 2008. USITC Interactive Tariff and Trade Data Web. http://dataweb.usitc.gov/scripts/user_set.asp

Douglas A. Irwin

The Employment Rationale for Trade Protection

Economic analysis has long established free trade as a desirable economic policy. This conclusion has been reinforced by mounting empirical evidence on the benefits of free trade, and yet protectionism is far from vanquished in the policy arena. Of course, this is nothing new: as Adam Smith observed more than two hundred years ago, "not only the prejudices of the public, but what is much more unconquerable, the private interests of many individuals, irresistibly oppose" free trade (Smith 1976, 471). Industries that compete against imports will always actively promote their own interests by seeking trade restrictions. But, as Smith acknowledges, the general public also has concerns about foreign competition. The argument that resonates most strongly with the public and with politicians is that imports destroy jobs. Is this an accurate view of trade as a whole? And if so, are import restrictions the remedy? . . .

Does Free Trade Affect Employment?

The claim that trade should be limited because imports destroy jobs has been trotted out since the sixteenth century (see e.g., Viner 1937, 51–52; Irwin 1996, 36ff). And imports do indeed destroy jobs in certain industries: for example, employment in the Maine shoe industry and in the South Carolina apparel industry is lower to the extent that both industries face competition from imports. So, we can understand why the plant owners and workers and the politicians who represent them prefer to avoid this foreign competition.

But just because imports destroy some jobs does not mean that trade reduces overall employment or harms the economy. After all, imports are not free: in order to acquire them a country must sell something in return. Imports are usually paid for in one of two ways: the sale of goods and services or the sale of assets to foreign countries. In other words, all of the dollars that U.S. consumers hand over to other countries in purchasing imports do not accumulate there, but eventually return to purchase either U.S. goods (exports) or U.S. financial assets (foreign investment). Both exports and foreign investment create new jobs: employment in export-oriented sectors such as farming and aircraft production is higher because of those foreign sales, and foreign investment either contributes directly to the national capital stock with new plants and equipment or facilitates domestic capital accumulation by reducing the cost of capital.

Thus, the claim that imports destroy jobs is misleading because it ignores the creation of jobs elsewhere in the economy as a result of trade. Similarly, while trade proponents like to note that exports create jobs, which is true, they generally fail to note that this comes at the expense of employment else-where. Export industries will certainly employ more workers because of the foreign demand for their products, but exports are used to purchase the very imports that diminish employment in other domestic industries.

Since trade both creates and destroys jobs, the pertinent question is whether trade has a net effect on employment. The public debate over NAFTA consisted largely of claims and counterclaims about whether it would add or subtract from total employment. NAFTA opponents claimed that free trade with Mexico would destroy jobs: the Economic Policy Institute put the number at 480,000. NAFTA proponents countered with the claim that it would create jobs: the Institute for International Economics suggested that 170,000 jobs would be created (Orme 1996, 107).

In fact, the overall impact of trade on the number of jobs in an economy is best approximated as zero. Total employment is not a function of interna-tional trade, but the number of people in the labor force. . . . Employment in the United States since 1950 has closely tracked the number of people in the labor force. And while there is always some unemployment, . . . this is determined by the business cycle, demographics, and labor market policies rather than changes in trade flows or trade policy. For example, unemploy-ment rose in the early 1980s and the early 1990s because the economy fell into recession, not because of the behavior of imports.

• • •

Yet there remains deep-seated inclination to frame the trade policy debate in terms of its impact on employment. This has motivated many attempts, how-ever futile, to quantify the overall employment effects of trade. Analysts at sev-eral Washington think tanks (both favorable and unfavorable to NAFTA) have settled upon the rule of thumb that every $1 billion in exports generates or supports thirteen thousand jobs (implying conversely that every $1 billion in imports eliminates thirteen thousand jobs) as a way of evaluating the employ-ment effects of trade agreements. Some NAFTA proponents argued that, because Mexico was to eliminate relatively high tariffs against U.S. goods while U.S. tariffs against Mexican goods were already very low, the agreement would generate more exports to than imports from Mexico. Using the rule of thumb, it was therefore reasoned that NAFTA would result in net job cre-ation. Anxious to sell NAFTA to a wary Congress, Mickey Kantor, the Clinton administration's trade representative, claimed that two hundred thousand jobs would be created by 1995 as a result of the agreement.[1]

Such formulaic calculations were publicized to fight the dire forecasts that thousands of jobs would be lost as a result of NAFTA. But even if tariff reductions are asymmetric, exports may not grow more rapidly than imports. Trade agreements themselves have little effect on any bilateral trade balance or the overall trade balance, as we will see shortly. And it is a mistake to think that changes in the trade balance translate into predictable changes in employment; a booming economy with low unemployment may be accompanied by a growing trade deficit because people have more money to spend on imports. Thus, any attempt to isolate the portion of the change in overall employment that is due to changes in trade is immediately suspect: it is bound to rest on implausible and arbitrary assumptions, and the predictions are ultimately unverifiable. In addition, stressing the positive employment effects of trade gives the false impression that achieving a higher level of employment is the principal motivation for pursuing more open trade policies. . . . The reason for pursuing more open trade policies is not to increase employment but to facilitate the more productive employment that comes with mutually beneficial exchanges that raise aggregate income.

• • •

Employment and the Trade Deficit

Does the trade deficit injure domestic industries and have adverse effects on employment? In every year since 1976, the value of goods and services imported into the United States has exceeded the value of goods and services exported. Should the trade deficit be a matter of concern and reversing it an objective for trade policy?[2]

The connection between the trade deficit and employment is more complex than the simple view that jobs are lost because imports exceed exports. . . . The correlation between the merchandise trade deficit and the unemployment rate is actually negative: the trade deficit has risen during periods of falling unemployment and has fallen during periods of rising unemployment. As noted earlier, the business cycle may be driving this relationship: a booming economy in which many people are finding employment is also an economy that sucks in many imports, whereas a sluggish economy is one in which expenditures on imports slacken.

A deeper understanding of the trade deficit, however, requires some familiarity with balance of payments accounting. Balance of payments accounting may be a dry subject, but it helps lift the fog that surrounds the trade deficit. That accounting also suggests which remedies are likely to be effective in reducing the deficit, should that be considered desirable.

The balance of payments is simply an accounting of a country's international transactions. All sales of U.S. goods or assets to nonresidents constitute a receipt to the United States and are recorded in the balance of payments as a positive entry (credit); all purchases of foreign goods or assets by U.S. residents constitute a payment by the United States and are recorded as a negative entry (debit). The balance of payments is divided into two broad categories of transactions: the current account, which includes all trade in goods and services, plus a few smaller categories; and the capital account, which includes all trade in assets, mainly portfolio and direct investments.

The first accounting lesson is that the balance of payments always balances. By accounting identity, which is to say by definition, the balance of payments always sums to zero. This implies that

Current account + capital account = 0.

Because the overall balance of payments always balances, a country with a current account deficit must have an offsetting capital account surplus. In other words, if a country is buying more goods and services from the rest of the world than it is selling, then the country must also be selling more assets to the rest of the world than it is purchasing.[3]

To make the link clearer, consider the case of an individual. Each of us as individuals exports our labor services to others in the economy. For this work, we receive an income that can be used to import goods and services produced by others. If an individual's expenditures exactly match his or her income in a given year, that person has "balanced trade" with the rest of the economy: the value of exports (income) equals the value of imports (expenditures). Can individuals spend more in a given year than they earn in income, in other words, can a person import more than he or she exports? Of course, by one of two ways: either by receiving a loan (borrowing) or by selling existing financial assets to make up the difference. Either method generates a financial inflow—a capital account surplus—that can be used to finance the trade deficit while also reducing the individual's net assets. Can an individual spend less in a given year than that person earns in income? Of course, and that individual exports more than he or she imports, thereby running a trade surplus with the rest of the economy. The surplus earnings are saved, generating a financial outflow—a capital account deficit—due to the purchase of financial investments.

What does this mean in the context of the United States? In 2000, the United States had a merchandise trade deficit of about $450 billion and a services trade surplus of $80 billion. The balance on goods and services was therefore a net deficit of about $370 billion, but owing to other factors (net income payments and net unilateral transfers) the current account deficit was nearly $435 billion, or 4.4 percent of that year's GDP. This implies that there must have been a capital account surplus of roughly the same magnitude. Sure enough, in that year U.S. residents (corporations and households) increased their ownership of foreign assets by just over $550 billion while foreigners increased their ownership of U.S. assets by over $950 billion. Therefore, the capital account surplus was approximately $400 billion. In other words, foreigners increased their ownership stake in U.S. assets more than U.S. residents increased their holdings of foreign assets, the mirror image of the current account deficit (Joint Economic Committee 2001, 36–37).

The balance of payments "balances" in the sense that every dollar we spend on imported goods must end up somewhere. Here's another way of thinking about it: in 2000, the United States imported almost $1,440 billion in goods and services from the rest of the world, but the rest of the world only purchased $1,070 billion of U.S. goods and services. What did the other countries do with the rest of our money? They invested it in the United States. In essence, for every dollar Americans handed over to foreigners in buying their goods (our imports), foreigners used seventy-five cents to purchase U.S. goods (our exports) and the remaining twenty-five cents to purchase U.S. assets. What assets are foreign residents purchasing? Some are short-term financial assets (such as stocks and bonds) for portfolio reasons; some are direct investments (such as mergers and acquisitions) to acquire ownership rights; and some are real assets (such as buildings and land) for the same reasons. . . .

In running a current account deficit, the United States is selling assets to the rest of the world. These foreign purchases of domestic assets allow the United States to finance more investment than it could through domestic savings alone. In essence, the United States is supplementing its domestic savings with foreign investment and thus is able to undertake more investment than if it had relied solely on domestic savings. The equation that expresses this relationship is

$$\text{Current account} = \text{savings} - \text{investment}.$$

Once again, this equation is an identity, meaning that it holds by definition. A current account deficit (the capital account surplus) implies that domestic investment exceeds domestic savings. Conversely, countries with current account surpluses have domestic savings in excess of domestic investment, the excess being used to purchase foreign assets via foreign investments (capital account deficit).

• • •

Because the United States is a net recipient of foreign investment, it is difficult to say much about the impact of the trade deficit on the number of jobs in the economy. The Economic Policy Institute, a Washington think tank aligned with organized labor, regularly issues reports stating that the trade deficit has destroyed American jobs. So why has the unemployment rate fallen during periods of large trade deficits? In recent years, [the Economic Policy Institute has] argued that job losses due to trade have been more than offset by job creation due to consumer spending and business investment (e.g., Scott and Rothstein 1998). And yet that higher business investment is made possible precisely because of foreign capital inflows, the flip side of the current account deficit. If the United States took action to reduce the trade deficit (supposedly reducing the number of jobs lost to trade), those capital inflows would necessarily fall. Then domestic investment would have to be financed by domestic savings, implying higher interest rates, which would reduce the number of jobs created by business investment. In the end, a lower trade deficit's positive impact on employment would be offset by the negative impact of lower domestic investment and higher interest rates.

• • •

So what are the implications for trade policy? The current account is fundamentally determined by international capital mobility and the gap between domestic savings and investment. The main determinants of savings and investment are macroeconomic in nature. Current account imbalances have nothing to do with whether a country is open or closed to foreign goods, engages in unfair trade practices or not, or is more "competitive" than other countries. If net capital flows are zero, the current account will be balanced. Japan's $11 billion current account deficit grew to an $87 billion current account surplus in 1987 not because it closed its market, or because the United States opened its market, or because Japanese manufacturers suddenly became more competitive in international markets. The surplus emerged because of financial and macroeconomic reasons in Japan and the United States.[4]

Trade policy cannot directly affect the current account deficit because trade policy has little influence on the underlying determinants of domestic savings and investment, the ultimate sources of the current account. If a country wishes to reduce its trade deficit, then it must undertake macroeconomic measures to reduce the gap between domestic savings and investment. . . .

REFERENCES

Hufbauer, Gary C. and Jeffrey J. Schott. 1993. NAFTA: An Assessment. Revised Edition. Washington, D.C.: Institute for International Economics.

Irwin, Douglas A. 1996. Against the Tide: An Intellectual History of Free Trade. Princeton: Princeton University Press.

Joint Economic Committee and Council of Economic Advisers. 2001. Economic Indicators (April).

Orme, William A. Jr. 1996. Understanding NAFTA: Mexico, Free Trade, and the New North America. Austin: University of Texas Press.

Scott, Robert E. and Jesse Rothstein. 1998. "American Jobs and the Asian Crisis: The Employment Impact of the Coming Rise in the U.S. Trade Deficit," Economic Policy Institute Briefing Paper, January.

Smith, Adam. 1976. An Inquiry into the Nature and Causes of the Wealth of Nations. Oxford: Clarendon Press.

Viner, Jacob. 1937. Essays on the Intellectual History of Economics. Princeton: Princeton University Press.

ENDNOTES

1. Hufbauer and Schott (1993, 14), for example, conclude that NAFTA and Mexican economic reforms "will create about 170,000 net new U.S. jobs in the foreseeable future. . . . Our job projections reflect a judgment that, with NAFTA, U.S. exports to Mexico will continue to outstrip Mexican imports to the United States."

2. To investigate the causes and consequences of the trade deficit, Congress set up the Trade Deficit Review Commission, which issued its report in November 2000. Unfortunately, the commission split along partisan lines. Democrats viewed the deficit as malign (a serious threat to employment in trade-affected industries), while Republicans viewed the deficit as benign (as reflecting the good state of the economy). The commission's report is available at http://govinfo.library.unt.edu/tdrc/index.html.

3. A country therefore cannot experience a "balance of payments deficit" unless one is using the old nomenclature that considers official reserve transactions (an important component of the balance of payments under fixed-exchange-rate regimes) as a separate part of the international accounts.

4. Japanese exporters became more price competitive in the U.S. market due to the appreciation of the dollar in the early to mid-1980s, but this appreciation was driven by capital flows into the United States. While trade policy cannot directly affect the current account deficit, the deficit does affect trade policy. A large trade deficit puts a competitive squeeze on both exporting and import-competing industries resulting mainly from the exchange rate appreciation that usually accompanies the rising deficit. This pressure fuels protectionist sentiment, as seen by the experience of the early and mid-1980s.

CHAPTER 2 RETRAIN WORKERS v. REDISTRIBUTE INCOME

Retrain Workers with Better Trade Adjustment Assistance Programs

Advocate: Howard F. Rosen

Source: Strengthening Trade Adjustment Assistance, Policy Brief #PB08-2 (Washington, DC: Peterson Institute for International Economics, January 2008)

Redistribute Income with a More Progressive Income Tax System

Advocate: Kenneth F. Scheve and Matthew J. Slaughter

Source: "A New Deal for Globalization," *Foreign Affairs,* July/August 2007: 34–47

The American public is increasingly anxious about participation in the global economy. Recent public opinion polls administered by the Pew Center found that almost half of the American population believes that participation in the World Trade Organization (WTO) and free trade agreements is bad for the country as a whole and for themselves individually.[1] More than 60 percent of the respondents stated that trade reduces American wages and eliminates jobs. Growing skepticism about the benefits of globalization have in turn made Americans reluctant to support additional trade liberalization through the WTO or free trade agreements and more receptive to protectionist measures.

The re-emergence of widespread protectionist sentiment has stimulated concern about whether the U.S. government can maintain its commitment to open trade. The fear that a protectionist public must ultimately generate protectionist governments has caused analysts to propose programs and policy changes that would transform a public skeptical of global markets into free trade supporters. Such proposals share a desire to use government policy to ease the negative impact of global economy on individual workers. Proposals differ on what policies are best suited to this purpose.

RETRAIN WORKERS WITH BETTER TRADE ADJUSTMENT ASSISTANCE PROGRAMS

One approach to ease the negative impact of global economy on workers involves the strengthening of programs specifically and narrowly directed at workers displaced by international trade. This approach rests on the assumption

---

[1]Pew Research Center for the People and the Press, "Obama's Image Slips, His Lead Over Clinton Disappears; Section 4: Trade and the Economy," May 1, 2008, http://people-press.org/report/?pageid=1295.

that public anxiety reflects falling job security in the face of international competition. Such anxieties may be eased by government programs that facilitate the transition to employment in expanding industries—programs known in the United States as Trade Adjustment Assistance.

Howard Rosen, a resident fellow at the Peterson Institute of International Economics, embraces this strategy. Rosen argues that American workers face more intense competition today than they have in the past. Their anxiety about this competition is lessened, he argues, when government programs help them acquire skills needed to find employment in the expanding higher technology industries. Thus, the appropriate response to public skepticism is an expansion of the trade adjustment assistance programs that help workers transition from declining to expanding industries.

REDISTRIBUTE INCOME WITH A MORE PROGRESSIVE INCOME TAX SYSTEM

Others suggest that American anxiety is driven by widening income inequality rather than uncertainty about job security. Income inequality in the United States has widened substantially during the last twenty-five years. Some portion of this greater inequality is a consequence of international trade. Those groups whose incomes have stagnated are increasingly skeptical about globalization because they perceive that its benefits accrue to a narrow segment of society. Shoring up public support for free trade therefore requires a more fundamental redistribution of income so that the gains from globalization are more broadly shared.

Matthew Slaughter and Kenneth Scheve develop an argument along precisely these lines. They suggest that growing public support for protectionism is a consequence of the rising income inequality. Moreover, they argue that trade adjustment assistance programs are too narrowly targeted to remedy the underlying problem. Building strong public support for globalization will require a substantial redistribution of income—the creation of what they call a "New Deal for Globalization."

POINTS **TO PONDER**

1. Rosen argues that Americans would be more supportive of free trade if the government strengthened trade adjustment assistance programs. Do you agree or disagree? Why?

2. Scheve and Slaughter argue that expanded trade adjustment assistance programs will do little to stem contemporary protectionism. Why do they believe this is the case? Do you agree or disagree?

3. Are trade adjustment assistance and income redistribution substitutes for or compliments to one another?

Howard F. Rosen

Strengthening Trade Adjustment Assistance

In 1962, when the United States was running a trade surplus, imports were barely noticeable, and manufacturing employment was increasing, Congress made a commitment to assist American workers, firms, and communities hurt by international trade, by establishing the Trade Adjustment Assistance (TAA) program. This commitment was based on an appreciation that despite their large benefits, widely distributed throughout the economy, international trade and investment could also he associated with severe economic dislocations. President John F. Kennedy best enunciated this commitment when he wrote,

> Those injured by trade competition should not be required to bear the full brunt of the impact. Rather, the burden of economic adjustment should he borne in part by the federal government. . . . [T]here is an obligation to render assistance to those who suffer as a result of national trade policy.[1]

More than 40 years later, with a trade deficit above 5 percent of GDP [gross domestic product], with imports as a percent of GDP five times what they were in 1962, and with manufacturing employment falling, this commitment is more important than ever before.

The U.S. economy is currently facing significant pressures from intensified domestic and international competition. There is no "magic bullet" to deal with the pressures from globalization. More worker training alone will not be sufficient to address the large adjustment burden placed on workers and their families. A comprehensive set of integrated efforts is necessary to help the economy adjust to the enormous pressures from globalization. These efforts should not be handouts, but rather targeted, yet flexible assistance aimed at raising productivity and enhancing U.S. competitiveness.

The TAA for Workers, TAA for Firms, and TAA for Farmers and Fishermen programs are part of this strategy. Although the impact of globalization on the U.S. economy calls for strengthening these programs, sound economic policies are the most important prerequisite for responding to the pressures from globalization. In that regard, TAA is a complement to trade policy, not a substitute for it.

Why Targeted Assistance for Those Affected by Globalization?

Assisting workers [to] move from declining, inefficient industries to growing, highly efficient industries, although painful to workers and their families, can contribute to increasing national productivity and raising living standards. Efforts aimed at encouraging this adjustment are central to any effort at enhancing U.S. competitiveness.

The benefits of international trade to the U.S. economy are large and widely distributed. One such study finds that international trade contributes approximately $1 trillion a year to the U.S. economy. These benefits are five times the estimated costs, primarily from job and earnings losses, associated with trade (Bradford, Grieco, and Hufbauer 2005).

Although the costs associated with opening the economy to increased international competition are significant to those incurring them, relative to the benefits and the size of the economy, they tend to be smaller and more highly concentrated. TAA is one means of sharing some of the benefits of trade with those workers and communities paying a heavy price for that policy. . . .

TAA for Workers

The TAA for Workers program is by far the largest of the three existing programs. In order to receive assistance, workers must show that they lost their jobs due to one of three criteria:

- an increase in imports;
- laid off from either an upstream or downstream producer; or
- a shift in production to another country.[2]

Each of these criteria must have "contributed importantly" to a firm's decline in production and sales. Table 2.1 presents the distribution of certified petitions by reason. In contrast to estimates made during the congressional debate over the 2002 reforms, the number of certified petitions related to shifts in production is much larger than the number of certified petitions for secondary workers.

Workers covered by certified petitions are currently eligible for the following assistance:

- 78 weeks of income maintenance payments, in addition to an initial 26 weeks of Unemployment Insurance (UI), if enrolled in training;
- all training expenses;
- a Health Coverage Tax Credit (HCTC), which provides a 65 percent advanceable, refundable tax credit to offset the cost of maintaining health insurance for up to two years;

Table 2.1 Distribution of certified petitions by reason, 2002–07

Grouping	2002	2003	2004	2005	2006	2007
Number of all petitions submitted	2,796	3,585	3,215	2,594	2,488	1,086
Number of workers covered by all petitions submitted	336,833	304,126	210,153	155,712	168,871	93,903
Percent of petitions certified	59	53	56	60	58	63
Percent of certified petitions due to increased imports	n.a.	47	55	55	53	46
Percent of certified petitions due to secondary workers	n.a.	8	9	6	8	9
Percent of certified petitions due to shifts in production	n.a.	30	36	39	39	44

n.a. = not available
SOURCE: U.S. Department of Labor.

- the Alternative Trade Adjustment Assistance (ATAA) program, commonly known as wage insurance, under which workers over 50 years old and earning less than $50,000 a year may be eligible to receive half the difference between their old and new wages, subject to a cap of $10,000, for up to two years;
- 90 percent of the costs associated with job search, up to a limit of $1,250; and
- 90 percent of the costs associated with job relocation, up to a limit of $1,500.

The TAA for Workers program has had a rocky history, including liberalization of eligibility criteria in 1974, cutbacks in assistance in 1981, and the establishment of a special program just for workers affected by trade with Canada and Mexico—i.e., the NAFTA-TAA for Workers program.[3] In 2002 Congress enacted the most expansive set of reforms in the TAA for Workers program since it was established. The reform . . . included:

- The TAA for Workers program and the NAFTA-TAA for Workers program were merged. The eligibility criteria and the assistance package under both programs were harmonized and unified in one program.
- Eligibility criteria were expanded to include workers who lost their jobs from companies producing inputs for goods that face significant import competition, and workers who lost their jobs due to shifts in production to countries with which the United States has a preferential trade agreement or "where there has been or is likely to be an increase in imports. . . ."[4]
- The HCTC was established.
- ATAA was established.
- The training appropriation cap was increased to $220 million.

- Income support payments were extended by 26 weeks to enable workers to be enrolled in training and receive income maintenance for up to two years.
- Workers undertaking remedial education can postpone their entry into the TAA for Workers program for up to six months.
- The amounts provided for job search assistance and relocation assistance were increased to keep up with inflation. . . .

ATAA and HCTC are two examples of how assistance under the TAA for Workers program has shifted from traditional income transfers to more targeted, cost-effective assistance. Despite the benefits associated with these new forms of assistance, however, enrollment in ATAA and the HCTC is disappointingly low. . . . Less than half of those TAA-eligible workers who visited one-stop career centers were even informed of the HCTC [GAO 2006]. A little over half of eligible workers were aware of the ATAA program.

Wage Insurance (ATAA)

Many workers who lose their jobs due to import competition and shifts in production pay a heavy price in terms or short- and long-term earnings losses. . . . Only two-thirds of dislocated workers from high import-competing industries find a new job within one to three years after layoff (Kletzer 2001). Of those workers reemployed, more than half experience no earnings loss or an improvement in earnings. Wage insurance is designed to assist the remaining 40 percent of dislocated workers. . . .

For example, the average weekly wage before layoff for workers displaced from high import-competing manufacturing industries was $402.97 between 1979 and 2001. Workers who found new jobs faced, on average, a 13 percent loss in earnings. Under the current wage insurance program, these workers would be eligible to receive an additional $5,532 for the first two years after reemployment, an 8 percent increase in their new wage.

Despite its benefits, wage insurance is not a perfect solution to addressing the costs associated with unemployment. The 26-week deadline for eligibility and the inability to enroll in training while receiving wage insurance are two examples of shortcomings in the current program. One option to address these problems would be to remove the 26-week requirement and allow workers to enroll in training while receiving wage insurance. A more ambitious proposal would be to enable workers, with the approval of their one-stop career counselor, to design a mix of income support, training, and wage insurance over a two-year period. The benefits of the program suggest that eligibility should also be expanded to those younger than 50 years old.

Health Coverage Tax Credit

The . . . average cost of health insurance for a family of four in 2006 was $11,500.[5] This equals 85 percent of the average amount of annual income support provided under the TAA for Workers program. For many workers, maintaining health insurance can be one of the largest, if not the largest, expense during unemployment. As a result many workers forgo health insurance. Unemployed workers and their families comprise a large share of the uninsured.[6]

The HCTC provides workers a 65 percent advanceable, refundable tax credit to offset the cost of maintaining health insurance for up to two years. The Internal Revenue Service (IRS) reports that since 2003, approximately 22,000 workers have used the credit, or about 500 to 600 new enrollees per month.[7] This constitutes only a small percentage of eligible workers. . . .

Of those workers who did not use the credit, the GAO [U.S. Government Accountability Office] found that between 50 to 82 percent of workers were covered by other health insurance—i.e., from a spouse. Forty-seven to 79 percent of respondents claimed that they could not afford to maintain their health insurance, despite the credit. Fifteen to 33 percent of workers found the credit too complicated.

. . . The IRS has implemented an outreach effort to inform each worker directly about the HCTC. Despite this effort, additional efforts appear necessary to ensure that all workers are aware of the credit. Congress should also consider raising the amount of the credit in order to make maintaining health insurance more affordable to unemployed workers and their families. Technical problems relating to waiting periods and health insurance options for workers not covered by their previous employer's health insurance need to also be addressed.

The Next Round of Reforms

For the most part, the 2002 reforms "fought the last battle" and did not fully address more recent economic developments, such as international outsourcing of services. In addition, several technical problems were discovered while implementing the 2002 reforms. Following are the major issues that still need to be addressed[8]:

Service Workers

The service sector is increasingly under pressure from outward shifts in investment and international outsourcing.[9] Based on its current interpretation of the statute, DOL [U.S. Department of Labor] denies assistance to workers who lose their jobs from the service sector. DOL argues that workers in the service sector do not produce items that are "similar or like an imported *good* (emphasis added)." Although the law does not specifically restrict TAA eligibility to workers employed in manufacturing industries per se, over the years DOL's interpretation of the law has de facto resulted in such a restriction. A recent GAO study finds that denying assistance to service-sector workers currently accounts for almost half of petition denials.[10]

In response to several recent appeals brought before the Court of International Trade, DOL recently announced that that it would consider petitions on behalf of software workers.

The statute governing the TAA for Workers program needs to be updated to explicitly cover workers who lose their jobs from service industries. A simple change in legislative language alone will not be sufficient to achieve this goal, since data do not currently exist to measure the importation of services. The administration and Congress may need to consider alternative methodologies for determining trade impact in order to adequately cover workers who lose their jobs in service industries.

Industry Certification

Petitions for TAA eligibility are currently filed according to firm-related layoffs, meaning that multiple petitions must be submitted by different groups of workers employed in the same firm as well as in the same industry. In an effort to streamline the petition process and remove arbitrary discrimination between workers from the same firm and industry, industrywide certification should be added to the existing firm-related layoff certification.

For example, if the apparel industry was found to experience a decline in employment related to an increase in imports or outward shift in investment, then any worker subsequently laid off from the industry over the next two years or so would be automatically eligible for TAA without needing to go through the bureaucratic petition process. . . .

Training Appropriations

Allocating training funds to states to meet the needs of workers has been a challenge to DOL under successive administrations. . . . On average, states spent or obligated 62 percent of their training allocations in 2006, with a large range among the states (GAO 2007a). The GAO found that 13 states spent less than 1 percent of their training allocation while 9 states spent more than 95 percent of their training funds in 2006 (GAO 2007b).

Currently, DOL allocates 75 percent of TAA training funds according to a formula based on states' spending over the previous two and a half years. Thus states that experience large layoffs in a subsequent year may receive an inadequate amount of training funds to meet the needs of all TAA-eligible workers. Conversely, states that experience large layoffs in previous years may receive more training funds than needed in a subsequent year. GAO also reported that DOL allocates a significant amount of funds at the end of the fiscal year, making it difficult for states to utilize those funds. Since existing legislation does not address this issue, DOL has complete discretion in setting the method by which training funds are allocated to the states.

The allocation of training funds desperately needs improvement. Currently, DOL makes two disbursements—one at the beginning and the other at the end of the year. One recommendation would be to increase the number of disbursements, spread out more evenly throughout the year, based on shorter look-back periods—i.e., six months.

Currently the law sets a global cap of $220 million for training expenditures under the TAA for Workers program. The gap is not adjusted for inflation, changes in the economy, or major plant closings. At a minimum, the training cap needs to be raised on a regular basis. Ways to better link the training appropriation to the needs of TAA-eligible workers should also be explored.

Health Coverage Tax Credit (HCTC)

GAO's survey of workers involved in five plant closings found that almost 70 percent of those workers without alternate health insurance reported that they could not afford to maintain their previous health insurance, despite the HCTC (GAO 2006). In a subsequent report, GAO estimated that even with the 65 percent tax credit, the cost of maintaining health insurance in four sample states was equal to approximately 25 percent of a worker's average monthly UI [unemployment insurance] payment. Although the HCTC appears to have been an important addition to the package of assistance provided to workers, the amount of the credit needs to be increased in order to enable more workers to use it.

Currently, workers must receive income maintenance (or participate in ATAA), which means that they must be enrolled in training, in order to be eligible to receive the HCTC. This restriction severely limits the number of displaced workers who can receive the credit. GAO found that this requirement has forced workers to both enroll in training and receive income maintenance payments or to apply for a training waiver.[11] Some argue that requiring a worker to undertake training promotes "real adjustment," while others contend that it results in workers getting expensive assistance that they may not need or want. One proposal would be to provide the HCTC to all TAA-certified workers for up to two years or until the worker finds a new job, regardless of enrollment in training.

Other technical issues concerning the HCTC, such as the waiting period before enrollment, require immediate attention.

Wage Insurance (ATAA)

The current program is restricted to workers over the age of 50. Although there is some evidence that older workers may have a harder time finding a new job, ATAA can potentially benefit all workers. It is a cost-effective means of cushioning the costs associated with taking a new job. The age requirement for ATAA should be lowered or even eliminated in order to make more workers eligible.

Self-Employed

Under the current program, workers are discouraged from pursuing self-employment. One option would be to continue providing income support, training, and possibly wage insurance to workers starting their own businesses.

Outreach

GAO has consistently found that many workers are unaware of the assistance provided by the TAA for which they are eligible (GAO 2006). This lack of awareness may help explain why program take-up rates are so low. DOL's outreach efforts seem inadequate. More resources need to be devoted to informing workers about TAA and other forms of assistance for dislocated workers. . . .

International Comparisons

. . . Currently, other industrialized countries are devoting many more resources to labor-market adjustment programs than is the United States (see Table 2.2). Relative to six other major industrialized countries, the United States spends the least on active labor-market adjustment programs, even after taking into account each country's unemployment rate. France and Germany each devote about five times more to their active labor-market programs than does the United States.

On the other hand, the Danish "Flexicurity" system, which is currently getting a lot of attention, is not a magic bullet. In addition to differences in hiring and firing policies, the Organization for Economic Cooperation and

Table 2.2 Spending on active labor-market adjustment programs

Country	As a percent of GDP all labor–market	Ratio of spending as a percent of GDP rate	As a percent of total spending on the unemployment programs
France	1.32	0.14	44.4
Germany	1.21	0.16	38.6
Canada	0.41	0.06	36.4
United Kingdom	0.37	0.07	40.0
Korea	0.31	0.08	66.9
Japan	0.28	0.06	34.2
United States	0.15	0.03	32.9

SOURCE: Organization for Economic Cooperation and Development, *Employment Outlook 2003*, data for 2000–2001.

Development estimates that Denmark spends eight times more public funds, as a share of GDP, on labor-market programs than the United States.[12] The Danes spend ten times more public funds, as a share of GDP, on training and five times more, as a share of GDP, on income support than the United States.

Conclusion

Public opinion surveys find that Americans are willing to support trade liberalization *if* the government assists those workers, firms, and communities adversely affected by trade and offshore outsourcing. Despite significant changes in the U.S. economy over the last 45 years, including an increase in import penetration and a decline in manufacturing employment, efforts to assist workers adversely affected by increases in imports and shifts in production have remained modest at best. Efforts to reform and expand the program in 2002 were extremely useful in breathing new life into that commitment. But implementation of those reforms has been uneven at best. More effort must be undertaken to ensure that all workers, firms, farmers, and fishermen receive the assistance they need.

Several pieces of legislation have already been introduced, and several others are likely to be introduced, to continue the efforts begun in 2002 to reform and expand TAA. These proposals include extending eligibility criteria to cover workers who lose their jobs from service industries, establishing a process for certifying entire industries, increasing the budget cap on training expenditures, and expanding the HCTC and wage insurance programs. Congress should seriously consider enacting these proposals.

The increased importance of international trade to the U.S. economy and the growing concern over economic dislocations would seem to make assistance to workers, firms, and communities facing these pressures a more pressing issue in 2006 than it was in 1962. Yet despite public support for this kind of assistance and rhetoric on the need to increase worker training, expanding labor-market adjustment programs remains a low priority in the United States. This needs to change if the United States wants to pursue a competitiveness strategy that increases productivity and raises living standards.

ENDNOTES

1. Special Message to Congress on Foreign Trade Policy, January 25, 1962. See Kennedy (1963).
2. Current law limits this eligibility to shift in production to countries with which the United States has a preferential trade agreement or from which there is a prospect of an increase in imports.

3. See Rosen (2006) for a more detailed discussion of the history of the TAA for Workers program.
4. Public Law 107-210, Section 113(a).
5. See the Henry J. Kaiser Family Foundation, *Employee Health Benefits: 2006 Annual Survey*, September 26, 2006.
6. US Census Bureau (2007). More than one-quarter of those workers without health insurance, aged 18 to 64, were not working.
7. The number of people covered by the HCTC rises to 37,000 when family members of TAA-eligible workers are included.
8. See Kletzer and Rosen (2005) for additional recommendations.
9. Alan Blinder (2006) recently estimated that as many as 42 million to 56 million jobs, or 30 to 40 percent of total U.S. employment, could be under pressure from possible offshoring. This estimate includes 14 million manufacturing workers and 28 million to 42 million nonmanufacturing workers, primarily workers employed in the service sector.
10. GAO (2007a). Many more workers may be discouraged from submitting petitions.
11. GAO (2006). Some states have issued training waivers in order for more workers to receive the HCTC.
12. Danish labor laws are more protective of workers than U.S. labor laws.

REFERENCES

Blinder, Alan. 2006. Offshoring: The Next Industrial Revolution? *Foreign Affairs* (March/April).

Bradford, Scott C., Paul L. E. Grieco, and Gary Clyde Hufbauer, 2005. The Payoff to America from Global Integration. In *The United States and the World Economy: Foreign Economic Policy for the Next Decade*, ed. C. Fred Bergsten and the Institute for International Economics. Washington: Institute for International Economics.

GAO (U.S. Government Accountability Office) 2006. *Trade Adjustment Assistance: Most Workers in Five Layoffs Received Services, but Better Outreach Needed on New Benefits*. GAO-06-43. Washington.

GAO (U.S. Government Accountability Office). 2007a. *Trade Adjustment Assistance: Changes to Funding Allocation and Eligibility Requirements Could Enhance States' Ability to Provide Benefits and Services*. GAO-07-701. Washington.

GAO (U.S. Government Accountability Office). 2007b. *Trade Adjustment Assistance: States Have Fewer Training Funds Available Than Labor Estimates When Both Expenditures and Obligations Are Considered*. Report to the Chairman, Subcommittee on Trade, Committee on Ways and Means, House of Representatives. Washington.

Kennedy, John F. 1963. *Public Papers of the Presidents of the United States, 1963*. Washington: Government Printing Office.

Kletzer, Lori G. 2001. *Job Loss from Imports: Measuring the Costs*. Washington: Institute for International Economics.

Kletzer, Lori G., and Howard F. Rosen. 2005. Easing the Adjustment Burden on US Workers. In *The United States and the World Economy: Foreign Economic Policy for the Next Decade,* ed. C. Fred Bergsten and the Institute for International Economics. Washington: Institute for International Economics.

Rosen, Howard E. 2006. Trade Adjustment Assistance: The More We Change the More It Stays the Same. In *C. Fred Bergsten and the World Economy,* ed. Michael Mussa. Washington: Institute for International Economics.

U.S. Census Bureau. 2007. *Income, Poverty and Health Insurance Coverage in the United States—2006.* Washington (August).

Kenneth F. Scheve and Matthew J. Slaughter
A New Deal for Globalization

Globalization has brought huge overall benefits, but earnings for most U.S. workers—even those with college degrees—have been falling recently; inequality is greater now than at any other time in the last 70 years. Whatever the cause, the result has been a surge in protectionism. To save globalization, policymakers must spread its gains more widely. The best way to do that is by redistributing income.

Wages Falling, Protectionism Rising

Over the last several years, a striking new feature of the U.S. economy has emerged: real income growth has been extremely skewed, with relatively few high earners doing well while incomes for most workers have stagnated or, in many cases, fallen. Just what mix of forces is behind this trend is not yet clear, but regardless, the numbers are stark. Less than four percent of workers were in educational groups that enjoyed increases in mean real money earnings from 2000 to 2005; mean real money earnings rose for workers with doctorates and professional graduate degrees and fell for all others. In contrast to in earlier decades, today it is not just those at the bottom of the skill ladder who are hurting. Even college graduates and workers with nonprofessional master's degrees saw their mean real money earnings decline. By some measures, inequality in the United States is greater today than at any time since the 1920s.

Advocates of engagement with the world economy are now warning of a protectionist drift in public policy. This drift is commonly blamed on narrow industry concerns or a failure to explain globalization's benefits or the war on terrorism. These explanations miss a more basic point: U.S. policy is becoming more protectionist because the American public is becoming more protectionist, and this shift in attitudes is a result of stagnant or falling incomes. Public support for engagement with the world economy is strongly linked to labor-market performance, and for most workers labor-market performance has been poor.

Given that globalization delivers tremendous benefits to the U.S. economy as a whole, the rise in protectionism brings many economic dangers. To avert them, U.S. policymakers must recognize and then address the fundamental cause of opposition to freer trade and investment. They must also recognize that the two most commonly proposed responses—more investment in education and more trade adjustment assistance for dislocated workers—are nowhere near adequate. Significant payoffs from educational investment will take decades to be realized, and trade adjustment assistance is too small and too narrowly targeted on specific industries to have much effect.

The best way to avert the rise in protectionism is by instituting a New Deal for globalization—one that links engagement with the world economy to a substantial redistribution of income. In the United States, that would mean adopting a fundamentally more progressive federal tax system. The notion of more aggressively redistributing income may sound radical, but ensuring that most American workers are benefiting is the best way of saving globalization from a protectionist backlash.

Rising Protectionism

U.S. economic policy is becoming more protectionist. First, consider trade. The prospects for congressional renewal of President George W. Bush's trade promotion authority, which is set to expire this summer, are grim. The 109th Congress introduced 27 pieces of anti-China trade legislation; the 110th introduced over a dozen in just its first three months. In late March, the Bush administration levied new tariffs on Chinese exports of high-gloss paper—reversing a 20-year precedent of not accusing nonmarket economies of illegal export subsidies.

Barriers to inward foreign direct investment (FDI) are also rising. In 2005, the Chinese energy company CNOOC tried to purchase U.S.-headquartered Unocal. The subsequent political storm was so intense that CNOOC withdrew its bid. A similar controversy erupted in 2006 over the purchase of operations at six U.S. ports by Dubai-based Dubai Ports World, eventually causing the company to sell the assets. The Committee on Foreign Investments in the United States [CFIUS], which is legally required to review and approve certain foreign acquisitions of U.S. businesses, has raised the duration and complexity of many reviews. Both chambers of the 109th Congress passed bills to tighten CFIUS scrutiny even further; similar legislation has already passed in the current House.

This protectionist drift extends to much of the world. The Doha Development Round of trade negotiations, the centerpiece of global trade liberalization, is years behind schedule and now on the brink of collapse. Key U.S. trading partners are becoming increasingly averse to foreign investment, as expressed both in their rhetoric (recent public pronouncements by the governments of France and Germany) and in their actions (new restrictions in China on foreign retailers).

At first glance, this rise in protectionism may seem puzzling. The economic gains from globalization are immense. In the United States, according to estimates from the Peter G. Peterson Institute for International Economics and others, trade and investment liberalization over the past decades has added between $500 billion and $1 trillion in annual income—between $1,650 and $3,300 a year for every American. A Doha agreement on global free trade in goods and services would generate, according to similar studies, $500 billion a year in additional income in the United States.

International trade and investment have spurred productivity growth, the foundation of rising average living standards. The rate of increase in output per worker hour in the U.S. nonfarm business sector has doubled in the past decade, from an annual average of 1.35 percent between 1973 and 1995 to an annual average of 2.7 percent since 1995. Much of the initial acceleration was related to information technology (IT)—one of the United States' most globally engaged industries, at the forefront of establishing and expanding production networks linked by trade and investment around the globe.

Gains from globalization have been similarly large in the rest of the world. China and India have achieved stupendous rates of productivity growth, lifting hundreds of millions of people out of poverty. Central to this success has been the introduction of market forces, in particular international market forces related to trade and FDI. In Chinese manufacturing, foreign multinational companies account for over half of all exports. And in the Indian IT sector, Indian and foreign multinational firms account for two-thirds of sales.

Freer trade and investment can also enhance other foreign policy goals. The Doha Round was launched shortly after 9/11 because of the view that global poverty is intimately linked to international insecurity and instability. The Doha Round was also intended to remedy the widespread perception that previous rounds of trade negotiations had treated poor nations unfairly by failing to open the very sectors—such as agriculture—whose openness would most likely help the world's poor. Accordingly, it is believed that a successful Doha agreement would enhance the United States' image and promote its interests around the world.

There are three common explanations for why protectionism is on the rise in the United States even though globalization is good for both the U.S. economy and U.S. security interests. None, however, are convincing. The first is that a narrow set of industries, such as agriculture and apparel manufacturing, have been harmed by freer trade and, in response, have lobbied hard to turn lawmakers against liberalization. But the incentives for these industries to oppose globalization have not changed in recent years, and there are also many industries that have benefited from, and thus lobbied for, further liberalization. What is new today is that special-interest protectionists are facing a more receptive audience.

The second explanation is that policymakers and the business community have failed to adequately explain the benefits of freer trade and investment to the public. But in fact, public-opinion data show the opposite: large majorities of Americans acknowledge these broad benefits. If anything, the public seems to understand certain benefits better than ever—for example, that its enjoyment of relatively affordable toys, DVD players, and other products depends on globalization.

Finally, there is the security explanation: that the need to balance economic interests with national security concerns has resulted in a more protectionist stance. This may help explain policy debates on certain issues, such as immigration. But generally, security concerns strengthen rather than weaken the case for further trade and investment liberalization, as long as such liberalization is viewed as fair to the developing world.

The Roots of Protectionism

The fundamental explanation is much simpler: policy is becoming more protectionist because the public is becoming more protectionist, and the public is becoming more protectionist because incomes are stagnating or falling. The integration of the world economy has boosted productivity and wealth creation in the United States and much of the rest of the world. But within many countries, and certainly within the United States, the benefits of this integration have been unevenly distributed—and this fact is increasingly being recognized. Individuals are asking themselves, "Is globalization good for me?" and, in a growing number of cases, arriving at the conclusion that it is not.

This account of rising protectionism depends on two key facts. First, there is a strong link between individuals' labor-market interests and their policy opinions about globalization. Second, in the past several years labor-market outcomes have become worse for many more Americans—and globalization is plausibly part of the reason for this poor performance.

Research on polling data shows that opinions about trade, FDI, and immigration are closely correlated to skill and educational levels. Less skilled Americans—who make up the majority of the U.S. labor force—have long led opposition to open borders. Workers with only high school educations are almost twice as likely to support protectionist policies as workers with college educations are.

This divide in opinion according to skill level reflects the impact that less skilled Americans expect market liberalization to have on their earnings. It also reflects their actual poor real and relative earnings performance in recent decades. It is now well established that income inequality across skill levels has been rising since (depending on the measure) the mid- to late 1970s and that the benefits of productivity gains over this time accrued mainly to higher-skilled workers. For example, from 1966 to 2001, the median pretax inflation-adjusted wage and salary income grew just 11 percent—versus 58 percent for incomes in the 90th percentile and 121 percent for those in the 99th percentile. Forces including skill-biased technological change played a major role in these income trends; the related forces of globalization seem to have played a smaller role—but a role nonetheless.

There are two important points about this link between policy opinions and labor-market skills and performance. One is that it does not simply reflect different understandings of the benefits of globalization. Polling data are very clear here: large majorities of Americans acknowledge the many benefits of open borders—lower prices, greater product diversity, a competitive spur to firms—which are also highlighted by academics, policymakers, and the business community. At the same time, they perceive that along with these benefits, open borders have put pressures on worker earnings.

Second, a worker's specific industry does not appear to drive his or her view of globalization. This is because competition in the domestic labor market extends the pressures of globalization beyond trade- and foreign-investment-exposed industries to the entire economy. If workers in a sector such as automobile manufacturing lose their jobs, they compete for new positions across sectors—and thereby put pressure on pay in the entire economy. What seems to matter most is what kind of worker you are in terms of skill level, rather than what industry you work in.

The protectionist drift also depends on worsening labor-market outcomes over the past several years. By traditional measures, such as employment growth and unemployment rates, the U.S. labor market has been strong of late. Today, with unemployment at 4.5 percent, the United States is at or near full employment. But looking at the number of jobs misses the key change: for several years running, wage and salary growth for all but the very highest earners has been poor, such that U.S. income gains have become extremely skewed.

Of workers in seven educational categories—high school dropout, high school graduate, some college, college graduate, nonprofessional master's, Ph.D., and M.B.A./J.D./M.D.—only those in the last two categories, with doctorates or professional graduate degrees, experienced any growth in mean real money earnings between 2000 and 2005. Workers in these two categories comprised only 3.4 percent of the labor force in 2005, meaning that more than 96 percent of U.S. workers are in educational groups for which average money earnings have fallen. In contrast to in earlier decades, since 2000 even college graduates and those with nonprofessional master's degrees—29 percent of workers in 2005—suffered declines in mean real money earnings.

The astonishing skewness of U.S. income growth is evident in the analysis of other measures as well. The growth in total income reported on tax returns has been extremely concentrated in recent years: the share of national income accounted for by the top one percent of earners reached 21.8 percent in 2005—a level not seen since 1928. In addition to high labor earnings, income growth at the top is being driven by corporate profits, which are at nearly 50-year highs as a share of national income and which accrue mainly to those with high labor earnings. The basic fact is clear: the benefits of strong productivity growth in the past several years have gone largely to a small set of highly skilled, highly compensated workers.

Economists do not yet understand exactly what has caused this skewed pattern of income growth and to what extent globalization itself is implicated, nor do they know how long it will persist. Still, it is plausible that there is a connection. Poor income growth has coincided with the integration into the world economy of China, India, and central and eastern Europe. The IT revolution has meant that certain workers are now facing competition from the overseas outsourcing of jobs in areas such as business services and computer programming. Even if production does not move abroad, increased trade and multinational production can put pressure on incomes by making it easier for firms to substitute foreign workers for domestic ones.

These twin facts—the link between labor-market performance and opinions on globalization and the recent absence of real income growth for so many Americans—explain the recent rise in protectionism. Several polls of U.S. public opinion show an alarming rise in protectionist sentiment over the past several years. For example, an ongoing NBC News/Wall Street Journal poll found that from December 1999 to March 2007, the share of respondents stating that trade agreements have hurt the United States increased by 16 percentage points (to 46 percent) while the "helped" share fell by 11 points (to just 28 percent). A 2000 Gallup poll found that 56 percent of respondents saw trade as an opportunity and 36 percent saw it as a threat; by 2005, the percentages had shifted to 44 percent and 49 percent, respectively. The March 2007 NBC News/Wall Street Journal poll found negative assessments of open borders even among the highly skilled: only 35 percent of respondents with a college or higher degree said they directly benefited from the global economy.

Given the lack of recent real income growth for most Americans, newfound skepticism about globalization is not without cause. Nor is it without effect: the change in public opinion is the impetus for the protectionist drift in policy. Politicians have an incentive to propose and implement protectionist policies because more citizens want them, and protectionist special interests face an audience of policymakers more receptive to their lobbying efforts than at any time in the last two decades.

Inadequate Adjustments

Because the protectionist drift reflects the legitimate concerns of a now very large majority of Americans, the policy debate needs fresh thinking. There is reason to worry even if one does not care about social equity. When most workers do not see themselves as benefiting from the related forces of globalization and technology, the resulting protectionist drift may end up eliminating the gains from globalization for everybody. Current ignorance about the exact causes of the skewed income growth is not reason for inaction. Policymakers may not be able to attack the exact source (or sources) and likely would not want to even if they could identify them, because doing so could reduce or even eliminate the aggregate gains from globalization.

Supporters of globalization face a stark choice: shore up support for an open global system by ensuring that a majority of workers benefit from it or accept that further liberalization is no longer sustainable. Given the aggregate benefits of open borders, the preferable option is clear.

Current policy discussions addressing the distributional consequences of globalization typically focus on the main U.S. government program for addressing the labor-market pressures of globalization—Trade Adjustment Assistance (TAA)—and on investing more in education. These ideas will help but are inadequate for the problem at hand.

The problem with TAA is that it incorrectly presumes that the key issue is transitions across jobs for workers in trade-exposed industries. Established in the Trade Act of 1974 (with a related component connected to the North American Free Trade Agreement), the program aids groups of workers in certain industries who can credibly claim that increased imports have destroyed their jobs or have reduced their work hours and wages. TAA-certified workers can access supports including training, extended unemployment benefits while in full-time training, and job-search and relocation allowances.

In short, TAA is inappropriately designed to address the protectionist drift. The labor-market concern driving this drift is not confined to the problem of how to reemploy particular workers in particular sectors facing import competition. Because the pressures of globalization are spread economy-wide via domestic labor-market competition, there is concern about income and job security among workers employed in all sectors.

Today many are calling for reform and expansion of TAA. For example, President Bush has proposed streamlining the processes of eligibility determination and assistance implementation to facilitate reemployment. This year, TAA is due to be reauthorized by Congress, and many legislators have proposed broadening the number of industries that are TAA-eligible. TAA improvements like these are surely welcome. But they alone cannot arrest the protectionist drift.

The idea behind investing in education is that higher-skilled workers generally earn more and are more likely to directly benefit from economic openness. The problem with this approach, however, is that upgrading skills is a process that takes generations—its effects will come far too late to address today's opposition to globalization. It took 60 years for the United States to boost the share of college graduates in the labor force from six percent (where it was at the end of World War II) to about 33 percent (where it is today). And that required major government programs, such as the GI Bill, and profound socioeconomic changes, such as increased female labor-force participation.

If the United States today undertook the goal of boosting its college-graduate share of the work force to 50 percent, the graduation of that median American worker would, if the rate of past efforts are any indication, not come until about 2047. And even this far-off date might be too optimistic. In the past generation, the rate of increase in the educational attainment of U.S. natives has slowed from its 1960s and 1970s pace, in part because college-completion rates have stalled. Rising income inequality may itself be playing a role here. Since 1988, 74 percent of American students at the 146 top U.S. colleges have come from the highest socioeconomic quartile, compared with just 3 percent from the lowest quartile. Moreover, even college graduates and holders of nonprofessional master's degrees have experienced falling mean real money earnings since 2000. If this trend continues, even completing college will not assuage the concerns behind rising protectionism.

Globalization and Redistribution

Given the limitations of these two reforms and the need to provide a political foundation for engagement with the world economy, the time has come for a New Deal for globalization—one that links trade and investment liberalization to a significant income redistribution that serves to share globalization's gains more widely. Recall that $500 billion is a common estimate of the annual income gain the United States enjoys today from earlier decades of trade and investment liberalization and also of the additional annual income it would enjoy as a result global free trade in goods and services. These aggregate gains, past and prospective, are immense and therefore immensely important to secure. But the imbalance in recent income growth suggests that the number of Americans not directly sharing in these aggregate gains may now be very large.

Truly expanding the political support for open borders requires a radical change in fiscal policy. This does not, however, mean making the personal income tax more progressive, as is often suggested. U.S. taxation of personal income is already quite progressive. Instead, policymakers should remember that workers do not pay only income taxes; they also pay the FICA (Federal Insurance Contributions Act) payroll tax for social insurance. This tax offers the best way to redistribute income.

The payroll tax contains a Social Security portion and a Medicare portion, each of which is paid half by the worker and half by the employer. The overall payroll tax is a flat tax of 15.3 percent on the first $94,200 of gross income for every worker, with an ongoing 2.9 percent flat tax for the

Medicare portion beyond that. Because it is a flat-rate tax on a (largely) capped base, it is a regressive tax—that is, it tends to reinforce rather than offset pretax inequality. At $760 billion in 2005, the regressive payroll tax was nearly as big as the progressive income tax ($1.1 trillion). Because it is large and regressive, the payroll tax is an obvious candidate for meaningful income redistribution linked to globalization.

A New Deal for globalization would combine further trade and investment liberalization with eliminating the full payroll tax for all workers earning below the national median. In 2005, the median total money earnings of all workers was $32,140, and there were about 67 million workers at or below this level. Assuming a mean labor income for this group of about $25,000, these 67 million workers would receive a tax cut of about $3,800 each. Because the economic burden of this tax falls largely on workers, this tax cut would be a direct gain in after-tax real income for them. With a total price tag of about $256 billion, the proposal could be paid for by raising the cap of $94,200, raising payroll tax rates (for progressivity, rates could escalate as they do with the income tax), or some combination of the two. This is, of course, only an outline of the needed policy reform, and there would be many implementation details to address. For example, rather than a single on-off point for this tax cut, a phase-in of it (like with the earned-income tax credit) would avoid incentive-distorting jumps in effective tax rates.

This may sound like a radical proposal. But keep in mind the figure of $500 billion: the annual U.S. income gain from trade and investment liberalization to date and the additional U.S. gain a successful Doha Round could deliver. Redistribution on this scale may be required to overcome the labor-market concerns driving the protectionist drift. Determining the right scale and structure of redistribution requires a thoughtful national discussion among all stakeholders. Policymakers must also consider how exactly to link such redistribution to further liberalization. But this should not obscure the essential idea: to be politically viable, efforts for further trade and investment liberalization will need to be explicitly linked to fundamental fiscal reform aimed at distributing globalization's aggregate gains more broadly.

Saving Globalization

Averting a protectionist backlash is in the economic and security interests of the United States. Globalization has generated—and can continue to generate—substantial benefits for the United States and the rest of the world. But realizing those broad benefits will require addressing the legitimate concerns of U.S. voters by instituting a New Deal for globalization.

In many ways, today's protectionist drift is similar to the challenges faced by the architect of the original New Deal. In August 1934, President Franklin Roosevelt declared:

> Those who would measure confidence in this country in the future must look first to the average citizen. . . .

This government intends no injury to honest business. The processes we follow in seeking social justice do not, in adding to general prosperity, take from one and give to another. In this modern world, the spreading out of opportunity ought not to consist of robbing Peter to pay Paul. In other words, we are concerned with more than mere subtraction and addition. We are concerned with multiplication also—multiplication of wealth through cooperative action, wealth in which all can share.

Today, such multiplication will depend on striking a delicate balance—between allowing globally engaged companies to continue to generate large overall gains for the United States and using well-targeted fiscal mechanisms to spread the gains more widely.

Would addressing concerns about income distribution make voters more likely to support open borders? The public-opinion data suggest that the answer is yes. Americans consistently say that they would be more inclined to back trade and investment liberalization if it were linked to more support for those hurt in the process. The policy experience of other countries confirms this point: there is greater support for engagement with the world economy in countries that spend more on programs for dislocated workers.

U.S. policymakers face a clear choice. They can lead the nation down the dangerous path of creeping protectionism. Or they can build a stable foundation for U.S. engagement with the world economy by sharing the gains widely. A New Deal for globalization can ensure that globalization survives.

CHAPTER 3 MIGRATION BRINGS ECONOMIC GAINS *v.* MIGRATION REDUCES CULTURAL COHESION

Dismantle Immigration Restrictions to Reap the Economic Gains

Advocate: Philippe LeGrain

Source: "The Case for Immigration," *The International Economy,* Summer 2007: 26–29

Restrict Migration to Maintain Societal Cohesion

Advocate: David Goodhart

Source: "Too Diverse?" *Prospect Magazine,* no. 95 (February 2004), http://www.prospect-magazine.co.uk/article_details.php?id=5835

Although the world's governments have greatly liberalized the cross-border flow of goods, services, technology, and financial capital, they continue to tightly restrict the flow of people. Indeed, government restriction on migration is perhaps the feature that most distinguishes contemporary globalization from the "first wave." In the late nineteenth and early twentieth centuries, approximately 60 million people migrated from Europe to Argentina, Australia, Brazil, Canada, and the United States. Most governments restricted inward migration following World War I and have continued to do so ever since.

In spite of government efforts to restrict migration, however, people have been migrating from less to more developed countries in large numbers. According to the International Organization for Migration, some 500,000 people migrated in 1960.[1] The number has grown steadily during the last forty years, and in the 2000–2005 period, the latest period for which data are available, 3.3 million per year moved from developing to developed countries. The re-emergence of substantial migrant flows has kindled a policy debate in the United States and in European countries.

---

[1] International Organization for Migration, *World Migration 2008: Managing Labour Mobility in the Evolving Global Economy* (Geneva: International Organization for Migration, 2008), 36.

DISMANTLE IMMIGRATION RESTRICTIONS TO REAP THE ECONOMIC GAINS

Proponents of liberalization focus on the economic benefits migration delivers. Foreign-born workers play an important role in their host economies. In the United States' case, they account for 15 percent of all workers and 40 percent of Ph.D. research scientists. They thus contribute to national income and they help raise productivity. Moreover, immigrants typically compliment rather than substitute for native workers. That is, immigrants do not take jobs from the local population. Instead, they help the native population produce more.

Philippe LeGrain, a British journalist, develops an argument along these lines. He argues that migration delivers clear economic benefits to the foreign-born workers and the native population. Such potential gains, he suggests, should convince governments to abandon their efforts to limit migration.

RESTRICT MIGRATION TO MAINTAIN SOCIETAL COHESION

Opposition to migration focuses on its potential negative economic and cultural consequences. Those who focus on possible negative economic consequences argue that immigrants take jobs from natives and push wages down. Those who focus on the cultural consequences voice concerns that the influx of large numbers of people with distinct cultural-linguistic traditions may undermine the social and cultural cohesiveness in the host country with eventual consequences for political cohesion. Examples might include the large North African community in France, the large Pakistani community in England, and the large Turkish population in Germany. The central question in each instance is the extent to which migrants, their children, and their grandchildren and the local population encourage assimilation that produces a cohesive society.

David Goodhart develops a variant of the cultural consequences argument by focusing on what he asserts is an inherent tension between the twin progressive values of risk sharing and multicultural diversity. Goodhart explores the degree to which migration to Great Britain from its former colonies (as well as migration to other West European societies from developing societies) is reducing the social cohesion required to foster public support for the welfare state. The "progressive dilemma," he argues, is that one value—a diverse multicultural society—might come at the expense of another value—a society in which individuals are willing to pay high taxes to insure each other from the risks associated with a market economy. He concludes that governments must restrict inward migration and encourage assimilation of new immigrants into the local culture—and thereby reduce diversity—to sustain social solidarity.

POINTS **TO PONDER**

1. What, according to LeGrain, are the principal benefits of migration?

2. Think of some other countries to which one can apply Goodhart's argument. What lessons, if any, might one draw from these cases that have relevance to the American case?

3. How do you balance the benefits from migration against the potential costs? Can you think of policy measures that might minimize the risk that migration will have the consequences Goodhart fears?

Philippe Legrain
The Case for Immigration

There is a contradiction at the heart of our globalizing world: while goods, services, and capital move across borders ever more freely, most people cannot. No government except perhaps North Korea's would dream of banning cross-border trade in goods and services, yet it is seen as perfectly normal and reasonable for governments to outlaw the movement across borders of most people who produce goods and services. No wonder illegal immigration is on the rise: most would-be migrants have no other option.

This is perverse. Immigrants are not an invading army: they are mostly people seeking a better life. Many are drawn to rich countries such as the United States by the huge demand for workers to fill the low-end jobs that their increasingly well-educated and comfortable citizens do not want. And just as it is beneficial for people to move from Alabama to California in response to market signals, so too from Mexico to the United States.

Where governments permit it, a global labor market is emerging: international financiers cluster in New York and London, information technology specialists in Silicon Valley, and actors in Hollywood, while multinational companies scatter skilled professionals around the world. Yet rich-country governments endeavor to keep out Mexican construction workers, Filipino care workers, and Congolese cooks, even though they are simply service providers who ply their trade abroad, just as American investment bankers do. And just as it is often cheaper and mutually beneficial to import information technology services from Asia and insurance from Europeans, it often makes sense to import menial services that have to be delivered on the spot, such as cleaning. Policymakers who want products and providers of high-skilled services to move freely but people who provide less-skilled services to stay put are not just hypocrites, they are economically illiterate.

From a global perspective, the potential gains from freer migration are huge. When workers from poor countries move to rich ones, they too can make use of advanced economies' superior capital and technologies, making them much more productive. This makes them—and the world—much better off. Starting from that simple insight, economists calculate that removing immigration controls could more than double the size of the world economy. Even a small relaxation of immigration controls would yield disproportionately big gains.

Yet many people believe that while the world would gain, workers in rich countries would lose out. They fear that foreigners harm the job prospects of local workers, taking their jobs or depressing their wages. Others fret that immigrants will be a burden on the welfare state. Some seem to believe that immigrants somehow simultaneously "steal" jobs and live off welfare.

Governments increasingly accept the case for allowing in highly skilled immigrants. The immigration bill before the Senate would tilt U.S. policy in that direction, establishing a points system that gives preference to university graduates. Such skills-focused points systems are in vogue: Canada and Australia employ one, Britain is introducing one, and other European countries are considering them.

For sure, as the number of university graduates in China, India, and other emerging markets soars in coming decades, it will be increasingly important for the United States to be able to draw on the widest possible pool of talent—not just for foreigners' individual skills and drive, but for their collective diversity.

It is astonishing how often the exceptional individuals who come up with brilliant new ideas happen to be immigrants. Twenty-one of Britain's Nobel Prize winners arrived in the country as refugees. Perhaps this is because immigrants tend to see things differently rather than following the conventional wisdom, perhaps because as outsiders they are more determined to succeed.

Yet most innovation nowadays comes not from individuals, but from groups of talented people sparking off each other—and foreigners with different ideas, perspectives, and experiences add something extra to the mix. If there are ten people sitting around a table trying to come up with a solution to a problem and they all think alike, then they are no better than one. But if they all think differently, then by bouncing ideas off each other they can solve problems better and faster. Research shows that a diverse group of talented individuals can perform better than a like-minded group of geniuses.

Just look at Silicon Valley: Intel, Yahoo!, Google, and eBay were all co-founded by immigrants, many of whom arrived as children. In fact, nearly half of America's venture capital-backed start-ups have immigrant founders. An ever-increasing share of our prosperity comes from companies that solve problems, be they developing new drugs, video games, or pollution-reducing technologies, or providing management advice. That's why, as China catches up, America and Europe need to open up further to foreigners in order to stay ahead.

Diversity also acts as a magnet for talent. Look at London: it is now a global city, with three in ten Londoners born abroad, from all over the world. People are drawn there because it is an exciting, cosmopolitan place. It's not just the huge range of ethnic restaurants and cultural experiences on offer, it's the opportunity to lead a richer life by meeting people from different backgrounds: friends, colleagues, and even a life partner.

Yet it is incorrect to believe that rich countries only need highly skilled immigrants, still less that bureaucrats can second-guess through a points system precisely which people the vast number of businesses in the economy need. America and Europe may increasingly be knowledge-based economies, but they still rely on low-skilled workers too. Every hotel requires not just managers and marketing people, but also receptionists, chambermaids, and waiters. Every hospital requires not just doctors and nurses, but also many more cleaners, cooks, laundry workers, and security staff. Everyone relies on road-sweepers, cabdrivers, and sewage workers.

Many low-skilled jobs cannot readily be mechanized or imported: old people cannot be cared for by a robot or from abroad. And as people get richer, they increasingly pay others to do arduous tasks, such as home improvements, that they once did themselves, freeing up time for more productive work or more enjoyable leisure. As advanced economies create high-skilled jobs, they inevitably create low-skilled ones too.

Critics argue that low-skilled immigration is harmful because the newcomers are poorer and less-educated than Americans. But that is precisely why they are willing to do low-paid, low-skilled jobs that Americans shun. In 1960, over half of American workers older than 25 were high school dropouts: now, only one in ten are. Understandably, high-school graduates aspire to better things, while even those with no qualifications don't want to do certain dirty, difficult, and dangerous jobs. The only way to reconcile aspirations to opportunity for all with the reality of drudgery for some is through immigration.

Fears that immigrants threaten American workers are based on two fallacies: that there is a fixed number of jobs to go around, and that foreign workers are direct substitutes for American ones. Just as women did not deprive men of jobs when they entered the labor force too, foreigners don't cost Americans their jobs—they don't just take jobs; they create them too. When they spend their wages, they boost demand for people who produce the goods and services that they consume; and as they work, they stimulate demand for Americans in complementary lines of work. An influx of Mexican construction workers, for instance, creates new jobs for people selling building materials, as well as for interior designers. Thus, while the number of immigrants has risen sharply over the past twenty years, America's unemployment rate has fallen.

But do some American workers lose out? Hardly any: most actually gain. Why? Because, as critics of immigration are the first to admit, immigrants are different to Americans, so that they rarely compete directly with them in the labor market: often, they complement their efforts—a foreign child-minder may enable an American nurse to go back to work, where her productivity may be enhanced by hard-working foreign doctors and cleaners—while also stimulating extra capital investment.

Study after study fails to find evidence that immigrants harm American workers. Harvard's George Borjas claims otherwise, but his partial approach is flawed because it neglects the broader complementarities between immigrant labor, native labor, and capital. A recent National Bureau of Economic Research study by Gianmarco Ottaviano and Giovanni Peri finds that the influx of foreign workers between 1990 and 2004 raised the average wage of U.S.-born workers by 2 percent. Nine in ten American workers gained: only one in ten, high-school dropouts, lost slightly, by 1 percent.

Part of the opposition to immigration stems from the belief that it is an inexorable, once-and-for-all movement of permanent settlement. But now that travel is ever cheaper and economic opportunities do not stop at national borders, migration is increasingly temporary when people are allowed to move freely. That is true for globe-trotting businessmen and it is increasingly so for poorer migrants too: Filipino nurses as well as Polish plumbers.

Britain's experience since it opened its borders to the eight much poorer central and eastern European countries which joined the European Union in 2004 is instructive. All 75 million people there could conceivably have moved, but in fact only a small fraction have, and most of those have already left again. Many are, in effect, international commuters, splitting their time between Britain and Poland. Of course, some will end up settling, but most won't. Most migrants do not want to leave home forever: they want to go work abroad for a while to earn enough to buy a house or set up a business back home.

Studies show that most Mexican migrants have similar aspirations. If they could come and go freely, most would move only temporarily. But perversely, U.S. border controls end up making many stay for good, because crossing the border is so risky and costly that once you have got across you tend to stay.

Governments ought to be encouraging such international mobility. It would benefit poor countries as well as rich ones. Already, migrants from poor countries working in rich ones send home much more—$200 billion a year officially, perhaps twice that informally (according to the Global Commission on International Migration)—than the miserly $100 billion that Western governments give in aid. These remittances are not wasted on weapons or siphoned off into Swiss bank accounts; they go straight into the pockets of local people. They pay for food, clean water, and medicines. They enable children to stay in school, fund small businesses, and benefit the local economy more broadly. What's more, when migrants return home, they bring new skills, new ideas, and capital to start new businesses. Africa's first internet cafés were started by migrants returning from Europe.

The World Bank calculates that in countries where remittances account for a large share of the economy (11 percent of GDP [gross domestic product] on average), they slash the poverty rate by a third. Even in countries which receive relatively little (2.2 percent of GDP on average), remittances can cut the poverty rate by nearly a fifth. Since the true level of remittances is much higher than official figures, their impact on poverty is likely to be even greater.

Remittances can also bring broader economic benefits. When countries are hit by a hurricane or earthquake, remittances tend to soar. During the Asian financial crisis a decade ago, Filipino migrants cushioned the blow on the Philippines' economy by sending home extra cash—and their dollar remittances were worth more in devalued Filipino pesos. Developing country governments can even borrow using their country's expected future remittances as collateral. Even the poorest countries, which receive $45 billion in remittances a year, could eventually tap this relatively cheap form of finance, giving them the opportunity of faster growth.

By keeping kids in school, paying for them to see a doctor, and funding new businesses, remittances can boost growth. A study by Paola Guiliano of Harvard and Marta Ruiz-Arranz of the International Monetary Fund finds that in countries with rudimentary financial systems, remittances allow people to invest more and better, and thus raise growth. When remittances increase by one percentage point of GDP, growth rises by 0.2 percentage points.

John Kenneth Galbraith said, "Migration is the oldest action against poverty. It selects those who most want help. It is good for the country to which they go; it helps break the equilibrium of poverty in the country from which they come. What is the perversity in the human soul that causes people to resist so obvious a good?"

Part of the answer is that people tend to focus their fears about economic change on foreigners. Other fears are cultural; more recently, these have [been] mixed up with worries about terrorism. Mostly, this is illogical: Christian Latinos are scarcely likely to be a fifth column of al Qaeda operatives, as Pat Buchanan has suggested. But logic scarcely comes into it. Psychological studies confirm that opposition to immigration tends to stem from an emotional dislike of foreigners. Intelligent critics then construct an elaborate set of seemingly rational arguments to justify their prejudice.

In Who Are We: The Challenges to America's National Identity, Harvard academic Samuel Huntington warns that Latino immigrants are generally poor and therefore a drain on American society, except in Miami, where they are rich and successful, at Americans' expense. Ironically, when he shot to fame by warning about a global "clash of civilizations," he lumped Mexicans and Americans together in a single civilization: now he claims that Latinos in the United States threaten a domestic clash of civilizations. He frets that Latinos have until recently clustered in certain cities and states, and then that they are starting to spread out. Immigrants can't win: they're damned if they do and damned if they don't.

Rich-country governments should not let such nonsense define their policies. Opening up our borders would spread freedom, widen opportunity and enrich the economy, society and culture. That may seem unrealistic, but so too, once, did abolishing slavery or giving women the vote.

David Goodhart

Too Diverse?

Britain in the 1950s was a country stratified by class and region. But in most of its cities, suburbs, towns and villages there was a good chance of predicting the attitudes, even the behavior, of the people living in your immediate neighborhood.

In many parts of Britain today that is no longer true. The country has long since ceased to be Orwell's "family" (albeit with the wrong members in charge). To some people this is a cause of regret and disorientation—a change which they associate with the growing incivility of modern urban life. To others it is a sign of the inevitable, and welcome, march of modernity. After three centuries of homogenization through industrialization, urbanization, nation-building and war, the British have become freer and more varied. Fifty years of peace, wealth and mobility have allowed a greater diversity in lifestyles and values. To this "value diversity" has been added ethnic diversity through two big waves of immigration: first the mainly commonwealth immigration from the West Indies and Asia in the 1950s and 1960s, followed by asylum-driven migrants from Europe, Africa and the greater middle east in the late 1990s.

The diversity, individualism and mobility that characterize developed economies—especially in the era of globalization—mean that more of our lives is spent among strangers. Ever since the invention of agriculture 10,000 years ago, humans have been used to dealing with people from beyond their own extended kin groups. The difference now in a developed country like Britain is that we not only live among stranger citizens but we must share with them. We share public services and parts of our income in the welfare state, we share public spaces in towns and cities where we are squashed together on buses, trains and tubes, and we share in a democratic conversation—filtered by the media—about the collective choices we wish to make. All such acts of sharing are more smoothly and generously negotiated if we can take for granted a limited set of common values and assumptions. But as Britain becomes more diverse that common culture is being eroded.

And therein lies one of the central dilemmas of political life in developed societies: sharing and solidarity can conflict with diversity. This is an especially acute dilemma for progressives who want plenty of both solidarity—high social cohesion and generous welfare paid out of a progressive tax system—and diversity—equal respect for a wide range of peoples, values and ways of life. The tension between the two values is a reminder that serious politics is about trade-offs. . . .

It was the Conservative politician David Willetts who drew my attention to the "progressive dilemma." Speaking at a round table on welfare reform (Prospect, March 1998), he said: "The basis on which you can extract large sums of money in tax and pay it out in benefits is that most people think the recipients are people like themselves, facing difficulties which they themselves could face. If values become more diverse, if lifestyles become more differentiated, then it becomes more difficult to sustain the legitimacy of a universal risk-pooling welfare state. People ask, 'Why should I pay for them when they are doing things I wouldn't do?' This is America versus Sweden. You can have a Swedish welfare state provided that you are a homogeneous society with intensely shared values. In the U.S. you have a very diverse, individualistic society where people feel fewer obligations to fellow citizens. Progressives want diversity but they thereby undermine part of the moral consensus on which a large welfare state rests."

. . . Thinking about the conflict between solidarity and diversity is another way of asking a question as old as human society itself: who is my brother? With whom do I share mutual obligations? The traditional conservative Burkean view is that our affinities ripple out from our families and localities, to the nation and not very far beyond. That view is pitted against a liberal universalist one which sees us in some sense equally obligated to all human beings from Bolton to Burundi—an idea associated with the universalist aspects of Christianity and Islam, with Kantian universalism and with left-wing internationalism. Science is neutral in this dispute, or rather it stands on both sides of the argument. Evolutionary psychology stresses both the universality of most human traits and—through the notion of kin selection and reciprocal altruism—the instinct to favor our own. Social psychologists also argue that the tendency to perceive in-groups and out-groups, however ephemeral, is innate. In any case, Burkeans claim to have common sense on their side. They argue that we feel more comfortable with, and are readier to share with, and sacrifice for, those with whom we have shared histories and similar values. To put it bluntly—most of us prefer our own kind.

The category "own kind" or in-group will set alarm bells ringing in the minds of many readers. So it is worth stressing what preferring our own kind does not mean, even for a Burkean. It does not mean that we are necessarily hostile to other kinds or cannot empathize with outsiders. (There are those who do dislike other kinds but in Britain they seem to be quite a small minority.) In complex societies, most of us belong simultaneously to many in-groups—family, profession, class, hobby, locality, nation—and an ability to move with ease between groups is a sign of maturity. An in-group is not, except in the case of families, a natural or biological category and the people who are deemed to belong to it can change quickly, as we saw so disastrously in Bosnia. Certainly, those we include in our in-group could be a pretty diverse crowd, especially in a city like London.

Moreover, modern liberal societies cannot be based on a simple assertion of group identity—the very idea of the rule of law, of equal legal treatment for everyone regardless of religion, wealth, gender or ethnicity, conflicts with it. On the other hand, if you deny the assumption that humans are social, group-based primates with constraints, however imprecise, on their willingness to share, you find yourself having to defend some implausible positions: for example that we should spend as much on development aid as on the NHS [National Health Service], or that Britain should have no immigration controls at all. The implicit "calculus of affinity" in media reporting of disasters is easily mocked—two dead Britons will get the same space as 200 Spaniards or 2,000 Somalis. Yet everyday we make similar calculations in the distribution of our own resources. Even a well-off, liberal-minded Briton who already donates to charities will spend, say, 200 on a child's birthday party, knowing that such money could, in the right hands, save the life of a child in the third world. The extent of our obligation to those to whom we are not connected through either kinship or citizenship is in part a purely private, charitable decision. But it also has policy implications, and not just in the field of development aid. For example, significant NHS resources are spent each year on foreign visitors, especially in London. Many of us might agree in theory that the needs of desperate outsiders are often greater than our own. But we would object if our own parent or child received inferior treatment because of resources consumed by non-citizens.

Is it possible to reconcile these observations about human preferences with our increasingly open, fluid and value-diverse societies? At one level, yes. Our liberal democracies still work fairly well; indeed it is one of the achievements of modernity that people have learned to tolerate and share with people very unlike themselves. (Until the 20th century, today's welfare state would have been considered contrary to human nature.) On the other hand, the logic of solidarity, with its tendency to draw boundaries, and the logic of diversity, with its tendency to cross them, do at times pull apart. Thanks to the erosion of collective norms and identities, in particular of class and nation, and the recent surge of immigration into Europe, this may be such a time.

The modern idea of citizenship goes some way to accommodating the tension between solidarity and diversity. Citizenship is not an ethnic, blood and soil concept but a more abstract political idea—implying equal legal, political and social rights (and duties) for people inhabiting a given national space. But citizenship is not just an abstract idea about rights and duties; for most of us it is something we do not choose but are born into—it arises out of a shared history, shared experiences, and, often, shared suffering; as the American writer Alan Wolfe puts it: "Behind every citizen lies a graveyard."

Both aspects of citizenship imply a notion of mutual obligation. Critics have argued that this idea of national community is anachronistic—swept away by globalization, individualism and migration—but it still has political resonance. When politicians talk about the "British people" they refer not just to a set of individuals with specific rights and duties but to a group of people with a special commitment to one another. Membership in such a community implies acceptance of moral rules, however fuzzy, which underpin the laws and welfare systems of the state.

In the rhetoric of the modern liberal state, the glue of ethnicity ("people who look and talk like us") has been replaced with the glue of values ("people who think and behave like us"). But British values grow, in part, out of a specific history and even geography. Too rapid a change in the make-up of a community not only changes the present, it also, potentially, changes our link with the past. As Bob Rowthorn wrote (Prospect, February 2003), we may lose a sense of responsibility for our own history—the good things and shameful things in it—if too many citizens no longer identify with it.

Is this a problem? Surely Britain in 2004 has become too diverse and complex to give expression to a common culture in the present, let alone the past. Diversity in this context is usually code for ethnic difference. But that is only one part of the diversity story, albeit the easiest to quantify and most emotionally charged. The progressive dilemma is also revealed in the value and generational rifts that emerged with such force in the 1960s. At the Prospect roundtable mentioned above, Patricia Hewitt, now trade secretary, recalled an example of generational conflict from her Leicester constituency. She was canvassing on a council estate when an elderly white couple saw her Labour rosette and one of them said, "We're not voting Labour—you hand taxpayers' money to our daughter." She apparently lived on a nearby estate, with three children all by different fathers, and her parents had cut her off. (Evidence that even close genetic ties do not always produce solidarity.)

Greater diversity can produce real conflicts of values and interests, but it also generates unjustified fears. Exposure to a wider spread of lifestyles, plus more mobility and better education, has helped to combat some of those fears—a trend reinforced by popular culture and the expansion of higher education (graduates are notably more tolerant than non-graduates). There is less overt homophobia, sexism or racism (and much more racial intermarriage) in Britain than 30 years ago and racial discrimination is the most politically sensitive form of unfairness. But 31 percent of people still admit to being racially prejudiced. Researchers such as Isaac Marks at London's Institute of Psychiatry warn that it is not possible to neatly divide the population between a small group of xenophobes and the rest. Feelings of suspicion and hostility towards outsiders are latent in most of us.

The visibility of ethnic difference means that it often overshadows other forms of diversity. Changes in the ethnic composition of a city or neighborhood can come to stand for the wider changes of modern life. Some expressions of racism, especially by old people, can be read as declarations of dismay at the passing of old ways of life (though this makes it no less unpleasant to be on the receiving end). The different appearance of many immigrants is an outward reminder that they are, at least initially, strangers. If welfare states demand that we pay into a common fund on which we can all draw at times of need, it is important that we feel that most people have made the same effort to be self-supporting and will not take advantage. We need to be reassured that strangers, especially those from other countries, have the same idea of reciprocity as we do. Absorbing outsiders into a community worthy of the name takes time.

Negotiating the tension between solidarity and diversity is at the heart of politics. But both left and right have, for different reasons, downplayed the issue. The left is reluctant to acknowledge a conflict between values it cherishes; it is ready to stress the erosion of community from "bad" forms of diversity such as market individualism but not from "good" forms of diversity such as sexual freedom and immigration. And the right, in Britain at least, has sidestepped the conflict, partly because it is less interested in solidarity than the left, but also because it is still trying to prove that it is comfortable with diversity.

But is there any hard evidence that the progressive dilemma actually exists in the real world of political and social choices? In most EU [European Union] states the percentage of GDP [gross domestic product] taken in tax is still at historically high levels, despite the increase in diversity of all kinds. Yet it is also true that Scandinavian countries with the biggest welfare states have been the most socially and ethnically homogeneous states in the west. By the same token the welfare state has always been weaker in the individualistic, ethnically divided U.S. compared with more homogeneous Europe. And the three bursts of welfarist legislation that the US did see—Franklin Roosevelt's New Deal, Harry Truman's Fair Deal and Lyndon Johnson's Great Society—came during the long pause in mass immigration between the first world war and 1968. (They were also, clearly, a response to the depression and two world wars.)

In their 2001 Harvard Institute of Economic Research paper "Why Doesn't the U.S. Have a European-style Welfare State?" Alberto Alesina, Edward Glaeser and Bruce Sacerdote argue that the answer is that too many people at the bottom of the pile in the U.S. are black or Hispanic. Across the U.S. as a whole, 70 percent of the population are non-Hispanic whites—but of those in poverty only 46 percent are non-Hispanic whites. So a disproportionate amount of tax income spent on welfare is going to minorities. The paper also finds that U.S. states that are more ethnically fragmented than average spend less on social services. The authors conclude that Americans think of the poor as members of a different group, whereas Europeans still think of the poor as members of the same group. Robert Putnam, the analyst of social capital, has also found a link between high ethnic mix and low trust in the U.S. There is some British evidence supporting this link too. Researchers at Mori found that the average level of satisfaction with local authorities declines steeply as the extent of ethnic fragmentation increases. Even allowing for the fact that areas of high ethnic mix tend to be poorer, Mori found that ethnic fractionalization still had a substantial negative impact on attitudes to local government.

Finally, Sweden and Denmark may provide a social laboratory for the solidarity/diversity trade-off in the coming years. Starting from similar positions as homogeneous countries with high levels of redistribution, they have taken rather different approaches to immigration over the past few years. Although both countries place great stress on integrating outsiders, Sweden has adopted a moderately multicultural outlook. It has also adapted its economy somewhat, reducing job protection for older native males in order to create more low-wage jobs for immigrants in the public sector. About 12 percent of Swedes are now foreign-born and it is expected that by 2015 about 25 percent of under-18s will be either foreign-born or the children of the foreign-born. This is a radical change and Sweden is adapting to it rather well (the first clips of mourning Swedes after Anna Lindh's murder were of crying immigrants expressing their sorrow in perfect Swedish). But not all Swedes are happy about it.

Denmark has a more restrictive and "nativist" approach to immigration. Only 6 percent of the population is foreign-born and native Danes enjoy superior welfare benefits to incomers. If the solidarity/diversity trade-off is a real one and current trends continue, then one would expect in, say, 20 years' time that Sweden will have a less redistributive welfare state than Denmark; or rather that Denmark will have a more developed two-tier welfare state with higher benefits for insiders, while Sweden will have a universal but less generous system.

What are the main objections, at least from the left, to this argument about solidarity and diversity? Multiculturalists stress Britain's multiple diversities, of class and region, which preceded recent waves of immigration. They also argue that all humans share similar needs and a common interest in ensuring they are met with minimum conflict; this, they say, can now be done through human rights laws. And hostility to diversity, they conclude, is usually a form of "false consciousness."

Critics of the dilemma also say, rightly, that the moral norms underpinning a community need not be hard for outsiders to comply with: broad common standards of right and wrong, some agreement on the nature of marriage and the family, respect for law, and some consensus about the role of religion in public life. Moreover, they add, there are places such as Canada (even Australia) which are happily combining European-style welfare with an officially multicultural politics. London, too, has U.S. levels of ethnic diversity but is the most left-wing part of Britain. . . .

A further point made by the multiculturalists is more telling. They argue that a single national story is not a sound base for a common culture because it has always been contested by class, region and religion. In Britain, the left traces democracy back to the peasants' revolt, the right back to Magna Carta, and so on. But while that is true, it is also the case that these different stories refer to a shared history. This does not imply a single narrative or national identity any more than a husband and wife will describe their married life together in the same way. Nor does it mean that the stress on the binding force of a shared history (or historical institutions like parliament) condemns immigrants to a second-class citizenship. Newcomers can and should adopt the history of their new country as well as, over time, contributing to it—moving from immigrant "them" to citizen "us." Helpfully, Britain's story includes, through empire, the story of many of our immigrant groups—empire soldiers, for example, fought in many of the wars that created modern Britain.

I would add a further qualification to the progressive dilemma. Attitudes to welfare have, for many people, become more instrumental: I pay so much in, the state gives me this in return. As we grow richer the ties that used to bind workers together in a risk-pooling welfare state (first locally, later nationally) have loosened—"generosity" is more abstract and compulsory, a matter of enlightened self-interest rather than mutual obligation. Moreover, welfare is less redistributive than most people imagine—most of the tax paid out by citizens comes back to them in one form or another so the amount of the average person's income going to someone they might consider undeserving is small. This, however, does little to allay anxieties based on perceptions rather than fiscal truths. And poor whites, who have relatively little, are more likely to resent even small transfers compared with those on higher incomes.

Despite these qualifications it still seems to me that those who value solidarity should take care that it is not eroded by a refusal to acknowledge the constraints upon it. The politician who has recently laid most stress on those constraints, especially in relation to immigration, is the home secretary, David Blunkett. He has spoken about the need for more integration of some immigrant communities—especially Muslim ones—while continuing to welcome high levels of net immigration into Britain of over 150,000 a year.

Supporters of large-scale immigration now focus on the quantifiable economic benefits, appealing to the self-interest rather than the idealism of the host population. While it is true that some immigration is beneficial—neither the NHS nor the building industry could survive without it—many of the claimed benefits of mass immigration are challenged by economists such as Adair Turner and Richard Layard. . . .

But large-scale immigration, especially if it happens rapidly, is not just about economics; it is about those less tangible things to do with identity and mutual obligation—which have been eroded from other directions too. It can also create real—as opposed to just imagined—conflicts of interest. One example is the immigration-related struggles over public housing in many of Britain's big cities in the 1970s and 1980s. In places like London's east end the right to a decent council house had always been regarded as part of the inheritance of the respectable working class. When immigrants began to arrive in the 1960s they did not have the contacts to get on the housing list and so often ended up in low quality private housing. Many people saw the injustice of this and decided to change the rules: henceforth the criterion of universal need came to supplant good contacts. So if a Bangladeshi couple with children were in poor accommodation they would qualify for a certain number of housing points, allowing them to jump ahead of young local white couples who had been on the list for years. This was, of course, unpopular with many whites. Similar clashes between group based notions of justice and universally applied human rights are unavoidable in welfare states with increasingly diverse people.

The "thickest" solidarities are now often found among ethnic minority groups themselves in response to real or perceived discrimination. This can be another source of resentment for poor whites who look on enviously from their own fragmented neighborhoods as minorities recreate some of the mutual support and sense of community that was once a feature of British working-class life. Paradoxically, it may be this erosion of feelings of mutuality among the white majority in Britain that has made it easier to absorb minorities. The degree of antagonism between groups is proportional to the degree of co-operation within groups. Relative to the other big European nations, the British sense of national culture and solidarity has arguably been rather weak—diluted by class, empire, the four different nations within the state, the north-south divide, and even the long shadow of American culture. That weakness of national solidarity, exemplified by the "stand-offishness" of suburban England, may have created a bulwark against extreme nationalism. We are more tolerant than, say, France because we don't care enough about each other to resent the arrival of the other.

When solidarity and diversity pull against each other, which side should public policy favor? Diversity can increasingly look after itself—the underlying drift of social and economic development favors it. Solidarity, on the other hand, thrives at times of adversity, hence its high point just after the second world war and its steady decline ever since as affluence, mobility, value diversity and (in some areas) immigration have loosened the ties of a common culture. Public policy should therefore tend to favor solidarity in four broad areas.

Immigration and Asylum

About 9 percent of British residents are now from ethnic minorities, rising to almost one third in London. On current trends about one fifth of the population will come from an ethnic minority by 2050, albeit many of them fourth or fifth generation. Thanks to the race riots in northern English towns in 2001, the fear of radical Islam after 9/11, and anxieties about the rise in asylum-led immigration from the mid-1990s (exacerbated by the popular press), immigration has shot up the list of voter concerns, and according to Mori 56 percent of people (including 90 percent of poor whites and even a large minority of immigrants) now believe there are too many immigrants in Britain. . . .

Immigrants come in all shapes and sizes. From the American banker or Indian software engineer to the Somali asylum seeker—from the most desirable to the most burdensome, at least in the short term. Immigrants who plan to stay should be encouraged to become Britons as far as that is compatible with holding on to some core aspects of their own culture. In return for learning the language, getting a job and paying taxes, and abiding by the laws and norms of the host society, immigrants must be given a stake in the system and incentives to become good citizens. . . . Immigrants from the same place are bound to want to congregate together but policy should try to prevent that consolidating into segregation across all the main areas of life: residence, school, workplace, church. In any case, the laissez-faire approach of the postwar period in which ethnic minority citizens were not encouraged to join the common culture (although many did) should be buried. Citizenship ceremonies, language lessons and the mentoring of new citizens should help to create a British version of the old U.S. melting pot. This third way on identity can be distinguished from the coercive assimilationism of the nationalist right, which rejects any element of foreign culture, and from multiculturalism, which rejects a common culture. . . .

Welfare Policy

A generous welfare state is not compatible with open borders and possibly not even with U.S.-style mass immigration. Europe is not America. One of the reasons for the fragmentation and individualism of American life is that it is a vast country. In Europe, with its much higher population density and planning controls, the rules have to be different. We are condemned to share—the rich cannot ignore the poor, the indigenous cannot ignore the immigrant—but that does not mean people are always happy to share. A universal, human rights-based approach to welfare ignores the fact that the rights claimed by one group do not automatically generate the obligation to accept them, or pay for them, on the part of another group—as we saw with the elderly couple in Leicester. If we want high tax and redistribution, especially with the extra welfare demands of an aging population, then in a world of stranger citizens taxpayers need reassurance that their money is being spent on people for whose circumstances they would have some sympathy. For that reason, welfare should become more overtly conditional. The rules must be transparent and blind to ethnicity, religion, sexuality and so on, but not blind to behavior. People who consistently break the rules of civilized behavior should not receive unconditional benefits. . . .

Culture

Good societies need places like London and New York as well as the more homogeneous, stable, small and medium-size towns of middle Britain or the American midwest. But the emphasis, in culture and the media, should be on maintaining a single national conversation at a time when the viewing and listening public is becoming more fragmented. In Britain, that means strong support for the "social glue" role of the BBC. (The glue once provided by religion no longer works, and in any case cannot include immigrants of different faiths.) The teaching of multi-ethnic citizenship in schools is a welcome step. But too many children leave school with no sense of the broad sweep of their national history. The teaching of British history, and in particular the history of the empire and of subsequent immigration into Britain, should be a central part of the school curriculum. At the same time, immigrants should be encouraged to become part of the British "we," even while bringing their own very different perspective on its formation.

Politics and Language

Multiculturalists argue that the binding power of the liberal nation state has been eroded from within by value diversity and from without by the arrival of immigrant communities with other loyalties. But the nation state remains irreplaceable as the site for democratic participation and it is hard to imagine how else one can organize welfare states and redistribution except through national tax and public spending. Moreover, since the arrival of immigrant groups from non-liberal or illiberal cultures it has become clear that to remain liberal the state may have to prescribe a clearer hierarchy of values. The U.S. has tried to resolve the tension between liberalism and pluralism by developing a powerful national myth. Even if this were desirable in Britain, it is probably not possible to emulate. Indeed, the idea of fostering a common culture, in any strong sense, may no longer be possible either. One only has to try listing what the elements of a common culture might be to realize how hard it would be to legislate for. That does not mean that the idea must be abandoned; rather, it should inform public policy as an underlying assumption rather than a set of policies. Immigration and welfare policies, for example, should be designed to reduce the fear of free riding, and the symbolic aspects of citizenship should be reinforced; they matter more in a society when tacit understandings and solidarities can no longer be taken for granted. Why not, for example, a British national holiday or a state of the union address?

Lifestyle diversity and high immigration bring cultural and economic dynamism but can erode feelings of mutual obligation, reducing willingness to pay tax and even encouraging a retreat from the public domain. In the decades ahead European politics itself may start to shift on this axis, with left and right being eclipsed by value-based culture wars and movements for and against diversity. Social democratic parties risk being torn apart in such circumstances, partly on class lines: recent British Social Attitudes reports have made clear the middle class and the working class increasingly converge on issues of tax and economic management, but diverge on diversity issues.

The anxieties triggered by the asylum seeker inflow into Britain now seem to be fading. But they are not just a media invention; a sharp economic downturn or a big inflow of east European workers after EU enlargement might easily call them up again. The progressive centre needs to think more clearly about these issues to avoid being engulfed by them. And to that end it must try to develop a new language in which to address the anxieties, one that transcends the thin and abstract language of universal rights on the one hand and the defensive, nativist language of group identity on the other. Too often the language of liberal universalism that dominates public debate ignores the real affinities of place and people. These affinities are not obstacles to be overcome on the road to the good society; they are one of its foundation stones. People will always favor their own families and communities; it is the task of a realistic liberalism to strive for a definition of community that is wide enough to include people from many different backgrounds, without being so wide as to become meaningless.

CHAPTER 4 FREE TRADE AREAS ARE STEPPING STONES *v.* FREE TRADE AREAS ARE STUMBLING BLOCKS

Free Trade Agreements Are Stepping Stones toward Global Free Trade

Advocate: Dan T. Griswold

Source: *Free Trade Agreements: Steppingstones to a More Open World*, Trade Briefing Paper no.18 (Washington, DC: CATO Institute, July 10, 2003)

Free Trade Agreements Are Stumbling Blocks toward Global Free Trade

Advocate: Jagdish Bhagwati

Source: "Why PTAs Are a Pox on the World Trading System," in *Termites in the Trading System: How Preferential Agreements Undermine Free Trade* (New York: Oxford University Press, 2008), 49–88

The last twenty years have seen an explosion of preferential trade agreements (PTAs). PTAs, sometimes referred to as regional trade agreements, are trade agreements that discriminate between members and nonmembers. PTAs come in two basic forms. In a free trade agreement (FTA) governments eliminate tariffs on goods entering their markets from their FTA partners but each member retains independent tariffs on goods entering from non–FTA members. In a customs union, like the European Union, member governments combine an FTA with a common external tariff for goods entering the union from nonmembers. Although PTAs have been part of the global trade system throughout the postwar period, the number of such agreements accelerated rapidly during the 1990s. Today, approximately 180 PTAs are in force and all World Trade Organization (WTO) members except Mongolia belong to at least one PTA.[1]

The proliferation of PTAs has thus generated debate concerning their impact on the multilateral trade system. Article 24 of the General Agreement on Tariffs and Trade gives governments the right to create PTAs, so the central issue is not really about whether PTAs are consistent with WTO obligations.

---

[1] World Trade Organization, "Regionalism: Friends or Rivals?" http://www.wto.org/english/theWTO_e/whatis_e/tif_e/bey1_e.htm.

Instead, the debate focuses on whether PTAs, in spite of their seeming trade-liberalizing consequences, are stepping stones or stumbling blocks: Do they bring the world closer to or further from free trade?

FREE TRADE AGREEMENTS ARE STEPPING STONES TOWARD GLOBAL FREE TRADE

Proponents argue that PTAs are stepping stones to global free trade. Liberalizing trade within the WTO is difficult because negotiations must produce agreements that satisfy more than 150 governments. In this context, a strategy based on PTAs might gradually lead to global free trade. Each successive PTA will eliminate tariffs on trade between some countries. Each PTA that governments negotiate will exert a gravitational pull that attracts new members. Eventually, the global network of PTAs will eliminate tariffs between most countries. Governments thus achieve via PTAs what they cannot achieve as readily via multilateral negotiations within the WTO.

Daniel T. Griswold, an American economist, develops an argument along these lines. Griswold supports the American policy of negotiating FTAs as a second-best alternative to multilateral negotiations. He recognizes the legal and economic complexities that characterize PTAs: Are they consistent with WTO rules, and do they divert more trade than they create? Yet, he argues that on balance, the careful construction of FTAs is a useful policy tool that can advance American interests and promote gradual movement toward global free trade.

FREE TRADE AGREEMENTS ARE STUMBLING BLOCKS TOWARD GLOBAL FREE TRADE

Critics of PTAs argue that on balance the recent proliferation of such arrangements constitutes a real threat to the global multilateral trade system. On the one hand, critics argue that the logical evolution of a system based on PTAs is to three rival trade blocs, one based in Europe, one based in the Americas, and one based in Asia. These rivals would then engage in trade wars. One bloc might raise tariffs on imports from outside to protect local producers. The other blocs would respond by raising tariffs in return. The resulting trade wars would progressively reduce trade between the blocs and thus push the world toward a regional rather than a multilateral and global trade organization. And even if this worst case scenario does not arise, the negotiation of PTAs necessarily reduces the attention paid to the multilateral WTO. Consequently, PTAs gradually, even if unintentionally, erode support for the WTO–based trade system.

Jagdish Bhagwati is perhaps the most vocal critic of contemporary proliferation of PTAs. In the extract presented here, Bhagwati criticizes PTAs on three grounds. First, he asserts that the resulting trade diversion is much larger than commonly recognized. Second, he claims that the proliferation of PTAs has created an extraordinarily complex network of rules that make it impossible *ex ante* to determine which tariff rates apply to a particular product. Finally, PTAs enable the United States to use its power to extract concessions from smaller countries that it could not otherwise obtain. This power asymmetry creates the opportunity to use PTAs to establish "trade unrelated rules" such as common labor and environmental standards and protection of property rights.

POINTS **TO PONDER**

1. Does the United States, as a hegemon, have a responsibility to pursue liberalization exclusively through the multilateral system?

2. Which of the following do you believe more likely: The threat to liberalize through PTAs will spur WTO negotiations to successful conclusion, or the emergence of PTAs will cause governments to gradually place less emphasis on the WTO?

3. Which do you consider more worrisome: a world in which governments liberalize trade through PTAs rather than the WTO or a world in which they eschew PTAs but are unable to make progress within the WTO? Justify your selection.

Daniel T. Griswold

Free-Trade Agreements: Steppingstones to a More Open World

Introduction

. . . Since final passage of trade promotion authority in 2002, the Bush administration has launched an aggressive campaign to negotiate bilateral and regional free-trade agreements (FTAs). . . . Those agreements already negotiated or in the pipeline are sure to spark the usual debate about free trade versus fair trade, environmental standards and working conditions in poor countries, jobs and wages in the United States, and the other issues that inevitably swirl around any trade agreement before Congress.[1] But bilateral and regional trade agreements also raise a peculiar set of policy issues, economic and noneconomic alike, that are generally neglected when deals are debated and voted on.

Even for supporters of trade expansion, not every bilateral and regional free-trade agreement proposed is necessarily good economic policy. Despite the name, free-trade agreements do not always promote more trade, nor do they necessarily leave parties to the agreement or the rest of the world better off. Beyond the economic ambiguities of FTAs are a number of important strategic and foreign policy considerations that cannot be ignored.

This paper examines the merits of negotiating free-trade agreements. It analyzes both the economic and noneconomic implications of FTAs, weighs the costs and benefits of the specific agreements put forward by the Bush administration in light of those implications, and proposes guidelines for future negotiations to maximize the benefits and minimize the costs to both the U.S. economy and our broader national interests.

On balance, . . . bilateral and regional agreements . . . further our national interests. If crafted properly, those agreements would strengthen the U.S. economy by injecting new import competition into domestic markets and opening markets abroad more widely to U.S. exports. More important, they would encourage economic reform abroad and cement economic and foreign policy ties between the United States and key allies.

The Peculiarities of FTAs

For anyone who supports free trade, support for free-trade agreements would at first glance seem to be automatic. Such agreements by definition lower barriers to trade between participants, and lowering or eliminating

barriers altogether has been the aim of the whole trade liberalization movement. Yet regional and bilateral trade agreements raise legal and economic
questions that should be addressed.

Departing from Multilateral Trade

FTAs are an exception to the basic legal principle of nondiscrimination in
international trade. Article III of the basic charter [of] the World Trade
Organization ([WTO;] the General Agreement on Tariffs and Trade
[GATT] 1947 as amended by the 1994 Uruguay Round Agreement)
declares as a fundamental principle that market access should be extended
to all members on a most-favored-nation, or nondiscriminatory, basis.
Specifically, "any advantage, favor, privilege or immunity granted by any contracting party to any product originating in or destined for any other country
shall be accorded immediately and unconditionally to the like product originating in or destined for the territories of all other contracting parties."[2]

Of course, FTAs explicitly deviate from that principle. They grant an
advantage (lower or zero tariffs) to parties to an agreement that are not
granted to other members of the WTO that are not parties to the agreement.
But free-trade agreements and customs unions, when properly crafted, are
consistent with GATT rules.

When the GATT was originally signed in 1947, its founding members
carved out an exception for free-trade areas. Article XXIV of the GATT allows
customs unions or free-trade agreements between members,[3] recognizing
"the desirability of increasing freedom of trade by the development, through
voluntary agreements, of closer integration between the economies of the
countries [party] to such agreements."[4] Such agreements are allowed
provided they (1) do not result in higher trade barriers overall for WTO
members outside the agreement,[5] (2) eliminate "duties and other restrictive
regulations of commerce" on "substantially all the trade between the con-
stituent territories . . . in products originating in such territories,"[6] and (3) do
so "within a reasonable length of time."[7] Article XXIV can be waived entirely
by a two-thirds vote of WTO members.[8]

The most obvious exception under Article XXIV has been the European
Union, which began in the 1950s as the six-member European Economic
Community. Other well-known FTAs or customs unions among WTO mem-
bers are the European Free Trade Association, the North American Free
Trade Agreement, the Southern Common Market, the Association of
Southeast Asian Nations Free Trade Area, and the Common Market of
Eastern and Southern Africa.

In fact, free-trade agreements have been proliferating among WTO
members. Today more than 150 such agreements are in effect, and the trend
has been accelerating in the last decade. In the first 46 years of the GATT,
between 1948 and 1994, 124 such agreements were signed (many of which

have since expired), an average of 2.7 per year. Since 1995 the WTO has been notified of 130 such agreements, an average of more than 15 per year.[9] Today an estimated 43 percent of international trade occurs under free-trade agreements, and that share would reach 55 percent if agreements currently being negotiated worldwide were to be implemented.[10]

Despite Article I, free-trade agreements are a legal fact of life in international trade. More and more WTO members are choosing to negotiate FTAs. The question for U.S. trade policy is whether we should join or resist the trend.

The Messy Economics of FTAs

The economics of FTAs is more ambiguous than the legalities. Even though FTAs by definition result in lower trade barriers between member countries, they do not necessarily result in economic gains for all members or the world as a whole.

Economists have been investigating this phenomenon since 1950, when Jacob Viner published his seminal study, *The Customs Union Issue.*[11] Viner noted that customs unions can promote new trade among members, but they can also divert trade from more efficient producers outside the agreement.

If signed with a low-cost foreign producer, an agreement can result in *trade creation* by allowing the low-cost producer to enter the domestic market tariff free, reducing domestic prices, and displacing higher-cost *domestic* producers. But if signed with a relatively high-cost foreign producer, an agreement can result merely in *trade diversion* by allowing the higher-cost importer to displace lower-cost *foreign* importers simply because producers in the new FTA partner can import tariff free. As Viner concluded, customs unions are likely to yield more economic benefit than harm when "they are between sizeable countries which practice substantial protection of substantially similar [that is, competing] industries."[12]

To maximize trade creation, FTAs should unleash real competition in previously protected markets. From an economic perspective, the essential purpose and principal payoff of international trade is expanded competition within the domestic economy and expanded markets abroad for domestic producers. Increased import competition results in lower prices for consuming households and businesses, more product choice, higher quality, and increased innovation. By stimulating more efficient production, import competition increases the productivity of workers, real wages, living standards, and the long-run growth of the economy.

If an FTA does not result in lower prices for the importing country but merely reshuffles imports from the rest of the world to FTA partners, the importing country can suffer a welfare loss. Its government loses tariff revenue, but its consumers do not reap any gain from lower prices. In effect, the importing country's treasury subsidizes less efficient production in the partner country. If global prices outside the FTA fall because of the diverted demand, then the rest of the world loses from lost producer surplus.

To minimize trade diversion, the best FTAs allow a large and competitive foreign producer to displace domestic producers in a large and protected domestic market, thus delivering lower prices and higher real incomes to workers and families. The worst allow less competitive foreign producers to replace more competitive foreign producers in a large and protected domestic market, costing the treasury tariff revenue without delivering lower domestic prices or more efficient domestic production.

Free-trade economists argue among themselves about whether trade creation or trade diversion usually predominates under free-trade agreements. Settling that dispute definitively is beyond the scope of this paper.[13] But we do know that the evidence is mixed and that the short-term, static economic impact of a free-trade agreement is only one factor in deciding whether a particular FTA meets the test of good public policy. The possibility of trade diversion is not sufficient reason to reject the Bush administration's policy of pursuing FTAs.

How FTAs Advance Trade Liberalization

Even if trade diversion occurs, free-trade agreements can advance the goals of expanding free markets, individual liberty, and more peaceful cooperation among nations. In addition to their short-term economic effects, free-trade agreements can advance American interests in several ways.

A Safety Valve for the Multilateral System

One, FTAs provide an important safety valve if multilateral negotiations become stuck—an all-too-real possibility. Multilateral negotiations through the GATT and now the WTO can be long, tortuous, and uncertain. Since the Kennedy Round concluded in 1967, only two other comprehensive multilateral agreements have been reached—the Tokyo Round Agreement in 1979 and the Uruguay Round Agreement in 1994. And because of the need for consensus, it takes only one of the 146 nations in the WTO to scuttle a new agreement.

To cite one plausible scenario, the French government could prevent completion of a Doha Round Agreement because of its long-standing objections to liberalization of agricultural trade. Negotiators have already missed a March 31, 2003, deadline for preliminary agreements on agriculture, and doubt is widespread that the round will be concluded by 2005 as agreed in the 2001 agreement that launched it. The Uruguay Round, it should be remembered, almost foundered on the subject of agriculture. Given the history of multilateral negotiations, it would be unwise to put all of our tradable eggs in the Doha Round basket.

FTAs provide institutional competition to keep multilateral talks on track. If other WTO members become intransigent, the United States should have the option of pursuing agreements with a "coalition of the willing" in pursuit of trade liberalization. Negotiating FTAs, or at least retaining the option to do so, can send a signal to other WTO members that, if they are unwilling to negotiate seriously to reduce trade barriers, we retain the right to find bilateral and regional partners who will. Knowing that WTO members, including the United States, can pursue FTAs outside the multilateral process can focus the minds and wills of negotiators to reach an agreement.

Fears that FTAs could divert attention from the multilateral track are unfounded. Most WTO members that have pursued regional and bilateral FTAs have not abandoned their commitment to multilateral negotiations. The U.S. government signed agreements with Israel, Canada, and Mexico during the Uruguay Round negotiations from 1986 to 1994 without reducing its commitment to a final multilateral agreement. And there is no evidence that pursuit of FTAs today has distracted the Bush administration from the ongoing Doha Round of WTO negotiations. Indeed, U.S. Trade Representative Robert Zoellick has been leading the charge in the Doha Round with aggressive proposals to liberalize global trade in manufactured goods, agricultural products, and services.

A Level Playing Field for U.S. Exporters

Two, FTAs can level the playing field for U.S. exporters who have been put at a disadvantage by free-trade agreements that do not include the United States. The United States is party to only 3 of the 150 or so FTAs currently in force around the world—NAFTA [North American Free Trade Agreement] and bilateral agreements with Israel and Jordan. Even though American producers may be the most efficient in the world in a certain sector, our exporters may not be able to overcome the advantage of rival foreign producers who can export tariff free to countries with which their governments have signed an FTA.

In Chile, for example, U.S. exporters encounter a uniform 6 percent tariff. Competing exporters in the European Union, Canada, and Brazil, in contrast, sell duty-free in the same market because their governments have signed free-trade agreements with Chile. According to the National Association of Manufacturers, U.S. exporters have lost market share in Chile since its government began to aggressively pursue free-trade agreements with its non-U.S. trading partners in 1997. Especially hard-hit by the tariff differential have been U.S. exports to Chile of wheat, soybeans, corn, paper products, plastics, fertilizers, paints and dyes, and heating and construction equipment.[14] All those sectors have seen their market share drop significantly in the absence of a U.S.-Chile free-trade agreement.

Institutionalizing Reforms Abroad

Three, FTAs can help less-developed countries lock in and institutionalize ongoing economic reforms. A signed agreement prevents nations from back-sliding in times of economic or political duress. Agreements assure foreign investors that reforms mark a permanent commitment to liberalization. For example, when Mexico suffered its peso crisis in 1994–95, its NAFTA commitments kept its market open to U.S. exports. The assurance of an FTA also works the other way, guaranteeing that exporters in the partner country will enjoy duty-free access to the large American market. By signing an FTA with the United States, less-developed countries signal to the rest of the world that they are serious about embracing global competition. That signal, combined with access to the U.S. market, can help to attract foreign investment and spur faster development.

Blazing a Trail for Broader Negotiations

Four, FTAs can provide useful templates for broader negotiations. As the members of the WTO grow in number and diversity, reaching consensus among all 146 members becomes more difficult. Negotiators can be forced to consider only the lowest common denominator acceptable to all members. Negotiating with only one country or a small group of like-minded countries can allow more meaningful liberalization in areas such as sanitary and phytosanitary (i.e., animal and plant) regulations, technical barriers to trade, service trade and investment, electronic commerce, customs facilitation, labor and environmental standards, dispute settlement, and market access for politically sensitive sectors.

Those agreements, in turn, can blaze a trail for wider regional and multilateral negotiations. The U.S.-Chile FTA provides an example of how to incorporate labor and environmental standards into the text of an agreement without threatening to hold trade hostage to rich-country demands for higher standards in less-developed countries. FTAs can provide creative solutions to sticky political problems that can then be adapted in other agreements.

Internal Competition and Integration

Five, FTAs can spur internal reform and consolidation within member states, enhancing economic growth and support for more liberalization. By encouraging regional integration, FTAs hasten the consolidation of production within the FTA, increase economies of scale, and create a more integrated production process. Consolidation may be most pronounced in more heavily protected service sectors such as telecommunications, financial services, and transportation. More efficient industries and infrastructure can yield dynamic gains year after year, boosting growth, investment, and demand for imports from FTA partners as well as the rest of the world.

For all those reasons, the Bush administration's agenda of negotiating free-trade agreements is worth pursuing. Under the right conditions, FTAs can inject new competition into our domestic economy, lowering prices for consumers and shifting factors of production to more efficient uses, while leveling the playing field for U.S. exporters. Beyond those immediate benefits, FTAs can provide institutional competition for multilateral talks, spurring integration among FTA countries and liberalization abroad and blazing a trail through difficult areas for broader negotiations in the future. As a foreign policy tool, FTAs can cement ties with allies and encourage countries to stay on the trail of political and economic reform.

Conclusion

As a tool for expanding freedom and prosperity, regional and bilateral free-trade agreements are useful if less than ideal. They complicate the international trading system by deviating from the most-favored-nation principle of nondiscrimination, and they can blunt the benefits of international trade by diverting it from the most efficient foreign producers to those that are favored but less efficient. But FTAs can produce compensating benefits by opening domestic markets to fresh competition, encouraging economic liberalization abroad, cementing important foreign policy and security ties, integrating regional economies, opening markets to U.S. exports, and providing healthy institutional competition for multilateral negotiations.

To maximize the economic benefits of free-trade agreements, the U.S. government should focus its efforts on negotiations with countries that provide new opportunities for U.S. exporters and whose producers would be most likely to enhance competition in our own market. That approach requires that U.S. negotiators not duck politically sensitive sectors through long phase-in periods for or exemptions from liberalization. Instead, they should tout the immediate liberalization of those sectors as offering the best opportunities to reap the benefits of trade.

As a broader foreign policy tool, free-trade agreements should reward and solidify market and political reform abroad. If FTA partners are not major export markets or significant producers of goods that compete in our domestic market, they should be moving decisively toward free markets and representative government. They should be reform leaders in regions of the world where models of successful reform are most needed. In this way, free-trade agreements can serve as carrots to encourage the spread of political and economic freedom abroad.

Despite their peculiarities and incremental nature, free-trade agreements can serve the cause of freedom and development by breaking down barriers to trade between nations. If crafted according to sound principles, free-trade agreements can serve America's economic and foreign policy interests.

ENDNOTES

1. For articles and studies on those more general trade issues, see previous materials published by the Cato Institute's Center for Trade Policy Studies available at www.freetrade.org.
2. General Agreement on Tariffs and Trade 1947, Part I, Article I, Section 1, www.wto.org/english/docs_e/legal_e/gatt47_01_e.htm.
3. Members of a customs union adopt a common external trade policy with uniform tariffs applying to imports of all members. Members of a free-trade agreement retain independent external trade policies while eliminating barriers among themselves.
4. General Agreement on Tariffs and Trade 1947, Part III, Article XXIV, Section 4.
5. Ibid., Part III, Article XXIV, Section 5 (a) and (b).
6. Ibid., Part III, Article XXIV, Section 8(a)i.
7. Ibid., Part III, Article XXIV, Section 5(c).
8. Ibid., Part III, Article XXIV, Section 10.
9. World Trade Organization, "Regional Trade Agreements: Facts and Figures," www.wto.org/english/tratop_e/region_e/regfac_e.htm.
10. Organization for Economic Cooperation and Development, "Regional Trade Agreements and the Multilateral Trading System," November 20, 2002, p. 12.
11. Jacob Viner, *The Customs Union Issue* (New York: Carnegie Endowment for International Peace, 1950).
12. Ibid., p. 135.
13. For a favorable assessment of free-trade agreements, see Robert Z. Lawrence, "Emerging Regional Arrangements: Building Blocks or Stumbling Blocks?" in *International Political Economy: Perspectives on Global Power and Wealth,* ed. Jeffry A. Frieden and David A. Lake, 3d ed. (New York: Routledge, 1995), pp. 407–15; and Lawrence H. Summers, "Regionalism and the World Trading System," in *Trading Blocs: Alternative Approaches to Analyzing Preferential Trade Agreements,* ed. Jagdish Bhagwati, Pravin Krishna, and Arvind Panagariya (Cambridge, Mass.: MIT Press, 1999), pp. 561–66. For a negative assessment, see Jagdish Bhagwati and Arvind Panagariya, *The Economics of Preferential Trade Agreements* (Washington: AEI Press, 1996), especially pp. 1–78.
14. National Association of Manufacturers, "Absence of Chilean Trade Agreement Costing U.S. over $1 Billion per Year," Washington, February 4, 2003, www.nam.org/Docs/ITIA/25837_ABSENCEOFCHILEANTRADEAGREEMENT.pdf.

Jagdish Bhagwatil

Why PTAs Are a Pox on the World Trading System

The worries over PTAs [preferential trade agreements] have increased dramatically in the past two decades as PTAs have proliferated. What exactly are the downsides of this phenomenon, which has gathered speed and become an addiction of the politicians, even as economists (with few exceptions) have expressed alarm at the development? What exactly are they worried about?

Trade Diversion

The traditional objection to PTAs was simply that . . . they could divert trade from the cost-efficient nonmember countries to the relatively inefficient member countries. The reason, of course, is that the nonmembers continue to pay the pre-PTA tariffs, whereas the higher cost member countries no longer have to.

It is easy to see that such a shift in production to a higher cost member country must sabotage the efficient allocation among countries and thus undermine what economists call "world welfare," or, in more palatable language, "cosmopolitan advantage." Recall that Jacob Viner was the first to draw attention to the possibility of trade diversion arising with discriminatory reduction of trade barriers in PTAs. He had focused mainly on PTAs' impact on cosmopolitan advantage, but it was pretty obvious to economists that such trade discrimination could hurt the liberalizing country itself. Why? Because when a country (call it the "home" country) shifts to a higher cost within-the-PTA supplier, it is buying its imports more expensively, incurring what economists call a "terms of trade" loss.

Trade diversion is not a slam-dunk argument against PTAs, for offsetting the loss from trade diversion can be a gain if trade creation takes place. Trade may grow because consumers in the home country now pay lower prices in their own markets; the higher cost supply from the member country is still cheaper than what the domestic consumers had to pay before the PTA was formed. Again, the import-competing producers in the home country will reduce their own inefficient production as the domestic price of imports falls after the PTA comes into operation; this also leads to welfare-enhancing trade creation. Therefore, whether a specific trade-diverting PTA brings loss or gain to a country depends on the relative strengths of the trade diversion and trade creation effects.[1]

The really important implication of the "trade diversion" analysis, however, was that informed economists could no longer pretend that it did not matter how one liberalized trade, that preferential trade liberalization was possibly a two-edged sword on which one could impale oneself. Thus, when some policy makers said that all trade liberalization was good, whether it was through bilateralism, plurilateralism, or multilateralism, they were really flying in the face of science. . . .

As it happens, the proponents of PTAs are too complacent about the phenomenon of trade diversion. Consider seven principal arguments.

1. There is evidence of fierce competition in many products and sectors today, with few managing to escape with "thick" margins of competitive advantage that provide comforting buffers against loss of comparative advantage.2 Thus, even small tariffs are compatible with trade diversion as tariffs are removed from members of a PTA while they remain in place on nonmembers.

2. The thinness of comparative advantage also implies that today we have what I have called kaleidoscopic comparative advantage, or what in jargon we economists call "knife-edge" comparative advantage. Countries can easily lose comparative advantage to some "close" rivals, who may be from any number of foreign suppliers. So even if preferences today do not lead to trade diversion, the menu of products where you develop comparative advantage in a world of volatility and rapidly shifting comparative advantage will be forever changing, and any given preferences may lead to trade diversion in the near future, if not today.

3. While Article 24 requires that the external tariffs not be raised when the PTA is formed so as not to harm nonmembers,[3] the fact is that they can be raised when the external (MFN [most favored nation]) tariffs are bound at higher levels than the actual tariffs. In these cases, a member of the PTA is free to raise the external MFN tariffs up to the bound levels, whereas typically the scheduled tariff reductions in the PTA, when a hegemonic power is involved, will be hard to suspend.[4] This is in fact what happened during the Mexican peso crisis of 1994, when external tariffs were raised on 502 items from 20 percent or less to as much as 35 percent, while the NAFTA [North American Free Trade Agreement]-defined reductions in Mexican tariffs on U.S. and Canadian goods continued. So the prospect of trade diversion actually increased, despite the intent of those who drafted Article 24.

4. Article 24 freezes only external tariffs when the PTA is formed, with no increase in the external tariff allowed. But it does not address the modern reality that "administered protection" (i.e., antidumping and other actions by the executive) . . . can be used and abused more or less freely in practice. Once you take into account the fact that trade barriers can

take the form of antidumping measures, . . . initially welfare-enhancing trade creation can be transformed into harmful trade diversion through antidumping actions taken against nonmembers. . . .

5. There is plenty of evidence that trade diversion can occur through content requirements placed on member countries to establish "origin" so as to qualify for the preferential duties. . . . To qualify for the preferential tariffs in PTAs that include the United States, one must satisfy requirements such as that the imports of raw materials and components . . . come from the United States. For example, if apparel exports to the United States are accorded preferential tariffs, they must be made with U.S. textiles. This naturally diverts trade in textiles from efficient nonmember suppliers to inefficient U.S. textile producers.

6. Many analysts do not understand the distinction between trade diversion and trade creation and simply take all trade increase as welfare-enhancing. However, some recent analysts who are familiar with the phenomenon of trade diversion have tried to estimate it using what is called the "gravity model." Dating back some decades, this equation simply explains trade between two countries as a function of income and distance. Adapting this simple equation to their use, the economists Jeffrey Frankel and Shang-Jin Wei, who pioneered the use of gravity analysis to estimate trade creation and trade diversion, estimated total bilateral trade between any pair of countries as a function of their income and per capita incomes, with bilateral distance accounted for by statistical procedures.[5] If the countries belonged to, say, the Western hemisphere and they traded more with each other than with a random pair of countries located outside the region, that would mean that the PTA between countries in the Western hemisphere had led to trade creation. . . . The real problem with the analysis is that more trade between partners in a PTA can take place with *both* trade creation and trade diversion, so that one simply cannot infer trade creation alone from this procedure. Hence, the recent estimates based on gravity equation, . . . which sometimes (but not always) suggest that PTAs in practice have led to more trade creation than diversion, cannot be treated as reliable guides to the problem of determining whether or not a PTA has led to trade diversion.[6]

7. Several economists have suggested that we need not worry about trade diversion and that beneficial effects will prevail if PTAs are undertaken with "natural trading partners." The initial proponents of this idea, Paul Wonnacott and Mark Lutz, declared, "Trade creation is likely to be great and trade diversion small if the prospective members of an FTA [free trade agreement] are natural trading partner,"[7] One criterion proposed

for saying that PTA partners are natural trading partners is the volume of trade already between them; the other is geographic proximity. Neither really works.[8]

. . . There is no evidence that pairs of contiguous countries or countries with common borders have larger volumes of trade with each other than do pairs that are not so situated, or that trade volumes of pairs of countries arranged by distance between the countries in the pair will also show distance to be inversely related to trade volumes.[9] . . .

The "Spaghetti Bowl": A Systemic Concern

. . . The systemic problem from discriminatory trade liberalization under PTAs arises in two ways. First, when a country enters into multiple FTAs, it is evident that the same commodity will be subjected to different tariff rates if, as is almost always the case, the trajectories of tariff reduction vary for different FTAs. Second, and much more important, is the . . . fact that . . . tariffs on specific commodities must depend on where a product . . . originates (requiring inherently arbitrary "rules of origin").

With PTAs proliferating, the trading system can then be expected to become chaotic. Crisscrossing PTAs, where a nation had multiple PTAs with other nations, each of which then had its own PTAs with yet other nations, was inevitable. Indeed, if one only mapped the phenomenon, it would remind one of a child scrawling a number of chaotic lines on a sketch pad. . . .

. . . Crisscrossing PTAs, causing in turn the mish-mash of preferential trade barriers, prompted me to christen them the "spaghetti bowl" phenomenon and problem. . . . The phrase has caught on famously. . . . Then again, in the Far East, and in the context of Asian PTAs, it is now referred to as the "noodle bowl," and each PTA that contributes to the chaos is called a "noodle."[10] Of course, Marco Polo is reputed to have brought noodles, eaten since the Han Dynasty, back from China, giving us the Italian spaghetti. So perhaps this Asian shift of terminology from spaghetti to noodles is only a matter of extended reciprocity spanning two millennia.

The chaos resulting from arbitrary rules of origin, designed to establish which product is whose—what I have called the "who is whose" question . . . would be considerable even if the rules of origin were unique and uniformly applied. Typical rules of origin require what are called "substantial transformation" tests to decide whether a product is eligible for the preferential tariff rate. Thus, if a Canadian product is to be certified as eligible for NAFTA preferential tariffs when entering the U.S. market, and it uses imported components or raw materials (e.g., Honda in Canada uses steel that may be imported), the product must generally satisfy one of the following criteria:

1. A change in tariff classification: Under the Harmonized System of Tariffs [HST] (which is also used for other purposes such as trade negotiations, according to transformation by HST categories, at an agreed level of product classification), of the imported component into the final product; or
2. Value content: The domestic content must be no less than a certain proportion of the value of the final product.[11]

But it is immediately obvious that, even when such common rules are imposed, there are impossible ambiguities in application that lead to chaos. Thus, if Canada imports and also produces steel ingots, how do we decide what imports went into the production of Toyota transplants in Canada? Do we apply the required domestic component value to NAFTA, or to Canadian production alone? Even if that were settled, there is the problem that Japanese steel ingots may have used iron ore from the United States and chemicals from Canada; these in turn may have used components from non-NAFTA sources, in an endless regress as one goes back into the product chain. The mind reels as one contemplates the level of ambiguity and the scope for skullduggery and corruption at every stage.

In fact, in the modern age, where multinationals source components from around the world and trade has expanded among many countries, it is a . . . folly to run your trade policy on the basis of preferences. . . . There are in fact numerous cases where such questions have led to disputes that come for resolution before . . . dispute settlement panels. In a classic case, the U.S. Customs Service refused to certify Hondas produced in Ontario, Canada, as "North American," and hence eligible for duty-free exports from Canada to the United States, on the grounds that . . . Canadian Hondas did not meet the local content requirement of more than 50 percent imposed by the Canada–U.S. Free Trade Agreement (CUFTA). Honda countered that its estimates showed that they did. There is no surefire, analytically respectable way to determine the truth in such a case: it all boils down to who has greater stamina and whether Honda is willing to put moneys into legal costs.

But the reality also is far more complex than even this neat but sorry situation. For, in practice, the rules of origin vary between members and nonmembers, across different FTAs by the same country, and across different products within each FTA. For instance, the United States generally applies the substantial transformation test to nonmembers, but, as in the Honda case, it uses the value content test for members of CUFTA and other bilaterals.

Again, in nearly all FTAs worldwide, the rules of origin vary by product. The reason, of course, is that while trade is being freed in these products for imports from member countries, the ability to exploit this opportunity is being undercut by imposing cost-raising rules of origin as required by the specific products. In short, the rules of origin . . . vary as necessary to . . . offset . . . the freeing of trade. They take away with one hand what they give with the other. . . .

In fact, the insertion of these extensive product-specific rules of origin, with their deleterious effect on cross-sector uniformity of protection, creates massive treaties that have prompted cynical comments, such as "If NAFTA was really about free trade, you would need only one page, not a document hundreds of pages long." I have seen the NAFTA treaty volume, or I think I have. In some of my debates with the foe of the WTO [World Trade Organization] and free trade Lori Wallach, an articulate and assertive chief of the trade policy division at Ralph Nader's NGO [nongovernmental organization], Public Citizen, she would often carry a fat volume, plonk it down on the table, and announce that it was the NAFTA treaty. Her point was the only one that I wholeheartedly agreed with: that the treaty's bulk reflected the fact that it was freighted with numerous rules of origin and the intrusion of several extraneous issues that had nothing to do with the freeing of trade. . . .

The complexity that the spaghetti bowls create for international trade causes distortions in trade and investment. Much energy and many resources must be expended to discover the optimal sourcing of large numbers of components with a view to minimizing the cost of manufacture plus transportation and the differential tariffs and charges levied by origin.[12]

. . . The Hong Kong businessman Victor Fung has written eloquently . . . about the distortions and costs imposed on businesses by the spaghetti bowls:

> Bilateralism distorts the flow of goods, throws up barriers, creates friction, reduces flexibility and raises prices. In structuring the supply chain, every country of origin rule and every bilateral deal [have] to be tacked on as an additional consideration, thus constraining companies in optimizing production globally. In each new bilateral agreement, considerations relating to "rules of origin" multiply and become more complex. . . .[13]

As Fung notes, these problems and costs created by the spaghetti bowl are particularly onerous for small enterprises. But they are appallingly difficult for the poorer countries. . . . Because of the spaghetti bowl, and because hegemonic powers use PTAs to impose a host of expensive trade-unrelated demands on the poor-country partners in PTAs that reflect lobbying demands in the hegemon, PTAs are a particularly unattractive trade option for the poor countries relative to multilateralism.

Trade-Unrelated Issues: Turning the Trade Game into a Shell Game

When poor countries enter into PTAs with one another . . . the agreements almost always address trade liberalization. But when they enter into PTAs with . . . the United States and often the European Union, the lobbies in the hegemon countries insist on inserting into the agreements a number of "trade-unrelated" demands on the poor countries. How and why?

First, the lobbies that wish to advance their trade-unrelated agendas by incorporating them into trade treaties and institutions typically mislead by claiming that their agendas are "trade-related." Thus, intellectual property protection has to do with collecting royalties, not with trade. . . . By inserting the phrase "trade-related" into the agreement on trade-related intellectual property (TRIPs), the pharmaceutical and software lobbies managed to get the U.S. trade representative at the Uruguay Round to get the issue into the newly formed WTO in 1995. . . . The process by which trade-unrelated issues are turned into trade-related matters is a cynical one and an inversion of the truth. In fact, when the phrase "trade-related" is used, you can be sure that the issue is trade-unrelated. . . .

Second, it is noteworthy that the PTAs among the poor countries are almost never characterized by the inclusion of such trade-unrelated issues. They concentrate exclusively on trade liberalization. It is only when the hegemonic powers, especially the United States and occasionally the European Union, are involved that one finds the inclusion of such extraneous matters. When important developing countries such as India and Brazil refuse to accommodate these demands and insist on keeping trade negotiations free from such extraneous issues, the reaction is frequently to dismiss these objections as "rejectionist." When President Lula of Brazil refused to extend the proposed Free Trade Agreement of the Americas (FTAA) to include these lobby-driven issues, Washington lobbies and the U.S. trade representative condemned Brazil as embracing an FTAA Lite. . . .

Third, it has become customary to pretend that these trade-unrelated conditions are being imposed "in your interest," that they are really "good for you." Thus, when the software and pharmaceutical industries were advocating intellectual property protection (IPP) during the Uruguay Round, the U.S. trade representative claimed the existence of a study, seen by no one I know, in which benefits had been empirically established for countries moving to adopt IPP. Not content with such propaganda, U.S. legislators also enacted, as part of the 1988 Omnibus Trade and Competitiveness Act, . . . Section 301 which would legitimate the use of retaliatory tariffs against countries that the United States unilaterally decided were indulging in "unreasonable practices." Part of this legislation was specifically aimed at countries that did not provide intellectual property protection. It was a unilateral measure that had no legitimacy since these countries had not entered into any treaty or even an agreement to adopt such protection.[14]

Finally, the U.S. trade representative made it clear during the negotiations in the Uruguay Round that IPP had to be included in the new WTO if the Uruguay Round was to be concluded. It was a position that all other producers of intellectual property signed on to as in their interest, while pretending publicly that it was also in the interest of the poorer nations themselves, even if they were not producers of intellectual property. Having managed to get TRIPs inserted thus into the WTO, in violation of the fact that royalty collection is not a trade isssue. The IPP lobby proceeded to use PTAs to advance their agendas beyond what the multilateral negotiations had yielded. . . .

[Negotiations for an FTA with the Southern Africa Customs Union sought] IPP in excess of those agreed to, under de jure and de facto duress in the first instance, at the WTO under the TRIPs agreement. The SACU countries were to be asked to agree on IPP standards "similar to that found in U.S. law" and that exceeded standards agreed to under the TRIPs agreement.[15]

The problem of inclusion of labor and domestic environmental standards in trade treaties is [even] more complex. . . . These are what Robert Hudec and I have called "values-related" demands.[16] . . . Because these demands are "values-based" (e.g., that workers deserve adequate labor standards), it is also easy to present the hegemonic countries' self-serving demands (motivated by the desire to moderate foreign competition) as if they are really demands made for altruistic reasons aimed at benefiting foreign workers. There are in fact a number of bad arguments for bringing these trade-unrelated issues into trade treaties, in one form or another. Such arguments have been floating around for years in the rich-country public domain; they are not compelling and should be rejected.

Take domestic environmental standards (as distinct from international standards, such as to reduce global warming, which involves all nations, or to reduce acid rain, which involves two or more but not all nations).[17] Why does it matter what a producer of steel in Brazil pays by way of a pollution tax for dumping carcinogens in a lake in Brazil that probably no one in the United States has even heard of? . . . Yet if your competitor in Country A pays a lower tax rate than you do, your lobby will insist that this amounts to "unfair trade" and will demand that before trade is freed, Country A must impose an identical burden on your rival.

This sounds reasonable until you spend some time thinking seriously about it. What the pollution tax rate should be (relative to yours) for your foreign rival in your industry cannot be determined except in the total context of the two countries' endowments and preferences. Thus, for instance, even if Mexico and the United States have an identical absolute preference for doing something for the environment, Mexico may have worse water and better air than the United States. . . . So it may make perfect sense for Mexico to worry about polluted water and for the United States to worry about polluted air. Correspondingly, it would make perfect sense for Mexico to have higher pollution taxes for industries generating water pollution than the United States does, and for the United States to have higher taxes for industries generating air rather than water pollution. To insist then that . . . pollution taxes be equalized for each industry everywhere is to ignore this elementary piece of logic. Even so, it is the principal driver of demands that domestic environmental standards must be forced via trade treaties and institutions to be identical across countries for the same industry.

When it comes to labor standards, the rationale for legitimate cross-country diversity, reflecting different stages of development and differential economic contexts, is equally pertinent. Generally speaking, countries will have different sequences by which they approach . . . labor standards, as well as different needs and capabilities. For example, the AFL-CIO has insisted on inclusion of labor standards in trade treaties, given its huge concern that competition from the poor countries is hurting U.S. workers' wages and threatens their hard-won standards, and bringing foreign countries' labor standards to the level of those in the United States has often been their desire. Yet many have asked: What is so sacrosanct about the labor standards of the United States, where workers' right to strike is badly crippled by half-century-old restrictions, and where the net result has been that union membership has shrunk steadily to almost a tenth of the labor force? It is truly ironic if U.S. labor standards are to be the gold standard for its trading partners.

As it happens, . . . the PTA negotiators of the United States with the developing countries initially settled—on the principle of "getting a foot in the door"—for enacting, despite Mexican hesitations, an agreement in an annex to the NAFTA treaty: that each country would enforce its own standards.[18] This agreement was then moved to the main text in the PTAs with Jordan and Morocco. In . . . PTAs with Peru and Colombia, the U.S. legislators have sought to raise the standards. . . .

But it is pretty clear that, no matter how flawed are the demands to include labor and domestic environmental issues in trade treaties, PTAs with weaker nations offer the best way of getting these demands accepted. And every lobby in Washington, D.C., is playing this game, regardless of the interests of these partner nations themselves. Thus, when the PTAs with Chile and Singapore were being negotiated, the U.S. position was that the use of capital account controls during financial crises ought to be proscribed. This ideological position, favorable to the interests of our financial lobbies, was at variance with even the IMF's [International Monetary Fund's] latest thinking. . . .

Astonishingly, the Australia–U.S. Free Trade Agreement was also witness to lobbying to get Australia's medicine policy, much admired in many circles, changed under pressure from the pharmaceutical lobby in the United States. Entering into force on January 1, 2005, the FTA has been much criticized within Australia. It contains many intellectual property provisions and others related to altering pharmaceutical regulation and public health policy in Australia, as embodied in its Pharmaceutical Benefits Scheme, which had been designed with a view to ensuring equitable and affordable access to essential medicine.[19]

While the PTAs are clearly being used by lobbies in the United States and, to a lesser degree, by the European Union to secure their agendas in one-on-one negotiations with weak nations, one must also entertain the thought that the aim of these lobbies is surely more ambitious. What they cannot secure immediately at the WTO, because the developing countries are there in greater numbers and can resist the pressure from the hegemonic powers by the sheer force of their numbers and some ability and willingness to take concerted stands in their own interest, the hegemonic powers can hope to secure by breaking away the developing countries one by one through the PTAs. Thus, if a developing country has signed a PTA with the United States that includes labor standards provisions, that country is unlikely to say at the WTO: We will not have labor standards at the WTO. This is in fact a strategy of "divide and conquer." The United States can be interpreted as playing this strategic game, hoping to get its lobbies' agendas on to the WTO by using the PTAs as a mechanism by which the opposition to these lobbies' agendas is steadily eroded at the WTO. Charles Kindleberger wrote about "altruistic hegemons" providing leadership for the world trading system; here we have the strategic behavior of what I have called a "selfish hegemon."[20]

Are PTAs Building Blocks or Stumbling Blocks to Multilateral Free Trade?

Recall that the original embrace of PTAs by the United States in the early 1980s was a result of frustration with the inability to get multilateral talks started under GATT [General Agreement on Tariffs and Trade] auspices. Once the Uruguay Round was launched, the United States should have reverted to its traditional "multilateralism only" doctrine that it adhered to for over 30 years. But it did not. In fact, its leadership, mainly Secretary of State Baker and his deputy, Robert Zoellick, decided that the United States should do both. Their argument was that PTAs would . . . serve as "building blocks" toward multilateral freeing of trade, that the two trade policies were complementary. . . . They would soon call it the theory of "competitive liberalization."

As Zoellick put it eloquently in 2003:

> When the Bush administration set out to revitalize America's trade agenda almost three years ago, we outlined our plans

clearly and openly: We would pursue a strategy of "competitive liberalization" to advance free trade globally, regionally, and bilaterally. By moving forward simultaneously on multiple fronts the United States can overcome or bypass obstacles; exert maximum leverage for openness, *target the needs of developing countries,* especially the most committed to economic and political reforms; establish models of success, especially in cutting-edge areas; strengthen America's ties with all regions within a global economy; and create a fresh political dynamic by putting free trade on the offensive.[21]

Zoellick thus argued that the United States would use the FTAs to advance a number of trade-unrelated objectives, and (astonishingly) that these issues were in fact addressing the "needs of developing countries," when in fact (as discussed earlier) they were being imposed by the United States as a precondition to signing an FTA with [the developing country]. In addition, Zoellick and his U.S. trade representative deputies also claimed that such initiatives would prompt other countries to seek trade liberalization, first in the shape of FTAs with the United States, and second, by embracing the multilateral system and negotiations at the WTO.

The former is surely an exaggerated claim, at best. While preferences are a wasting asset as MFN tariffs come down over time, the willingness of the United States to sign more FTAs implies that the preferences earned by signing an FTA with the United States are also a wasting asset, insofar as your close rivals may also join an FTA. Simon Evenett and Michael Meier in fact find far too few public statements by policy makers worldwide to the effect that they would like an FTA with the United States because their rivals have one.[22]

. . . The . . . claim that . . . FTAs . . . advance WTO negotiations is even more problematic. Fred Bergsten, a prominent trade expert in Washington, D.C., is a leading exponent of this view. His principal claim of a positive link between PTAs and multilateral trade negotiations is the assertion that the Uruguay Round was brought to a close because the APEC [Asia-Pacific Economic Cooperation] Summit in Seattle in November 1993 was used by the United States to threaten the recalcitrant European Union that if the EU did not close the Round, the United States would have a competing alternative: APEC liberalization. I have asked many European trade officials about his claim, and they simply laugh at it. . . . Surely, everyone could see that there was not the slightest chance that APEC, with its many disparate economies and political differences, would turn into an FTA. . . .

The implausibility of the benign Bergsten argument leaves one with a whole range of arguments that suggest instead that the effect of PTAs on the multilateral trade negotiations is malign. . . .

1. Consider that a dollar's worth of lobbying on opening up Mexico under a PTA will get the Mexican market opened to you. But if you spend the same dollar in Geneva, opening up the Mexican market on an MFN basis, your benefit will be diluted by the "free riders," your rivals from EU, Japan, and elsewhere who have not spent any money to open the Mexican market. So you will spend the dollar on PTAs, not on MTN [multilateral trade negation].
2. Although there are any number of routine bureaucrats available to negotiate trade deals, the supply of skilled bureaucrats is always limited. If PTAs are being pursued simultaneously with MTN, you can be sure that the talented bureaucrats' attention will be split, at best. I saw this in Seattle in November 1999 when the WTO meeting erupted under protests. U.S. Trade Representative Charlene Barshefsky arrived just in time, after long trade negotiations with China: her eye was not on the WTO ball.
3. Politicians often equate all kinds of trade deals, so if you nail down a PTA, no matter how negligible in trade volume, that is a feather in your cap. In fact, I was once at a Bureau of Labor function to honor a bureaucrat whom U.S. Trade Representative Mickey Kantor congratulated for participating in negotiations of over 250 trade deals. Of these, one was the Uruguay Round, another was NAFTA (much less important and, in fact, arguably even a mistake), and the rest were trade-restricting, quota-setting textiles deals under the Multi-Fiber Arrangement!
4. Lobbies provide the foot soldiers in the battles to open trade, and I have already documented that several lobbies with trade-unrelated causes also find PTAs, where weak countries can be intimidated into making concessions, a more agreeable way to go. These lobbies use the PTAs to provide templates—"Ah, we now have our agenda accepted as a part of trade liberalization, and that is the way it will be for other PTAs from now on"—and to steadily encircle the WTO to push their agendas. Aside from the AFL-CIO, few groups are spending as much time and money on Doha as on the PTAs with Peru and Colombia.
5. In the United States, given the general anxiety over trade, it has been a mistake to ask politicians (especially Democrats who have unions among their constituents) to repeatedly spend their limited pro-trade political capital on a succession of trivial PTAs, leading to "trade fatigue" that afflicts then the Doha Round as well.
6. Finally, recent empirical analysis by Nuno Limao, using tariff reduction data during the most recent MTN, demonstrates that PTAs by the

United States were a stumbling block to multilateral trade liberalization.[23] The adverse effect operates through the mechanism that the hegemon maintains higher multilateral tariffs on products imported from the preferential trade partner relative to those on similar products imported from the rest of the world. These higher MFN tariffs act virtually as bargaining chips to be used in negotiating PTAs, because the value of the preference increases the higher the MFN tariff is. This provides an incentive not to reduce MFN tariffs relative to the situation where PTAS were not permitted.

It is hard indeed to contemplate the consequences of PTAs with equanimity. The most important item on our policy agenda has to be to devise an appropriate response to their spread and the damage they impose on the multilateral trading system.

ENDNOTES

1. This analysis of trade diversion and creation is in a simplified framework, designed to convey the essence of the trade-diversion issues raised by PTAs. For a theoretically tight treatment, the reader is referred to the extended analysis by Panagariya and me in Bhagwati, Krishna, and Panagariya, *Trading Blocs*, chapter 2.

2. I have discussed the reasons for this phenomenon and its consequence for coping with globalization in my book, *In Defense of Globalization* (New York: Oxford University Press, 2007), afterword.

3. This restriction is compatible with trade diversion even when the external terms of trade are inflexible and the damage is to the member rather than the non-member countries. But the nonmember countries also can be hurt when the terms of trade are variable. The empirical evidence of such nonmember terms of-trade effects is provided in W. Chang and Alan Winters, "How Regional Blocs Affect Excluded Countries: The Price Effects of MERCOSUR," *American Economic Review* 92, no. 4 (2001). Recent theoretical work by Masahiro Endoh, Koichi Hamada, and Koji Shimomura, "Can a Preferential Trade Agreement Benefit Neighbor Countries without Compensating Them?" unpublished manuscript, Yale University, December 2007, demonstrates in fact that PTAs, unless accompanied by tariff concessions or compensatory transfers, will generally speaking hurt nonmember countries under reasonable restrictions.

4. As Petros Mavroidis has reminded me, when PTAs are formed under Article 24, the members of the PTA are free to raise their external tariffs from the applied levels to the higher bound levels. So the discipline on external tariffs essentially does not operate when the bound levels are higher than the applied tariffs, which is almost always the case, though in varying degrees for different countries.

5. In technical terms, the Frankel-Wei estimating equation uses dummy variables that take a value of 1 if both countries are in Western Europe and zero otherwise. I am grateful to Arvind Panagariya, who took me through the statistical procedures and

their rather drastic limitations, in both the original Frankel-Wei analysis and its later variants by themselves, Gary Hufbauer, and others.

6. Some economists have posed the question of the welfare effects directly by using computable general equilibrium (CGE) models to compare the welfare outcomes under different trade policies, such as multilateral free trade under the Doha Round and current and potential preferential trade agreements. Using the Michigan CGE model of world production and trade developed by Robert Stern, Alan Deardorff, and Drusilla Brown, the economists Kozo Kiyota and Stern have calculated that the gains under multilateral trade liberalization dominate significantly those from a policy of PTAs.

7. Paul Wonnacott and Mark Lutz, "Is There a Case for Free Trade Areas?," in Jeffrey Schott, ed., *Free Trade Areas and U.S. Trade Policy* (Washington D.C.: Institute for International Economics, 1989).

8. The following discussion draws on the far more thorough analysis of the "natural trading partner" hypothesis by Panagariya and me in Bhagwati, Krishna, and Panagariya, *Trading Blocs,* chapter 2.

9. This would generally be true, I am sure, even if one were to take the measure just for one individual country with every other country instead of pooling all possible pairs together. I might add that the gravity equation that shows distance to matter for the volume of trade is taking only a "partial derivative," so to speak, with regard to distance; the discussion in the text relates instead, as is proper in the matter of the equation of the "volume of trade" and "geographical proximity" by Krugman and Summers, simply to the relationship between distance and observed trade volumes.

10. The phrase was introduced by President Haruhiko Kuroda of the Asian Development Bank in July 2006 in a speech delivered to the Jeju Summer Forum in South Korea.

11. There can also be some technical requirements for eligibility, such as meeting certain technical standards on safety, but it is obviously rare for such requirements to be imposed differentially against members of the FTA and not against nonmembers.

12. Sometimes the cost of establishing origin is so high for a firm that it decides instead to forgo the process and to pay the MFN tariff. It is not clear how significant this "opting out" is, however.

13. Victor Fung, "Bilateral Deals Destroy Global Trade," *Financial Times,* November 3, 2005.

14. For an analysis of 301 legislation, and the dangers it posed for the world trading system, see Jagdish Bhagwati and Hugh Patrick, eds., *Aggressive Unilateralism* (Ann Arbor: University of Michigan Press, 1991), especially the chapters by Robert Hudec and by me.

15. See Jonathan Berger and Achal Prabhala, "Assessing the Impact of TRIPs–Plus Rules in the Proposed U.S.-SACU Free Trade Agreement," Working Paper, preliminary draft, Center for Applied Legal Studies, University of Witwatersrand, Johannesburg, South Africa, February 2005.

16. There is a huge literature on this subject, which includes several of my writings in the past fifteen years in places as diverse as the *American Journal of*

International Law and two substantial volumes based on a research project involving several of the leading international economists and trade jurists today: Jagdish Bhagwati and Robert Hudec, eds., *Fair Trade and Harmonization: Prerequisites for Free Trade?* (Cambridge, Mass.: MIT Press, 1996). See, in particular, the extensive analytical discussion of the issues involved in Bhagwati and T.N. Srinivasan, "Trade and the Environment: Does Environmental Diversity Detract from the Case for Free Trade?" chapter 4 of Vol. I.

17. International pollution raises a different set of analytical issues than domestic pollution and is usually negotiated in self-standing treaties, such as Kyoto on global warming and the Montreal Protocol on the ozone layer. There are implications for the WTO, for sure, but these have little to do with the question of PTAs versus multilateralism. For instance, see Jagdish Bhagwati and Petros Mavroidis, "Is Action against U.S. Exports for Failure to Sign Kyoto Protocol WTO–Legal?" *World Trade Review* 6, no. 2 (2007): 299–310; and Bhagwati and Srinivasan, "Trade and the Environment: Does Environmental Diversity Detract from the Case for Free Trade?"

18. This sounds innocuous but is not. Often, legislation is not expected to be enforced. For that reason, it is often pitched high, with minimum wages, for example, being defined at sumptuous levels that no one expects to pay. Again, laws are left on the books because taking them off would be politically difficult, but no one expects them to be enforced. Thus, there are still laws against adultery in some states, but President Clinton can confidently expect to go to these states without being handcuffed and produced in court because the laws are dormant. Asking developing countries, with their low enforcement ability besides, to enforce their own laws on labor standards is therefore either naive or cynical.

19. Among numerous articles on the subject, I found the following most informative: Thomas Faunce, Evan Doran, David Henry, Peter Drahos, Andrew Searles, Brita Pekarsky, Warwick Neville, and Andrew Searles, "Assessing the Impact of the Australia—United States Free Trade Agreement on Australian and Global Medicines Policy," *Globalization and Health* 15 (2005): 1–10.

20. The phrase and idea of a "selfish hegemon" was introduced by me in "Threats to the World Trading System: Income Distribution and the Selfish Hegemon," *Journal of International Affairs* 48 (1994): 279–285.

21. Cited in Evenett and Meier, "An Interim Assessment of the U.S. Trade Policy of 'Competitive Liberalization,'" emphasis added. It is from a report by the U.S. General Accounting Office on international trade, January 2004. Other such pronouncements by Zoellick are on record as well. Perhaps the most remarkable one is from Zoellick's Op Ed piece, "Our Credo: Free Trade and Competition," *Wall Street Journal,* July 10, 2003: "FTAs break new ground—they establish prototypes for liberalization in areas such as services, e-commerce, intellectual property for knowledge societies, transparency in government regulation, and better enforcement of labor and environmental protections."

22. Perhaps the most dramatic such statements are from New Zealand vis-à-vis the Australia-U.S. FTA and the plaintive worries of Colombia, struggling to

get its FTA with the United States, over the fact that Peru has gotten ahead in the queue.

23. Nuno Limao, "Preferential Trade Agreements as Stumbling Blocks for Multilateral Trade Liberalization: Evidence for the U.S.", *American Economic Review* 96, no. 3 (June 2006), 896–914. This paper's brilliant empirical analysis nicely complements the theoretical analyses such as those of Phil Levy and Pravin Krishna . . . on the question of the dynamic time-path issues concerning PTAs.

CHAPTER 5 THE WORLD TRADE ORGANIZATION UNDERMINES ENVIRONMENTAL REGULATION v. THE WORLD TRADE ORGANIZATION IS GREENING

The World Trade Organization Undermines Environmental Regulation

Advocate: Lori Wallach and Michelle Sforza

Source: "The WTO's Environmental Impact," in *Whose Trade Organization? Corporate Globalization and the Erosion of Democracy* (Washington, DC: Public Citizen, 1999), 12–51

The World Trade Organization Is Becoming More Sensitive to Environmental Concerns

Advocate: Michael M. Weinstein and Steve Charnovitz

Source: "The Greening of the WTO," *Foreign Affairs* 80 (November/December 2001): 147–156

The international trade system affects the environment in at least two distinct ways. International trade itself has environmental consequences. Trade can have negative consequences: Goods are transported by fossil-fueled vehicles, and this increases carbon dioxide emissions. Trade can also have positive consequences: Given that New Englanders want to eat tomatoes in January, importing tomatoes from Mexico or Chile may be less harmful than using energy to produce tomatoes in hothouses in the northern United States in the dead of winter. Trade, and the economic activity it encourages, thus affects the natural environment in complex and not always obvious ways.

The international trade system's rules also have environmental consequences. The rules that governments accept as World Trade Organization (WTO) members constrain their ability to restrict trade. As a possible unintended consequence of such constraints, governments might find that they cannot use trade restrictions to achieve a desired environmental objective. In two famous cases, for example, the WTO ruled that the United States could not restrict imports of foreign tuna not certified to have been caught in a dolphin-safe method or shrimp not certified to have been caught in a sea turtle–safe manner. Similarly, WTO rules prevented the European Union from prohibiting the import of genetically modified organisms. Trade rules thus seem to interfere with and sometimes stymie governments' efforts to protect endangered species or prevent potential negative environmental consequences from new technologies.

THE WORLD TRADE ORGANIZATION UNDERMINES ENVIRONMENTAL REGULATION

Environmental activists argue that international trade rules are unnecessarily constraining because they focus too narrowly on a single objective—trade liberalization—at the expense of legitimate environmental goals. The prioritization of trade liberalization over other goals undermines existing regulations, makes it difficult for governments to implement new regulations, and discourages efforts to create multilateral environmental agreements. They argue that WTO rules should be reformed to allow for environmental exceptions. That is, trade rules should allow governments to restrict trade or discriminate against WTO members in the pursuit of legitimate environmental goals.

Lori Wallach and Micelle Sforza, both researchers at the Washington, DC–based nongovernmental organization (NGO) Public Citizen, are among the harshest critics of the WTO's environmental impact. Focusing on a few of the most prominent WTO disputes that involve environmental goals, they argue that the WTO dispute settlement panels unravel national regulations. They then argue that WTO rules weaken the incentive for governments to negotiate new multilateral environmental agreements (MEAs) because MEAs can run afoul of the WTO's principle of nondiscrimination. Finally, they are quite critical of the WTO's Committee on the Environment, arguing that it has done little to heighten environmental awareness among WTO members.

THE WORLD TRADE ORGANIZATION IS BECOMING MORE SENSITIVE TO ENVIRONMENTAL CONCERNS

Other analysts argue that the WTO's rather exclusive focus on trade is appropriate and should be altered only with very careful consideration. Opponents of a link between trade and the environment within the WTO argue that governments will use environmental objectives to justify simple protectionist measures. A government fearful of foreign competition, in other words, might point to supposed negative environmental consequences that may or may not exist to justify a restriction of trade designed to protect local producers. Such disguised protectionism would enable governments to reconstruct protectionist barriers.

Moreover, opponents argue that governments are not prohibited from developing other agreements to achieve their environmental objectives; they just need to use policies other than trade barriers.

Michael Weinstein and Steve Charnovitz develop a variant of this argument. Focusing on the evolution of environmental issues in the General Agreement on Tariffs and Trade (GATT)/WTO since the late 1980s, they argue that the WTO has become increasingly sensitive to environmental concerns. Mindful of the need to balance its goal of trade liberalization with growing concern about the environment, the WTO has shown a greater willingness to consider environmental concerns into account when ruling on trade disputes. The authors conclude by suggesting a number of moderate reforms that would further strengthen the environmental component of the WTO.

POINTS **TO PONDER**

1. Wallach and Sforza focus most attention on a few important cases. What conclusions can be drawn about the WTO and the environment in general from these few cases?

2. Weinstein and Charnovitz argue that although environmentalists have lost many key battles in the WTO, they have won the war. What do they mean by this, and do you agree with them?

3. How can two sets of authors reach such diametrically opposed conclusions from the examination of essentially the same record?

Lori Wallach and Michelle Sforza
The WTO's Environmental Impact

When the legislation implementing the General Agreement on Tariffs and Trade (GATT) Uruguay Round and establishing the World Trade Organization (WTO) was approved in the U.S. Congress in 1994, it was done without the support of a single environmental, conservation, or animal welfare group.

While the year before, several environmental groups split away from the majority of U.S. nongovernmental organizations to support the North American Free Trade Agreement (NAFTA), environmentalists were unified in opposition to the Uruguay Round Agreements. Then-U.S. Trade Representative Mickey Kantor claimed that no U.S. environmental or health laws would be undermined by the WTO, testifying, "The . . . [WTO] clearly recognizes and acknowledges the sovereign right of each government to establish the level of protection of human, animal, and plant life and health deemed appropriate by that government."[1] But these assurances failed to persuade the environmental community.

The environmentalists' skepticism was not surprising. Some of the groups that had supported NAFTA the year before—in exchange for an environmental "side agreement"—felt betrayed. First, early indications were that the side agreement would be ineffective.[2] Second, the groups had been promised by the Clinton administration that the NAFTA model would establish a "floor" for environmental protection in trade agreements that would be strengthened in subsequent trade pacts.[3] Instead, NAFTA's environmental side pact turned out to be the high-water mark. The next year it became clear that the Uruguay Round Agreements contained numerous provisions limiting the actions governments could take to protect the public and the environment—but included no environmental safeguards at all.

In addition, environmentalists had witnessed the negative impacts of GATT provisions in effect before the Uruguay Round. In several instances, countries had challenged environmental laws as violating GATT rules. GATT dispute resolution tribunals had agreed that the environmental laws violated GATT rules and also made extremely narrow interpretations of several GATT "exception" provisions that theoretically could be relied upon to protect environmental safeguards from such challenges.

Environmentalists feared that the expansive new powers of enforcement that were granted to the WTO, combined with the anti-environmental bias already evident in the GATT, would produce dire consequences for global environmental protection. Environmentalists implored the Uruguay Round negotiators to refashion their approach to environmental issues.[4]

These entreaties were ignored by the negotiators, who produced an agreement that built upon the GATT's foundation of rules prioritizing commercial prerogatives over conservation and environmental protection. In an effort to counter the potential political problems that environmental concerns could cause with parliaments faced with approval of the Uruguay Round, the future WTO Member countries made a last-minute decision at the Marakesh, Morocco, WTO signing ceremonies to establish a Committee on Trade and Environment (CTE). The committee was given the mandate to study ways to make trade and environmental goals mutually compatible. The CTE was designated a WTO study group (not a negotiating group, meaning it was not empowered to develop new WTO rules for environmental protection). It has proven entirely ineffective as a mechanism for promoting environmental interests within the WTO.

Five years of experience under the WTO have confirmed environmentalists' fears. In case after case, the WTO is being used to threaten or has upheld formal challenges to environmental safeguards, doing far more damage than what occurred under the pre-Uruguay Round regime.

Threats—often by industry but with government support—of WTO illegality are being used to chill environmental innovation. Increased trade flows also are leading to greater biodiversity problems caused by invasive species infestations, and the status of multilateral environmental agreements is being undermined by the WTO. . . .

Through the threat of sanctions, the WTO has compelled countries to repeal or rewrite key environmental laws or has chilled innovations. Particularly disturbing, most challenges to date have merely involved the application of the WTO's new enforcement powers to long-standing, anti-environmental GATT rules. The new, stronger, anti-environmental provisions developed through the Uruguay Round have, with limited exceptions, only been brought to bear in the context of threats. These new agreements, as they are fully implemented, will provide new, far broader opportunities for anti-environmental interests to use the WTO to attack environmental safeguards—a process already under way.

Gatt and the Environment: Pre-Uruguay Round

The GATT's anti-environmental bent was apparent prior to negotiations of approval of the Uruguay Round, as exemplified by high-profile challenges to two key U.S. environmental laws—the Marine Mammal Protection Act (MMPA) and the Corporate Average Fuel Efficiency (CAFE) standards for automobiles.

In 1991, GATT Article III on National Treatment (nondiscrimination) was interpreted to prohibit governments from treating goods differently based on the way they are produced or harvested. This interpretation arose from a successful GATT challenge by Mexico to the MMPA—an effective, long-standing U.S. statute banning the U.S. sale of tuna caught by domestic or foreign fishers using purse seines. Purse seines are massive nets that are laid over schools of dolphins to catch tuna swimming below. The technique had resulted in millions of dolphin nets.[5] A GATT tribunal ruled that the U.S. law violated GATT rules by distinguishing tuna caught in a dolphin-safe manner from tuna caught using deadly encirclement seines.

Then, in 1994, a GATT panel ruled against U.S. CAFE regulations on a challenge brought by the European Economic Community (EEC). The GATT panel concluded that although the CAFE rules were facially neutral— i.e., they treated domestic and foreign cars alike—they had a discriminatory effect on European cars. Under the regulation, a manufacturer's entire fleet of cars sold in the U.S. was required to meet a combined average fuel efficiency. European auto manufacturers had made the marketing decision to sell only the larger, high-end (and thus more profitable) models of their cars in the United States. An unintended consequence of that marketing decision was the requirement under the CAFE standards that such models be more fuel efficient than comparable American or Japanese luxury cars, whose efficiency could be averaged against smaller, cleaner models that the American and Japanese makers also sold on the U.S. market.

In both the dolphin and the automobile fuel efficiency cases, the U.S. tried to invoke exceptions to the GATT that are contained in Article XX of the agreement. Article XX "exceptions" are supposed to allow countries to adopt and/or maintain laws that contradict GATT rules in certain narrowly defined circumstances.[6] In theory, the exceptions protect countries from inappropriate infringements on the capacity of policymakers to protect the public interest in vital areas such as national security and, theoretically, health or environmental protection. However, in both of these cases, the exceptions were so narrowly interpreted as to render them moot.

Thus, before the Uruguay Round talks were complete, environmentalists had witnessed successful attacks on environmental laws using GATT rules and had seen that the existing GATT exceptions provided no protection for such laws.

The WTO and the Environment: Strong Enforcement of Anti-Environmental Laws

Mindful of this disturbing pre-Uruguay Round track record, environmentalists urged Uruguay Round negotiators to strengthen the weak Article XX exceptions so that they might be used effectively to safeguard WTO-challenged environmental laws. They also sought to amend GATT provisions that had been—or could be—the basis for attacks on environmental policies. Since a central objective of the Uruguay Round was to make the GATT and other related agreements strongly enforceable through the WTO by use or threat of trade sanctions, environmentalists considered it to be critical that the new regime not include provisions that could undermine domestic and international environmental laws and policy.

Uruguay Round negotiators refused to remedy the existing problems. Rather, in the Uruguay Round Agreements, they added a vast array of new anti-environment, anti-conservation provisions to the existing GATT rules. These new rules subject a wider array of hard-won environmental laws to scrutiny as so-called "non-tariff barriers" to trade. . . .

The WTO agreement on Sanitary and Phytosanitary Measures (SPS) explicitly restricts the actions that governments can take relating to food and agriculture in an effort to protect the environment, human, plant, and animal health, and the food supply. As a result, many policies that governments use to avoid or contain invasive species infestations from undermining biodiversity can run afoul of SPS rules. The WTO agreement on Technical Barriers to Trade (TBT) requires that product standards—a nation's rules governing the contents and characteristics of products—be the least restrictive version and, with extraordinarily limited exceptions, be based on international standards. The WTO agreement on Government Procurement (AGP) requires that governments take into account only "commercial considerations" when making purchasing decisions. The agreement on Trade Related Aspects of Intellectual Property Rights (TRIPS) requires that WTO Members provide property rights protection to genetically modified plant varieties even though their long-term environmental impacts have not been established. All of these agreements are enforceable, by threat of sanction, through the WTO's dispute resolution system.

A crucial difference between the GATT and the WTO trade regimes is the legal status of their respective dispute settlement panel rulings. Both systems include the possibility of challenging other countries' laws before trade tribunals, when one country thinks another's law violates GATT rules. Under GATT, however, the emphasis was on cooperation and negotiated settlements to trade agreements. The WTO, in contrast, is "self-executing," which means its panels are empowered to make binding decisions, enforceable through trade sanctions.

Under pre-Uruguay Round rules, a dispute panel report was adopted only if there was consensus by all GATT Contracting Parties. Requiring consensus for action is a typical sovereignty protection found in many international agreements. Under the previous GATT rules, a country whose domestic regulations were under fire could essentially block the enforcement of a ruling (although, in order to avoid undermining GATT's legitimacy, countries rarely exercised this option).

The Uruguay Round Agreements turned the sovereignty safeguard of consensus on its head by requiring unanimous consensus to stop adoption of any WTO panels' ruling. This would require 134 [now 155] WTO Members, including the victorious country, to all agree to stop adoption of a panel ruling. The intention of this change was to create a rule-based system in which all WTO Members were equal, since the former cooperative system was seen to give too much negotiating power to the financially stronger countries [that] had more political ability to decide to follow or ignore rulings. Unfortunately, the effect of the new binding system has been to consolidate the dominant position of countries that can afford permanent representation at the WTO and expert help at the panel hearings.[7] Worse still, the outcomes of trade battles are now being sold to the public as technical, legal interpretations of commercial law and not recognized as what they are: political and policy decisions.

While the WTO publicly states its support for the principles of sustainable development in the WTO ("the [environment] has been given and will continue to be given a high profile on the WTO agenda"),[8] the track record suggests an altogether different set of priorities. Indeed, in a revealing attack of candor, then-WTO Secretary General Renato Ruggiero stated that environmental standards in the WTO are "doomed to fail and could only damage the global trading system."[9]

WTO's New Binding Rules have Weakened Environmental Safeguards

• • •

Case 2: Clinton Administration Guts Dolphin Protection

Under amendments to the U.S. Marine Mammal Protection Act (MMPA), the sale by domestic or foreign fishers of tuna caught with encirclement nets, known as purse seines, was banned in the U.S. in 1988 because the nets killed millions of dolphins in the Eastern Tropical Pacific.[10] For reasons marine biologists have never determined, schools of tuna in that region congregate under schools of dolphins. Thus, the fishing industry began using mile-long nets deployed by speedboats to encircle the dolphins on the surface. In this method, the weighted bottoms of the massive nets are drawn short, creating huge sacks in which both the dolphins and tuna are trapped.

Over 30 years, seven million dolphins were drowned, crushed, or otherwise killed as a result of purse seine tuna fishing.[11]

The slaughter was captured on videotape by an environmentalist who slipped aboard a fishing boat as a cook.[12] The resulting furor—including millions of children writing to Congress to "Save the Dolphins"—led to the dolphin-safe tuna provisions of the MMPA.[13] Two of the four affected species of dolphin, the eastern spinner and northeastern offshore spotted dolphins, have been designated "depleted" under the MMPA due to purse seine fishing methods.[14]

The GATT Dolphin Cases

In 1991, a GATT panel ruled against Section 101(a)(2) of the U.S. MMPA[15]—which excluded from the U.S. market tuna caught by domestic or foreign fishers using purse seines. The panel interpreted language in GATT's Article III, which prohibits discrimination between products on the basis of *where* they are produced, to also forbid distinguishing between products based on *how* they are produced (called production processes and methods or PPMs). Specifically, the GATT panel interpreted language in GATT Article III requiring "like products" produced domestically or abroad to be given equal treatment. By deciding that the notion of "like product" only pertained to a product's physical characteristics, the panel ruling placed a long list of U.S. and other countries' laws that focus on *how* tuna is caught or *how* paper is manufactured in violation of GATT rules. Thus, unless there is literally dolphin meat in a can of tuna, making it physically different, a can of tuna caught with dolphin-deadly nets must be treated exactly the same as one caught by dolphin-safe methods.

The next year the European Community, which sought to export prepared tuna processed from fish obtained from Pacific Ocean stocks, launched its own challenge to the law.[16] In its 1994 ruling, the GATT panel on the European challenge again ruled against dolphin protection.[17]

In both cases, the U.S. argued that because dolphin protection is a legitimate environmental objective and the embargo was applied to both the domestic and foreign tuna industries, the law would fall well within the protections of GATT Article XX. Both GATT panels rejected this argument. The first panel found that the law was not "necessary" to protect dolphin health because, in the panel's opinion, the United States could have attempted to protect dolphins through other measures that would not have violated GATT.[18] It also found that the U.S. law targeted tuna fishing largely outside U.S. borders and ruled that Article XX applied only to actions taken inside a nation's borders.[19] This ruling is astounding, given that fish are migratory and are not confined to the territory of one country.

The panel in the European challenge disagreed with the first panel's conclusion that a country can never, under GATT rules, protect resources outside of its territory if such protections limit trade. However, it agreed with the first panel that the dolphin-safe law was not "necessary" to protect dolphin health and thus that the U.S. law was GATT-illegal.

In addition, the panel in the European challenge concluded that a nation cannot require another country to change domestic laws—in this case adopt regulations on tuna fishing to protect dolphins—in exchange for market access.[20] The U.S. could pressure individual tuna producers to change their behavior but could not condition access to the U.S. market for these producers on their home country governments' taking concrete action to enforce U.S. dolphin protection standards. This line of reasoning would be recycled in a similar WTO case involving a U.S. embargo on shrimp from countries that do not require fishers to protect sea turtles (see [next case]).

Given that the rulings against the U.S. dolphin-safe law were issued by GATT—and not WTO—panels, they were not automatically enforceable. Indeed, worried that implementation of the controversial 1991 GATT case that had been dubbed GATTzilla vs. Flipper could threaten NAFTA's 1993 congressional approval, the U.S. and Mexico originally agreed to block further GATT action.

However, in 1995, with NAFTA already implemented and the WTO enforcement mechanism now in effect, Mexico threatened a WTO enforcement case against the United States for continuing failure to implement the 1991 GATT dolphin ruling. In order to avoid the political embarrassment of having the WTO order the U.S. to rescind the highly popular dolphin protection (or face millions of dollars in trade sanctions) the Clinton administration launched a two-year campaign that ultimately resulted in the gutting of the MMPA.

Clinton Administration Guts Dolphin Law to Comply with GATT

President Clinton was so anxious to avoid the public spectacle of a dolphin protection law being eviscerated again by the WTO, he sent a letter to Mexican President Ernesto Zedillo declaring that the weakening of the standard "is a top priority for my Administration and for me personally."[21] Clinton promised to take action within the first thirty days of his second term.[22] It would not prove easy to comply with the ruling or this promise, as this required the United States to amend the [MMPA] through an act of Congress.

The administration recruited several members of Congress with notoriously bad environmental voting records, such as Rep. Randy "Duke" Cunningham, a California Republican, and Sen. John Breaux, a Louisiana

Democrat, to introduce a bill weakening the MMPA to make it conform to the GATT ruling. That legislation was quickly nicknamed the "Dolphin Death Act" by many environmental groups.[23]

Under the leadership of the [MMPA]'s original champions, such as Sen. Barbara Boxer and Rep. George Miller, both California Democrats, a coalition of environmental, consumer, and other public interest groups—the Dolphin Safe Fair Trade Campaign—was able to stall the Dolphin Death Act in 1996. However, a slightly different version of the legislation was passed in August 1997[24] after a huge push by the Clinton administration, led by then-Undersecretary of State Timothy Wirth and Vice President Al Gore. The amendment would allow tuna caught with the deadly nets to be sold in the United States. Moreover, it would even allow tuna caught with such nets to carry the "dolphin safe" label that consumers have come to know and trust—provided the tuna is certified as coming from a catch where a single monitor on a football field–length fishing boat did not observe any dolphin deaths.

On April 29, 1999, the Commerce Department announced that based on the results of a study by the National Marine Fisheries Service (NMFS)[25] in consultation with the Marine Mammal Commission and the Inter-American Tropical Tuna Commission (IATTC), it would implement the 1997 law and weaken the labeling standard for "dolphin safe" tuna.[26] The study, mandated by the 1997 legislation, concluded that dolphin mortality has declined in areas where purse seines are used when monitors are aboard fishing fleets.[27] The study also found, however, that the dolphin population in the Eastern Tropical Pacific was not recovering, despite the use of monitors. The study showed that although mortality rates declined relative to unmonitored purse seine fishing, the decline was not sufficient to replace the damage that purse seines had already wrought on the dolphin population. Nonetheless, the Commerce Department decided to move ahead, and tuna caught with purse seines was slated to be back on the U.S. market by the fall of 1999—for the first time in over a decade. (Meanwhile, the IATTC will continue to study dolphin mortality until 2002, at which time, if the results are the same, the United States will make the new U.S. standard permanent.)[28]

The U.S. Commerce Department claims that the new regulation will allow only tuna from catches during which no dolphin deaths were observed to bear the "dolphin safe" label.[29] However, tuna boats are a football field in length, the nets are miles in circumference, and only one observer is required per ship—making it physically impossible to monitor thoroughly. Moreover, to enforce this policy, the United States would have to track all tuna imports from the moment they are caught in the Eastern Tropical Pacific to the time they enter the U.S. consumer market. This presents an enormous task for regulators, which is why the old law operated on a country-by-country basis, not on a catch-by-catch basis. It remains unclear how the United States can, with any confidence, distinguish among tuna shipments that have involved the death of dolphins and those that have not. Instead, regulators will have to rely on the "dolphin safe" reports of the producers themselves—those with the greatest incentive to downplay dolphin deaths. Consumer and environmental groups say that this new policy degrades the "dolphin safe" label from an effective way in which to hold the tuna industry accountable to consumers to a cynical marketing ploy rewarding unsafe fishing practices.[30]

The precedent set in the GATT panel's ruling has widespread implications.[31] It declares import bans designed to further a legitimate social or environment aim by eliminating objectionable production methods to be outside GATT/WTO permissible policy. Under such reasoning, prohibiting the use of fur harvested by clubbing of harp seals could be GATT-illegal. Similarly, bans on products involving child labor or even slave labor could be prohibited by the WTO.

Case 3: The WTO Rules against Endangered Species Act

Provisions of the Endangered Species Act allow sale of shrimp in the United States only if the shrimp is caught in nets equipped with turtle excluder devices, or TEDs.[32] These devices are designed to allow sea turtles to escape from shrimp nets. In late 1998, a WTO panel ruled that the U.S. law violated trade rules and ordered the United States to rewrite its turtle protection policy. Worldwide, the turtle population has plummeted, and all sea turtles that inhabit U.S. waters are listed as endangered or threatened.[33] Shrimp nets entangle, drown, dismember, and kill as many as 55,000 endangered or threatened sea turtles each year.[34] Indeed, shrimping kills more sea turtles than all other human threats to turtles combined.[35]

In an effort to minimize the decline in the sea turtle populations, the National Marine Fisheries Service promoted the use of TEDs to U.S. shrimpers. After few shrimpers installed TEDs in their nets, U.S. law was changed in 1980 to require shrimpers to operate in a manner that did not harm turtles.[36] Under section 609 of the Endangered Species Act,[37] all shrimp sold in the United States must be caught using TEDs, any of several trapdoor-like devices that shunt sea turtles out of shrimp nets before they drown. Costing from $50 to $400, TEDs are a relatively inexpensive way to reduce sea turtle deaths by as much as 97%—without appreciably decreasing shrimp catches.[38]

The governments of India, Malaysia, Pakistan, and Thailand joined forces to challenge the U.S. law, arguing that WTO rules prohibit limitations on imports based on the way products are produced.[39] Australia, El Salvador, the EU [European Union], Guatemala, Hong Kong, Japan, Nigeria, the Philippines, Singapore, and Venezuela made third-party submissions to the WTO panel arguing that the U.S. law violated WTO rules.

Under the argument used by these nations—the same one used in the tuna-dolphin case—all shrimp are "like products" and therefore must be allowed into the U.S. market, regardless of whether the shrimp are caught using methods that kill sea turtles.

The United States argued that it was allowed under WTO rules to protect animal life, as long as the law was applied equally to U.S. and foreign shrimp producers. Indeed, unlike the MMPA challenge in the tuna-dolphin case, which had a potential for technical discrimination in how one aspect was implemented, the turtle policy was exactly the same for foreign and domestic fishers. Thus, the United States argued that the shrimp law qualified for an exception under Article XX.

The WTO panel disagreed. "We note that the issue in dispute was not the urgency of protection of sea turtles, . . . It was not our task to review generally the desirability or necessity of the environmental objectives of the U.S. policy on sea turtle conservation. In our opinion, Members are free to set their own environmental objectives. However, they are bound to implement these objectives in such a way that is consistent with their WTO obligations, not depriving the WTO Agreement of its object and purpose."[40]

The panel ruled that the U.S. law was designed to interfere with trade and thus the Article XX exceptions were inapplicable. Of course, this interpretation eviscerates the entire exceptions clause of GATT. The panel also declared that because the regulations were unilaterally imposed on U.S. trading partners, the law deprived the WTO of its object and purpose of establishing a multilateral trade regime, regardless of the nontrade-related objective that was being pursued and the lack of discrimination between domestic and foreign fisheries.

Major U.S. environmental organizations quickly denounced the decision and urged the Clinton administration to continue to implement the sea turtle protections and attempt to reform the WTO substantially—or withdraw from it.[41] Even the pro-WTO *New York Times* editorialized about the "Sea Turtles Warning," contradicting its past admonitions about WTO critics' unfounded concerns by urging the WTO to reconsider and the United States not to change the law.[42] The U.S. government appealed the WTO decision.[43]

In October 1998, the WTO Appellate Body reaffirmed the decision that the U.S. law is WTO-illegal.[44] However, the Appellate Body reversed the lower panel as to whether the Endangered Species Act theoretically could be covered by Article XX exceptions.[45] Reaching impressive heights of legal sophistry, the panel held that the law could indeed have qualified for an environmental exception under Article XX but did not do so in this case because the law was implemented in a way that was unjustifiably and arbitrarily discriminatory.[46]

The Appellate Body's ruling has been viewed as an attempt to defuse the criticism of environmentalists while still advancing the GATT agenda of primacy of trade over all other policy goals. The panel acknowledged that sea turtles are endangered and that there is a legitimate interest in protecting and preserving them. It also acknowledged the appropriateness of the U.S. turtle excluder device policy. The ruling included language aimed at pacifying environmentalists, stating, "We have not decided that the protection and preservation of the environment is of no significance to the Members of the WTO. Clearly, it is. We have not decided that the sovereign nations that are Members of the WTO cannot adopt effective measures to protect endangered species, such as sea turtles. Clearly they can and should."[47] Despite the positive sounding political rhetoric, the WTO Appellate Body ultimately ruled that the measure violated WTO rules.

The Appellate Body recommended that the United States change its turtle protection measures to comply with the ruling, leading one trade policy expert to quip, "Good dicta for environmentalists, but I wouldn't want to be a sea turtle."[48]

If implemented, the WTO ruling against the Endangered Species Act could severely hamper efforts to protect sea turtles. Perversely, it could also put the U.S. producers who have already invested in TEDs technology at a competitive disadvantage for having complied with the law of the land. According to one shrimper, "We are the ones who have to pay the price to save the turtle. I thought we were going to have a level playing field to compete, but apparently not."[49]

As domestic industry learns the lesson that the WTO is hostile to strong environmental safeguards, affected domestic industries will question environmental legislation on the basis that it disadvantages them vis-à-vis their foreign competitors, whose noncompliance is effectively sanctioned by the WTO. The combination of WTO environmental hostility and related industry pressure will make it increasingly difficult for countries to assert environmental leadership in the absence of often slow or impossible international consensus.

Initially, the United States agreed to comply with the WTO ruling against the Endangered Species Act by revising regulations to allow

shipment-by-shipment certification of TED use. Under the original regulation, a country seeking to send shrimp to the United States was responsible
for requiring its shrimp fleet to have sea turtle protections comparable to
the Endangered Species Act standard. Environmental groups charged that
the new regulation would violate the Endangered Species Act. In April
1999, the U.S. Court of International Trade (CIT) sided with environmental groups, interpreting Section 608 of the [Endangered Species Act]
as requiring countries to have fleet-wide TED regulations in place before
any boat could export shrimp to the United States.[50] That would stop
shrimpers who don't use TEDs from evading U.S. law by purchasing
export permits that say they do or by shipping their product on boats that
do use TEDs.[51]

The Clinton administration faces a stark choice. The administration
agreed to comply with the WTO ruling by taking regulatory action, thus
limiting the role of Congress and the public. The [CIT] ruling removes this
option. Now, the administration must bow to the WTO and prepare for a
bruising congressional battle to change the Endangered Species Act or face
WTO sanctions.

Multilateral Environmental Agreements Run Afoul of WTO

The negotiation of multilateral environmental agreements (MEAs) represents a recognition of the fact that natural resources like air, water, and
wildlife are not constrained by national borders. When these resources are
threatened by pollution or with extinction, nations must cooperate to forestall the damage. These are numerous multilateral efforts under way to
address global environmental issues such as climate change, air pollution,
endangered species, and the trade in hazardous waste.

MEAs are the embodiment of global progress toward, and commitment
to, the preservation of the environment. Yet many WTO rules explicitly contradict MEAs, including those in effect long before the WTO's formation. As
a matter of international law, the WTO automatically supersedes MEAs
signed before the WTO. Uruguay Round negotiators refused to include
language in the WTO to make MEAs and their domestic enforcement
immune to WTO challenge.

There are several ways in which MEAs can run afoul of WTO rules. First,
some of the international environmental agreements explicitly restrict trade.
For instance, the Convention on International Trade in Endangered Species
(CITES) bans trade in endangered species; the Basel Convention on the
Transboundary Movement of Hazardous Waste bans the export of toxic
waste from rich countries—which produce 98% of the world's hazardous

waste—to developing nations; and the Montreal Protocol bans trade in ozone-depleting chemicals and also products made with those chemicals. Second, these treaties and others sometimes employ the use of trade sanctions to enforce their objectives. Still other [MEAs] do not involve trade sanctions but may require countries to adopt policies that affect the potential products (asbestos, for example) of one country more than those of another. Thus, MEAs of all stripes have a significant chance of coming into conflict with GATT/WTO rules.

Finally, unlike the WTO, which is self-executing, . . . the MEAs provide commitments that each country agrees to enforce. For instance, CITES lists species for which its signatory countries have agreed that protection is needed. But, the enforcement of CITES comes not through a central CITES tribunal but rather under the domestic laws of each signatory. Thus, many U.S. CITES obligations are enforced through the Endangered Species Act. [Endangered Species Act] provisions ban import of CITES-listed species and products made from them and endorse embargoes against countries that violate the rules.[52] Other countries have similar domestic laws implementing their CITES obligations. Yet, under WTO rules, such domestic laws can—and have—been challenged as illegal trade barriers.

WTO dispute panels are not required to interpret the existence of MEAs as evidence in favor of environmental laws that are challenged as WTO violations. Indeed, the rules of international law stipulate that the "latest in time" of international obligations trumps previous obligations unless an exception is taken.[53] While a very limited "saving" clause—giving some precedence to the three MEAs over conflicting rules—was forced in the North American Free Trade Agreement,[54] it is conspicuously absent in the WTO or other Uruguay Round Agreements. To date there have been several rulings both under GATT and the WTO that have been detrimental to domestic efforts to implement obligations undertaken under MEAs.

• • •

Misguided WTO Committee on the Environment

Environmentalists had hoped that the WTO's Committee on Trade and the Environment (CTE) would provide a forum for WTO Members to devise new WTO rules to safeguard MEAs. Indeed, the original CTE work plan prioritized the issue. But when the EU offered proposals in 1996 for WTO recognition of MEAs that allow the imposition of trade sanctions, the United States neither supported the EU nor produced any proposals of its own.[55] Other countries grew bitter at the lack of leadership from the

United States, the country that had called for the creation of the CTE in the first place.[56]

Indeed, in its somewhat beleaguered four years of operation, the CTE has failed to agree to any recommendations for pro-environment changes to the GATT/WTO system. Some environmentalists criticize it as being used primarily to identify environmental measures that distort trade and to propose ways to get rid of them.[57]

Recently, the CTE has shifted the entire approach to its work. Dubbed the "win-win" strategy, the new approach abandons the goal of protecting environmental regulations from WTO challenge and instead focuses on identifying and eliminating trade barriers (like subsidies for fisheries) that are also bad for the environment.

At the March 1999 high-level WTO meeting on the environment in Geneva, WTO officials sought out environmental groups to give this strategy their support.[58] A few groups such as World Wildlife International did issue positive statements on the idea of cutting fisheries subsidies,[59] but the environmental community as a whole criticized the WTO's failure to make progress on the issue of safeguarding existing environmental policies coming under increasing WTO attack worldwide.[60]

Now the Clinton administration is shifting its environmental strategy for WTO in the same direction, specifically as regards to its position in the WTO's Seattle Ministerial, where the WTO's future agenda will be set.[61] Indeed, some environmental groups view the shift to the so-called "win-win" strategy as a way to buy off environmental opposition to the European proposal to launch further liberalization talks and to make use of environmentalists to further aspects of the WTO's agenda.[62] Ironically, even as the WTO staff and now the Clinton administration are calling for such a "win-win" strategy, the United States is moving forward with its efforts to make liberalization in forest products—which is vigorously opposed by environmentalists and has been estimated by the industry to increase depletion of forests by 3%–4%[63]—a high priority for future WTO negotiations.[64]

ENDNOTES

1. U.S. Trade Representative Michael Kantor, Testimony to the House Ways and Means Committee, Jan. 26, 1994.
2. The North American Agreement on Environmental Cooperation (NAAEC) is ancillary to NAFTA, meaning its terms are not binding over any of NAFTA's core provisions. The NAAEC created the Commission for Environmental Cooperation (CEC), which can investigate citizens' complaints that a NAFTA member-country is not enforcing its environmental laws. The side agreement does not cover environmental problems caused by the *absence* of regulation. The

NAFTA environmental side agreement also specifically excludes laws on natural resources, endangered species, and other vital environmental issues. The process for seeking review of the limited areas covered is long and tortured. In the five years that NAFTA has been in effect, the CEC has issued a total of two fact-finding reports out of over 20 citizen submissions alleging government non-enforcement of environmental laws. The first report took the CEC over two years to complete, and though it found that Mexico was not enforcing its environmental laws in allowing the construction of a pier requiring the destruction of ecologically critical coral reefs in the port of Cozumel, the pier had been built and the reefs had been destroyed for over a year before the report was even issued. See "NAFTA Environmental Agreement: A Paper Tiger?" *News-Journal Wire Services*, Jul. 29, 1988. All petitions to use the limited provision that could result in actual enforcement actions (versus the issuance of reports on the matter) have been refused to date.

3. The Clinton Administration, *The NAFTA: Expanding U.S. Exports, Jobs, and Growth*, U.S. Government Printing Office, Nov. 1993, at 1.

4. Letter to President Clinton, April 21, 1998, Signed by the Center for International Environmental Law, Center for Marine Conservation, Community Nutrition Institute, Defenders of Wildlife, Earth Island Institute, Earthjustice Legal Defense Fund, Friends of the Earth, Humane Society of the United States, National Audubon Society, National Wildlife Federation, Natural Resources Defense Council, Sierra Club, on file at Public Citizen.

5. Between 1958 and 1994, at least 6 million dolphins in the Eastern Tropical Pacific have been killed by purse seine nets. See Shannon Brownlee, "A Political Casserole of Tuna and Greens," *U.S. News and World Report*, Aug. 11, 1997, at 53.

6. [Note deleted. See original article for note.]

7. American Electronics Association (AEA), *Legality Under International Trade Law of Draft Directive on Waste From Electrical and Electronic Equipment*, Mar. 1999, prepared by Rod Hunter and Marta Lopez of Hunton & Williams, Brussels, on file with Public Citizen.

8. See Chapter 8 [of *Whose Trade Organization? Corporate Globalization and the Erosion of Democracy*] on the WTO's Dispute Resolution System.

9. Robert Evans, "Green Push Could Damage Trade Body—WTO Chief," *Reuters*, May 15, 1998.

10. Shannon Brownlee, "A Political Casserole of Tuna and Greens," *U.S. News and World Report*, Aug. 11, 1997, at 53.

11. John Malek and Dr. Peter Bowler, *Dolphin Protection in the Tuna Fishery, Interdisciplinary Minor in Global Sustainability*, Seminar, Irvine: University of California Press (1997), at 1.

12. *Id.*

13. The key provision that was the target of challenges under GATT is 16 U.S.C. Section 1371(a)(2), prohibiting the importation of tuna from countries that harvest tuna using purse seine nets.

14. See Statement for the Inter-American Tropical Tuna Commission Meeting, Oct. 21–23, 1996.

15. GATT, United States—Restrictions on Imports of Tuna (DS21/R), Report of the Panel, Sep. 3, 1991.

16. See GATT, United States—Restrictions on Imports of Tuna (DS29/R), Report of the Panel, Jun. 1994.

17. See *id*. at Para. 6.0.

18. See GATT, Findings on U.S. Tuna Ban, Report of Dispute Panel, Aug. 16, 1991 at Paras. 5.24–5.29.

19. See *id*. at Paras. 5.30–5.34.

20. GATT, United States—Restrictions on Imports of Tuna (DS29/R), Report of the Panel, Jun. 1994, at Para. 5.24.

21. "Clinton Pledges Early, Renewed Effort to Pass Tuna-Dolphin Bill," *Inside U.S. Trade*, Oct. 1996.

22. *Id*.

23. See 104th Congress, H.R. 2179, Sponsor: Rep. "Duke" Cunningham (R-CA); see also S.1420, Sponsors: Sen. Ted Stevens (R-AK), Co-sponsor: Sen. John Breaux (D-LA).

24. See 105th Congress, H.R. 408, Sponsor: Rep. Gilchrest (R-MO); see also S.39, Sponsor: Sen. Ted Stevens (R-AK).

25. See 64 *Fed. Reg.* 24590, May 7, 1999. In its initial finding NMFS concluded that there was insufficient evidence to show that catching tuna by encircling dolphins has a significant adverse impact on dolphin stocks.

26. See U.S. Department of Commerce, "Commerce Department Issues Initial Finding on Tuna/Dolphin Interactions—Will Adopt New Dolphin-Safe Label Standard," Press Release, Apr. 29, 1999.

27. 64 *Fed. Reg.* 24590, May 7, 1999.

28. *Id*.

29. See U.S. Department of Commerce, "Commerce Department Issues Initial Finding on Tuna/Dolphin Interactions—Will Adopt New Dolphin-Safe Label Standard," Press Release, Apr. 29, 1999.

30. Scott Harper, "Rule Revised for Tuna Fishing, Encirclement Will be Allowed with Oversight to Help Protect Dolphins," *The Virginian Pilot*, May 18, 1999. A campaign by Earth Island Institute has resulted in commitments by some major tuna canners to use only tuna caught without purse seine nets.

31. A WTO Appellate Body has stated that adopted reports of either GATT or WTO "create legitimate expectations among Members and, therefore, should be taken into account where they are relevant to a dispute." Japan—Taxes on Alcoholic Beverages, (WT/DS10/AB/R), Report of the Appellate Body, Oct. 4, 1996, at 14. In practice, panels have cited previous reports as precedents and have supported subsequent rulings by referring to previous decisions.

32. Public Law 93–205, 16 U.S.C. 1531 *et.seq*; see also 52 *Fed. Reg.* 24244, Jun. 29, 1987.

33. *52 Fed. Reg.* 24244, Jun. 29, 1987. Five species of sea turtles fell under the Endangered Species Act regulations: loggerhead (Caretta caretta), Kemp's ridley (Lepidochelys kempi), green (Chelonia mydas), leatherback (Dermochelys coriacea), and hawksbill (Eretmochelys imbricate).

34. National Research Council, Committee on Sea Turtle Conservation, *Decline of the Sea Turtle: Causes and Prevention* (1990) at 5.

35. *Id*.

36. *Id.* at 17–18.

37. Pub. L. 101–162.

38. National Research Council, Committee on Sea Turtle Conservation, *Decline of the Sea Turtle: Causes and Prevention* (1990) at 11.

39. WTO, United States—Import Prohibition of Certain Shrimp and Shrimp Products (WT/DS58), Complaint by India, Malaysia, Pakistan, and Thailand.

40. WTO, United States—Import Prohibition of Certain Shrimp and Shrimp Products (WT/DS58/R), Final Report, May 15, 1998, at Para 9.1 (Concluding Remarks).

41. See Letter to President Clinton, Apr. 21, 1998, signed by the Center for International Environmental Law, Center for Marine Conservation, Community Nutrition Institute, Defenders of Wildlife, Earth Island Institute, Earthjustice Legal Defense Fund, Friends of the Earth, Humane Society of the United States, National Audubon Society, National Wildlife Federation, Natural Resources Defense Council, and Sierra Club, on file at Public Citizen.

42. "The Sea Turtles Warning," *The New York Times*, Apr. 10, 1998.

43. WTO, United States—Import Prohibition of Certain Shrimp and Shrimp Products (WT/DS58), Appealed on Jul. 13, 1998.

44. WTO, United States—Import Prohibition of Certain Shrimp and Shrimp Products (WT/DS58/AB/R), Report of the Appellate Body, Oct. 12, 1998, at Para. 187.

45. *Id.* at Para. 122.

46. *Id.* at Para. 184.

47. *Id.* at Para. 185.

48. Jock Nash, Trade Analyst, written communication with Michelle Sforza, Research Director, Public Citizen's Global Trade Watch, Oct. 13, 1998.

49. "Louisiana Shrimpers Threatened By Ruling on Turtle Excluder," *States News Service*, Apr. 14, 1998.

50. *Earth Island Institute vs. William M. Daley*, U.S. Court of International Trade, Case No. 98–09–02818, Apr. 2, 1999, at 35.

51. The U.S. government had initially refused to implement the shrimp-turtle policy's country-based certification requirements in favor of shipment-by-shipment certification. In 1996, three environmental groups sued to force implementation of the law as written. The U.S. Court of International Trade (ICT) ruled in 1997 for the environmentalists, and ordered the State Department to rewrite the rule to require country-based certification. This CIT ruling triggered the WTO challenge. The CIT overturned its earlier ruling on a technicality in 1998, but in April 1999, an appellate judge ruled that the law allowed the U.S. sale of shrimp only from countries that have regulations mandating TEDs. If the CIT affirms its interim ruling, the State Department will have no choice but to scrap its proposal to certify shrimp on a shipment-by-shipment basis.

52. 16 U.S.C. Chapter 35, Section 1538.

53. 1969 Vienna Convention on the Law of Treaties at Article 30(2).

54. North American Free Trade Agreement (NAFTA) at Para. 104.

55. Dan Seligman, *Broken Promises: How the Clinton Administration is Trading Away our Environment*, Sierra Club Responsible Trade Campaign, May 13, 1998.

56. *Id.*

57. See "U.S. Business, Environmental Groups Divided on Shrimp-Turtle Case," *BRIDGES Weekly Trade News Digest*, vol. 2, no. 15, Apr. 27, 1988.

58. "WTO Enviro Groups Getting Closer Together," *Washington Trade Daily*, Mar. 17, 1999.

59. "Green Groups Challenge WTO," *Financial Times*, Mar. 17, 1999.

60. "Cuts Urged in Fishing and Farm Aid," *Financial Times*, Mar. 16, 1999.

61. Statement by the U.S. delegation to the WTO General Council Session, Geneva, Switzerland, Jul. 29, 1999.

62. See e.g., Friends of the Earth International. The U.S. government was speaking about reconciling the WTO and the environment at the WTO high-level environmental meeting while it was negotiating with other countries in an attempt to secure a final forestry deal as an "early harvest" at the Seattle Ministerial.

63. The American Forest & Paper Association, "Forest Industry Leader Urges Worldwide Tariff Elimination," Press Release, Apr. 28, 2000, citing study by the international consultant firm of Jaakko Poyry.

64. Statement by the U.S. delegation to the WTO General Council Session, Geneva, Switzerland, Jul. 29, 1999.

Michael M. Weinstein and Steve Charnovitz

The Greening of the WTO

Save the Turtles

Anyone who has followed the negative press coverage of the World Trade Organization [WTO] over the last few years would be shocked to learn that the WTO has started to develop an environmental conscience. With only a few tweaks, it can turn greener still.

The most memorable assault on the WTO's environmental record came at its 1999 meeting in Seattle, where antiglobalization demonstrators dressed as sea turtles to highlight the alleged damage wrought by the organization's policies. Similar protests have dogged multilateral trade meetings ever since. But a careful look at the WTO's record shows that such attacks are unwarranted. The organization is in fact developing constructive principles for accommodating both trade and environmental concerns. A series of rulings by the WTO's dispute-resolution bodies—judicial panels that settle conflicts among member states—has established the principle that trade rules do not stand in the way of legitimate environmental regulation.

The gradual greening of the WTO throughout its seven-year life reflects changes made to international rules when the organization was created in 1994. In particular, the preamble to the WTO agreement noted the importance of protecting the environment and the need for enhanced means of doing so. Environmental sensitivity has also been heightened by the stalwart efforts of environmentalists in and out of government to influence the system of global trade. The environmental movement has, in fact, achieved most of the goals it pursued in the early 1990s—although the need to keep their supporters energized makes some groups loath to say so.

Moreover, and contrary to what protesters often claim, further progress can take place within the current system. This is reassuring, because modest reform is the only politically realistic way to further the green agenda. The WTO's rules can be changed only by a consensus of its 142 [now 147] members, and many developing nations want no part of a costly environmental program they regard as an imposition by the wealthy industrialized powers. Radical demands in this area would increase friction between rich and poor countries and sabotage efforts to start a new round of global trade negotiations—a round that the WTO's director-general proposes be focused on the needs of the poorest countries. Moderate proposals, backed by sound public explanations, have a much better chance of achieving significant results.

As the WTO struggles to handle environmental concerns, one issue looms above all others: the organization needs to figure out how to manage the clash between its open trade agenda and unilateral attempts by some member governments to protect the environment through trade restrictions. The WTO must strike a balance between two extremes. Cracking down too hard on the use of environmental trade restrictions invites environmental damage. But excessive leniency in imposing sanctions invites two other abuses: pressure on poorer countries to adopt standards that are ill suited to their strained economies, and suppression of trade that will lead to higher prices and stunted growth.

Seductive Sanctions

Trade policy must have an environmental dimension because the environment is a global collective resource. To manage it properly, governments must cooperate on all policies—including trade—that can threaten fisheries, forests, air quality, and endangered species. Without collective agreements, countries will be tempted to lower their environmental standards in an effort to increase their competitive advantage. The question is not whether there should be some form of international cooperation on environmental issues, but what kind of cooperation there should be, and under what institutional auspices.

Purists want environmental regulations left to specialized agencies, whereas many environmentalists want them enforced by the WTO. The argument for using the WTO is simple, for unlike most other international organizations, the WTO has a mechanism for enforcing its rulings: trade sanctions. The WTO convenes panels of experts to rule on trade disputes among member governments. If the losing government refuses to comply with the ruling, the panel authorizes the winning government to impose trade sanctions.

The recent transatlantic flap over hormones shows how the system works. Claiming that beef from cows fed with artificial hormones posed a health hazard, the European Union (EU) blocked imports of such beef from the United States in 1989. The U.S. government brought the dispute before a WTO panel, which ruled in Washington's favor. The panel, however, had no power to change Europe's laws. All it could do was authorize the United States to retaliate—which Washington did, by imposing stiff tariffs on meat products, cheeses, and several other European exports. Punishment through sanctions was quick and easy. That is why environmentalists, along with organized labor and many other groups, want to use the international trading system to advance their missions.

Trade sanctions come at a cost, however. They often backfire, hurting a country's own consumers while aiding a politically powerful group of domestic producers. They can drive up prices and threaten the living standards of workers in both rich and poor countries, as well as provide cover for protectionists. In the beef-hormone case, for example, U.S. sanctions did indeed hurt European farmers and ranchers. But they also raised food prices in the United States, punishing American consumers. And the sanctions have not forced the Europeans to back down. They continue to ban beef produced with artificial hormones.

Trade sanctions are at best crude weapons, and environmentalists should reconsider their enthusiasm for them. Sanctions are ill suited to the subtleties of environmental policymaking and unlikely to persuade developing countries to undertake environmentally sensitive policies. Even if sanctions might ultimately play some role in a few unusual cases, in general environmentalists ought to focus primarily on education, persuasion, and mediation.

Losing Battles, Winning the War

According to its critics, the WTO interferes with legitimate efforts by the United States and other countries to block imports that harm the environment. For example, Lori Wallach and Michelle Sforza of Public Citizen, a group affiliated with Ralph Nader, argue that "in case after case, the WTO is being used to threaten or has upheld formal challenges to environmental safeguards, doing far more damage than occurred under the [pre-WTO] regime." Using similar arguments, the Humane Society of the United States has labeled the WTO "the single most destructive international organization ever formed" when it comes to animals.

To prove their case, critics point to several controversial decisions made over the past decade by trade panels, each of which ruled against attempts by the United States to protect the environment through unilateral measures. Reading just the headlines, these decisions may indeed appear to have undermined conservation. But closer inspection reveals a different picture. As Professor John Jackson of the Georgetown University Law Center has said, environmentalists "lost the battles but won the war."

In the first set of cases, known as tuna-dolphin, two pre-WTO trade panels in 1991 and 1994 rejected U.S. bans on imports of tuna caught with nets that unintentionally also trapped dolphins, a threatened (although not endangered) species. Environmental advocates howled. But the decisions were never formally adopted by the then-governing body and therefore established no legal precedent. Besides, the tuna-dolphin panels predate the creation of the WTO and its improved recognition of environmental concerns. Nevertheless, critics of the WTO cite this case as evidence of the threat that trade-dispute panels continue to pose to the environment.

In the second case, a WTO trade panel ruled that the United States had wrongfully blocked imports of Venezuelan and Brazilian gasoline, which the United States claimed violated its clean-air laws. The United States appealed the decision to the organization's Appellate Body, where it lost again. Environmental activists angrily accused the WTO of trampling Washington's right to protect the American environment. But the appellate decision was actually a step forward because it rejected some of the key findings of the lower panel. The appellate jurists found no problem with the U.S. clean-air law itself, declaring it legitimate under the provision of the WTO agreement that permits trade barriers "relating to the conservation of exhaustible natural resources." They merely disapproved of the regulations the United States used to administer the law, in particular the fact that the rules subjected foreign gasoline suppliers to tougher standards than were applied to domestic suppliers. All that Washington had to do to bring its policy into compliance was correct its administrative procedures, and it has since done so.

In the third case, known as shrimp-turtle, a WTO trade panel in 1998 ruled that the United States was wrongfully blocking imports of shrimp from countries that did not require fishing fleets to use devices designed to safeguard endangered sea turtles. Once again the WTO's Appellate Body upheld the ruling—but once again it rejected some of the lower panel's key arguments. The appellate judges acknowledged that an import ban might sometimes be justified and thus found nothing inherently wrong with the U.S. law in question. But it sharply criticized Washington for using administrative procedures that lacked due process and for making insufficient efforts to negotiate a conservation agreement with the Asian governments filing the complaint. As in the gasoline case, the WTO ruled that the United States needed to change only its procedures, not its law, to bring itself into compliance, and the United States has done so. Last year Malaysia challenged the revised U.S. regulations, but this time the WTO panel sided with the United States. Indeed, the judges went so far as to declare that "sustainable development is one of the objectives of the WTO agreement." This decision is now under appeal.

The Appellate Body's judgment in the shrimp-turtle case demonstrates that trade law may permit a nation to impose an import ban even when the primary purpose of the ban is to safeguard an endangered species found outside that nation's territory. In terms of environmental protection, that stance is light-years ahead of the tuna-dolphin ruling from ten years ago. Another milestone was reached this year in a dispute over asbestos, a carcinogen. The WTO Appellate Body upheld France's policy of blocking imports from Canada that contain the material—the first time the WTO has approved the use of a trade restriction to protect human health.

Precautionary Puzzle

Although the WTO has begun to embrace environmental protection, it certainly can and should do more. The challenge will be to find an effective middle ground among the rival parties in this debate: environmentalists and free traders, the United States and the EU, and the industrialized and developing worlds.

One proposal favored by European governments and environmental advocates on both sides of the Atlantic is to write a "precautionary principle" into WTO rules. This measure would protect the right of countries to block imports of products they deem a threat to public health, safety, or the environment even when no existing scientific evidence supports the feared threat. Had this concept prevailed when the beef-hormone case was decided, the Europeans would have won. Lurking behind the proposal to adopt the precautionary principle is the dispute over genetically modified organisms (GMOs). The United States is a large producer of food products incorporating GMOs, and American industry, citing a lack of evidence to the contrary, insists that they are safe. Europeans respond that GMOs are too new for scientists to know what their long-term consequences might be.

Two aspects of the WTO framework bear on this issue. First, the Agreement on the Application of Sanitary and Phytosanitary Measures (SPS) governs a country's rules for protecting the health of its people, animals, and plants from listed risks such as toxins, disease, and pests. The SPS requires that these rules be based on scientific evidence showing that a risk to health exists, although scientific certainty is not required. Once a risk has been established, individual countries can set their standards as high as they like. In the beef-hormone case the SPS agreement was invoked successfully against the Europeans because the EU did not produce scientific evidence to support its claims. Another accord, the Agreement on Technical Barriers to Trade (TBT), governs general health and safety standards. The TBT does not require a country to produce a scientifically backed assessment of risk, but it does insist, among other conditions, that standards be set in a way that restricts trade as little as possible to achieve the intended goal.

Neither the SPS nor the TBT threatens legitimate environmental or health measures. Neither puts environmental restrictions into a scientific straitjacket. Both permit countries to set high standards even when the scientific evidence on risk is uncertain. For example, the SPS calls for making the standards provisional and subject to modification once more evidence becomes available. That approach provides for balance and is the reason that the Appellate Body ruled that the precautionary principle already "finds reflection" in the SPS.

Explicitly embedding a precautionary principle in the SPS or TBT sections of the WTO framework would, by contrast, allow countries to block imports on environmental or health grounds in the absence of any scientific evidence of a significant risk. This would be a step backward. The current WTO rules have not been abused to undermine any country's legitimate environmental or health standards. Furthermore, no one has determined how to define a precautionary principle that would not provide a gaping loophole for protectionism, health fads, or environmental zealotry. Finally, because of the provisions in the SPS and the TBT, the WTO does not need an explicit precautionary principle. What the EU and others should pursue instead is getting future judicial panels to provide plenty of legal room for countries to set high health standards when scientific evidence of risk exists but is uncertain.

It's Easy Being Green

The WTO can take several concrete steps to answer its critics. These need not be dramatic policy modifications, such as an ill-considered adoption of a precautionary principle. Instead, a series of measured, incremental changes could pass the twin tests of environmental effectiveness and political viability.

First, the organization should make some accommodation for multilateral environmental agreements—treaties among groups of countries that can call for trade restrictions to protect the environment. For example, the Montreal Protocol blocks trade in ozone-depleting chemicals with nonsignatory countries, and the Convention on International Trade in Endangered Species (often referred to by its acronym, CITES) bans trafficking in endangered species. Europe has lobbied within the WTO for giving deference to these agreements, a step that could lead the WTO to bless trade restrictions that would otherwise violate its rules.

The European position makes good sense in cases where trade controls are imposed by one signatory against another according to rules set out in a multilateral agreement both have ratified. But the issue becomes knottier when a signatory applies trade restrictions to a nonparty. Permitting this type of sanction would turn the WTO into a tool for coercing nonsignatory countries to join, or at least adhere to, the agreement in question. Complicating the matter further is the question of what precisely constitutes a multilateral environmental agreement. If two countries form a cartel and erect import barriers to protect domestic industry, should the WTO go along blindly so long as the countries label their agreement "environmental"? Although such shenanigans cannot be allowed, the EU makes a strong case for putting the WTO on the side of multilateral environmental cooperation. But a complete plan for doing so remains elusive.

Another needed step would open the WTO dispute-resolution process to public participation. The WTO's newfound sensitivity toward the environment has shallow roots. Several times the Appellate Body has had to overrule misguided judgments by lower panels, and nothing guarantees that future appellate jurists will be as wise or as shrewd as their predecessors. Environmentalists have been able to pull WTO jurisprudence away from the tuna-dolphin rulings, but advocates need to remain vigilant and fight any sign of backtracking if the trade body is to continue on its green trend. Yet WTO rules make public oversight difficult by keeping most deliberations secret, thereby breeding distrust. The organization has made some efforts to answer its critics. Recently, panels have been permitted to review unsolicited "friend of the court" briefs submitted by nongovernmental organizations. Yet this practice is hotly contested within the organization and may not continue. For reasons of both sound jurisprudence and sound public relations, the WTO ought to routinely accept briefs by independent experts.

Additionally, the WTO needs procedures specially crafted to handle environmental disputes. The shrimp-turtle case showed that the United States exploited its market power too quickly by imposing unilateral sanctions, and that the Asian plaintiffs complained to the WTO too quickly rather than examining their own fishing practices. When environmental disputes are brought to the WTO, the organization's director-general should push the parties, publicly if necessary, toward mediation. If that fails, then the WTO should steer the dispute to an appropriate environmental forum before getting involved itself.

The WTO should also explicitly authorize "eco-labeling." The EU wants to clarify WTO rules for labeling goods, protecting a country's right to require disclosure of potential health, safety, or environmental threats so that consumers can decide for themselves what risks to take. But labeling can create problems. For example, simply telling consumers when beef contains artificial hormones suggests that the hormones are dangerous, even though the scientific evidence says otherwise. For this reason, the U.S. Food and Drug Administration carefully regulates labels on food and drugs and prohibits claims that it deems misleading or scaremongering. On balance, however, giving countries wide latitude to label products would be a smart reform that would keep markets open while allowing countries to respect the wishes of concerned citizens.

The WTO should also appoint a commission of experts to monitor future trade negotiations in order to inform countries of the potential environmental impact of the measures under discussion. The goal would be to press negotiators to take account of environmental consequences before trade accords are signed. Such a review process would increase public confidence that environmental concerns had not been ignored.

Pressuring countries to adopt clean technologies would be another effective measure. This step would require member countries to lower tariffs and remove needless regulations that impede imports of pollution-control equipment and other environmental technologies and services. In addition, the industrialized countries should comply with an existing WTO rule calling for the transfer of technology to the developing world.

The WTO also needs to root out environmentally harmful national subsidies. Government subsidies to domestic fishing industries worsen the depletion of fishery stocks. Subsidies to other sectors, such as agriculture, can cause harm by encouraging overuse and excessive consumption of other natural resources. In 1999, the U.S. government joined several other countries in proposing that the WTO consider curbing fishing subsidies. The proposal was shelved after the failed Seattle conference. The initiative needs to be relaunched, and the WTO should combat other subsidies that harm both trade and the environment.

Defer to multilateral environmental agreements. Invite legal briefs from outside experts. Mediate before litigating disputes. Monitor the environmental impacts of proposed trade agreements. Allow eco-labeling. Promote technology transfer and trade in environmental services. Curb environmentally damaging subsidies. None of these ideas sound earth-shattering, because none are. Radical steps are not needed. For seven years, the WTO has moved toward a responsible environmental posture. The best way to continue that green trend is for the industrialized powers to latch onto a modest set of reforms that are affordable for developing nations, protect the environment and public health, and keep zealots and protectionists at bay.

PART II
MULTINATIONAL CORPORATIONS

Multinational corporations (MNCs) have always been highly controversial. MNCs are firms with production facilities in two or more countries. Corporations of this type have been part of the global economy from the early days of the British Empire, but the number of such firms operating in the global economy has grown rapidly during the last twenty-five years. Almost 80,000 MNCs are active today, up sharply from the 18,000 active in the late 1980s. MNCs spark controversy in part because they are very large actors that extend managerial control across national borders. MNCs, therefore, are vehicles through which foreign residents acquire the ability to make decisions about local resource use.

Chapter 6 examines the debate over whether MNCs create "sweatshops" in developing societies. The growth of MNC investment in manufacturing activities in developing societies has generated substantial concern about how MNCs treat workers in the factories they build. Such concern has focused on how much MNCs paid their developing-country workers and on the safety of the conditions in the factories. Paul Krugman argues that much of this concern is misplaced. The jobs that MNCs provide are better than the other jobs available to developing-country residents. Krugman suggests that trying to raise standards will merely reduce MNC investment in developing countries, thereby reducing the number of jobs created. John Miller counters Krugman. He argues that even if current MNC jobs are better than the alternatives, the jobs still can be made safer and be made to pay more. Doing so will not reduce investment by MNCs in developing countries.

Chapter 7 explores the impact of MNCs on national labor and environmental regulations. A concern commonly voiced is that MNCs will invest heavily in countries with lax regulatory standards and invest little in countries with more stringent regulations. Debora Spar and David Yoffie argue that the ability to invest where regulatory regimes are weakest creates a "race to the bottom" wherein governments relax regulations to attract investment. Daniel Drezner argues that fears of such dynamics are baseless. There is no evidence, he argues, that MNCs make decisions about where to invest based on regulatory regimes. Nor, he argues, is there evidence that governments relax standards to attract investment. Instead, he claims that the race to the bottom is merely a useful myth for proponents and opponents of globalization.

Chapter 8 focuses on a relatively new debate over sovereign wealth funds (SWFs). SWFs are not MNCs; they are state-owned investment funds. But SWFs raise many of the same concerns as MNCs. As Gal Luft argues, SWFs transfer control over domestic productive assets to foreigners. Moreover, foreign control rests in state hands and thus SWFs can be used to achieve political rather than economic objectives. Edwin Truman argues that concerns about SWFs becoming instruments for political influence are overstated. Instead, the dangers of SWFs rest in their relatively opaque decision-making process.

CHAPTER 6

SWEATSHOP REGULATION IS COUNTERPRODUCTIVE *v.* GOVERNMENTS MUST REGULATE SWEATSHOPS

Regulating Sweatshops Is Counterproductive

Advocate: Paul Krugman

Source: "In Praise of Cheap Labor: Bad Jobs at Bad Wages Are Better than No Jobs at All," *Slate* March 27, 1997, http://www.slate.com/id/1918

Governments Must Regulate Sweatshops

Advocate: John Miller

Source: "Why Economists Are Wrong about Sweatshops and the Antisweatshop Movement," *Challenge* 46 (January/February 2003): 93–122

As western multinational corporations (MNCs) move manufacturing production to developing countries, they face mounting criticism about working conditions in the factories they establish there. MNCs are often accused of running "sweat-shops." Although there is disagreement about what constitutes a sweatshop, an acceptable definition might be a manufacturing facility that requires its workers to work long hours for low wages, often in unsafe conditions. Though we lack extensive and systematic research to determine the prevalence of such factories, considerable evidence documents such practices in footwear, apparel, toys, and sporting goods industries. They seem also to be more common in locally owned firms than in MNC–owned subsidiaries.

The emergence of sweatshops in developing societies has generated sub-stantial discussion and debate about whether and how governments should respond. Two questions are central. The first question is whether governments should create a set of global labor regulations to reduce the incidence of sweat-shops. The question of whether regulations are necessary is tightly linked to the kind of regulation contemplated. Is it a matter of broad human rights principles, or should governments craft very specific rules that regulate wages and work-place practices? The second question is where to pursue such regulations. Should global labor standards remain the exclusive purview of the International Labor Organization (ILO), or should governments make labor standards an inte-gral part of the World Trade Organization (WTO)?

REGULATING SWEATSHOPS IS COUNTERPRODUCTIVE

Developing-country governments are among the most vocal opponents of global labor standards. They oppose such regulation for two primary reasons. First, they argue that current wages and workplace conditions reflect their underlying comparative advantage in low-skill labor. Global standards that raise the cost of labor in developing societies therefore make it more difficult for developing countries to capitalize on their current comparative advantage. Moreover, developing-country governments believe that western efforts to bring labor standards into the WTO reflect protectionist orientations. As Marin Khor, the Director of Third World Network, has argued, "developing countries fear that the objectives of the northern governments that back [global labor standards] are ... to protect jobs in the North by reducing the low-cost incentive that attracts global corporations to developing societies."[1]

Paul Krugman develops this line of argument in detail. He suggests that rather than lamenting these factories, we should recognize that they represent a positive step on the path of economic development. Working in such factories may not be pleasant, and the wages may not be high by western standards, but the jobs available in these factories are better than any of the available alternatives. Moreover, sweatshop conditions will gradually disappear as developing countries transition from low-skill labor-intensive industries to higher skill types of production. In this context, implementing standards via the WTO will be counterproductive.

GOVERNMENTS MUST REGULATE SWEATSHOPS

Northern labor unions have been among the greatest advocates of international labor regulation. They wish to expand global labor regulations beyond the four core standards currently embodied in the ILO's Declaration on the Fundamental Principles and Rights at Work. These "Core Labor Standards" require governments to respect and promote principles and rights in four categories: freedom of association and collective bargaining, elimination of compulsory labor, elimination of child labor, and elimination of discrimination in the workplace. Many in the antisweatshop movement would like to expand these core standards to include minimum pay and workplace safety regulations. Advocates of regulation have also sought to make core labor standards an integral part of the WTO in order to compensate for the ILO's lack of enforcement capability. The WTO could enforce compliance through its dispute settlement mechanism. Governments would gain the right to suspend tariff concessions to countries that violated commonly agreed standards.

---

[1] Martin Khor, "How the South Is Getting a Raw Deal at the WTO," in *Views from the South: the Effects of Globalization and the WTO on the Third World*, ed. Sarah Anderson, 1–49 (San Francisco: International Forum on Globalization, 1999).

John Miller develops this proregulation perspective. He claims that available evidence does not suggest that global labor standards will reduce the number of manufacturing jobs available in developing countries. Nor does he believe that sweatshops will disappear as a natural consequence of development. Sweatshops will disappear, he argues, only if governments use regulation—national and international—to eliminate them.

POINTS TO PONDER

1. What economic concept underlies Paul Krugman's assertion that sweatshop jobs should be seen as good rather than bad jobs?

2. What argument does John Miller advance to counter Krugman? How do you think Krugman would respond?

3. How does Miller define the concept "living wage"? Is this a good definition? What are the arguments for and against an internationally regulated minimum wage using the living wage standard?

4. Should developing countries be required to have the same labor standards as advanced industrialized countries? Why or why not?

Paul Krugman

In Praise of Cheap Labor: Bad Jobs at Bad Wages Are Better than No Jobs at All

For many years a huge Manila garbage dump known as Smokey Mountain was a favorite media symbol of Third World poverty. Several thousand men, women, and children lived on that dump—enduring the stench, the flies, and the toxic waste in order to make a living combing the garbage for scrap metal and other recyclables. And they lived there voluntarily, because the $10 or so a squatter family could clear in a day was better than the alternatives.

The squatters are gone now, forcibly removed by Philippine police last year as a cosmetic move in advance of a Pacific Rim summit. But I found myself thinking about Smokey Mountain recently, after reading my latest batch of hate mail.

The occasion was an op-ed piece I had written for the *New York Times,* in which I had pointed out that while wages and working conditions in the new export industries of the Third World are appalling, they are a big improvement over the "previous, less visible rural poverty." I guess I should have expected that this comment would generate letters along the lines of, "Well, if you lose your comfortable position as an American professor you can always find another job—as long as you are 12 years old and willing to work for 40 cents an hour."

Such moral outrage is common among the opponents of globalization—of the transfer of technology and capital from high-wage to low-wage countries and the resulting growth of labor-intensive Third World exports. These critics take it as a given that anyone with a good word for this process is naive or corrupt and, in either case, a de facto agent of global capital in its oppression of workers here and abroad.

But matters are not that simple, and the moral lines are not that clear. In fact, let me make a counter-accusation: The lofty moral tone of the opponents of globalization is possible only because they have chosen not to think their position through. While fat-cat capitalists might benefit from globalization, the biggest beneficiaries are, yes, Third World workers.

After all, global poverty is not something recently invented for the benefit of multinational corporations. Let's turn the clock back to the Third World as it was only two decades ago (and still is, in many countries). In those days, although the rapid economic growth of a handful of small Asian nations had started to attract attention, developing countries like Indonesia or Bangladesh were still mainly what they had always been: exporters of raw materials, importers of manufactures. Inefficient manufacturing sectors served their domestic markets, sheltered behind import quotas, but generated few jobs. Meanwhile, population pressure pushed desperate peasants into cultivating ever more marginal land or seeking a livelihood in any way possible—such as homesteading on a mountain of garbage.

Given this lack of other opportunities, you could hire workers in Jakarta or Manila for a pittance. But in the mid-1970s, cheap labor was not enough to allow a developing country to compete in world markets for manufactured goods. The entrenched advantages of advanced nations—their infrastructure and technical know-how, the vastly larger size of their markets and their proximity to suppliers of key components, their political stability and the subtle-but-crucial social adaptations that are necessary to operate an efficient economy—seemed to outweigh even a tenfold or twentyfold disparity in wage rates.

And then something changed. Some combination of factors that we still don't fully understand—lower tariff barriers, improved telecommunications, cheaper air transport—reduced the disadvantages of producing in developing countries. (Other things being the same, it is still better to produce in the First World—stories of companies that moved production to Mexico or East Asia, then moved back after experiencing the disadvantages of the Third World environment, are common.) In a substantial number of industries, low wages allowed developing countries to break into world markets. And so countries that had previously made a living selling jute or coffee started producing shirts and sneakers instead.

Workers in those shirt and sneaker factories are, inevitably, paid very little and expected to endure terrible working conditions. I say "inevitably" because their employers are not in business for their (or their workers') health; they pay as little as possible, and that minimum is determined by the other opportunities available to workers. And these are still extremely poor countries, where living on a garbage heap is attractive compared with the alternatives.

And yet, wherever the new export industries have grown, there has been measurable improvement in the lives of ordinary people. Partly this is because a growing industry must offer a somewhat higher wage than workers could get elsewhere in order to get them to move. More importantly, however, the growth of manufacturing—and of the penumbra of other jobs that the new export sector creates—has a ripple effect throughout the economy. The pressure on the land becomes less intense, so rural wages rise; the pool of unemployed urban dwellers always anxious for work shrinks, so factories start to compete with each other for workers, and urban wages also begin to rise. Where the process has gone on long enough—say, in South Korea or

Taiwan—average wages start to approach what an American teenager can earn at McDonald's. And eventually people are no longer eager to live on garbage dumps. (Smokey Mountain persisted because the Philippines, until recently, did not share in the export-led growth of its neighbors. Jobs that pay better than scavenging are still few and far between.)

The benefits of export-led economic growth to the mass of people in the newly industrializing economies are not a matter of conjecture. A country like Indonesia is still so poor that progress can be measured in terms of how much the average person gets to eat; since 1970, per capita intake has risen from less than 2,100 to more than 2,800 calories a day. A shocking one-third of young children are still malnourished—but in 1975, the fraction was more than half. Similar improvements can be seen throughout the Pacific Rim, and even in places like Bangladesh. These improvements have not taken place because well-meaning people in the West have done anything to help— foreign aid, never large, has lately shrunk to virtually nothing. Nor is it the result of the benign policies of national governments, which are as callous and corrupt as ever. It is the indirect and unintended result of the actions of soulless multinationals and rapacious local entrepreneurs, whose only concern was to take advantage of the profit opportunities offered by cheap labor. It is not an edifying spectacle; but no matter how base the motives of those involved, the result has been to move hundreds of millions of people from abject poverty to something still awful but nonetheless significantly better.

Why, then, the outrage of my correspondents? Why does the image of an Indonesian sewing sneakers for 60 cents an hour evoke so much more feeling than the image of another Indonesian earning the equivalent of 30 cents an hour trying to feed his family on a tiny plot of land—or of a Filipino scavenging on a garbage heap?

The main answer, I think, is a sort of fastidiousness. Unlike the starving subsistence farmer, the women and children in the sneaker factory are working at slave wages *for our benefit*—and this makes us feel unclean. And so there are self-righteous demands for international labor standards: We should not, the opponents of globalization insist, be willing to buy those sneakers and shirts unless the people who make them receive decent wages and work under decent conditions.

This sounds only fair—but is it? Let's think through the consequences.

First of all, even if we could assure the workers in Third World export industries of higher wages and better working conditions, this would do nothing for the peasants, day laborers, scavengers, and so on who make up the bulk of these countries' populations. At best, forcing developing countries to adhere to our labor standards would create a privileged labor aristocracy, leaving the poor majority no better off.

And it might not even do that. The advantages of established First World industries are still formidable. The only reason developing countries have been able to compete with those industries is their ability to offer employers cheap labor. Deny them that ability, and you might well deny them the prospect of continuing industrial growth, even reverse the growth that has been achieved. And since export-oriented growth, for all its injustice, has been a huge boon for the workers in those nations, anything that curtails that growth is very much against their interests. A policy of good jobs in principle, but no jobs in practice, might assuage our consciences, but it is no favor to its alleged beneficiaries.

You may say that the wretched of the earth should not be forced to serve as hewers of wood, drawers of water, and sewers of sneakers for the affluent. But what is the alternative? Should they be helped with foreign aid? Maybe—although the historical record of regions like southern Italy suggests that such aid has a tendency to promote perpetual dependence. Anyway, there isn't the slightest prospect of significant aid materializing. Should their own governments provide more social justice? Of course—but they won't, or at least not because we tell them to. And as long as you have no realistic alternative to industrialization based on low wages, to oppose it means that you are willing to deny desperately poor people the best chance they have of progress for the sake of what amounts to an aesthetic standard—that is, the fact that you don't like the idea of workers being paid a pittance to supply rich Westerners with fashion items.

In short, my correspondents are not entitled to their self-righteousness. They have not thought the matter through. And when the hopes of hundreds of millions are at stake, thinking things through is not just good intellectual practice. It is a moral duty.

John Miller

Why Economists Are Wrong about Sweatshops and the Antisweatshop Movement

The student-led antisweatshop movement that took hold on many college campuses during the late 1990s should have pleased economists. Studying the working conditions faced by factory workers across the globe offered powerful lessons about the workings of the world economy, the dimensions of world poverty, and most students' privileged position in that economy.

On top of that, these students were dedicated not just to explaining sweatshop conditions, but also to changing them. They wanted desperately to do something to put a stop to the brutalization and assaults on human dignity suffered by the women and men who made their jeans, t-shirts, or sneakers.[1] On many campuses, student activism succeeded in pressuring college administrators by demanding that clothing bearing their college logo not be made under sweatshop conditions, and, at best, that it be made by workers earning a living wage (Featherstone and United Students Against Sweatshops 2002). But most mainstream economists were not at all pleased. No, they did not dispute these tales from the factory floor, many of which had been confirmed in the business press (Roberts and Bernstein 2000) and by international agencies (ILO 2000). Rather, mainstream economists rushed to defend the positive role of low-wage factory jobs, the very kind we usually call sweatshops, in economic development and in alleviating poverty.

What is more, these economists were generally dismissive of the student-led antisweatshop movement. In Summer 2000, the Academic Consortium on International Trade (ACIT), a group of advocates of globalization and free trade made up mostly of economists, took it upon themselves to write directly to the presidents of universities and colleges (see www.spp.umich.edu/rsie/acit/). The ACIT letter warned presidents that antisweatshop protesters on college campuses were often ill informed and that adopting codes of conduct requiring multinational corporations to pay higher wages recommended by the protesters may cost workers in poor countries their jobs.

The response of mainstream economists to the antisweatshop movement was hardly surprising. Economists have a penchant for playing the contrarian, and, for the most part, they oppose interventions into market outcomes, even interventions into the labor markets of the developing world.

No matter how predictable, their response was profoundly disappointing. Although it contains elements of truth, what economists have to say about sweatshops misses the mark. . . . First, the propositions that mainstream economists rely on to defend sweatshops are misleading, rooted in an exchange perspective that obscures sweatshop oppression. Sweatshop oppression is not defined by labor market exchanges but by the characteristics of a job. Second, policy positions based on these propositions are equally flawed. Economists' claim that market-led economic development, independent of labor and social movements and government regulation, will put an end to sweatshop conditions distorts the historical record. Finally, their assertion that demands for better working conditions in the world-export factories will harm third-world workers and frustrate poverty alleviation is also suspect.

With that said, the challenge issued by mainstream economists to the antisweatshop movement remains a formidable one. What economists have to say about the sweatshops has considerable power in the way of persuasion and influence, the protestations of Bhagwati and the ACIT notwithstanding. Often it is their writings that are being distilled in what journalists, government officials, and the general public have to say about sweatshops.

Supporters of the antisweatshop movement, and instructors of sweatshop seminars, need to be able to answer each count of the economists' indictments of their movement with arguments that are equally persuasive.

Today a group of economists is dedicated to doing just that. In the fall of 2001, Scholars Against Sweatshop Labor (SASL) issued a response to the ACIT indictment of the antisweatshop movement (SASL 2001). Its lead author, economist Robert Pollin, made the case that "the anti-sweatshop movement is taking constructive steps toward improving living and working conditions for millions of poor people throughout the world."

Teaching about sweatshops also convinced me that supporters of the antisweatshop movement need to respond to the criticisms of mainstream economists with actions as well as words. We need to link antisweatshop campaigns for the betterment of the women and men who toil in the world-export factories with efforts to improve the lot of their brothers and sisters, who often work under even more oppressive conditions in the informal and agricultural sectors of the developing world.

Just Enforce the Law

What to do about sweatshops? That is not a difficult question for most mainstream economists to answer. Just enforce the law, they say (Weidenbaum 1999, 26–28). And avoid other "institutional interventions" that might impair a market-led development that will enhance productivity and thereby raise wages and improve working conditions (Irwin 2002, 214; Sengenberger 1994, 10). By law, they mean local labor law, not some labor standard that ill-informed protesters (or even the International Labor Organization, for that matter) would impose on multinational corporations and their subcontractors in developing economies.

No one in the antisweatshop movement would quarrel with the insistence that the law be obeyed. In fact, several U.S. antisweatshop groups define a sweatshop in legal terms. According to Feminists Against Sweatshops (2002), for instance, sweatshop operators are employers who violate two or more labor laws, from the prohibition of child labor, to health, safety, fire, and building codes, to forced overtime and the minimum wage.[2]

Effective enforcement of local labor law in the developing world, where labor legislation in many countries—on paper, at least—is quite extensive, would surely help to combat sweatshop abuse as well (Portes 1994, 163). For instance, *Made in China,* a report of the National Labor Committee, the leading U.S.-based antisweatshop group, found that subcontractors producing goods for U.S. corporations, including Wal-Mart and Nike, "routinely violate" Chinese labor law. In some of these factories, young women work as long as seventy hours a week and are paid just pennies an hour after pay deductions for board and room, clear violations of China's labor law (Kernaghan 2000). A three-month *Business Week* investigation of the Chun Si Enterprise Handbag Factory in southern China, which makes Kathie Lee Gifford handbags sold by Wal-Mart stores, confirmed that workers there confronted labor practices that included illegally collected fines, confiscated identity papers, and beatings (Roberts and Bernstein 2000).

But the limitations of this legal prescription for curing sweatshop abuse become obvious when we go to apply it to countries where local labor law, even on paper, does not measure up to the most minimal, internationally agreed-upon labor standards. Take the case of the high-performance economies of Southeast Asia, Indonesia, Malaysia, and Thailand. In those countries, several core labor conventions of the International Labour Organization (ILO) have gone unratified—including the right to organize. Minimum wages are well below the level necessary to lift a family of three above the poverty line, the usual definition of a living wage. And in those countries (as well as China), independent trade union activity is systematically and sometimes brutally suppressed.[3]

When labor law protections are limited and international labor conventions are neither ratified nor respected, then insisting "the law should be fully obeyed" will do little to prevent sweatshop abuse. In those cases, enforcing the law would seem to be a shaky foundation on which to build a strategy of alleviating sweatshop labor through improved market outcomes.[4]

A Defense of Sweatshops?

The defense of sweatshops offered up by mainstream economists turns on two elegantly simple and ideologically powerful propositions. The first is that workers freely choose to enter these jobs, and the second is that these sweatshop jobs are better than the alternative employments available to them in developing economies. Both propositions have a certain truth to them.

An Exchange Perspective

From the perspective of mainstream economics, every exchange, including the exchange between worker and boss, is freely entered into and only takes place because both parties are made better off. Hiring workers to fill the jobs in the world-export factories is no exception.

Of course, in some cases, workers do not freely enter into sweatshop employment even by the usual standards of wage labor. Sometimes workers are held captive. For example, a 1995 police raid of a fenced-in compound of seven apartments in El Monte, California, found a clandestine garment sweatshop where some seventy-two illegal Thai immigrants were held in virtual captivity as they sewed clothes for brand-name labels (Su 1997, 143). Other times, workers find themselves locked into walled factory compounds surrounded by barbed wire, sometimes required to work fifteen hours a day, seven days a week, subject to physical abuse, and, after fines and charges are deducted from their paycheck, left without the money necessary to repay exorbitant hiring fees. That was the case for the more than 50,000 young female immigrants from China, the Philippines, Bangladesh, and Thailand who were recently discovered in Saipan (part of the Commonwealth of the Northern Mariana Islands, a territory of the United States) working under these near-slavelike conditions as they produced clothing for major American distributors bearing the label "Made in the United States" (ILO 2000).

But in most cases, workers do choose these jobs, if hardly freely or without the coercion of economic necessity. Seen from the exchange perspective of mainstream economics, that choice alone demonstrates that these factory jobs are neither sweatshops nor exploitative.

Listen to how mainstream economists and their followers make this argument. In response to the National Labor Committee's exposé of conditions in the Honduran factories manufacturing Kathie Lee clothing for Wal-Mart, El Salvadoran economist Lucy Martinez-Mont assured us that "People choose to work in maquila shops of their own free will, because those are the best jobs available to them" (Martinez-Mont 1996, sec. A, p. 14). For economic journalist Nicholas Kristof (1998), the story of Mrs. Tratiwoon, an Indonesian woman, makes the same point. She sustains herself and her son by picking through a garbage dump outside of Jakarta in search of metal scraps to sell. She tells Kristof of her dreams for her three-year-old son as she works. "She wants him to grow up to work in a sweatshop."

Stories such as this one are powerful. The fact that many in the developing world are worse off than workers in the world-export factories is a point that economists supportive of the antisweatshop movement do not deny. For instance, a few years back, economist Arthur MacEwan . . . made much the same point. He observed that in a poor country like Indonesia, where women working in agriculture are paid wages one-fifth those of women working in manufacturing, sweatshops do not seem to have a hard time finding workers (MacEwan 1998). And the Scholars Against Sweatshop Labor statement (2001) admits that "even after allowing for the frequent low wages and poor working conditions in these jobs, they are still generally superior to 'informal' employment in, for example, much of agriculture or urban street vending."

This is not meant to suggest that these exchanges between employers and poor workers with few alternatives are in reality voluntary or that world-export factory jobs are not sweatshops or places of exploitation. Rather, as political philosopher Michael Waltzer argues, these exchanges should be seen as "trades of last resort" or "desperate" exchanges that need to be protected by labor legislation regulating such things as limits on hours, a wage floor, and guaranteed health and safety requirements (Rodrik 1997, 35).[5]

Prevailing Wages and Working Conditions

What mainstream economists say in defense of sweatshops is limited in other ways as well. For instance, an ACIT letter (2000) misstates the argument. The ACIT writes that multinational corporations "commonly pay their workers more on average in comparison to the prevailing market wage for similar workers employed elsewhere in the economy." But, as the SASL authors correctly point out, "While this is true, it does not speak to the situation in which most garments are produced throughout the world—which is by firms subcontracted by multinational corporations, not the [multinational corporations] themselves." The ACIT authors implicitly acknowledge as much, for in the next sentence they write that, "in cases where subcontracting is involved, workers are generally paid no less than the prevailing market wage."[6]

The SASL statement also warns that the ACIT claim that subcontractors pay the prevailing market wage does not by itself make a persuasive case that the world export factories we commonly call sweatshops are anything but that. The SASL authors (2001) emphasize that "the prevailing market wage is frequently extremely low for garment workers in less developed countries. In addition, the recent university-sponsored studies as well as an

October 2000 report by the International Labor Organization consistently find that serious workplace abuses and violations of workers' rights are occurring in the garment industry throughout the world."

The same can be said about other world-export factories. Consider for a minute the working conditions at the Indonesian factories that produce footwear for Reebok, the Stoughton, Massachusetts–based international corporation that "goes to great lengths to portray itself as a conscientious promoter of human rights in the Third World" (Zuckoff 1994). Despite its status as a model employer, working conditions at factories that make Reebok footwear became the focus of the *Boston Globe* 1994 series entitled "Foul Trade" (Zuckoff 1994). The *Globe* tells the story of Yati, a young Indonesian woman in Tangerang, Indonesia. She works sewing bits of leather and lace for tennis shoes sold as Reeboks.

Yati sits at a sewing machine, which is one of sixty in her row. There are forty-six rows on the factory floor. For working sixty-three hours a week, Yati earns not quite $80 a month—just about the price of a pair of Reeboks in the United States. Her hourly pay is less than 32 cents per hour, which exceeds the minimum wage for her region of Indonesia. Yati lives in a nearby ten-by-twelve-foot shack with no furniture. She and her two roommates sleep on the mud and tile floor.

A factory like the one Yati works in is typically owned by an East Asian company. For instance, PT Tong Yang Indonesia, a South Korean–owned factory, pumped out 400,000 pairs of Reeboks a month in 1993. In return, Reebok paid its owner, Tan Chuan Cheng, $10.20 for each pair of shoes and then sold them for $60 or more in the United States. Most of Tan's payment went to purchase materials. Tan told the Globe that wages accounted for as little as $1.40 of the cost of a pair of shoes (Zuckoff 1994).[7]

A More Effective Response

As I taught my seminar on sweatshops, I settled on a more effective response to the mainstream economic argument. It is simply this: Their argument is irrelevant for determining if a factory is a sweatshop or if workers are exploited. Sweatshop conditions are defined by the characteristics of a job. If workers are denied the right to organize, suffer unsafe and abusive working conditions, are forced to work overtime, or are paid less than a living wage, then they work in a sweatshop, regardless of how they came to take their jobs or if the alternatives they face are worse yet.

A careful reading of what the mainstream exchange perspective suggests about sweatshop jobs is not they are "good news" for the world's poor but "less bad news" than the usual conditions of work in the agricultural and informal sectors. The oppressive conditions of the work in the world-export factories are not denied by their argument. For instance, ACIT leader

Jagdish Bhagwati says sweatshop jobs are a "ticket to slightly less impoverishment" (Goldberg 2001, 30).

Confronting Critics of the Antisweatshop Movement

Still, none of the above speaks directly to the contention of mainstream economists that imposing "enlightened standards" advocated by the antisweatshop activists onto conditions for employment in the export factories of the developing world will immiserate the very workers the movement intends to help (ACIT 2000).

Core Labor Standards

To begin with, as labor economist Richard Freeman (1994, 80) writes, "Everyone, almost everyone is for *some* standards" (emphasis in the original). Surely that includes economists who would combat sweatshops by insisting that local labor law be respected. Even their position recognizes that the "voluntary" exchange of labor for wages must be delimited by rules, collectively determined and obeyed by all.

The relevant question is, What are those rules, and are any so basic that they should be applied universally, transcending the normal bounds of sovereignty? For the most part, economists, trained after all as economists and not political philosophers, have little to say on this matter other than to caution that outside of the condemnation of slavery, there is no universal agreement about the appropriateness of labor standards even when it comes to bonded labor and child labor (Bhagwati 1995, 754; Brown 2001, 94; Irwin 2002, 216).

Nonetheless, other economists, even some critical of the antisweatshop movement, are favorably disposed toward international labor standards about safety and health, forced labor, and the right to organize. For instance, Alice Amsden, an economist who opposes establishing wage standards on developing economies, favors the imposition of other labor standards. "The issue," she says, "is not health and safety conditions, the right of workers to be treated like human beings—not to be murdered for organizing unions, for example. These rights are inviolate" (Amsden 1995). At times, even Jagdish Bhagwati has taken a similar position (Bhagwati 2002, 60).

The ILO, in its 1998 Declaration on Fundamental Principles at Work, took a similar position. The ILO held that each of its 175 members (even if they have not ratified the conventions in question) was obligated "to respect, to promote, and to realize" the fundamental rights of "freedom of association and the effective recognition of the right to collective bargaining, the elimination of all forms of forced or compulsory labor, the effective abolition of child labor and the elimination of discrimination in respect of employment and occupation" (2002a).

The empirical evidence of the effect of these core labor standards on economic development is ambiguous. For instance, the Organization for Economic Cooperation and Development (OECD) found that countries that strengthen these core labor standards "can increase economic growth and efficiency" (OECD 2000, 14). International trade economist Jai Mah, on the other hand, found that ratification of the ILO Conventions on freedom of association and on the right to nondiscrimination negatively affected the export performance of developing countries (Mah 1997, 781). And a study conducted by Dani Rodrik, another international trade economist, suggested that low core labor standards enhanced a country's comparative advantage in the production of labor-intensive goods but deterred rather than attracted direct foreign investment (Rodrik 1996, 59).

The Living Wage

Nevertheless, almost all mainstream economists draw the line at labor codes designed to boost wages as opposed to leaving the determination of wages to labor market outcomes. That surely goes for labor codes that call for the payment of a living wage, usually defined as a wage adequate to lift a worker and two dependents out of poverty. The ACIT worries that if multinational corporations are persuaded to increase their wages (and those of their subcontractors) "in response to what the ongoing studies by the anti-sweatshop movement may conclude are appropriate wage levels, the net result would be shifts in employments that will worsen the collective welfare of the very workers who are supposed to be helped" (2001). And ACIT leader Bhagwati dismisses the call for multinationals and their subcontractors to pay a living wage as so much first-world protectionism cloaked in the language of "social responsibility" (Bhagwati 2000, 11). As he sees it, students' demand that a "living wage" be paid in developing countries would dull the one competitive advantage enjoyed by these countries—cheap labor.

But, in practice, would a labor standard demanding that multinational corporations and their subcontractors boost their wages beyond the local minimum wage and toward a living wage be a jobs killer? On that point the ACIT letter is silent . . .

Still, we can ask just how responsive are the hiring decisions of multinational corporations and their subcontractors to higher wages. There is real reason to believe that the right answer is, not very responsive.

Economists Robert Pollin, James Heintz, and Justine Burns recently looked more closely at this question (Pollin et al. 2001). They examined the impact that a 100 percent increase in the pay for apparel workers in Mexico and in the United States would have on costs relative to the retail price those garments sell for in the United States. Their preliminary findings are that doubling the pay of nonsupervisory workers would add just 50 cents to the production costs of a men's casual shirt sold for $32 in the United States, or just 1.6 percent of the retail price. And even if the wage increase were passed on to consumers, which seems likely because retailers in the U.S. garment industry enjoy substantial market power, Pollin et al. argue that the increase in price is well within the amount that recent surveys suggest U.S. consumers are willing to pay to purchase goods produced under "good" working conditions as opposed to sweatshop conditions. (See Elliot and Freeman [2000] for a detailed discussion of survey results.) More generally, using a sample of forty-five countries over the period 1992–1997, Pollin et al. found no statistically significant relationship between real wages and employment growth in the apparel industry. Their results suggest that the mainstream economists' claim that improving the quality of jobs in the world-export factories (by boosting wages) will reduce the number of jobs is not evident in the data (Pollin et al. 2001).

Even if this counterexample is not convincing, it is important to recall that the demand curve that defines the responsiveness of multinational corporations and their subcontractors to wage increases for factory workers is a theoretical device drawn while holding other economic circumstances constant, including public policy. In reality, those circumstances are neither fixed nor unalterable. In fact, to counteract any negative effect that higher wages might have on employment, the SASL statement calls for the adoption of new polices, which include "measures to expand the overall number of relatively high quality jobs; relief from excessive foreign debt payments; raising worker job satisfaction and productivity and the quality of goods they produce; and improving the capacity to bring final products to retail markets" (SASL 2001).

"Shifting the demand curve for labor outward," says economic sociologist Peter Evans (2002), "is almost the definition of economic development—making people more valuable relative to the commodities they need to live." This "high road" approach to development, adds Evans, has the additional benefit of augmenting the demand for the commodities that workers produce.

Historical Change and Social Improvement

A labor code that requires multinational corporations and their subcontractors to pay a living wage, provide safe and healthy working conditions, and allow workers to organize would be likely to have yet more profound effects on these developing economies. On this point, the antisweatshop activists and their critics agree. What they disagree about is whether these broader effects will be a help or hindrance to economic development and an improved standard of living in the developing world (Freeman 1992).

Mainstream critics argue that labor codes are likely to have widespread debilitating effects. The institutionalization of these labor standards proposed by activists, they argue, would derail a market-led development process (Irwin 2002, 214; Sengenberger 1994, 10–11).

As they see it, labor-intensive sweatshops are good starter jobs—the very jobs that successful developing economies and developed countries used as "stepping-stones" to an improved standard of living for their citizens. And in each case, these countries outgrew their "sweatshop phase" through market-led development that enhanced productivity, not through the interventions of an antisweatshop movement (Krugman 1994, 116).

These economists often use the Asian economies as examples of national economies that abandoned "sweatshop practices" as they grew. Their list includes Japan, which moved from poverty to wealth early in the twentieth century, and the tiger economies—South Korea, Hong Kong, Singapore, and Taiwan—which grew rapidly in the second half of the century to become middle-income countries (Irwin 2002; Krugman 1994; Krugman 1997; Lim 1990; Weidenbaum 1999). Paul Krugman (1997) allows that some tigers relied on foreign plant owners (e.g., Singapore) while others shunned them (e.g., South Korea). Nonetheless, he maintains that their first stage of development had one constant: "It's always sweatshops" (Meyerson 1997).

• • •

But these arguments distort the historical record and misrepresent how social improvement is brought about with economic development. First, the claim that developed economies passed through a sweatshop stage does not establish that sweatshops caused or contributed to the enhanced productivity that they say improved working conditions. Second, in the developed world, the sweatshop phase was not extinguished by market-led forces alone but when economic growth combined with the very kind of social action, or enlightened collective choice, that defenders of sweatshops find objectionable.

Even Nobel Prize–winning economist Simon Kuznets, whose work did much to inspire economists' faith in the moderating effects of capitalist development on inequality, would find the mainstream economists' story of market-led social progress questionable. Kuznets based his famous hypothesis—that after initially increasing, inequality will diminish with capitalist economic development—not on the operation of market forces alone, but on the combined effect of economic growth and social legislation.[8] For instance, in his famous 1955 American Economic Review article, Kuznets writes, "In democratic societies the growing political power of the urban lower-income groups led to a variety of protective and supporting legislation, much of it aimed to counteract the worst effects of rapid industrialization and urbanization and to support the claims of the broad masses for more adequate shares of the growing income of the country" (1955, 17). The labor codes called for by the antisweatshop movement would seem to be an example of the "protective and supporting legislation" that Kuznets says is key to spreading the benefits of economic growth more widely.

To be sure, labor standards in the absence of economic growth will be hard put to make workers better off. Economist Ajit Singh and Ann Zammit of the South Centre, an intergovernmental organization dedicated to promoting cooperation among developing countries, make exactly this point in their article opposing compulsory labor standards (Singh and Zammit 2000, 37). As they note, over the last few decades, wages in rapidly growing South Korea increased much more quickly than those in slowly growing India, even though India had much better labor standards in the 1950s than South Korea did.[9] . . .

Fastidiousness or Commodity Fetishism?

Mainstream economists have one last probing question for antisweatshop activists: Why factory workers? Krugman (1997) asks the question in a most pointed way: "Why does the image of an Indonesian sewing sneakers for 60 cents an hour evoke so much more feeling than the image of another Indonesian earning the equivalent of 30 cents an hour trying to feed his family on a tiny plot of land, or of a Filipino scavenging on a garbage heap?"

It is a good question. There are plenty of poor people in the world. Some 1.2 billion people, about one-fifth of the world population, had to make do on less than U.S. $1 a day in 1998 (World Bank 2001). The world's poor are disproportionately located in rural areas. Most scratch out their livelihood from subsistence agriculture or by plying petty trades, while others on the edge of urban centers work in the informal sector as street-hawkers or the like (Todaro 2000, 151). In addition, if sweat is the issue, journalist Kristof (1998) assures us that "this kind of work, hoeing the field or working in paddies, often involves more perspiration than factory work."

So why has the plight of these rural workers, who are often poorer and sweat more than workers in the world-export factories, not inspired a first-world movement dedicated to their betterment?

"Fastidiousness" is Krugman's answer. "Unlike the starving subsistence farmer," says Krugman, "the women and children in the sneaker factory are working at slave wages *for our benefit*—and this makes us feel unclean. And so there are self-righteous demands for international labor standards" (1997; emphasis in the original).

Ironically, Krugman's answer is not so different from the one Marx would have given to the question. Marx's answer would be commodity fetishism or that commodities become the bearers of social relations in a capitalist economy (Marx 1967). Purchasing commodities brings us in contact with the lives of the factory workers who manufacture them. Buying jeans, t-shirts, or sneakers made in Los Angeles, Bangkok, or Jakarta, or the export zones of southern China and Latin America, connected students in my seminar to the women and men who work long hours in unhealthy and dangerous conditions for little pay in the apparel and athletic footwear industries. And it was the lives of those workers that my most political students sought to improve through their antisweatshop activism. Beyond that, as consumers and citizens they are empowered to change the employment practices of U.S. corporations and their subcontractors.

Krugman's complaint is no reason to dismiss the concerns of the antisweatshop movement. Historically, the organization of factory workers has been one of the most powerful forces for changing politics in the democratic direction that Kuznets outlines. Krugman's complaint does, however, suggest that the plight of sweatshop workers needs to be seen in the context of pervasive world poverty and the gaping inequalities of the global economy.

The global economy, to the extent that we live in a truly unified marketplace, connects us not just with sweatshop workers, but with oppressed workers outside the factory gates as well. By pointing out these connections to my students, I hoped to demonstrate the need to build a movement that would demand more for working people across the multiple dimensions of the world economy. Campaigns to improve conditions in the world-export factories should, of course, be part of that movement. But that movement must also tackle the often worse conditions of low-wage agricultural workers, poor farmers, street vendors, domestic servants, small-shop textile workers, and prostitutes. Only when conditions for both groups of workers improve might economists be able to say honestly, as something other than a Faustian bargain, that more world-factory jobs are good news for the world's poor.

ENDNOTES

1. While men and women suffer sweatshop abuse, young women overwhelmingly constitute the workforce of the "world market factories" in the developing world (Elson and Pearson 1997, 191). Women workers have also been the focus of the antisweatshop movement. Female employment is generally high in the clothing industry and in export-processing zones. In 1995, women made up 74 percent of the global workforce in the clothing industry (ILO 2000, 26).

2. There is no universal agreement about the definition of a sweatshop in the antisweatshop movement. For instance, sociologists Roger Waldinger and Michael Lapp argue that sweatshop labor is a form of what the Organisation for Economic and Cooperative Development (OECD) calls "concealed employment," which escapes state regulation (Waldinger and Lapp 1993, 8–9). Their definition would cover the return of sweatshops to the United States. It also covers subcontractors of first-world multinational corporations who employ workers

in the formal sector of the third world under lax regulatory standards, as well as the minuscule firms in informal sectors of the developing world that are not subject to regulation. Other sweatshop critics, such as labor economist Michael Piore, insist that the term "sweatshop" should be reserved for "a specific organization of work" characterized by "very low fixed costs" (Piore 1997, 136). In sweatshops, workers are usually paid by the piece. Other fixed costs—rent, electricity, heat—are held to a minimum by operating substandard, congested, unhealthy factories, typically overseen by a "sweater" or subcontractor (Piore 1997, 135). Still others use the term sweatshop as a vivid metaphor to describe lousy jobs ranging from bicycle messengers who work in "Sweatshops of the Streets" (Lipsyte 1995), to cruise workers who endure "Sweatshops at Sea" (Reynolds and Weikel 2000), to adjunct professors at colleges "who might as well be sweatshop workers" (Scarff 2000).

3. In the case of China, the ILO writes that "the existence of a single trade union linked to the Communist Party [the All-China Federation of Trade Unions] in itself says much about freedom of association in the country" (ILO 2000, 66). The Organisation for Economic Cooperation and Development reports that in China "the right to strike is not recognized" (OECD 2000, 101). In Indonesia, several core ILO conventions remained unratified until June 1999, when then President J. B. Habibie faced a national election. The Suharto regime never signed ILO labor convention 87, which recognizes the right of workers to organize; convention 138, establishing a minimum age of employment; convention 105, outlawing forced labor; and convention 111, banning discrimination in employment (ILO 1998; ILO 1999a; ILO 1999b). Thailand's and Malaysia's records are similarly dismal. Thailand has failed to ratify both ILO conventions recognizing the right of workers to organize (conventions 87 and 98) and the minimum age convention, 138. The right to strike is not recognized in Thailand's state enterprises, and authorities can prohibit strikes in the Thai private sector (OECD 2000, 104). Malaysia has not ratified ILO convention 87 and not only has failed to sign convention 105 calling for the abolition of forced labor, but has condemned it (ILO 1998). And the right to strike in Malaysia is "severely limited" (OECD 2000, 106). According to a study of wages at Indonesian factories producing Nike footwear, the minimum wage for Jakarta in 1997 provided a family of three less than $1 per day for each family member, the United Nations' definition of extreme poverty (Benjamin 1998). The same study found that to meet the minimum physical needs of a woman working for Nike in the Indonesian area required $35 month and that the usual wage paid by Nike subcontractors fell well below even that amount (Benjamin 1998). In Thailand, Bangkok's minimum wage, which kept pace with inflation during the 1990s boom, never extended to most of the 800,000 Thai garment workers, the great bulk of whom were employed by subcontractors (Pasuk and Baker 1998, 139–40).

4. These arguments also apply to countries in the developed world. For instance, the United States has failed to ratify six of the ILO's eight Fundamental Human Rights Conventions, covering freedom of association and collective bargaining, elimination of forced and compulsory labor, elimination of discrimination in respect to employment and occupation, and the abolition of child labor (ILO

2002b). Bhagwati rightly complains that discussions of international labor standards have focused on conditions in the developing world while remaining silent about "the much-documented quasi-slavery conditions for migrant labor in American agriculture in Georgia and Mississippi" (Bhagwati 2002, 71–72). He adds that a recent Human Rights Watch report, *Unfair Advantage,* documents how U.S. legal doctrine violates internationally recognized workers' rights to organize by allowing employers to permanently replace workers on strike and by banning secondary boycotts (Bhagwati 2002, 77). Bhagwati's complaint makes it clear that merely enforcing local labor law, even in the United States, is insufficient for combating abusive working conditions.

5. This sort of "asymmetric bargaining power," actually any sort of bargaining power, goes unrecognized in standard economic models (Stiglitz 2000).

6. When correctly stated, the limitations of the claim that working for these manufacturing subcontractors is better than the other opportunities available to the sons and daughters of recyclers and other poor workers are evident in the writings of defenders of sweatshops. For instance, the writings of economist Linda Lim, an ACIT signatory who is dismissive of the efforts of the antisweatshop movement (which she describes as "patronizing white-man's-burden stuff"), convinced several students in my sweatshop seminar that women who work in the world's export factories are exploited (Featherstone and Henwood 2001).
   In her earlier work, Lim reports that in East Asia, "the wages earned by women in export factories are usually higher than what they could earn as wage laborers in alternative low-skilled female occupations" (Lim 1990, 109). But at the same time, the wages of women in the export industries are lower than the wages of men who work in those industries and lower than those of first-world women who work in the same industries. That is true, even though third-world women's productivity "is acknowledged to be higher than that of either of these other groups" (Lim 1997, 223). Even for Lim, that makes these women "the most heavily exploited group of workers relative both to their output and other groups" (Lim 1997, 223). Whatever Lim's work suggests about the relative attractiveness of these factory jobs, it went a long way toward convincing my students that these workplaces are sites of exploitation and properly described as sweatshops.

7. How is Yati likely to be faring today? Thanks in part to aggressive consumer campaigns in the United States, spearheaded by such groups as Global Exchange, campus organizations, and unions, Reebok commissioned an independent Indonesian firm to study conditions in factories that do business with Reebok. Murray Weidenbaum acted as a consultant for that report. One of the factories investigated was PT Tong Yang. According to the *London Guardian* (October 19, 1999), the fourteen-month study "found evidence of health and safety abuses, sexual discrimination and communication problems. Safety notices were often handed out in English, for example." Other safety problems include "lack of labels for dangerous chemicals . . . and inadequate ventilation." According to the report, women face special problems, such as access to few toilets despite the fact that they represent 80 percent of the workforce, and under-representation among higher-ranking workers. In response, Tong Yang Indonesia introduced new machinery that used safer water-based solvents,

installed a new ventilation system, and bought new chairs with backs that provided more support than the older ones. Despite those efforts, more basic problems remain. Wages still hover just above the inadequate Jakarta-area minimum wage, and workers continue to go without effective collective bargaining, denied the right to form independent unions (Bernstein 2000).

8. For a thoroughgoing analysis of the progressive underpinnings of Kuznets's article and its subversive implications for the neoliberal policy agenda, see the third chapter of Arthur MacEwan's *Neo-Liberalism or Democracy? Economic Strategy, Markets, and Alternatives for the 21st Century* (1999).

9. For these reasons, Singh and Zammit favor measures intended to promote more equitable and stable economic growth in the developing world, such as managed world trade and controls on international capital movements, instead of compulsory labor standards (Singh and Zammit 2000, 67).

REFERENCES

Academic Consortium on International Trade (ACIT). 2000. Letter to Presidents of Universities and Colleges, July 29 (www.spp.umich.edu/rsie/acit/).

Amsden, Alice. 1995. "International Labor Standards: Hype or Help?" *Boston Review* 20, no. 6 (bostonreview.mit.edu/BR20.6/amsden.html). . . .

Benjamin, Medea. 1998. San Francisco: Global Exchange (www.globalexchange.org).

Bernstein, Aaron. 2000. "A World of Sweatshops: Progress Is Slow in the Drive for Better Conditions." *Business Week*, November 6: 84.

Bhagwati, Jagdish. 1995. "Trade Liberalization and 'Fair Trade' Demands: Addressing the Environmental and Labour Standards Issues." *World Economy* 18, no. 6: 745–59. . . .

———. 2000. "Nike Wrongfoots the Student Critics." *Financial Times*, May 2: 11.

———. 2002. *Free Trade Today*. Princeton: Princeton University Press.

Brown, Drusilla K. 2001. "Labor Standards: Where Do They Belong on the International Trade Agenda?" *Journal of Economic Perspectives* 15, no. 3 (summer): 89–112. . . .

Elliot, K.A., and R.B. Freeman. 2000. "White Hats or Don Quixotes? Human Rights Vigilantes in the Global Economy." National Bureau of Economic Research Conference on Emerging Labor Market Institutions (www. nber. org/ ~confer/2000/si2000/elliot. pdf).

Elson, Diane, and Ruth Pearson. 1997. "The Subornation of Women and the Internationalization of Factory Production." In *The Women, Gender, and Development Reader*, ed. Naline Visvanathan et al., pp. 191–202. London: Zed Books.

Evans, Peter B. 2002. Personal communication, April. . . .

Featherstone, Liza, and Doug Henwood. 2001. "Clothes Encounters: Activists and Economists Clash Over Sweatshops." *Lingua Franca* 11, no. 2 (March): 26–33 (www.linguafranca.com).

Featherstone, Liza, and United Students Against Sweatshops. 2002. *Students Against Sweatshops*. New York: Verso.

Feminists Against Sweatshops. 2002. www. feminist.org/other/sweatshops. html. . . .

Freeman, Richard B. 1992. "Labour Market Institutions and Policies: Help or Hindrance to Economic Development?" In *Proceedings of the World Bank Annual Conference on Development Economics*, pp. 117–56. Washington, DC: World Bank.

_____. 1994. "A Hard-Headed Look at Labour Standards." In *International Labour Standards and Economic Interdependence*, ed. Werner Sengenberger and Duncan Campbell, pp. 79–92. Geneva: International Labor Organization (International Institute for Labor Studies).

Goldberg, Jonah. 2001. "Sweatshop Chic: The Know-Nothings Find a Cause." *National Review*, April 4 . . . .

International Labour Organization (ILO). 1998. *The Social Impact of the Asian Financial Crisis*. Bangkok, Thailand.

_____. 1999a. *Toward Full Employment: Prospects and Problems in Asia and the Pacific*. Bangkok, Thailand.

_____. 1999b. "Indonesia Ratifies Core ILO Conventions." Press release, June 7.

_____. 2000. *Labour Practices in the Footwear, Leather, Textiles and Clothing Industries*. Geneva: International Labor Organization.

_____. 2002a. Declaration on Fundamental Principles at Work.ilo.org/ public/english/standards/deci/declaration/index.htm.

_____. 2002b. Ratifications. ilolex. ilo. ch:1567/english/docs/declworld. htm.

Irwin, Douglas A. 2002. *Free Trade Under Fire*. Princeton: Princeton University Press.

Kernaghan, Charles. 2000. *Made in China: The Role of U.S. Companies in Denying Human and Worker Rights*. New York: National Labor Committee . . . .

Kristof, Nicholas. 1998. "Asia's Crisis Upsets Rising Effort to Confront Blight of Sweatshops." *New York Times*, June 15: sec. A, p. 1.

Krugman, Paul. 1994. "Does Third World Growth Hurt First World Prosperity?" *Harvard Business Review* (July–August): 113–21.

_____. 1997. "In Praise of Cheap Labor: Bad Jobs at Bad Wages Are Better Than No Jobs at All." *Slate*, March 27.

Kuznets, Simon. 1955. "Economic Growth and Income Inequality." *American Economic Review* 45, no. 1 (March): 1–28.

Lim, Linda. 1990. "Women's Work in Export Factories." In *Persistent Inequalities*, ed. Irene Tinker, pp. 101–19. New York: Oxford University Press.

_____. 1997. "Capitalism, Imperialism, and Patriarchy." In Visvanathan et al., ed., *The Women, Gender, and Development Reader*, pp. 216–29.

Lipsyte, Robert. 1995. "Voices from the 'Sweatshop of the Streets.'" *New York Times*, May 14: sec. A, p. 18.

MacEwan, Arthur. 1998. "Ask Dr. Dollar." *Dollars & Sense*, no. 219 (September/October): 51.

_____. 1999. *Neo-Liberalism or Democracy? Economic Strategy, Markets, and Alternatives for the 21st Century*. London: Zed Books.

Mah, Jai S. 1997. "Core Labor Standards and Export Performance in Developing Countries." *World Economy* 20, no. 6 (September): 773–85.

Marx, Karl. 1967. *Capital*. Vol. 1. New York: International . . . .

Martinez-Mont, Lucy. 1996. "Sweatshops Are Better Than No Shops." *Wall Street Journal,* June 25: sec. A, p. 14 . . . .

Meyerson, Allen R. 1997. "In Principle, a Case for More 'Sweatshops,'" *New York Times,* June 22: sec. 4, p. 5 . . . .

Organisation for Economic Cooperation and Development (OECD). 2000. *International Trade and Core Labour Standards.* Paris: OECD.

Pasuk Phongpaichit and Chris Baker. 1998. *Thailand's Boom and Bust.* Chiang Mai, Thailand: Silkworm Books.

Piore, Michael. 1997. "The Economics of the Sweatshop." In Ross, ed., *No Sweat,* pp. 135–42.

Pollin, Robert, Justine Burns, and James Heintz. 2001. "Global Apparel Production and Sweatshop Labor: Can Raising Retail Prices Finance Living Wages?" Political Economy Research Institute, Working Paper series, no. 19.

Portes, Alejandro. 1994. "By-Passing the Rules: The Dialectics of Labour Standards and Informalization in Less Developed Countries." In Sengenberger and Campbell, ed., *International Labour Standards and Economic Interdependence,* pp. 159–76.

Reynolds, Christopher, and Dan Weikel. 2000. "For Cruise Ship Workers, Voyages Are No Vacations." *Los Angeles Times,* May 30: pt. A, p. A-1.

Roberts, Dexter, and Aaron Bernstein. 2000. "A Life of Fines and Beatings." *Business Week,* October 2: 122.

Rodrik, Dani. 1996. "Labor Standards in International Trade: Do They Matter and What Do We Do About Them?" In *Emerging Agenda for Global Trade: High Stakes for Developing Countries,* ed. Robert Z. Lawrence, Dani Rodrik, and John Walley, pp. 35–79. Washington, DC: Johns Hopkins University Press for the Overseas Development Council.

————. 1997. *Has Globalization Gone Too Far?* Washington, DC: Institute for International Economics . . . .

Scarff, Michelle. 2000. "The Full-Time Stress of Part-Time Professors: For the Pittance They're Paid, Adjunct Profs at Our Colleges Might as Well Be Sweatshop Workers." *Newsweek,* May 15: 10.

Scholars Against Sweatshop Labor (SASL). 2001. October (www. umass. edu/peri/sasl/).

Sengenberger, Werner. 1994. "International Labour Standards in a Globalized Economy: The Issues." In Sengenberger and Campbell, ed., *International Labour Standards and Economic Interdependence,* pp. 3–16.

Singh, A., and A. Zammit. 2000. "The Global Labour Standards Controversy: Critical Issues for Developing Countries." Geneva: South Centre (www. southcentre.org/publicatons/labour/toc.htm).

Stiglitz, Joseph. 2000. "Democratic Development as the Fruits of Labor." Keynote address of the annual meetings of the Industrial Relations Research Association, Boston (available at www.globalpolicy.org/socecon/bwi-wto/wbank/stieg2. htm).

Su, Julie. 1997. "El Monte Thai Garment Workers: Slave Sweatshops." In Ross, ed., *No Sweat,* pp. 143–50 . . . .

Todaro, Michael. 2000. *Economic Development*. 7th ed. New York: Addison Wesley. . . .

Waldinger, Roger, and Michael Lapp. 1993. "Back to the Sweatshop or Ahead to the Informal Sector?" *International Journal of Urban and Regional Research* 17, no. 1: 6–29.

Weidenbaum, Murray. 1999. "A Defense of Sweatshops." In *Child Labor and Sweatshops*, ed. Mary Williams, pp. 26–28. San Diego: Greenhaven.

World Bank. 2001. *World Development Report 2000/2001*. New York: Oxford University Press.

Zuckoff, Mitchell. 1994. "Taking a Profit, and Inflicting a Cost." First part of a series titled "Foul Trade." *Boston Globe*, July 10: sec. A, p. 1.

CHAPTER 7 THE MULTINATIONAL CORPORATION RACE TO THE BOTTOM *v.* THE MYTH OF THE MULTINATIONAL CORPORATION RACE TO THE BOTTOM

The Multinational Corporation Race to the Bottom

Advocate: Debora Spar and David Yoffie

Source: "Multinational Enterprises and the Prospects for Justice," *Journal of International Affairs* 52 (Spring 1999): 557–81

The Myth of the Multinational Corporation Race to the Bottom

Advocate: Daniel W. Drezner

Source: "Bottom Feeders," *Foreign Policy* (November/December 2000): 64–70

The growth of multinational corporations (MNCs) prompts concerns about a "race to the bottom" dynamic in government regulation. Governments maintain different regulatory standards. At a broad level, labor and environmental regulations tend to be stricter in advanced industrialized countries than in developing countries. Governments in advanced industrialized countries enact and enforce stringent regulations that tightly constrain how firms can treat workers, how they must handle toxic waste and other environmental pollutants, and other business activities. Governments in developing societies adopt less stringent regulations and have less capacity to enforce even these laws. These different regulatory frameworks affect firms' production costs. It is more expensive, for example, for a firm to treat hazardous waste than simply to dump it in a landfill. Differences in regulatory standards can make it cheaper to produce in a developing country than in an advanced industrialized country.

Not only might firms shift their operations to countries with lax regulation, governments in advanced industrialized countries might also alter their regulatory standards. To prevent existing factories from moving offshore and to attract new investments from domestic and foreign firms, governments in high-standard countries might find it necessary to relax their labor and environmental regulations. Governments in developing countries might then respond by further relaxing their regulations, prompting governments in advanced industrialized countries to relax theirs still further. Competition between governments to maintain and attract investment will thus drive regulator frameworks down toward the lowest common denominator.

THE MULTINATIONAL CORPORATION RACE TO THE BOTTOM

Those who first enunciated the race-to-the-bottom hypothesis argued that it is the dominant characteristic of the contemporary global economy. The "global economy has allowed multinational companies to escape developed countries' hard-won labor standards. Today these companies choose between workers in developing countries that compete against each other to attract foreign investment. . . . Multinational companies have turned back the clock, transferring production to countries with labor conditions [like those in nineteenth-century America]."[1] Confident that footloose companies were forcing governments to compete to attract investment by relaxing regulatory standards, these same analysts called for governments to develop common global standards to end such races.

Deborah Spar and David Yoffie advance a much more sophisticated and substantially more nuanced version of this argument. They posit that races to the bottom are a possible but hardly inevitable consequence of globalization. Whether firms engage in such races depends on a range of incentives that the authors separate into necessary and sufficient conditions. In addition, the authors suggest that government-led efforts to stem such races by crafting global regulatory regimes may be helpful and even necessary in some cases. But they also highlight how firms can craft private agreements that limit races to the bottom. Such efforts, be they government or firm led, produce what they call a "race to the top."

THE MYTH OF THE MULTINATIONAL CORPORATION RACE TO THE BOTTOM

Perhaps the greatest challenge confronting those who voice concerns about races to the bottom is the absence of compelling evidence that firms in fact relocate production in response to regulatory differences. That is, there doesn't seem to be much racing going on. Indeed, the effort by Spar and Yoffie to develop a more sophisticate framework to think about races to the bottom

---

[1]Terry Collingsworth, J. William Goold, and Pharis J. Harvey, "Time for a Global New Deal," *Foreign Affairs* 73 (January/February 1994): 8.

reflects this lack of convincing evidence of such races. And if multinational companies are not moving production to countries with lax regulatory regimes, advanced industrialized countries need not worry that competition for investment will force them to dismantle the regulatory structures created over the last fifty years. Consequently, elaborate global efforts to harmonize regulations internationally are simply not necessary.

Daniel Drezner argues this position forcefully. He asserts that there is no evidence to support the claim that firms move production to countries with lax regulatory standards. He suggests that the race-to-the-bottom logic has become popular because it enables groups with competing interests to advance their political agendas. Opponents of globalization use the race-to-the-bottom myth to attempt to block further market-based integration. Deregulating politicians embrace the myth to avoid bearing political responsibility for their deregulatory orientation. The myth persists not because it is true, but because it is useful.

POINTS **TO PONDER**

1. According to Spar and Yoffie, under what conditions are we most and least likely to see races to the bottom? What industries are most and least likely to meet these conditions?

2. Why does Drezner believe that the race to the bottom is a myth? Why does the argument retain favor even though it is a myth?

3. Do you believe that the global economy is characterized by races to the bottom? What evidence would you need to collect to confidently answer this question?

4. If we assume that races to the bottom do occur, must governments take steps to prevent them? What would happen if governments did nothing?

Debora Spar and David Yoffie

Multinational Enterprises and the Prospects for Justice

One of the defining features of the modern era is the spread of business enterprises across international borders. Markets once considered peripheral or exotic are now often viewed as integral to a firm's success, and a global corps of businesses has replaced the once-scattered legion of expatriate firms. As corporations increasingly define their markets to encompass wide swathes of the globe, cross-border flows of capital, technology, trade, and currencies have skyrocketed. Indeed, cross-border activities of multinational firms are an integral piece—perhaps the integral piece—of globalization. They are also, in some quarters at least, highly controversial.

One of the controversies centers on the impact of global mobility. According to some scholars, the corporate scramble for ever-wider markets has a dark side. In addition to creating economies of scale and enhancing efficiency, globalization may create a deleterious "race to the bottom," a downward spiral of rivalry that works to lower standards among all affected parties. As described by proponents of this view, the dynamic behind such races is straightforward and compelling. As corporations spread throughout the international economy, their constant search for competitive advantage drives down all those factors that the global players seek to minimize. Tax and labor rates are pushed down, and health and environmental regulation are kept to a bare minimum. In the process, crucial functions of governance effectively slip from the grasp of national governments, and corporations and capital markets reap what societies and workers lose. Since justice is hardly a central concern of the modern corporate enterprise, it presumably gets lost in the shuffle.

Does corporate expansion necessarily lead to such race-to-the-bottom behavior? Or are there situations in which multinational enterprises might actually contribute to the pursuit of international justice? Common wisdom would probably suggest that because corporations are motivated solely by the desire to maximize profits, it would be unrealistic to expect them to play any positive role in the pursuit of international justice. This paper seeks to unbundle such arguments and looks in greater detail at races to the bottom and their impact on affected nations. In particular, it seeks to examine when such races really do occur and when they do not; when corporate expansion is liable to drive global standards to rock-bottom lows; and when it can, paradoxically perhaps, actually enhance prospects for global governance and international justice. . . .

. . . This article proposes a series of hypotheses about the impact of corporate mobility on international standards and international governance. Specifically, we suggest that races to the bottom only occur when border controls are minimal and regulation and factor costs differ across national markets. Once these preconditions are met, races will most likely occur when products are relatively homogeneous, cross-border differentials are significant, and both sunk costs and transaction costs are minimal. Likewise, we suggest that "governance from the top" will be facilitated by the strong presence of externalities within a particular issue area, by a cascading process that affects several states (racing that occurs in steps), by the presence of cross-cutting and powerful domestic coalitions, and occasionally, by incentives for self-governance among the racing firms.

Taken together, these hypotheses imply a more nuanced combination of races to the bottom and governance from the top. They describe globalization as a complex process with no determinate outcome and few clear winners. Sometimes, the integration of capital flows and corporate structures can indeed produce a deleterious spiral and an erosion of governance mechanisms. Yet sometimes it can also culminate in increased governance and more stringent international standards. The challenge for both scholars and policymakers is to separate these effects and probe their disparate causes.

Global Races

In an influential 1994 *Foreign Affairs* article, Terry Collingsworth, J. William Goold, and Pharis J. Harvey laid forth a bleak logic of globalization. According to the authors, the advent of the global economy has enabled multinational companies to escape from developed countries' labor standards and to depress working conditions and wages around the world. As corporations have ventured abroad, they have encouraged a fierce rivalry among the developing countries that seek to win their investment capital. In the process of wooing multinationals, countries "compete against each other to depress wages."[1] As a result, "First World components are assembled by Third World workers who often have no choice but to work under any conditions offered them. Multinational companies have turned back the clock, transferring production to countries with labor conditions that resemble those in the early period of America's own industrialization."[2] . . .

More specific arguments focus on the impact of globalization on labor, suggesting that, in a bid to attract multinational investment, countries may race to the regulatory bottom, lowering wages and abandoning any labor protection they might have offered in the past. In the process, international economic justice is almost certainly compromised, as labor demands give way to corporate rivalry.[3] In the environmental realm, numerous studies have likewise suggested that international competition for investment will compel governments to create "pollution havens," lowering their environmental regulations far below socially desirable levels.[4] These havens will, in turn, lure multinational firms, causing them to flee from more stringent environments. The result of this migration will be more lax standards around the world, increased environmental degradation and a massive migration of jobs and capital from the industrialized states.

Though "justice" is not an explicit theme in this work, the implications in its direction are clear: as corporations race around the world, they weaken the ability of governments to address social issues. Concerns about income distribution, for example, will be muted by a desire to retain multinational investment, and demands for unionization or free association will fall prey to corporate preferences for low wages and docile labor pools. As a result, society at large is bound to suffer and justice will take a back seat to profits. This is the basic logic that connects globalization with race-to-the-bottom effects.

Empirically, evidence of races is more difficult to discern.[5] Indeed, most of the research done tends to dispute the race-to-the-bottom hypothesis, arguing that firms do not actually trawl around the global economy looking for lower labor standards or weaker environmental regimes.[6] Admittedly, finding empirical evidence of race-to-the-bottom effects is bound to be a difficult endeavor since so many variables and motives are involved. Firms choose locations for a wide variety of reasons: to expand markets, to be close to customers, to follow competitors, and to reduce factor and regulatory costs. In most instances, it will be difficult to discern from aggregate data which motives predominate and how important cost or regulatory reduction has been in prompting firms' overseas movements. . . .

Yet even if the empirical evidence is somewhat dismissive, races to the bottom remain a troubling element of the global economy. Theoretically, they are also quite plausible. Firms undeniably seek to increase profits and create a competitive advantage, and if moving to less expensive or less onerous locations would serve these aims, then it is only logical to expect them to do so. It is also reasonable to expect these cross-border movements to increase as globalization tears down old barriers to international flows of capital, people, and technology. If these movements occur, and if they force governments to restrict their own policy options, then the outcomes will be distinctly troubling. In short, even the possibility of race-to-the-bottom effects is important enough to demand continued attention and rigorous inquiry.

At the same time, though, such inquiries must also not lose sight of a parallel possibility. Sometimes it appears that the very same forces that lead to downward spirals can simultaneously produce pressures for higher standards and increased levels of international governance.[7] In other words, some races to the bottom have let loose a countervailing force: supranational regulation, either by governments or by the firms themselves. Rather than directly competing for multinational investment, countries can sometimes agree to common standards for the treatment of multinationals and protocols for taxation. Rather than using wage differentials to compete in the trading arena, national governments can negotiate agreements that regulate their trade and promote more just outcomes. In at least a few cases, governance from the top has mitigated races to the bottom.

In the discussion below, we try to separate out these two effects and the relationship between them. What factors lead, theoretically, to a race to the bottom, and what factors can transform this dynamic into governance from the top?

Racing to the Bottom

. . . A race to the bottom is the progressive movement of capital and technology from countries with relatively high levels of wages, taxation, and regulation to countries with relatively lower levels. . . . Under what conditions, and in what areas, is a race to the bottom most likely to occur? Logically, the answers seem to fall into two distinct tiers: necessary conditions and facilitating factors.

Necessary Conditions

The necessary conditions for races to the bottom are fairly obvious. The first is simply mobility. As with any race, races to the bottom depend critically on the participants' ability to move. Corporations can only launch a race to the bottom once they are free to move across national borders.[8] This essential assumption is evident in many more formal treatments of races.[9] Practically, it also implies that races to the bottom can occur only where border controls are minimal. As countries remove barriers to trade and, particularly, investment, they fire the starting gun that allows corporations to race abroad. . . .

. . . By itself, however, the freedom to move is not sufficient to launch a full-scale race. For a race to occur, corporations must also have some incentives to search for lower cost or more attractive locations: there must be lower taxes and/or lower wage costs in an overseas location, less expensive inputs, and/or less onerous regulations. If these factors are the same across borders, then there is little incentive for firms to race across them.[10] Firms race only when regulation and factor costs are heterogeneous—and when this heterogeneity leaves gaps that can be turned to the firms' competitive advantage.

At a minimum, racing to the bottom demands that two necessary conditions be met. Firms must be mobile and markets must be heterogeneous; there must either be differential factor costs or regulatory differences that affect product costs. Without these conditions, firms either will not be able to move across international borders or will have no incentive to do so. Yet does the mere existence of these conditions ensure that such races will occur? Empirically, it seems not. As mentioned above, numerous studies have demonstrated that even when the conditions for racing are met, races do not necessarily occur.[11] Less formally, we can observe that races simply do not happen everywhere and in every industry. . . . Clearly, there are other factors at work.

Facilitating Factors

We hypothesize that four variables raise the incentives for races to occur: homogeneity of products, regulatory differentials, transaction costs, and sunk costs. While all four capture different elements of the interaction between firms and states in a global economy, we believe that races are more likely when multiple combinations of these variables are present.

Homogeneity of Products

The first variable is what we label as homogeneity of products. In some industries, firms compete across a wide range of dimensions. They may have sharply different products, marketing operations, or research foci. For these firms, marginal cost differentials are unlikely to be all that important to their competitive performance. Intel, for example, does not compete with other semiconductor manufacturers by shaving a few pennies off the price of its Pentium chip. Merck does not undercut its rivals through cut-throat pricing on cancer drugs. These firms still compete, and they still worry about relative cost structures, but they are probably not predisposed to race across the world in order to seize either a cost or a regulatory advantage.

By contrast, firms that manufacture homogeneous products will be more inclined to leap for any advantages that location hopping might bring. If firms produce essentially the same product, and if their internal cost structures are similar, they will feel obligated to compete more at the margin, seizing whatever relative advantage they can find. Thus, firms such as Sony and Matsushita, which produce television sets, may well be tempted to search for lower labor costs in their assembly plants; bulk chemical producers may look for regulatory gaps that help to reduce their relative costs. The more homogeneous the products in any industry, the more we would expect to see competition lured by races toward the bottom.

An interesting twist here concerns the homogeneity of products within a firm's production chain. In developed economies many firms produce high-profile brand goods: Nike shoes or Izod shirts, for example. At the product level, these goods are not homogeneous. A customer may refuse, for example, to purchase anything but Air Jordan shoes. Yet if we separate the marketing and distribution of these brand goods from their production, homogeneity becomes relevant once more. Only here homogeneity exists at the level of the supplier. Nike and Izod, after all, essentially still produce homogeneous goods—sneakers and T-shirts—that are sourced and assembled by a range of virtually interchangeable suppliers. Nike, for example, purchases nearly all its footwear from relatively small suppliers scattered across Asia. From Nike's perspective, these suppliers are basically homogeneous. Nike can pick and choose among them, chasing whatever cost advantages a particular subcontractor might provide. Nike can then act as an oligopolist in its own market, and can pocket the profit differential that lower-cost suppliers can offer. This combination of oligopolistic industry structure at home combined with homogeneity of international suppliers sharply increases the incentives for Nike (and indeed any firm from the apparel or footwear industries) to pursue lower-cost suppliers—that is, to race toward the bottom. Thus, races can occur not only when final products are homogeneous, but also when the producers of non-homogeneous products can disaggregate their own supply chain and wring advantages from the homogeneous components they employ.

Regulatory Differentials

A second factor concerns the relative cost of regulatory differentials. . . . If factor and regulatory costs vary widely across borders, and if these costs are important to the affected firms, then firms will have an incentive to follow these costs to their lowest possible point. If the differences are small and/or unimportant, firms will generally be more content to remain where they are or base any relocation decisions on a range of other factors. Consider, for example, the impact of regulatory variation on firms from two very different industries: toys and paper. For the paper firm, environmental regulation is a critical component of doing business. Under certain circumstances, therefore, it may be in the paper firm's interest to search the globe for more lax regulatory regimes and to invest wherever environmental regulation is least stringent. In this case, a race to the bottom is likely to occur. For a toy producer, however, environmental regulation is generally not that important. If being in a more lax regulatory regime does not affect a firm's way of doing business—or if this effect is minimal—a firm is unlikely to race toward a more lax country, in which case no race to the bottom will ensue. This dynamic may help to explain why evidence of industrial flight to "pollution havens" is limited, despite the obvious logic behind such proposed flights. In most industries, it appears that the costs of complying with pollution control measures are simply not that high.[12]

Transaction Costs and Sunk Costs

The third and fourth factors relate to the economists' well-worn notion of stickiness. In most cases, empirical evidence indicates that firms do not move with the ease suggested by economic models. Changes in production costs do not instantaneously manifest themselves in price changes, wage increases do not create instant layoffs, and firms do not change suppliers or supply patterns to accord perfectly with their relative prices. Such stickiness is particularly relevant for investment decisions, since investment involves a considerable outlay of firm resources. In the race-to-the-bottom literature, there is an underlying sense that firms move at the speed of relative cost change: they hop across borders as soon as they perceive a financial advantage. Yet the stickiness of investment is bound to slow the pace of relocation. Most firms cannot switch plant locations at will as most will incur substantial costs from any move across borders. The higher these costs, the stickier existing investments will prove to be—and stickier investments will decrease the momentum for any race to the bottom.

In particular, we can imagine two kinds of stickiness that would affect firms' propensity to engage in a race to the bottom. The first is that which arises from sunk costs: the more expensive and capital-intensive an operation is, the less likely its parent firm will be to relocate.[13] The second comes from transaction costs: the more difficult and time-consuming a move will be, the less likely it is to occur. Both of these points are largely intuitive, yet they explain considerable differences in industry structure and incentives.

Consider again the gap that separates apparel firms from paper mills. An apparel firm is a highly labor-intensive venture, with only a limited amount of in-the-ground capital investment. It may lease a building or a few floors and own some machinery, the total cost of which can be as low as $100,000. Neither relocating its operations nor opening additional facilities in a new location is particularly daunting. The sunk costs are low and the stickiness of the investment is thus minimal. Similar characteristics would adhere to firms in the footwear industry and many low-technology assembly operations. A paper mill, by contrast, has much lower levels of labor intensity and correspondingly higher levels of capital intensity. Instead of housing primarily laborers and easily duplicated machinery, a paper plant (or a chemical processing plant or semiconductor fabrication facility) typically contains highly specific machinery and complex interlocked processes. Such plants can be moved; they can also be closed in one location and supplanted by newer facilities elsewhere. Yet the propensity for such changes is significantly lower than in the apparel industry, since the sunk costs of any particular plant are much greater. We should expect, therefore, that paper mills are less likely to race abroad than apparel firms. . . .

A similar logic adheres to the stickiness created by transaction costs. As the literature on institutional economics makes clear, not all costs borne by firms are explicitly financial. There are also invisible costs such as the costs of hiring and training new employees, suffering productivity losses after introducing new technologies, and building contacts and reputation. All of these costs will be present, and frequently heightened, as firms move to new locations. The higher these costs, the more reluctant firms should be to engage in race-to-the-bottom behavior.[14] . . .

Taken together, these hypotheses sketch a two-tiered view of races and an argument that industry structure matters. In any industry, races can occur only when two key necessary conditions are met: corporations must be free to move their capital and technology across borders, and government regulation and factor costs must be heterogeneous across those borders. Once these conditions are in place, though, industry variation comes into play, meaning that not all firms will be equally predisposed to chase each other toward the lowest common denominator. Firms will be most inclined to race when they produce homogeneous, commodity-type products; when the costs that matter most to them are sharply divergent across national borders; and when their sunk costs of investment and transaction costs of relocation are both relatively low. When these conditions are not in place, races to the bottom are less likely to occur.

Racing Toward Justice?

Thus far, we have described only how races to the bottom might be forestalled by the internal dynamics of various industries. Yet, as mentioned at the outset, there exists another realm of possibilities: races, once launched, might be curtailed by the imposition of external standards. A race to the bottom, in other words, can be transformed into governance from the top.[15] In the process, the prospects for justice are bound to increase.

To imagine how this transformation might occur, consider the dynamics of the race. Essentially, regulatory and/or factor arbitrage facilitates a downward spiral. In the absence of high sunk or transaction costs, firms chase competitive advantage to the lowest possible point; they will move investment to whatever location will support their operations at the lowest cost. Countries can reinforce the game by depressing the cost of factors under their control (taxes, regulation, minimum wages) and watering down standards in order to compete for scarce capital.

What would slow the race down, then, is any constraint that either prevents the firm from seizing the arbitrage opportunity or prevents the state from creating it. Theoretically, such possibilities are relatively easy to imagine. Consider the situation from the firm's perspective. What drives the race here is rivalry and relative costs. Firms need to chase lower costs primarily to keep (or get) a cost advantage relative to their competitors. If everyone were to stop chasing, then no one would be at a particular disadvantage. It is precisely the dynamic that describes cartels, the dynamic captured in Rousseau's classic parable of the stag hunt.[16] If firms were to cooperate and hold to a common standard, the race would stop. The problem, though, is that firms are rarely able to form this kind of collective endeavor. Indeed, as we know, the record of cartels is dismally poor: most succumb early on to the pressures of competition and defection.[17]

Where national governments are concerned, however, the prospects are considerably brighter. As the vast literature on international organizations and regimes makes clear, it is eminently possible for governments not only to govern effectively at home, but also to establish governance structures that stretch across borders. . . .

We know . . . that, in numerous cases, governments have . . . agreed on common, higher standards; and they have achieved (varying) degrees of compliance with the rules they set. The GATT [General Agreement on Tariffs and Trade], the World Trade Organization, the Nuclear Nonproliferation Treaty and the European Union all . . . enforce common standards that collectively enhance their members' well-being while simultaneously denying these members the advantages of certain unilateral actions. Conceptually, there is no reason to suspect that the global playing field could not be similarly leveled with regard to multinational investment and corporate mobility.

More challenging, though, is to imagine the precise conditions under which this "race to the top" might emerge to regulate races to the bottom. As a first cut, we might expect that a necessary condition for any kind of international governance is the strong presence of externalities within a particular issue area. Realistically, governance efforts are likely to cluster where state borders are most porous. The more that events in one country affect outcomes or welfare in another, the greater the need for cross-border governance to address any problems that might arise. . . . States, in short, will be more inclined to pursue international governance when the effect of races to the bottom is to damage their own domestic economy. The greater the damage, the greater their incentive to stop the race.

A final point along these lines, though, is that state identity matters. While all states may have similar interests in stopping races or forging governance structures, not all states will be similarly equipped to address these issues. . . . It seems reasonable to assume that some states will be better positioned to create and enforce arrangements of international governance. States that are more powerful in the international arena simply will carry more clout in the formation of cross-border rules. They will be better able to set higher standards, abide by them, and persuade others to do likewise. They will also generally be better prepared to perform the duty of enforcer, punishing those who wander too far from the rules established at the international level.[18] . . .

A second hypothesis concerns what might be labeled "cascading." When races occur, they rarely sweep downward in a single motion. Rather, firms move through a series of steps: from their home country to a less expensive, less onerous foreign location; from that spot to an even more lax alternative; then on to the next contender; and so forth. This is the process by which the spiral is widened and accelerated. Governments are most likely to get involved only after the process has already moved down several of the early steps. If firms move only from their home market to an overseas facility, pressure for governance will be muted by the inherent ambiguities described earlier. The firms may have moved for a whole range of reasons, and the state is unlikely to get involved. If these same firms move on from destination to destination, then the pressure for governance is likely to mount. There are more states that feel the negative consequences of [the firms'] movement, and more evidence that the movement is being driven by a race-to-the-bottom rivalry. Critically, in order for international governance to succeed, multiple states must share a common interest in arresting the race at any particular point and preventing any further downward movement. We should therefore expect to see more concerted efforts at international governance as the race cascades beyond its initial stages. . . .

A third hypothesis brings domestic politics back into the . . . picture. . . . Domestic groups typically put international governance issues on the state's agenda. The Multifiber Arrangement is the end result of extensive lobbying by U.S. textile firms and (particularly) their labor unions; pressure for environmental regulation has for decades been the work of concerted activist groups such as Greenpeace and the Environmental Defense Fund, and pressure for international labor standards comes from human rights groups, as well as labor organizations.[19] When these domestic groups have already forged their own alliances at the international level, the political pressure is likely to be even more effective and the governance swifter. The more that domestic groups care about a particular issue, and the more powerful these groups are, the higher levels of international governance we should expect to see.

A final hypothesis returns us to . . . firms. While it is easy to paint firms as the malevolent drivers of these downward spirals, . . . firms could play some role in redirecting their races back toward the top—that is, toward global regulation and higher international standards. Under some circumstances, firms might choose to self-regulate, settling upon common standards rather than competing for relative advantage along these lines. Admittedly, these circumstances are bound to be rare. Given the collective action dilemma . . . , firms generally will be wary of defection and thus not eager to bind themselves to a set of prescribed rules. Nevertheless, in some cases rules may triumph over races. If firms suspect that formal international governance is imminent, then they may choose to self-regulate in the hopes of pre-empting a more onerous set of restrictions. Likewise, if the race is becoming too costly for all of the players, or even for a solid and powerful majority of them, then they may choose again to self-regulate and set a common floor below which none of the players will compete.

Cases of this sort are actually quite common, more common by far than the race-to-the-bottom literature would suggest. As early as 1981, for example, when pressure for environmental regulation was just beginning to spread around the world, the International Chamber of Commerce (a private business group) passed its own set of environmental guidelines supporting the harmonization of global pollution regulations. After the 1984 disaster in Bhopal, India, the U.S.-based Chemical Manufacturers Association (CMA) enacted a set of environmental guidelines known as "Responsible Care" that applied to all of the association's 180 member firms. Consisting of ten "guiding principles" and six management codes, Responsible Care specifies requirements for many different aspects of the chemicals business, from community awareness and emergency response to pollution control and employee health and safety. While the initiative was largely a response to negative public opinion within the United States, its effects have ranged far beyond national borders. By mandating that Responsible Care be extended to cover the numerous foreign manufacturing facilities of member firms, the CMA has successfully exported United States environmental standards to developing nations.[20] Similar guidelines were adopted subsequently by the European Chemical Industries Council (CEFIC).[21] More recently, major producers of chemicals and pesticides adopted a voluntary and apparently highly effective system to ensure that exports of these substances follow certain well-defined rules and procedures.[22]

In the area of human rights and labor standards, private initiatives are also playing an increasingly important role. In 1997, for example, both the World Federation of Sporting Goods Industry and the U.S.-based Sporting Goods Manufacturers Association pledged to eradicate child labor in the Pakistani soccer ball industry. Spurred by Reebok, a U.S. firm that had been hard hit by accusations that it had purchased balls made by 12-year-old workers, all members of the private industry associations eventually agreed to establish a system of independent monitors to ensure that no children were involved in the production of soccer balls. The firms also joined forces in establishing schools and other programs for the former child workers.[23] Similarly, public pressure in the United States has recently led to the formation of a private Apparel Industry Partnership, under which firms such as Liz Claiborne and L.L. Bean have agreed to ensure that all of their suppliers comply with specific workplace codes of conduct.[24] In the rug industry, importers in both the United States and Germany have agreed to monitor the source of the products they sell, affixing a "Rugmark" label to those carpets that are guaranteed to have been made without the use of child labor.[25] At the most general level, a number of major multinationals such as Toys'R'Us and Avon announced in the spring of 1998 that their suppliers will henceforth need to comply with the provisions of SA8000, a certifiable set of labor and human rights standards. Modeled on the International Organization for Standardization system for ensuring compliance with technical and environmental standards, SA8000 is an ambitious attempt to create private standards for social accountability.[26] Under this system, corporations voluntarily agree to adhere to a list of social standards, for example, provisions regarding the use of child labor, the right to collective bargaining, nondiscrimination and so forth. Independent auditors then visit the firms and their suppliers to ensure compliance with the SA8000 code. . . .

Clearly, any scheme for private corporate governance must be regarded with some degree of caution. None of these arrangements have any formal structure around them, and all lack stringent enforcement mechanisms. They can all easily disintegrate into public relations efforts and will always bear the stigma of this possibility. Yet private corporate arrangements also have a number of advantages. They appear easier to forge than governmental structures, since the negotiation process involves fewer parties and does not have the same measure of public accountability as would a governmental initiative.[27] According to some evidence, they also actually have higher rates of compliance over a harder range of issues.[28]

Finally, from the firms' perspective, self-regulation can be an effective means of restoring or enhancing profitability. If racing becomes too costly, or if firms fear that governments are prepared to impose collective regulation upon them, then self-regulation can make sense. By leveling the playing field, firms can solve the collective action dilemma that binds them all. They can also use harmonized policies to shift the cost of compliance from producers to consumers: if all producers are held to the same standard, then the world price of their good is likely to rise. Finally, if firms are already adhering to their own cross-national standards (a common practice for many firms from industrialized countries), then encouraging other firms to agree to these same standards can convey a significant advantage. As one American CEO recently commented in response to a U.S. proposal to include environmental standards in trade legislation: "We already have environmental standards . . . we want a level playing field."[29] Cooperation under these circumstances can prove a powerful competitive weapon.

Firms, States, and the Pursuit of Justice

Drawing a connection between multinational enterprises and international justice is no easy task. As stated at the outset, corporations are not designed as emissaries of justice. . . . Corporations can exploit host countries and peoples; they can capitalize on whatever advantages a location offers to them; and they can chase each other round the globe in a downward spiraling search for more lax regulations and lower costs. Yet they also can eschew all of these activities—not because they find them unsavory, but because it may be in their own best interest to do so. Under some circumstances, corporations may even act to raise global standards. Working either through national governments or private associations, corporations may cooperate to enact tougher environmental standards, bans on child labor, and tighter health and safety regulations. . . .

As a policy issue, of course, the key question is "how?" How can governments prod multinational firms into a race to the top rather than the bottom? How can they compel multinationals to work toward justice rather than against it? . . . The dilemma for government policy is that races to the bottom are largely driven by factors inherent in industry structure. Some industries— footwear, apparel, and toys, for example—are more likely to engage in this type of behavior than others. If countries explicitly woo these industries, then they should expect, eventually, that they will either be outbid by countries offering even more attractive terms, or that they will progressively have to lower their own standards in order to compete. Not surprisingly, it is also these industries that have witnessed some of the greatest allegations of labor abuse and unjust practices. If countries truly want to end corporate racing (and this, after all, remains an open question), they would be wise to promote investment in other spheres and to resist the temptation of using competitive deregulation as a sustainable policy tool.

Finally, if the arguments laid forth in this paper are correct, then multinationals may hold the most powerful key to their own regulation. To forestall racing to the bottom and enhance the prospects for corporate self-governance, states may want to facilitate a process in which multinationals forge their own common standards. They may wish, for example, to host or encourage intra-industry negotiations, perhaps even conducting these negotiations under governmental auspices. Such has been the case with the U.S. Apparel Industry Partnership, which was launched by (though not controlled by) the U.S. Department of Labor. Governments may also want to keep regulation as an ever-ready possibility, since a concern for impending formal regulation seems often to coalesce industry interest in informal self-regulation. . . .

Ultimately, it is unrealistic to expect that corporations will be leaders in the pursuit of international economic justice. Yet corporations are neither an impediment to justice nor an irrelevant instrument in its pursuit. Under certain conditions and with the prodding of concerned voices in both the public and private arenas, multinational enterprises may be surprisingly forceful means for pushing global standards to a higher, and more just, plateau.

ENDNOTES

1. . . . Terry Collingsworth, J. William Goold and Pharis J. Harvey, "Labor and Free Trade: Time for a Global New Deal," *Foreign Affairs*, 73, no. 1 (January/ February 1994) p. 9.

2. Ibid. . . .

3. See Dani Rodrik, *Labour Standards and International Trade: Moving Beyond the Rhetoric* (Washington, DC: Institute for International Economics, 1995); Ethan B. Kapstein, "Workers and the World Economy," *Foreign Affairs*, 75, no. 3 (May/June 1996) pp. 16–37; Adrian Wood, *North-South Trade, Employment and Inequality: Changing Fortunes in a Skill-Driven World* (New York: Oxford University Press, 1994); Richard B. Du Boff, "Globalization and Wages: The Down Escalator," *Dollars and Sense*, no. 213 (September/October 1997) pp. 36–40; and Werner Sengenberger, "Local Development and International Economic Competition," *International Labour Review*, 132, no. 3 (1993) pp. 313–329.

4. Eric Bond and Larry Samuelson, "Strategic Behavior and Rules for International Taxation of Capital," *Economic Journal*, 99, no. 398 (December 1989) pp. 1099–1111; Herman E. Daly, "The Perils of Free Trade," *Scientific American*, 269, no. 5 (November 1993) pp. 24–29. See also Arik Levinson, "Environmental Regulations and Industry Location: International and Domestic Evidence," in *Fair Trade and Harmonization: Prerequisites for Free Trade*, ed. Jagdish Bhagwati and Robert E. Hudec (Cambridge: The MIT Press, 1996) pp. 429–457; and H. Jeffrey Leonard, *Pollution and The Struggle for World Product* (Cambridge: Cambridge University Press, 1988).

5. See Eddy Lee, "Globalization and Labour Standards: A Review of Issues," *International Labour Review*, 136, no. 2 (Summer 1997) pp. 173–189; Maureen Cropper and Wallace Oates, "Environmental Economics: A Survey," *Journal of Economic Literature*, 30, no. 2 (June 1992) pp. 675–740; and Charles S. Pearson, "Environmental Standards, Industrial Relocation, and Pollution Havens," in *Multinational Corporations, Environment, and the Third World: Business Matters*, ed. Charles S. Pearson (Durham, NC: Duke University Press, 1987) pp. 113–128.

6. See Cletis Coughlin, Joseph V. Terza and Vachira Arromdee, "State Characteristics and the Location of Foreign Direct Investment Within the United States," *Review of Economics and Statistics*, 73, no. 4 (November 1991) pp. 675–683; Timothy J. Bartik, "Business Location Decisions in the United States: Estimates of the Effects of Unionization, Taxes, and Other Characteristics of States," *Journal of Business and Economic Statistics*, 3, no. 1 (January 1985) pp. 14–22; Richard B. Freeman, "Comments," in *Labor Markets and Integrating National Economies*, ed. Ronald G. Ehrenberg (Washington, DC: The Brookings

Institution, 1994) pp. 107–110; G. Knogden, "Environment and Industrial Siting," *Zeitschrift fur Umweltpolitik* (December 1979); and Gene M. Grossman and Alan B. Krueger, "Environmental Impacts of a North American Free Trade Agreement," Woodrow Wilson School Discussion Papers in Economics, no. 158 (November 1991).

7. David Vogel, *Trading Up: Consumer and Environmental Regulation in a Global Economy* (Cambridge: Harvard University Press, 1995).

8. For a discussion of mobility and its dangers, see Daly, pp. 24–29.

9. William A. Fischel, "Fiscal and Environmental Considerations in the Location of Firms in Suburban Communities," in *Fiscal Zoning and Land Use Controls,* ed. Edwin S. Mills and Wallace Oates (Lexington, MA: DC Heath & Co., 1975) pp. 119–174; and Michelle J. White, "Firm Location in a Zoned Metropolitan Area," in Mills and Oates, eds., pp. 175–201. . . .

10. Except, perhaps, to service these markets with lower transportation costs.

11. Joseph Freidman, Daniel A. Gerlowski and Johnathan Silberman, "What Attracts Foreign Multinational Corporations? Evidence From Branch Plant Location in the United States," *Journal of Regional Science,* 32, no. 4 (November 1992) pp. 403–418.

12. H. David Robison, "Who Pays for Industrial Pollution Abatement?" *Review of Economics and Statistics,* 67, no. 4 (November 1985) pp. 702–706; Cropper and Oates, p. 698.

13. For a discussion of sunk costs in multinational investment, see David B. Yoffie, "From Comparative Advantage to Regulated Competition," in *Beyond Free Trade: Firms, Governments, and Global Competition,* ed. David B. Yoffie (Boston: Harvard Business School Press, 1993) pp. 1–25.

14. Robert Wade, "Globalization and its Limits: Reports of the Death of the National Economy are Greatly Exaggerated," in *National Diversity and Global Capitalism,* ed. Suzanne Berger and Ronald Dore (Ithaca, NY: Cornell University Press, 1996) pp. 80–81.

15. Or as Vogel puts it, the "Delaware effect" is replaced by the "California effect." Businesses relocate to Delaware due to its low corporate taxation rate, while California's stringent environmental regulations raise the standards of regulation across the country. Vogel, pp. 5–6.

16. For more on Rousseau's idea of the stag hunt, see R. Harrison Wagner, "The Theory of Games and the Problem of International Cooperation," *American Political Science Review,* 77, no. 2 (June 1993) pp. 330–346.

17. See Debora L. Spar, *The Cooperative Edge: The Internal Politics of International Cartels* (Ithaca, NY: Cornell University Press, 1994); and Jock A. Finlayson and Mark W. Zacher, *Managing International Markets: Developing Countries and the Commodity Trade Regime* (New York: Columbia University Press, 1988).

18. For more on this relationship, see James Alt, Randall Calvert and Brian D. Humes, "Reputation and Hegemonic Stability: A Game Theoretical Analysis," *American Political Science Review,* 82, no. 2 (June 1988) pp. 445–466; Spar (1994).

19. See Peter J. Spiro, "New Global Communities: Nongovernmental Organizations in International Decision-Making Institutions," *Washington Quarterly,* 18, no.1 (Winter 1995) pp. 45–56; and Lester M. Salamon, "The Rise of the Nonprofit

Sector," *Foreign Affairs*, 73, no. 4 (July/August 1994) pp. 109–122. For an argument that these concerns are linked solely to organized labor's disguised desire for protection, see International Labor Organization, *Extracts From Statements Made at the Ministerial Conference of the World Trade Organization*, Singapore: 9–13 December 1996 (Geneva: International Labor Organization, 1997).

20. Forest L. Reinhardt, "Business and the Environment," forthcoming manuscript (Boston: Harvard Business School Press, 1999) pp. 3–12.

21. M. Baram, "Multinational Corporations, Private Codes, and Technology Transfer for Sustainable Development," *Environmental Law*, 24 (1994) pp. 33–65.

22. David Victor, "The Operation and Effectiveness of the Montreal Protocol's NonCompliance Procedure," in *The Implementation and Effectiveness of International Commitments: Theory and Practice*, ed. David Victor, Kal Rustilia and Eugene B. Sholnikoff (Cambridge: MIT Press, 1998) pp. 137–176.

23. Steven Greenhouse, "Sporting Goods Concerns Agree to Combat Sale of Soccer Balls Made by Children," *New York Times*, 14 February 1997, p. A12.

24. Debora L. Spar, "The Spotlight and the Bottom Line," *Foreign Affairs*, 77, no. 2 (March/April 1998) pp. 7–12; and Michael Posner and Lynda Clarizio, An Unprecedented Step in the Effort to End Sweatshops," *Human Rights*, 24, no. 4 (Fall 1997) p. 14.

25. Hugh Williamson, "Stamp of Approval," *Far Eastern Economic Review*, 158, no. 5 (2 February 1995) p. 26.

26. For more on the provisions of SA8000, see Pamela Sebastian, "A Special Background Report on Trends in Industry and Finance," *Wall Street Journal*, 16 July 1998, p. Al; and Aaron Bernstein, "Sweatshop Police," *Business Week* (20 October 1997) p. 39.

27. Richard Freeman also suggests that private standards are more market-friendly, since they essentially allow consumers to determine which standards they deem acceptable. See Richard Freeman, "A Hard-headed Look at Labor Standards," in *International Labour Standards and Economic Interdependence*, ed. Werner Sengenberger and Duncan Campbell (Geneva: International Institute for Labor Studies, 1994) pp. 79–92.

28. See Victor; for an opposing argument, see Baram, pp. 33–65.

29. W. Douglas Ellis Jr., CEO of Southern Mills, Inc., cited in Paul Magnusson, De'Ann Weimer and Nicole Harris, "Clinton's Trade Crusade," *Business Week* (8 June 1998) p. 35.

Daniel W. Drezner
Bottom Feeders

The "race to the bottom" in global labor and environmental standards has captivated journalists, politicians, and activists worldwide. Why does this myth persist? Because it is a useful scare tactic for multinational corporations and populist agitators peddling their policy wares.

The current debates over economic globalization have produced a seemingly simple and intuitive conclusion: Unfettered globalization triggers an unavoidable "race to the bottom" in labor and environmental standards around the world. The reduction of restrictions on trade and cross-border investment frees corporations to scour the globe for the country or region where they can earn the highest return. National policies such as strict labor laws or rigorous environmental protections lower profits by raising the costs of production. Multinational corporations will therefore engage in regulatory arbitrage, moving to countries with lax standards. Fearing a loss of their tax base, nation-states have little choice but to loosen their regulations to encourage foreign investment and avoid capital flight. The inevitable result: a Darwinian struggle for capital where all other values—including workers' rights and the environment—are sacrificed upon the altar of global commerce.

The fear of such a race to the bottom has helped forge an unlikely coalition of union leaders, environmentalists, and consumer groups; together, they have spearheaded significant public resistance to several recent international economic initiatives. These include the North American Free Trade Agreement (NAFTA), the abortive Multilateral Agreement on Investment (MAI), the 1999 World Trade Organization (WTO) talks in Seattle, China's admission into the WTO, and the African Growth and Opportunity Act that U.S. President Bill Clinton signed into law [in May 2000]. In each instance, protestors argued that unless globalization is reversed or at least slowed, a race to the bottom is inevitable.

At the opposite end of the political spectrum, the rhetoric and goals may differ, but the underlying imagery remains the same. Pro-market politicians and multinational corporations also cultivate the idea of an unstoppable global race—except they do so in order to advance environmental deregulation and "flexible" labor legislation that otherwise would become ensnared in fractious political debates. Multinational corporations argue that the pressures of the global marketplace force them to relocate or outsource their production to lower-cost facilities in poor nations.

The race-to-the-bottom hypothesis appears logical. But it is wrong. Indeed, the lack of supporting evidence is startling. Essayists usually mention an anecdote or two about firms moving from an advanced to a developing economy and then, depending on their political stripes, extrapolate visions of healthy international competition or impending environmental doom. However, there is no indication that the reduction of controls on trade and capital flows has forced a generalized downgrading in labor or environmental conditions. If anything, the opposite has occurred.

Given this dearth of evidence, why does the race to the bottom persist in policy debates? Because the image is politically useful for both pro- and antiglobalization forces. Unfortunately, by perpetuating the belief in a nonexistent threat, all sides contribute to a misunderstanding of both the effects of globalization and how governments in developing and advanced economies should—or should not—respond.

Running in Place

If economic globalization really does trigger a race to the bottom in regulatory standards, two trends should be evident. First, countries that are more open to trade and investment should have fewer and less demanding regulations affecting corporate production costs. Once barriers to trade and investment are lowered, the logic goes, nation-states must eliminate burdensome regulations or risk massive capital flight. Over time, therefore, more open economies should display lower labor and environmental standards. Second, multinational corporations should flock to countries with the lowest regulatory standards. The core of the race-to-the-bottom hypothesis is that profit-maximizing firms will locate to places where the production costs are relatively low. Since any regulatory standard presumably raises these costs, corporations will seek out countries with the weakest possible standards.

These predicted trends are, in fact, nonexistent. Consider labor standards. There is no real evidence that economic openness leads to the degradation of workers. In fact, some evidence suggests that openness actually improves worker standards. A comprehensive 1996 study by the Organisation for Economic Co-operation and Development (OECD) found that "successfully sustained trade reforms" were linked to improvements in core labor standards, defined as nondiscrimination in the workplace, the right to unionize, and the prohibition of forced labor and exploitative child labor. This linkage occurs because multinationals often pay higher-than-average wages in developing countries in order to recruit better workers. Moreover, since corporations have learned to work efficiently under rigorous regulatory standards in their home countries, they favor improving standards in their foreign production sites in order to gain a competitive advantage over local competitors, who are not accustomed to operating under such conditions. A recent World Bank survey of 3,800 workers in 12 Nike factories in Thailand and Vietnam found that 72 percent of Thai workers were satisfied with their overall income levels, while a majority of Vietnamese workers preferred factory employment over lower-wage jobs in their country's agricultural sector.

The case of export processing zones (EPZs) in developing economies underscores the spuriousness of the race-to-the-bottom argument. EPZs are areas established in order to attract foreign investment. Typically, governments entice investors into EPZs with infrastructure investment and duty-free imports and exports. There are more than 850 [EPZs] worldwide, employing some 27 million workers; in some developing nations, like Mauritius, EPZs account for a majority of a country's exports. If there is a race to the bottom in labor standards, it should be particularly evident in EPZs.

There are a few countries, such as Bangladesh and Zimbabwe, that have attempted to preempt competitive pressures by exempting their EPZs from regulations covering labor standards. However, contrary to the race-to-the-bottom hypothesis, such policies have not compelled other countries to relax labor standards in their own EPZs. Indeed, several nations, including the Dominican Republic and the Philippines, actually reversed course in the mid-1990s and established labor standards in their EPZs when none previously existed. A 1998 International Labour Organization report found no evidence that countries with a strong trade-union presence suffered any loss of investment in their EPZs, while a 1997 World Bank study noted a strong positive correlation between higher occupational safety and health conditions and foreign investment in EPZs. Analysts also have found that wages in EPZs actually tend to exceed average wages elsewhere in the host country.

Similarly, openness to trade and investment does not lead to a race to the bottom in environmental conditions or regulations. Countries most open to outside investment—OECD nations—also have the most stringent environmental regulations. Even developing countries such as Malaysia, the Philippines, Thailand, Argentina, and Brazil have liberalized their foreign investment laws while simultaneously tightening environmental regulations. In Latin America, there is clear evidence that more protectionist countries, such as pre-NAFTA Mexico and Brazil under military rule, have been the biggest polluters. This finding is hardly surprising; the most protectionist economies in this century—the Warsaw Pact bloc—displayed the least concern for the environment. Privatization programs in these countries, which help attract foreign direct investment, have contributed to improved environmental performance as multinational corporations have transferred cleaner technologies from the developed world. In Brazil, for instance, the privatization of the petrochemicals sector in the early 1990s led to a greater acceptance of environmentally safe practices.

Race-to-the-bottom critics counter that stringent labor and environmental standards in developing economies are backed by purely nominal enforcement capabilities. Although it is difficult to quantify compliance and enforcement in developing economies, the emergence of watchdog groups—analogous to election observers and human rights organizations—that scrutinize the enforcement of national labor and environmental legislation is a positive development. The United States has recently pursued this strategy by bolstering the role of the International Labour Organization in monitoring core labor standards around the world. And even in the absence of uniform national enforcement, many multinational corporations have embraced self-monitoring programs for the environment—an effective complement to government regulations.

Perhaps most damaging to the race-to-the-bottom proponents, there is no evidence that corporations direct their investment to developing countries with lower labor or environmental standards. Indeed, the relationship between foreign direct investment (FDI) and labor standards is strongly positive. During the 1990s, an overwhelming majority of global FDI was directed toward advanced economies (which tend to have higher labor standards), not to poor nations. A similar story can be told with environmental standards. Comparing data on U.S. FDI in developed and developing countries reveals that pollution-intensive U.S. firms tend to invest in countries with stricter environmental standards.

Profit-maximizing corporations invest in countries with high labor and environmental standards not out of a sense of obligation, but for hard-nosed business reasons. Consumption has gone global along with production; many firms base their investment decisions not just on likely production costs but also on access to sizable markets. A 1994 survey by the U.S. Department of Commerce found that more than 60 percent of the production of U.S. corporate affiliates in developing countries was sold in the host country and less than 20 percent was exported back to the United States. In Mexico, which provides an ideal platform for reexporting to the United States, only 28 percent of production by U.S. affiliates made it back to the United States; more than two thirds was marketed in Mexico. The great fear of the race-to-the-bottom crowd—that U.S. multinationals will locate production facilities in developing countries, exploit local resources, and reexport back to the United States—has not materialized. In fact, that type of activity characterizes less than 4 percent of total U.S. investment abroad. The oft-cited cases of garment facilities based in poor nations and geared to consumers in advanced economies are the exception, not the rule. This exception is largely due to the low capital investment and importance of labor costs in the textiles sector.

Since corporations invest overseas to tap into new, large markets, host countries actually wield considerable power. They can use that power to resist deregulatory pressures. Multinational corporations have invested large sums in China despite formidable regulatory hurdles, a blatant disregard for copyright laws, high levels of corruption, and strict requirements for technology transfers. The prospect of 1 billion consumers will cause that kind of behavior among chief executive officers. Mexico has enhanced its environmental protection efforts while trying to attract investment. The result? Foreign direct investment around Mexico City has exploded, while the air quality has actually improved.

Multinational firms are also well aware of the growing link between public opinion and profits. Increasingly, citizens care about the conditions under which their products are manufactured—an environmental or labor mishap can cripple a corporation's brand name. Thus, foreign investors in Costa Rican bananas or Asian lumber insist on higher standards than the local government in order to cater to environmentally savvy European consumers. And PepsiCo pulled out of Myanmar in 1997 because it did not want to be linked to that country's repressive regime. To be sure, some multinational corporations are hardly paragons of labor or environmental virtue, as the perilous labor conditions at Royal Dutch Shell and Chevron's operations in Nigeria make clear. But in general, corporations understand that it is smart business to stay in the good graces of their customers.

The lack of evidence for a race to the bottom is not surprising when put in historical perspective. In the late 19th century, there was an enormous increase in flows of capital, goods, and labor among countries in the Atlantic basin. On several dimensions, such as labor mobility and investment flows, the degree of market integration 100 years ago is much greater than today. Despite claims made at the time that these trends would lead to a world ruled by social Darwinism, the United States and Europe created national regulatory standards for consumer safety, labor, and the environment and developed regional institutions (including a predecessor to the European Central Bank) to cope with the vicissitudes of financial markets. Indeed, globalization does not eliminate the ability of sovereign states to make independent regulatory decisions. Nor does globalization render governments impervious to the preferences of their own citizens. Even authoritarian countries are not immune to public pressure; the beginning of the end of the Soviet bloc saw environmental protests against rising levels of pollution. Governments, particularly in democratic countries, must respond not only to domestic and foreign firms but also to the wishes of citizens who prefer stricter regulatory standards.

The Scapegoat Factory

Of course, one can hardly dispute that developing countries often display deplorable environmental and labor standards and conditions, far below those in the world's advanced economies. But the evidence thus far indicates that globalization itself does not cause or aggravate this disparity. If anything, the opposite is true. So why do so many people seem to believe in a hypothesis that has yet to attract any evidence? Because the myth is politically convenient for all sides. Nongovernmental organizations (NGOs), corporations, politicians, and academics use the race to the bottom as an excuse to peddle their policy wares.

Opponents of globalization—including environmentalists, labor unions, and a multitude of NGOs—advance the myth of a race to the bottom to oppose further global market integration. The race to the bottom is a wonderful rallying tool for fundraising and coalition building and also serves as the perfect bogeyman, allowing these groups to use scare tactics derived from previous domestic policy campaigns against nuclear power and acid rain. Such strategies are consistent with a pattern of exaggerating dangers to capture the attention of the press and the public: Only by crying that the sky is falling can antiglobalization forces rouse complacent citizens. For example, Public Citizen, one of the most vocal NGOs on trade issues, has argued that steps toward economic liberalization will have devastating social effects. Its Web site notes that the Multilateral Agreement on Investment would have "hasten[ed] the 'race to the bottom,' wherein countries are pressured to lower living standards and weaken regulatory regimes in an effort to attract needed investment capital." Whatever shortcomings the MAI may have displayed, it demanded discerning criticism, not knee-jerk attacks based on spurious reasoning.

The race to the bottom also provides a useful scapegoat for larger trends that adversely affect specific interest groups, such as labor unions. A recent statement by Philip Jennings, general secretary of the Geneva-based Union Network International, which represents more than 900 unions in 140 countries, provides an apt example. "Globalization is not working for working people," Jennings declared in July 2000. "It needs a human face." Similarly, union leaders in the United States have argued that globalization and the race to the bottom are responsible for the 30-year stagnation in the median real wages and the growing income inequality in the United States. Such simplistic views disregard other key factors—particularly advances in technology and the subsequent demand for high-skilled labor—affecting wage and employment levels. If, as race-to-the-bottom proponents suggest, U.S. workers are being replaced by their counterparts in developing economies, then the 2.6 million employees laid off by manufacturing multinationals in the United States over the past three decades were replaced with a mere 300,000 workers hired in developing nations over the same period. In other words, Third World laborers would have to be nearly nine times as productive as those in the United States—hardly a persuasive proposition. In fact, the U.S. labor force displays the highest productivity levels in the world.

The race-to-the-bottom myth also helps pro-globalization forces sell deregulatory policies that may result in short-term economic pain. But rather than take the responsibility of pushing for deregulation directly, advocates invoke globalization as an excuse. It does not matter whether one favors deregulation or not; globalization will punish those who fail to deregulate, so there is little choice in the matter. For example, Pacific Telesis (now part of SBC Communications) used globalization as an excuse for cutbacks and layoffs in its San Francisco offices and to lobby Washington for deregulation. Unocal has argued that because of the competitive pressures of globalization, it should not be forced by U.S. sanctions to pull out of Myanmar.

Politicians also exploit the need to compete in the global marketplace and the myth of a race to the bottom as excuses to support policies that would otherwise trigger fierce public debate. State governments in the United States have often claimed that widespread deregulation must occur in order to attract capital. Meanwhile, European politicians trotted out the specter of globalization to justify the Maastricht criteria, a series of stringent economic prerequisites for a European monetary union. It was a clever tactic; governments across the European Union were able to push through deregulation and painful spending cuts without an overwhelming electoral backlash.

Perhaps the most potent reason for deploying the race-to-the-bottom myth is the psychological effect it has on individuals. By depicting a world without choices, the race to the bottom taps into the primal fear of a loss of control. Governments and citizens appear powerless in a world dominated by faceless, passionless capital flows. This perceived lack of control prompts unease for the same reason that many people prefer driving a car to flying in an airplane even though the latter is safer: Even if driving is riskier, at least we are behind the steering wheel.

A Durable Myth

In his 1996 book *Jihad vs. McWorld*, Benjamin Barber warned that, by empowering owners of capital and disenfranchising voters, globalization would threaten democratic practices. Democracy may indeed be at risk, but not for the reasons Barber suggested. Globalization itself will not necessarily weaken democracy, but the rhetoric surrounding globalization may have that effect. If protestors persist in the indiscriminate trashing of multilateral institutions, they will only undermine the legitimacy of the mechanisms that democratic governments have established to deal with the very problems that concern them. And if enough leaders claim that globalization is an unstoppable trend demanding specific and formulaic policy responses, ordinary citizens will lose interest in a wide range of policy debates, believing their outcomes to be foregone conclusions determined by economic forces beyond their comprehension and control.

Can the race-to-the-bottom myth be debunked? In time, perhaps. As facts continue to contradict fiction, the claim will become untenable, much as the notion of Japan's global economic superiority died down by the mid-1990s. Ironically, some of the strongest voices speaking against the race-to-the-bottom myth emanate from the very developing countries that antiglobalization forces purport to defend. In a speech before the World Economic Forum in January 2000, Mexican President Ernesto Zedillo charged that antitrade activists wanted to save developing countries . . . from development. Even in Malaysia, where Prime Minister Mahathir Mohamad has become notorious for his diatribes against currency traders and global capitalism, the Federation of Malaysian Manufacturers recently stated that globalization and liberalization should be viewed "with an open mind and [in] an objective and rational manner." And economist Jagdish Bhagwati of Columbia University is spearheading the Academic Consortium on International Trade, a group of academic economists and lawyers arguing that the antisweatshop campaigns currently underway at several U.S. universities will only "worsen the collective welfare of the very workers in poor countries who are supposed to be helped."

Unfortunately, bad economics is often the cornerstone of good politics. The belief in a race to the bottom has helped cement an unwieldy coalition of interests and has enhanced the influence of antiglobalization activists both inside the corridors of power and in the mind of public opinion. Myths persist because they are useful; there is little incentive to abandon the race to the bottom now, even though there is no evidence to support it.

For those who wish to deepen the process of globalization, however, the implications are troubling. Historically, bouts of protectionism have occurred primarily during global economic downturns. But the rhetoric of a race to the bottom has gained adherents during a time of relative prosperity. If the current era has produced so many challenges for continued economic openness, what will happen when the economy hits the next speed bump? The image of a race to the bottom will likely endure in global policy debates well into the new century.

CHAPTER 8 SOVEREIGN WEALTH FUNDS THREATEN U.S. INTERESTS v. SOVEREIGN WEALTH FUNDS DO NOT THREATEN U.S. INTERESTS

Sovereign Wealth Funds Threaten U.S. Interests

Advocate: Gal Luft

Source: "Sovereign Wealth Funds, Oil, and the New World Economic Order," Testimony Before the Committee on Foreign Affairs, U.S. House of Representatives, Washington, DC, May 21, 2008. http://foreignaffairs.house.gov/110/luf052108.htm.

Sovereign Wealth Funds Do Not Threaten U.S. Interests

Advocate: Edwin M. Truman

Source: "The Rise of Sovereign Wealth Funds: Impacts on U.S. Foreign Policy and Economic Interests," Testimony before the Committee on Foreign Affairs, U.S. House of Representatives, Washington, DC, May 21, 2008. http://foreignaffairs.house.gov/110/tru052108.htm.

Sovereign wealth funds (SWFs) have generated increasing public and political scrutiny in the United States and the European Union (EU). SWFs are government-owned funds that purchase private assets in foreign markets. More than twenty governments currently have SWFs, which together control approximately $3 trillion; projections suggest that they could grow to $10 trillion by 2012. The single largest fund, the United Arab Emirate's Abu Dhabi Investment Authority, controls approximately $875 billion. Norway's SWF, the second largest, controls just shy of $400 billion. Many SWFs are funded with revenues generated by state-owned oil companies. Others, such as the China Investment Corporation, are funded with foreign exchange reserves generated by persistent balance of payments surpluses.

The growth of SWFs has raised political concerns similar to those generated by multinational corporations (MNCs). SWFs are instances in which concentrated foreign economic power gains some control over local productive assets. Thus, SWFs extend foreign control across national borders, just as

MNCs do. Second, foreign control could be used to advance foreign interests rather than, and in some case at the expense of, local interests, again just as with MNCs. Thus, even though SWFs are distinct from MNCs, their activities raise concerns and generate policy debates quite similar to those sparked by MNCs. The issue of foreign control is heightened in the case of SWFs, however, because foreign governments rather than foreign firms control the investments.

SOVEREIGN WEALTH FUNDS THREATEN U.S. INTERESTS

Some analysts fear that SWFs pose novel risks to U.S. economic and security interests. The core fear is that governments will use their investments to pursue political rather than economic objectives. Government-controlled investment funds might select which firms to invest in with an eye toward their political rather than economic value. Governments might use their investments once acquired as leverage in pursuit of political objectives. The businesses that are affiliated with a foreign SWF might also exploit that connection to advance its economic interests. In short, once governments become involved, cross-border investments are much less likely to be undertaken for purely economic gain and much more likely to have political ramifications.

Gal Luft, the executive director of the Institute for the Analysis of Global Security, expresses these concerns in his testimony to the U.S. House Committee on Foreign Affairs. Governments may use their SWFs to enhance their geopolitical influence and to advance anti-Western ideologies. Luft finds particularly worrying the fact that many of the largest SWFs are owned by Persian Gulf states. Although Luft recognizes that none of the threats he lists have yet materialized, he argues that they are likely to materialize in the future as SWFs continue to grow.

SOVEREIGN WEALTH FUNDS DO NOT THREATEN U.S. INTERESTS

Other observers believe that SWFs pose no threat to U.S. interests. But even these more sanguine observers do raise concerns about SWFs' impact on financial markets. Many of these concerns reflect the lack of transparency in SWF operations and the absence of a common regulatory framework. Few SWFs are open about the strategies that motivate their investment decisions or about the assets they own. As they grow in size, their investment decisions will increasingly affect markets. In the absence of better information about what they own and what motivates their purchases, other market participants will wind up guessing. Such dynamics could give rise to disruptive and potentially destabilizing trading activity.

Edwin Truman, a Senior Fellow at the Peterson Institute, advance this argument. He asserts that SWFs do not pose a substantial threat to American interests, but do raise a set of issues that require governmental responses. The central area for concern is the lack of transparency in SWF activities in conjunction with their growing importance in the global economy. The appropriate government response, Truman argues, includes efforts to promote a code of conduct to promote more transparency within SWF operations.

POINTS **TO PONDER**

1. In what ways are the issues raised by SWFs and MNCs similar and in what ways are they different?

2. Do you believe that SWFs are likely to emerge as significant security threats in the future? Would the remedies that Truman proposes help reduce the likelihood of this eventuality?

3. Luft distinguishes between the behavior of the Norwegian SWF and that of a Persian Gulf state. Do you agree that Norway's SWF constitutes a lower threat than a Persian Gulf SWF? Why or why not?

4. Which of Truman's proposals do you think the U.S. government should enact?

Gal Luft

Sovereign Wealth Funds, Oil, and the New World Economic Order

Mr. Chairman, members of the committee, less than a decade ago Washington was consumed by a debate on what would be the best policy to absorb the then multibillion dollar federal surplus. Reductions in outstanding debt, tax cuts, and spending increases were the most touted solutions. The least popular policy was for the government to invest the accumulated excess balances in private-sector financial markets. Former Office of Management and Budget (OMB) Director Alice Rivlin wrote in 1992, "No good would come of making the government a big shareholder in private companies or the principal owner of state and local bonds." [Federal Reserve] Chairman Alan Greenspan said in a 1999 testimony that federal investment in the private sector "would arguably put at risk the efficiency of our capital markets and thus our economy." Two years later, on January 25, 2001, he underscored this point at a Senate Budget Committee hearing: "The federal government should eschew private asset accumulation because it would be exceptionally difficult to insulate the government's investment decisions from political pressures. Thus, over time, having the federal government hold significant amounts of private assets would risk suboptimal performance by our capital markets, diminished economic efficiency, and lower overall standards of living than would be achieved otherwise." These words are worth remembering today as we are again facing a similar dilemma about what to do with government surpluses, just that this time it is not our own government's surplus that knocks on the door of our financial system but that of some of the world's least democratic, least transparent, and least friendly governments.

The rise of sovereign wealth funds (SWFs) as new power brokers in the world economy should not be looked at as a singular phenomenon but rather as part of what can be defined [as] a new economic world order. This new order has been enabled by several mega-trends [that] operate in a self-reinforcing manner, among them the meteoric rise of developing Asia, accelerated globalization, the rapid flow of information, and the sharp increase in the price of oil by a delta of over $100 per barrel in just six years which has enabled Russia and OPEC [Organization of Petroleum Exporting Countries] members to accumulate unprecedented wealth and elevate themselves to the position of supreme economic powers. Oil-rich countries of OPEC and Russia have more than quadrupled their revenues, raking some

$1.2 trillion in revenues last year alone. At $125-a-barrel oil they are expected to earn close to $2 trillion dollars in 2008.

The resulting transfer of wealth from consumers to exporters has already caused the following macroeconomic trends:

1. **Regressive tax on the world economy.** As a result [of] the rise in oil prices consuming countries face economic dislocations such as swollen trade deficits, loss of jobs, sluggish economic growth, inflation, and if prices continue to soar, inevitable recessions. The impact on developing countries, many of which still carry debts from the previous oil shocks of the 1970s, is the most severe. Three-digit oil will undoubtedly slow down their economic growth and exacerbate existing social illnesses; it would also make them economically and politically dependent on some of the world's most nasty petro-regimes.
2. **Change in the direction of the flow of capital.** Historically the flow of capital has always been from industrialized countries to the developing ones. The rise in oil prices coupled with growing dependence on oil and other commodities by the industrialized world have reversed this course, and today it is the developing world [that] feeds the industrialized world with capital.
3. **Change in ownership patterns.** During the post–Cold War era, there has been a decline in direct state ownership of business and a significant strengthening of the private sector. Throughout the world private businesses took ownership over what were once state-owned companies. In some cases, like Russia, such privatization happened too fast, leading to various socio-economic problems. The tide is now turning against the private sector as governments accumulate unprecedented wealth, which allows them to buy stakes in what were once purely private companies.

In this context, we should view SWFs as enablers of the new economic order. SWFs are pouring billions into hedge funds, private equity funds, real estate, natural resources, and other nodes of the West's economy. No one knows precisely how much money is held by SWFs, but it is estimated that they currently own $3.5 trillion in assets and [that] within one decade they could balloon to $10–$15 trillion, equivalent to America's gross domestic product. While much of the economic activity is generated by the Asian funds, particularly China's and Singapore's, I will focus my testimony on the activities of the SWFs from oil-producing countries, primarily the five Persian Gulf states that account for nearly half of the world SWF assets—Abu Dhabi, Dubai, Qatar, Kuwait, and Saudi Arabia—as well as SWFs owned by oil-producing countries like Nigeria, Oman, Kazakhstan, Angola, and Russia, which have been among the fastest growing over the last five years.

Before I delve into the specific issues related to SWFs, I would like to remind the Committee that those funds are not the only way states can exert influence in global financial markets. High net worth individuals, government controlled companies, and central banks are just as important in this context. Each one of the governments [that] are concentrating wealth has a different portfolio of investment instruments. Saudi Arabia, for example, accounts for roughly half of the GCC [Gulf Cooperation Council]'s private foreign wealth, yet unlike the UAE [United Arab Emirates], where SWFs control foreign assets, most Saudi foreign wealth is in the hands of private investors who are mostly members of the royal family. Only recently the Kingdom announced its intention to create a large SWF. While I applaud the Committee for holding this hearing on this important topic, we should realize that SWFs are only part of a much bigger problem.

The second thing to bear in mind is that to date there has been little evidence that SWFs attempt to assume control of firms they invest in or use their wealth to advance political ends. This is perhaps why so many experts dismiss the fear of foreign money acquiring portions of Western economies as a new form of jingoism, deriding the "fear mongers" as disciples of those who propelled the "Japanese-are-coming" hysteria of the 1980s. I do not share their dismissive view. The key issue to understand is that there is a fundamental difference between state versus private ownership, and that because governments operate differently from other private sector players, their investments should be governed by rules designed accordingly. Unlike ordinary shareholders and high–net-wealth private investors who are motivated solely by the desire to maximize the value of their shares, governments have a broader agenda—to maximize their geopolitical influence and sometime to promote ideologies that are in essence anti-Western. Nondemocratic and nontransparent governments can allow the use of their intelligence agencies and other covert as well as overt instruments of power to acquire valuable commercial information. Unlike pure commercial enterprises, state-owned investment funds can leverage the political and financial power of their governments to promote their business interests. Governments may enter certain transactions in order to extract a certain technology or alternatively in order to "kill" a competing one. The reason the Japan analogy is incorrect is that Mitsubishi Estate, the Japanese company that bought the Rockefeller Center in 1989 was not Tokyo's handmaid and Japan was—and still is—an American ally. This can hardly be said about Russia, Communist China, or OPEC members, some of whom use their revenues to fund the proliferation of an anti-Western agenda, develop nuclear capabilities, fan the flames of the Arab-Israeli conflict, and serially violate human rights. As it is now known to all, for decades the de facto leader of OPEC, Saudi Arabia, has been actively involved in the promotion of Wahhabism, the most puritan form of Islam, and its charities and other governmental and nongovernmental institutions have been bankrolling terrorist organizations and Islamic fundamentalism. To this day, the Kingdom's petrodollars pay for a hateful education system and fuel conflicts from the

Balkans to Pakistan. With a little over 1% of the world's Muslim population, Saudi petrodollars support today 90% of the expenses of the entire faith. U.S. Undersecretary of the Treasury in charge of fighting terrorist financing Stuart Levey recently said in an interview: "If I could snap my fingers and cut off the funding from one country, it would be Saudi Arabia."

Mr. Chairman, from an international relations perspective most of the concerns raised about SWFs only really matter if in the years to come the relations between the United States and the investing countries were to deteriorate. If tension between the United States and the Muslim world subsided and if China maintained its peaceful rise without undermining U.S. strategic interests there would hardly be a reason for concern; if the opposite occurs, then indulging on Arab or Chinese wealth could be outright dangerous. The best example here is CITGO. PDVSa's successful acquisition of CITGO in the United States (50% in 1986, the remainder in 1990) triggered very few concerns at the time. But if such a takeover were attempted by Hugo Chavez today, when U.S.–Venezuela relations are acrimonious, the public outcry would be huge. Therefore, our discussion on foreign investment should not be dominated only by "what is happening today" but also in view of "where we are headed," considering the trajectories and patterns we can already begin to observe, the most important of which are the unabated rise in oil prices combined with questionable international behavior of some of the major oil-producing countries.

Despite the attention given to SWFs, they are still relatively small players in the global economic system. Their assets exceed the $1.4 trillion managed by hedge funds, but they are far below the $15 trillion managed by pension funds, the $16 trillion managed by insurance companies, or the $21 trillion managed by investment companies. Here again it is more important to look at the trend rather than the present situation. At their current growth rate of 24% a year SWFs are beginning to present tough competition to other institutional investors over access to investment opportunities. To understand the anatomy of the competition between government entities and commercial firms one needs only to observe the process in which international oil Companies (IOC) have gradually lost their competitive edge vis-à-vis national oil companies (NOC). IOCs find themselves unable to compete against the deep-pocketed NOCs, which do not face the same regulatory limitations, do not have to provide the same measures of transparency, and do not have to abide by stringent environmental and humanitarian constraints. As SWFs gain strength and volume they could sideline other players vying for investments. Unlike pension funds and other institutional investors who are slow in their decision-making process, following strict timelines set by their investment committees, SWFs are agile. They have the in-house structure and the resources to make investment decisions quickly.

New Economic Balance of Power

No doubt perpetual high oil prices will shift the economic balance between OPEC and the West in the direction of those who own the precious commodity. As Robert Zubrin points out in his book *Energy Victory,* in 1972 the United States spent $4 billion on oil imports, an amount that equaled to 1.2% of our defense budget. In 2006, it paid $260 billion, which equals half of our defense budget. In 2008, it is likely to pay over $500 billion, which is equivalent to our full defense budget. Over the same period, Saudi oil revenues grew from $2.7 billion to roughly $400 billion and with it their ability to fund radical Islam. In the years to come this economic imbalance will grow by leaps and bounds. To understand the degree of the forces in play it is instructive to visualize the scale of OPEC's wealth in comparison to the consuming countries. The value of OPEC's proven oil and gas resources using today's prices is $137 trillion. This is roughly equivalent to the world's total financial assets—stocks, bonds, other equities, government and corporate debt securities, and bank deposits—or almost three times the market capitalization of all the companies traded in the world's top twenty-seven stock markets [see Figure 8.1]. Saudi Arabia's oil and gas alone is worth $36 trillion, ten times the total value of all the companies traded in the London Stock Exchange. If one adds the additional oil and gas reserves that have not yet been discovered, OPEC's wealth more than doubles. If oil

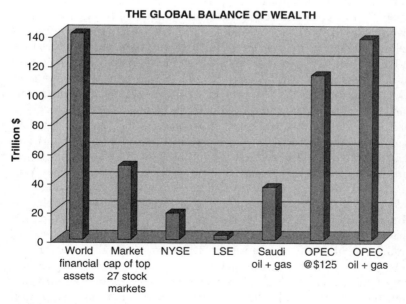

Figure 8.1

prices climb to $200, as OPEC's president Chakib Khelil recently warned, the wealth nearly doubles again. In an economic system of $200-barrel oil we can expect the value of financial institutions to shrink while the transfer of wealth to the oil-producing countries increases in velocity. Such monumental wealth potential will enable buying power of the oil countries that far exceeds that of the West. For demonstration sake, at $200 oil OPEC could potentially buy Bank of America in one month's worth of production, Apple Computers in a week, and General Motors in just three days. It would take less than two years of production for OPEC to own a 20% stake (which essentially ensures a voting block in most corporations) in every S&P 500 company. Of course, takeovers of such magnitude are unlikely, but $200 oil and additional trillions of dollars in search of a parking spot are very likely. What is clear about the new economic reality is that while the economic power of America and its allies is constantly eroding, OPEC's "share" price is on a solid upward trajectory and with it an ever-growing foreign ownership over our economy.

Vulnerable Sectors

SWFs have lost $25 billion on their recent investments in struggling banks and securities firms worldwide. In the near future, they are not likely to be as enthusiastic to bail out additional financial institutions. But with high oil prices here to stay and with the International Energy Agency projecting that "we are ending up with 95% of the world relying for its economic well-being on decisions made by five or six countries in the Middle East," it is hard to see how OPEC's massive buying power would not upset the West's economic and political sovereignty. This is particularly true in light of the prospects of potential future bailouts in sectors other than banking should the U.S. economy continue to decline. As populations in Western countries age and dwindle, it is only a matter of time before the under funded health care and retirement systems begin to face similar liquidity problems. Foreign governments have already put their sight on auto manufacturers, buying stakes in companies like Ferrari and Daimler. In 2004, Abu Dhabi attempted to buy 25% of Volkswagen's shares after the German automakers profits fell sharply. The danger here is that SWFs might be the first to step in to save the ailing U.S. auto industry from its pension obligations if the industry continues to underperform. What would this mean for the effort to make our cars less dependent on petroleum is a question policymakers should think about before such crisis occurs.

Media organizations are another sector worthy of attention. In September 2006, with mainstream news organizations in the United States reporting falling earnings and downbeat financial assessments, information ministers, tycoons, and other officials of the 57-nation Organization of the Islamic Conference (OIC) gathered in Saudi Arabia where OIC

Secretary General Ekmeleddin Ihsanoglu urged them to buy stakes in Western media outlets to help correct what he views as misconceptions on Islam around the world. To date, though private investors from the Middle East have made substantial acquisitions of global media, SWFs have not bought holdings in this sector. A change in SWF behavior [that] leads to attempts to gain control over media organizations could lead to an erosion in freedom of speech and freedom of information. Pervasive influence of Saudi money in the publishing world, coupled with growing number of litigations against scholars critical of Saudi Arabia, is shielding from public scrutiny the one country that is most responsible for the proliferation of radical Islam.

Opaque Investment Patterns and the Risk of Predatory Behavior

When it comes to governance, transparency, and accountability SWFs are not cut from the same cloth. There is a profound difference between SWFs of democratic countries like Norway and the United States and those of nondemocratic regimes. In some of the latter countries, like Kuwait, SWFs are barred by the country's laws from revealing their assets. The Linaburg-Maduell Transparency Index, which was developed at the Sovereign Wealth Funds Institute, shows significantly lower SWF transparency ranking among nondemocratic countries as opposed to democratic ones. Not surprisingly, nine out of the ten worst ranked funds are those of oil-producing nations. Lack of transparency and accountability among those SWFs makes them a disruptive factor in our overall highly transparent market economy. To avoid scrutiny, SWFs have fostered new alliances with private equity funds, which offer a culture of secrecy. SWFs already account for approximately 10% of private equity investments globally, and this number will grow further in the coming years. Last year, Chinese entities bought the largest external stake in Blackstone, [which], indirectly through its holdings, is one of the largest employers in the United States. Carlyle Group sold [a] 7.5% stake to a fund owned by Abu Dhabi, which also bought 9% of Apollo Management. The situation is similar in hedge funds. One of the dangers here is that through their investments SWFs can shape market conditions in sectors where their governments have economic and/or political interests or where they enjoy comparative advantage. In recent months, for example, commodity futures have increased dramatically, largely due to astronomical growth in speculation and bidding up of prices, while actual deliveries are far behind. Commodity markets are easily manipulated, and the impact of such manipulations could often reverberate throughout the world, as the current food crisis shows. While U.S. companies are not allowed to buy their own products and create shortage to increase revenues, foreign governments with economic interest in a particular commodity face no similar restrictions bidding on it, via their proxies, in the commodity market. Under the current system, oil countries can, via their SWFs as well as other investment vehicles that receive investment from SWFs, long future contracts and commodity derivatives and hence affect oil futures in a way that benefits them. This would be tantamount to the U.S. government using its position as the world's largest exporter of corn to bid up corn futures.

Boardroom Presence

To date, the influx of petrodollars has not translated into overbearing presence of government agents in corporate boardrooms. In fact, many of the SWFs buy holdings under the 5% benchmark that triggers regulatory scrutiny and forego board seats. But at the current rate of investment and many more years of three-digit oil combined with deepening geopolitical tensions, foreign governments might be more willing to translate their wealth into power, dictating business practices, vetoing deals, appointing officers sympathetic to their governments, and dismissing those who are critical of them. Direct influence of foreign government could lead to inefficiencies, capital misallocations, and political interference in business decisions. This is why it is my view that SWF acquisitions should be restricted to nonvoting stakes.

The Rise of Sharia Finance

The gradual penetration of Shariah (Islamic Law) into [the] West's corporate world is another characteristic of the new geo-economic order. Islamic countries operating on the basis of compliance with Shariah have strict guidelines of economic conduct. Banks and investment houses gradually employ a new breed of executive—the Chief Shariah Officer (CSO)—whose sole job is to ensure compliance with Islamic law and hence attract more business from the Muslim investors. Over time, such compliance could put pressure on companies not consistent with Islamic principles to become more "Islamic." Imams sitting on Shariah boards could be pressured to withhold their approval of any business dealing directly or indirectly connected with countries or institutions that are offensive to Islam. One can only guess what this would mean for publishing houses, Hollywood movie studios, the alcohol and gambling industries. A sure casualty of the Islamization of the corporate world would be Israel, which has for years been subjected to the Arab boycott. According to the U.S. Department of Commerce, last year American companies reported no fewer than 486 requests from UAE companies alone to boycott Israel.

Building a Fireless Firewall

None of the potential risks to which I alluded entail lifting the drawbridge and becoming economic hermits. America's commitment to open markets has been a source of respect and admiration around the world, and reversing it through investment protectionism would only hurt U.S. prestige while undermining economic growth and job creation at home. To arrest the current economic trend and to hedge the risk of sovereignty loss the United States should apply a healthy dosage of vigilance and develop a system of indicators to determine and examine when SWFs pursue different approaches from other institutional investors. Willingness to pay above-market prices, use government assets to back up financial deals, or manipulate prices to increase returns should all be red flags that trigger response. The United States already has rigorous safeguard mechanisms against undesirable foreign investors. The Committee on Foreign Investment in the U.S. (CFIUS) protects national security assets in sectors such as telecommunications, broadcasting, transportation, energy, and minerals in which there is a clear potential danger to national security. I am delighted that many of the concerns about foreign investments have already been addressed in the CFIUS reform legislation entitled the Foreign Investment and National Security Act of 2007. The range of regulatory and supervisory tools available to the Federal Reserve Board as described in the Federal Reserve Act are quite satisfactory [in] case SWFs make an investment in a U.S. banking organization that triggers one of the Fed's thresholds. But in order to protect ourselves against sovereignty loss more safeguards are needed.

Reciprocity

While enjoying almost unlimited access to investment opportunities in the West, oil-rich governments do not feel the need to reciprocate by opening their economies to foreign investment. The opposite is true: They obstruct international companies from investing in their midst, limiting them to, at best, minority share. This is the root cause of insufficient production of new oil. Oil countries, together owning 80% of the world's reserves, practice resource nationalism, stick to quotas, [and] refuse to provide transparency of oil activities including reserve studies and terms of contract with their own national oil companies, and they are riddled with corruption and cronyism.

The least we can do is demand that foreigners treat us as we treat them. Despite being the lead violator of free trade by dint of its leadership of the OPEC cartel, three years ago, with U.S. support, the Saudis were admitted to the World Trade Organization (WTO). This was a terrible mistake. Since the admission, the world's generosity toward the Saudis was rewarded with nothing but continuous manipulation of oil prices and behavior that can only be described as antithetical to free trade. Enjoying the benefits of free trade is an earned privilege, not an entitlement, and foreign governments wishing to acquire assets in the West should be obliged only if they show similar hospitality to Western companies. We should not be shy to use retaliatory measures against serial violators of free-trade principles. There are currently four OPEC members in waiting to accede to the WTO—Algeria, Iran, Iraq, and Libya. Oil-producing countries with growing SWFs like Russia, Kazakhstan, and Azerbaijan are also on the waiting list. These countries' admittance to the organization should be contingent on compliance with those principles and on an unequivocal commitment to refrain from noncompetitive behavior and anti-market activities. You cannot seek a seat at the WTO and at the same time promote a natural gas cartel.

Increase Transparency

The scope and growth rate of SWFs are so vast that their actions can have far-reaching influence on world financial markets, whether intentionally or mistakenly. This begs for the introduction of intermediary asset managers and the creation of disclosure standards for SWF as well as other foreign institutional investors that are at least as stringent as those applied to other regulated investors. However, any go-it-alone effort to force SWFs to adopt higher transparency standards would be unworkable and easy to circumvent. The guidelines of working with SWFs should therefore be drawn in collaboration with the EU and other countries on the receiving end of sovereign money.

Break the Oil Cartel

In the long run, the only way to roll back the new economic order and restrain OPEC's control over the world economy is to reduce the inherent value of its commodity. This cannot be done as long as we continue to put on our roads cars that can run on nothing but petroleum. Every year 17 million new cars roll onto America's roads. Each of these cars will have a lifespan of nearly 17 years. In the next Congressional session 35 million new cars will be added. If the next president presides for two terms he or she will preside over the introduction of 150 million new cars. If we allow all those cars to be gasoline only we are locking our future to petroleum for decades to come. I cannot think of something more detrimental to America's security than Congress allowing this to happen. Congress can break OPEC's monopoly over the transportation sector by instituting fuel choice. The cheapest, easiest, and most immediate step should be a federal Open Fuel Standard, requiring that every new car put on the road be a flex fuel car, which looks and operates exactly like a gasoline car but has a

$100 feature [that] enables it to run on any combination of gasoline and alcohol. Millions of flex fuel cars will begin to roll back oil's influence by igniting a boom of innovation and investment in alternative fuel technologies. The West is not rich in oil, but it is blessed with a wealth of other energy sources from which alcohol fuels—such as ethanol and methanol—capable of powering flexible fuel vehicles, can be affordably and cleanly generated. Among them: vast rich farmland, hundreds of years' worth of coal reserves, and billions of tons a year of agricultural, industrial, and municipal waste. Even better: In an alcohol economy, scores of poor developing countries, which right now struggle under the heavy economic burden caused by high oil prices, would be able to become net energy exporters. With hot climate and long rainy seasons, countries in south Asia, Africa, and Latin America enjoy the perfect conditions for the production of sugarcane ethanol, which costs roughly half the price and is five times more efficient than corn ethanol. Hence, a shift to alcohol-enabled cars will enable developing countries to generate revenues and emerge as a powerful force that could break OPEC's dominance over the global transportation sector.

In addition to alcohols, coal, nuclear power, [and] solar and wind energy can make electricity to power pure electric and plug-in hybrid cars. The latter have an internal combustion engine and fuel tank, and thus are not limited in size, power, or range, but also have a battery that can be charged from an electric socket and can power 20–40 miles of driving, giving the consumer the choice of driving on electricity or liquid fuel. Only 2% of U.S. electricity is generated from oil today. While plug-in hybrids have unlimited range and a cost premium of several thousand dollars, pure electric cars are planned to be sold at competitive prices in several countries, including the United States and Japan, as early as 2010. Because pure electric cars have a range limitation—at least two countries, Israel and Denmark, are now in the process of developing an infrastructure for battery replacement to address this problem—they may not satisfy the needs of many Americans. But electric cars can easily serve as a second or third family car. This "niche market" is roughly two thirds of America. Thirty-one percent of America's households own two cars, and an additional 35% own three or more vehicles. These are not the cars a family would use to visit Grandma out of town but cars that drive routinely well below the full battery range. There are over 75 million households in the United States that own more than one vehicle and that can potentially replace one or more gasoline-only cars with cars powered by made-in-America electricity.

Mr. Chairman, the new economic order is shaping up right before our eyes, increasingly invalidating much of the economic paradigm to which we have been accustomed. For America, a continuation of the petroleum standard guarantees economic decline and perpetual economic and political enslavement to the OPEC cartel and its whims. If we want to address the challenge of SWFs and increased foreign government control over our economy we must focus on policies that can empower countries that share our values rather than the petro-dictators of the world. We must bring down the price of oil before it hits a critical point beyond which sovereignty loss becomes inevitable.

Edwin M. Truman

The Rise of Sovereign Wealth Funds: Impacts on U.S. Foreign Policy and Economic Interests

The broadest definition of a sovereign wealth fund (SWF) is a collection of government-owned or government-controlled assets. Narrower definitions may exclude government financial or nonfinancial corporations, purely domestic assets, foreign exchange reserves, assets owned or controlled by subnational governmental units, or some or all government pension funds. I use "sovereign wealth fund" as a descriptive term for a separate pool of government-owned or government-controlled assets that includes some international assets. I include all government pension, as well as nonpension, funds to the extent that they manage marketable assets. The basic objectives of both types are essentially the same. They raise virtually identical issues of best practice—the focus of my research and analysis—in government control and accountability regardless of their specific objectives, mandates, or sources of funding.

SWFs are funded from foreign exchange reserves, earnings from commodity exports, receipts from privatizations, other fiscal revenues, or pension contributions. These funds have been around for more than half a century with a range of structures, mandates, and economic, financial, and political (domestic and international) objectives—normally a mixture. Consequently, it is perilous to generalize about SWFs and associated potential threats to U.S. foreign policy, national security, or economic interests.

Nevertheless, my summary conclusions are three:

First, SWFs do not pose a significant new threat to U.S. security or economic interests. We have adequate mechanisms to manage any potential threats they pose, which at this point are likely to be minimal.

Second, SWFs are one of the many challenges of global economic and financial change in the twenty-first century. Whether these particular challenges of globalization are appropriately addressed will have profound implications for the United States and for the world economy and financial system.

Third, the United States should continue to press countries with SWFs to design and embrace best practices for these funds to enhance their accountability to citizens of the countries with the funds as well as to the citizens and markets in which they invest. At the same time, the United States should continue to try to minimize economic and political barriers to foreign investment in all forms from all sources here and around the world. Financial protectionism is the wrong answer to the very real challenges of financial globalization and the associated potential for global financial turbulence. The United States cannot disengage from evolving changes in the global financial system. If we were merely to hint that we are tempted to do so, we would risk catastrophic damage to the U.S. and world economies.

It is useful to place the activities of SWFs in a broader perspective. At the end of 2006, the estimated size of global capital markets was $190 trillion. A conservative estimate of financial assets owned or controlled by governments is $15 trillion, or about 8% of global financial assets. Governments in the United States own or control more than $3 trillion (20%) of the total. Thus, the United States is in the business of sovereign wealth management. Consequently, we should be careful what we wish for.

International assets owned or controlled by governments are at least $10 trillion: $6 trillion in foreign exchange reserves, $2.7 trillion in assets of nonpension SWFs, and at least $1.3 trillion in government pension funds. Excluding our modest holdings of foreign exchange reserves, international assets of U.S. SWFs are about $800 billion mostly in the form of the pension funds of state and local governments. Thus, U.S. SWFs, as a group, are second to the United Arab Emirates in their holdings of international assets.

As an additional point of reference, at the end of 2006, U.S. total holdings of foreign assets were $13.8 trillion. About 92% was managed by the private sector. Foreign holdings of U.S. assets were $16.3 trillion. At least 17% was managed by the public sector. U.S. holdings of international financial assets are at least 20% of the global total. In other words, the U.S. economy is thoroughly intertwined with the global financial system on both the asset and liability side of our balance sheet through both the private and public sectors.

Over the past five years, the size of the global capital market has doubled, but asset holdings of SWFs have at least tripled. The explosive growth of SWFs reflects the sustained rise in commodity prices as well as global imbalances. However, the increased international diversification of financial portfolios—the weakening of so-called home bias—is at least as important as macroeconomic factors in explaining the growth of SWFs.

The increasing relative importance of SWFs has exposed two tensions as part of the ongoing globalization of the international financial system.

The first is the dramatic redistribution of international (or cross-border) wealth from the traditional industrial countries, like the United States, to countries that historically have not been major players in international finance. The newcomers have had little or no role in shaping the practices, nouns, and conventions governing the system.

The second is the fact that governments own or control a substantial share of the new international wealth. This redistribution from private to public hands implies a decision-making orientation that is at variance with the traditional private-sector, market-oriented framework with which most of us are comfortable even though [the] system does not fully conform to that ideal.

These twin tensions, in turn, are manifested in five broad concerns.

First, governments may mismanage their international investments to their own economic and financial detriment, including large-scale corruption in handling the huge amounts involved. It is a well known, though often ignored, regularity that governments are not good at picking economic winners; for example, government-owned banks tend to be less profitable than private banks. This concern about mismanagement is the principal reason why it is in the interests of every country with a SWF to favor the establishment of internationally agreed SWF best practices. Moreover, greater accountability of such funds is in the foreign policy interest of the United States because the mismanagement of SWF investments could lead to political as well as economic instability in countries with such funds.

Second, governments may manage SWF investments in pursuit of political objectives—raising national security concerns—or economic power objectives—for example, promoting state-owned or state-controlled national champions as global champions. Such behavior contributes not only to political conflicts between countries but also to economic distortions.

Third, financial protectionism may be encouraged in host countries in anticipation of the pursuit of political or economic objectives by the funds or in response to their actual actions. Development of and compliance with SWF best practices would help to diffuse this source of backlash against globalization. At the same time, countries receiving SWF investments should be as open as possible to such investments, subject to the constraints of national security considerations narrowly defined.

Fourth, in the management of their international assets, SWFs may contribute to market turmoil and uncertainty. They also may contribute to financial stability, but their net contribution is difficult to establish *a priori*, in particular if their operations are opaque, but also because judgments can only be reached on a case by case basis.

Fifth, foreign government owners of the international assets may come into conflict with the governments of the countries in which they are investing. For example, government ownership adds a further dimension in balancing open markets and appropriate macroprudential regulation.

At this point, these concerns, with the important exception of the first—potential adverse implications for the home countries—are largely in the realm of the hypothetical. The others are much more salient in the context of cross-border investments by government-owned or government-controlled financial or nonfinancial corporations. Nevertheless, a loud, often acrimonious public discourse about SWFs is underway in many countries, and not only in countries receiving SWF investments.

In my view, the challenge is to make the world safe for SWFs through the establishment of an internationally agreed voluntary set of best practices. The natural place to start is with the current practices of individual funds today. To this end, I have created with the assistance of Doug Dowson a scoreboard for the largest SWFs. The scoreboard rates funds on their current practices and includes thirty-three elements grouped in four categories: structure, governance, accountability and transparency, and behavior. We have scored the funds based on systematic, regularly available public information. At least one fund receives a positive score on each element. In fact, at least several do.

First, all SWFs are not the same. Nor is there one cluster of "good" funds and another cluster of "bad" funds. The overall scores range from 95 to 9 out a possible 100. The rating of each of them can be improved. The funds fall in three broad groups: twenty-two funds with scores above 60, fourteen funds with scores below 30, and ten funds in a middle group. Moreover, the grouping of scores is essentially identical if one examines only the category of accountability and transparency.

Second, although each of the twelve representative pension SWFs is in the top group, that group of twenty-two funds also includes ten nonpension SWFs. Thus, it is not unreasonable to hold nonpension SWFs to the standard of accountability of pension funds. Chile's pension and nonpension SWFs both score in the top group. On the other hand, China's National Social Security Fund is in the top group, but the China Investment Corporation is in the bottom group.

Third, it is essentially impossible to correlate the ratings of the individual funds with the economic or political characteristics of their government owners. For example, the top group includes seven of the fourteen funds with estimated assets of more than $100 billion, but four are in the second group, and two are in the third group. The top group includes funds of a number of developing countries, including Azerbaijan, Chile, China, Kazakhstan, Thailand, and Timor-Leste. The middle group includes funds of nonindustrial countries as diverse as Russia, Mexico, Kuwait, and Singapore, whose two funds are in this group. Singapore's two funds have close-to-identical overall scores, but their scores differ on many individual elements. The bottom group includes three funds from Abu Dhabi, each of which has an excellent reputation in financial markets.

For some this diversity of current practice illustrates the challenge in developing a common set of best practices. In my view, it illustrates the opportunity to converge on a common high standard. A senior representative of the Abu Dhabi Investment Authority is co-chairing, with the director of the IMF [International Monetary Fund]'s monetary and capital markets department, the International Working Group of Sovereign Wealth Funds to develop "a set of SWF principles that properly reflects their investment practices and objectives." The decision by the authorities of the United Arab Emirates to provide a co-chairman for this group implies a commitment by them to enhance substantially the accountability and transparency of their SWFs.

In his letter of invitation to testify before this committee today, Chairman Berman raised three issues, other than the phenomenon of SWFs and their accountability and transparency, on which I have not yet commented explicitly.

First, he asked whether SWFs have the potential to disrupt financial markets. All investors with large portfolios have the potential to disrupt financial markets whatever their motivation. However, the very size of their portfolios helps to inhibit them from doing so—in other words, discourages them from shooting themselves in their feet.

At the same time, it is inappropriate in my opinion to view SWFs as cornucopias available to be tapped to rescue the U.S. or the global financial system. For every SWF investment in a U.S. financial institution, that fund has to disinvest, or not invest, in some other asset, normally in the United States or at least in U.S. dollars.

Some observers of private equity firms and hedge funds have concerns about their implications for the stability of our economy and financial system. I do not share most of those concerns, though I have long favored increased transparency for large private equity firms and hedge funds. However, the facts do not support those who argue that SWFs are not like hedge funds and private equity firms in their speculative activities. SWFs invest in hedge funds, in private equity firms, and in other highly leveraged financial institutions whose activities, including the use of leverage, are indistinguishable from hedge funds and private equity firms. In effect, SWFs are providing the capital that those firms subsequently leverage to generate high rates of return for the funds. They are no different from other investors except that their stakes may be measured in the billions rather than in the hundreds of millions of dollars.

Second, Chairman Berman asked more generally whether the foreign policy and national security interests of countries with SWFs pose a threat to the United States. It follows from what I have already said that my short answer is no.

I am not an expert on the foreign policy and national interests of each of the more than 30 countries with nonpension SWFs, to say nothing of the additional countries that only have pension SWFs. However, it is clear that the interests [of] the individual countries are diverse, and perceptions of those countries fluctuate over time, in part, reflecting differences in the development and evolution of their political and social systems.

Policymakers are primarily interested in issues of underlying investment control even if they do not agree on how to define that concept. In this context, government-owned or -controlled financial and nonfinancial corporations are much more relevant because, in general, their activities are more focused and more easily integrated with foreign policy and national security objectives.

Although some SWFs do take controlling interests via their investments, more than half of the forty-six funds we scored have explicit policies against doing so. A substantial proportion of the remaining twenty-two funds also do not seek controlling interests, but they do not have explicit, public policies in this area. Of course, it is possible to pursue foreign policy or national security interests without taking a controlling investment interest, but it is more difficult, and the investment interest is likely to be more narrowly focused and more easily identified. The essential point is that the activities of a few countries that have SWFs and may use them to pursue political and economic interests should not be conflated with the motivations of the vast majority of countries that have such funds.

Finally, Chairman Berman asked for thoughts on how the U.S. Congress and the Administration can best "manage" SWF investing in the United States. I interpret his question as asking how the Congress and Administration should best respond to the phenomenon of SWFs.

Notwithstanding my view that the greatest risks associated with SWFs are to the citizens of the countries whose governments have accumulated the large stocks of international assets, authorities in the United States and other countries where those assets are invested also have legitimate concerns about how they will be managed. Those concerns focus primarily on acquisition of large or controlling stakes by foreign governments in private institutions. As noted, at present this is the exception not the rule for SWFs. However, one area of concern and potential conflict is the apparent use by a few countries, such as China and potentially Brazil, to use their SWFs to promote the expansion of their own economic enterprises.

Of course, the current, largely benign, pattern could change, and foreign government-owned or government-controlled financial and nonfinancial corporations do acquire stakes in companies in other countries, including controlling stakes. The 2007 Foreign Investment and National Security Act (FINSA) revised the framework and procedures of the Committee on Foreign Investment in the United States (CFIUS). With these changes and the existing powers of the Securities and Exchange Commission, as well as other U.S. financial regulators, we are well positioned to evaluate and, if necessary, to mitigate, to block, or to pursue any U.S. acquisitions or investment by an SWF or other foreign government entity to protect our national security or to enforce our laws and regulations governing financial markets and institutions.

With respect to economic security concerns, the greatest risk to the U.S. economy is that we will erect unnecessary barriers to the free flow of capital into our economy and, in the process, contribute to the erection of similar barriers in other countries to the detriment of the health and continued prosperity of the U.S. and global economies. We may not in all cases be comfortable with the consequences of the free flow of finance and investment either internally or across borders, but on balance it promotes competition and efficiency. We should exhaust all multilateral approaches before pursuing bilateral remedies, and any such bilateral remedies should be narrowly focused.

To this end, I endorse the Administration's support of the OECD [Organisation for Economic Co-operation and Development] process designed to strengthen the framework that the United States and other OECD member countries use to govern foreign investment, including by governmental entities. At present that framework does not, in principle, extend to nonmembers of the OECD, though often it does in practice. The United States should support its explicit extension to all countries.

My hope is that the OECD process will provide sufficient reassurance to countries with SWFs so that, with the facilitation of the IMF, they can reach agreement on and fully comply with a voluntary set of best practices for their funds.

How should that IMF–facilitated effort be judged when it is completed in the fall of this year?

One test is whether the resulting set of best practices covers substantively all the elements included in my scoreboard. Of course, it is not essential to cover them precisely in the form outlined. However, each element should be adequately addressed. A significant omission should be seen as falling short of expectations.

A second test of success is whether the best practices are embraced by substantially all countries with large SWFs. If each of them [the fourteen SWFs with more than $100 billion in total assets] were to adhere to the prospective set of best practices, it is less critical that the others do so immediately. For each country, including those that choose not to adhere fully or at all, the minimum expectation should be that the country would comply, or it should explain why it does not do so in whole or in part.

A third test is the quality of compliance by the countries that embrace the best practices. If they are drawn up properly, the best practices should be self-enforcing. Politicians, the media, financial-market participants, and the general public in the home and host countries should be able to determine the degree of compliance.

On the other hand, if the voluntary best practices agreed under the auspices of the IMF are less precise than they should be, it will be necessary to have some mechanism to report on compliance. That function might be lodged in the IMF or the World Bank, which have experience with respect to overseeing compliance with twelve of the many existing international standards and codes. As is the case with existing standards subject to IMF and World Bank surveillance and oversight, the resulting process of implicit naming and shaming, combined with peer pressure from other SWFs that want to avoid the application of draconian restrictions to their activities, should contribute to a high level of compliance within a short period.

Some may favor supervisory inspections of SWFs beyond those that would be covered by IMF and World Bank surveillance, plus published, independent audits as called for in my scoreboard. To my knowledge, no official has said so publicly. However, to advocate this type of supervision would sharply escalate the SWF debate from one about the content of and adherence to internationally agreed voluntary best practices to one about explicit regulation. At this point, such an escalation is neither appropriate nor justified on the merits.

On the recipient side, many countries today have (very diverse) regimes covering foreign direct investment in their countries. Pending the establishment of a broad consensus on those regimes as they apply to government investments, such as is being pursued within the OECD, and perhaps even in that context, the United States and other similarly situated countries might reasonably decide to take account of a country's voluntary compliance with the international best practices for SWFs as one of a number of factors considered in making determinations about whether a particular SWF's investment should be blocked because of a threat to national security. For example, in a March 13 letter sent to U.S. Treasury Secretary Henry Paulson, Representatives Barney Frank, Carolyn Maloney, and Luis Gutierrez suggested that a country's compliance with aspects of SWF best practices could be used by the CFIUS as a factor in determining whether the committee should grant that country a waiver from a full investigation under FINSA of an investment, for example, by a government-owned pension fund.

More controversially, some observers have suggested that an SWF that takes even a noncontrolling stake in a company should be forbidden from voting its shares, presumably increasing the probability that the investment is "passive." My understanding is that there is no generally accepted legal definition of a passive investment. (I note that the proposed CFIUS regulations implementing the FINSA instead seek to define interests that are "solely for the purpose of investment," which is a more limited approach.) To limit the voting rights of government investors, if applied uniformly, would disenfranchise as much as several trillion dollars of investments by U.S. state and local government pension funds. If the United States did not apply this type of restriction to domestic pension SWFs, it would still risk disenfranchising U.S. government pension funds in their investment operations abroad. The reason is that it would be difficult to apply such a restriction to foreign nonpension SWFs and not to foreign pension SWFs. As a consequence, foreign governments almost certainly would retaliate in kind.

U.S. Treasury Assistant Secretary Clay Lowery has suggested a more sensible approach: Either an SWF should choose voluntarily not to vote its shares or it should disclose how it votes, as is now done voluntarily by some U.K. institutional investors and is required by the Securities and Exchange Commission for U.S. mutual funds. The objective of the SEC rule for mutual funds is to address concerns about conflicts of interest and, as noted earlier, similar concerns arise with respect to SWFs. Presumably, the SWF would not face a formal SEC reporting requirement in this area; that would raise a host of other process and jurisdictional issues and also serve to escalate the SWF debate.

In conclusion, the phenomenon of SWFs is a permanent feature of our global economy and financial system. Their potential impacts on U.S. foreign policy, national security, and economic interests may be disquieting, but they do not endanger the United States. U.S. authorities should exhaust all multilateral approaches to make the world safe for SWFs—in the form of SWF best practices and open financial environments—before turning to any additional, bilateral remedies for concerns that to date are between minimal and nonexistent.

PART III
INTERNATIONAL MONETARY ISSUES

The international monetary system is supposed to facilitate international trade and promote adjustment of large trade imbalances. Our current international monetary system has been in place for thirty-five years. The current system facilitates trade by according the dollar a key role. Many internationally traded goods are priced in dollars—or at least relative to dollars—and most cross-border payments typically are made in dollars. The international monetary system is designed to promote adjustment of imbalances through exchange-rate movements. The currencies of countries with large surpluses should appreciate while currencies of countries with large deficits should depreciate. Contemporary debates about the international monetary system focus on whether the system will persist in its current form and whether it effectively promotes adjustment. This section examines two specific contemporary manifestations of these broader questions.

Chapter 9 explores the dollar's role as the system's key currency. The dollar has served in the privileged role of the world's key currency for the last seventy years. For this entire period, it has had no real rivals. The dollar inherited the role from the British pound, and the pound never regained the appeal it had held prior to World War I. At various times, the German mark and the Japanese yen seemed poised to emerge as possible rivals, but the possibility never materialized. Consequently, the dollar easily retained its privileged status even in periods of dollar weakness. The euro's creation provides a real alternative to the dollar as the world's key currency. Niall Ferguson argues that the euro is most likely to assume this role in a period of sustained dollar weakness. One might argue that the current financial weakness is exactly the conditions Ferguson had in mind. Benjamin Cohen and Paola Subacchi argue that the euro will not take over the dollar's role. The euro, they argue, is not supported by a political institutional framework capable of pushing the euro into the central role and sustaining it in that position over time.

Chapter 10 delves into the role of exchange-rate movements in promoting adjustment of the United States and China bilateral trade imbalance. Some economists, and many members of Congress, argue that the Chinese government has intentionally undervalued its currency, the renminbi, against the dollar. China's exchange-rate policy sits next to a very large U.S.–China trade imbalance. Indeed, the U.S. trade deficit with China—about $290 billion in 2007—accounts for a large share of the U.S. overall trade deficit. The question at the center of this debate is whether Chinese exchange-rate policy is the cause of the trade imbalance. C. Fred Bergsten argues that it is. The bilateral imbalance, he argues, is a direct consequence of China's exchange rate policy. Adjustment of this trade imbalance, therefore, requires the renminbi to appreciate against the dollar by a substantial amount. David Hale and Lyric Hughes Hale argue that the trade imbalance is not a consequence of China's exchange-rate policy. Instead, the trade imbalance is a consequence of macroeconomic imbalances—especially savings and investment rates—in the United States and China.

CHAPTER 9

THE EURO WILL SUPPLANT THE DOLLAR AS THE WORLD'S RESERVE CURRENCY *v.* THE DOLLAR WILL REMAIN THE WORLD'S RESERVE CURRENCY

The Euro Will Supplant the Dollar as the World's Reserve Currency

Advocate: Niall Ferguson

Source: "The Euro's Big Chance," *Prospect* 99 (June 7, 2004): 24–27.

The Dollar Will Remain the World's Reserve Currency

Advocate: Benjamin J. Cohen and Paola Subacchi

Source: "A One-and-a-Half Currency System," *Journal of International Affairs* 62 (Fall–Winter 2008): 151–153.

The dollar has served as the world's principal currency throughout the postwar period, a role that it took from the British pound in the early twentieth century. The dollar was used more than any other by governments and private individuals as a unit of account, a medium of exchange, and a store of value. In the private sector, the dollar has been the currency most often used to invoice international trade, to denominate international financial transactions, and to intervene in foreign exchange markets.

Is the euro poised to supplant the dollar in the international economy? The euro's launch in 1999 created, for the first time since 1945, a potential rival to the dollar. Yet, the euro weakened against the dollar after its creation, and few believed it could readily supplant the dollar. The recent turbulence in the U.S. financial system, the United States' persistent current account deficits, and the euro's strengthening since 2005 has reignited interest in the potential for a dollar-euro rivalry. Will there be a struggle for rivalry between these two currencies? Is the euro already challenging the dollar for the leading role in the global economy?

THE EURO WILL SUPPLANT THE DOLLAR
AS THE WORLD'S RESERVE CURRENCY

Some argue that the dollar is vulnerable to a challenge from the euro. Over the past twenty years or so, the United States has run persistent current account deficits financed by capital inflows. Since 2005 or so, these capital inflows have been provided to an increasing extent by Asian governments willing to accumulate dollar-denominated assets. The result has been a mutually beneficial relationship in which Asian countries run export surpluses with the United States and recycle these earnings by purchasing U.S. assets. Dangers arise if Asian governments cease being willing to accumulate additional dollar-denominated assets. They will then begin to accumulate new assets denominated in euros and also will begin to trade their stock of dollar-denominated assets for euros. The result will be a shift from the dollar to the euro as the principal reserve currency.

Niall Ferguson develops an argument along these lines. He compares the dollar's current predicament to the situation it faced in the mid-1960s. Although the dollar continued to serve as the world's most important currency in spite of its weakness in the early 1960s, its survival this time around is highly uncertain. The United States is running persistent current account deficits today, which it did not have in the 1960s, and these deficits are generating a mounting foreign debt burden. Moreover, today the world has something it lacked in the 1960s— a plausible replacement for the dollar.

THE DOLLAR WILL REMAIN THE WORLD'S
RESERVE CURRENCY

Other analysts believe the dollar's position is quite secure. Dollar enthusiasts point to the fact that the dollar remains very attractive as a reserve asset. The American economy is large, the United States has maintained a stable value for the dollar for the last twenty five years, and American financial markets are deep and liquid. Moreover, prior shifts from one reserve currency to another—such as the shift from the pound sterling to the dollar in the early twentieth century—were brought about by massive shocks, including world wars, the Great Depression, and the Suez Canal Crisis of 1956. Even were the euro to offer a viable alternative to the dollar, therefore, it would probably require some major systemic shock to prompt all participants in the global economy to abandon the dollar in favor of the euro.

Benjamin Cohen and Paola Subacchi take this line of argument one step further by suggesting that the euro may never be a plausible alternative to the dollar. The euro is "not yet ready for prime time," they argue, because European governments have not used monetary union as a vehicle to expand their political influence in the global economy, in large part because the system does not promote a single coherent EU position. The system lacks coherence because of the disjuncture between national governments and supranational currency and monetary policy. EU governments must find an institutional solution to this governance problem before the euro can play a large role in the global economy.

POINTS **TO PONDER**

1. What characteristics make a currency suitable for use as a reserve currency?

2. Why, according to Cohen and Subacchi, must the EU reform monetary institutions in order for the euro to assume a larger international role?

3. What are the stakes in the competition between the euro and the dollar? That is, what does the United States gain from the dollar's current role and therefore what does it stand to lose if the euro supplants the dollar in this role?

Niall Ferguson
The Euro's Big Chance

"The convention whereby the dollar is given a transcendent value as an international currency no longer rests on its initial base. . . . The fact that many states accept dollars in order to make up for the deficits of the American balance of payments has enabled the U.S. to be indebted to foreign countries free of charge. Indeed, what they owe those countries they pay in dollars that they themselves issue as they wish. . . . This unilateral facility attributed to America has helped spread the idea that the dollar is an impartial, international means of exchange, whereas it is a means of credit appropriated to one state." Thus spoke Charles De Gaulle in 1956, from a press conference often cited by historians as the beginning of the end of postwar international monetary stability. De Gaulle's argument was that the U.S. was deriving unfair advantages from being the principal international reserve currency. To be precise, it was financing its own balance of payments deficit by selling foreigners dollars that were likely to depreciate in value.

The striking thing about De Gaulle's analysis is how very aptly it describes the role of the dollar in 2004. That is itself ironic, since the general's intention was, if possible, to topple the dollar from its role as the world's number one currency. True, pressure on the dollar grew steadily in the wake of De Gaulle's remarks. By 1973, if not before, the system of more or less fixed exchanges rates, devised at Bretton Woods in 1944, was dead, and the world entered an era of floating exchanges rates and high inflation. Yet, even in the darkest days of the 1970s, the dollar did come close to losing its status as a reserve currency. Indeed, so successfully has it continued to perform this role that in the past decade some economists have begun speaking of Bretton Woods II—with the dollar, once again, as the key currency. The question is: how long can this new dollar standard last?

The existence of a dollar standard may come as a surprise to any American who has been considering a summer holiday in Europe. With the euro at $1.18 (compared with 90 cents two years ago), talk of a new era of fixed exchange rates seems far-fetched. But "son of Bretton Woods" is not a global system (nor, in fact, was Bretton Woods senior). It is primarily an Asian system. Pegged to the dollar are the currencies of China, Hong Kong, and Malaysia. Also linked, less rigidly, are the currencies of India, Indonesia, Japan, Singapore, South Korea, Taiwan, and Thailand.

As in 1960s, it is not difficult to make the case that this system is highly beneficial to the U.S. Over the past decade or so, the American current account deficit with the rest of the world for goods, services, and loans has grown dramatically. Add together the deficits of the past 12 years and you arrive at a total external debt of $2.9 trillion. At the end of 2002, according to the department of commerce, the net international indebtedness of the U.S. was equivalent to around a quarter of GDP [gross domestic product]. Yet as recently as 1988 the U.S. was still a global net creditor.

This rapid role reversal—from world's banker to world's biggest debtor—has had two advantages for Americans. First, it has allowed U.S. business to invest substantially (notably in information technology) without requiring Americans to reduce their consumption. Between 10 to 20 percent of all investments in the U.S. economy in the past decade has been financed out of the savings of foreigners, allowing Americans to spend and spend. The personal savings rate is less than half of what it was in the 1980s.

The second payoff, however, has taken the form of tax cuts rather than private sector investment. The dramatic shift in the finances of the federal government from surplus to deficit since 2000—a deterioration unprecedented in peacetime, according to the IMF [International Monetary Fund]—has been substantially funded from abroad. Had that not been the case, the combination of tax cuts, increased spending, and reduced revenue that has characterized President [George W.] Bush's fiscal policy would have led to much more severe increasing in long-term U.S. interest rates. Veterans of the Nixon and Reagan years can only shake their heads enviously at the way the . . . Republican administration has escaped punishment for its profligacy. To run deficits on this scale while enjoying long-term bond yields of under 5 percent looks like the biggest free lunch in modern economic history. The cost of servicing the federal debt has actually fallen under Bush, even as the total debt itself has risen.

The reason is simply that foreigners are willing to buy the new bonds issued by the U.S. treasury at remarkably high prices. In the past ten years, the share of the privately held federal debt in foreign hands has risen from 20 to nearly 45 percent. Just who is buying up all these dollar-denominated bonds, apparently oblivious to the possibly that, if past performance is anything to go by, their value could quite suddenly drop? The answer is that the purchases are being made not by private investors but by public institutions—the central banks of Asia.

Between January 2002 and December 2003, the Bank of Japan's foreign exchange reserves increased by $266 billion. Those of China, Hong Kong, and Malaysia rose by $224 billion. Taiwan acquired more than $80 billion. Nearly all of this increase took the form of purchases of U.S. dollars and dollar-denominated bonds. In the first three months of [2004] alone, the Japanese bought another $142 billion. The Asian central banks' motivation for doing so is simple: to prevent their own currencies from appreciating relative to the dollar—because a weak dollar would hurt their own exports to the mighty American market. Were it not for these interventions, the dollar would certainly have depreciated relative to the Asian currencies, as it has against the euro. But the Asian authorities are willing to spend whatever it takes of their own currency to keep the dollar exchange rate steady.

This, then, is Bretton Woods junior: an Asian system of pegged exchange rates [that] keeps the Asian economies' exports competitive in the U.S. while at the same time giving Americans a seemingly limitless low interest credit facility to run up huge private and public sector debts.

In one respect, at least, the claim that the world has unwittingly reinvented Bretton Woods is convincing. Taking a long view, the real trade-weighted exchange rate of the dollar has proved remarkably stable. It experienced bouts of appreciation in the early 1980s and the late 1990s, but then reverted to something like a mean value. Right now it is less than 10 percent below where it was [in] 1973. And where the new system differs from the old is to the advantage of the former. The original Bretton Woods was premised on a fixed link between the dollar and gold. Remember the plot of Goldfinger? The prosperity of the cold war era supposedly rested on the foundation of the Fort Knox gold reserve. But that made the system vulnerable to speculation by foreigners who, like De Gaulle, decided they would rather hold gold than dollars. This time around there is only the dollar. The world's monetary system is built on paper.

But here's the catch. The proponents of the new Bretton Woods seem to see it as a system with a boundless, rosy future. The Asians, so the argument goes, will keep on buying dollars and U.S. treasuries because they so desperately need to avoid a dollar slide, and because there is no theoretical limit on how much of their own currency they can print purely in order to make their dollar purchases. In any case, why should foreigners not want to invest in the U.S.? It is, as numerous Wall Street practitioners have told me over the past few months, the place to invest now that recovery is under way. "Where else are they going to go?" one Wall Street banker asked me last month, with a rather superior sneer. "Europe?"

But this optimistic conventional wisdom overlooks a number of big differences between the 1960s and the present. American deficits under the old Bretton Woods system were insignificant; the U.S. was running current account surpluses throughout the decade. People then were worried about the fact that Americans were investing quite substantially abroad, though that was counterbalanced by inflows of foreign capital. But mainly they were worried that overseas dollar holdings were outstripping the Federal Reserve's stock of gold. Today the U.S. is running up huge deficits, while international capital flows are much larger. So, consequently, are the potential strains on a system of fixed exchange rates.

Whatever its virtues, the Bretton Woods system did not last long. If you count only the period when the dollar and the major European currencies were truly convertible into gold at the agreed rates, it lasted ten years

(1958–68). There are reasons to think that this Asian son of Bretton Woods could prove equally ephemeral. And the aftermath of its breakdown could be as painful as the crisis of the mid-1970s.

For all the mystical appeal of the dollar bill, it is not a piece of gold. Since the end of gold convertibility, a dollar has been little more than a flimsy piece of printed paper that costs around three cents to manufacture. The design with which we are familiar dates back to 1957; since then, as a result of inflation, it [has] lost 84 percent of its purchasing power. Tell the Japanese that they are the lucky members of a "dollar standard" and they will laugh. In 1971 a dollar was worth more than 350 yen; today it hovers around 100.

Until very recently, the frailty of the dollar has not really mattered. We have forgiven it the periodic bouts of depreciation for the simple reason that there has been no alternative. The sheer scale of American trade (the prices of so many commodities from oil to gold are quoted in dollars) means the dollar has remained the world's favorite currency and the first choice for settling international balances.

Yet no monetary system lasts forever. A hundred years ago, sterling was the world's number one currency. Yet Britain's soaring indebtedness during and after the first world war created an opportunity for the dollar to stake a claim first to equality and then to superiority. This pattern could repeat itself, for there is a new kid on the international monetary block. And few Americans have grasped that this new kid, despite the flaws of his parents, is a plausible contender for the top job.

Whatever you may think about the EU [European Union] as a political entity, there is no denying that the currency it has spawned has what it takes to rival the dollar as the international reserve currency. First, eurozone GDP is not so very much less than that of the U.S.—16 percent of world output in 2002, compared with 21 percent for the U.S. Second, unlike the U.S., the eurozone runs current account surpluses; there is plenty of slack in European demand. Third, and in my view most important, since the creation of the euro, more international bonds have been issued in euros than dollars. Before 1999, around 30 percent of total international bonds were issued in the euro's predecessor currencies, compared with more than 50 percent in dollars. In the past five years, the euro has accounted for 47 percent to the dollar's 44 percent.

Could this mark a turning point? Last month, at a dinner held in London by one of the biggest U.S. banks for around 18 clients at other major City institutions, I posed the question: who thought the euro could plausibly replace the dollar as the principal international reserve currency? No fewer than six thought it could—and were prepared to admit it before their American hosts. When I asked a smaller group of Wall Street bankers the same question, they were more doubtful—though one observed that the euro is already the preferred currency of organized crime because, unlike the

Fed, which no longer issues bills with a value above $100, the European Central Bank issues a high-denomination E500 note. That makes it possible to cram around €7 million into a briefcase—which can come in useful in some parts of Colombia. Maybe on Wall Street too.

The future of the Asian Bretton Woods system—and indeed of this year's U.S. recovery—depends on the willingness of Asian institutions to go on (and on and on) buying dollars and dollar-denominated bonds. But why should they, if the Japanese economy is—as now seems to be the case—finally coming out of its deflationary slump? In any case, Japan's intervention has not been wholly successful in stemming the dollar's slide: over the past two years, the yen has gone from 135 to 110 against the dollar. In yen terms, the returns on the Bank of Japan's dollar portfolio have been decidedly negative.

Moreover, reliance on exports to the U.S. may not be a long-term option for Asia. In a recent lecture in Washington, Larry Summers, the former U.S. treasury secretary, argued that the U.S. has no alternative but to increase its savings rates if it is to extricate itself from "the most serious problem of low national saving, resulting in dependence on foreign capital, and fiscal unsustainability, that we have faced in the last 50 years." His conclusion is that the world can no longer count on the U.S. to be the consumer of first resort, which means in turn that "the growth plans of others that rely on export-led growth will need to be adjusted in the years ahead."

The Asian dollar dilemma is the euro's opportunity, both economically and politically. First, if the U.S. does cease to be the only functioning engine of global demand, it is imperative that the eurozone step up to the plate, and soon. For too long the European Central Bank [ECB] has made price stability the "magnetic north" of its policy compass. It has not spent enough time thinking about growth in Europe and the world. For too long ECB interest rates have been about a percentage point above the Fed's, despite the fact that deflation is a bigger threat to the core German economy that it ever has been to the U.S.

The president of the ECB is now a Frenchman. Maybe Jean-Claude Trichet should remind himself of some history. Thirty-nine years ago, the dollar was coming under pressure as U.S. entanglement in a messy postcolonial war began to grow. It was Charles De Gaulle who called time on the Bretton Woods system, which, he alleged, obliged European economies to import American inflation. This is the moment for someone to call time on Bretton Woods junior. Asians and Europeans alike need to sell their goods somewhere other than to profligate America. And they need to recognize that the emergence of the euro as an alternative reserve currency to the dollar creates a chance to fundamentally shift the center of gravity of the international economy.

If the Europeans seize their chance, Americans could face the end of half a century of dollar domination. Does it matter? You bet it does. For if Asian institutions start rebalancing their portfolios by switching from dollars to euros, it will become harder than it has been for many years for the U.S. to find its private and public sector consumption at what are, in terms of the returns to foreign lenders, low or negative real interest rates. (Do the math: the return on a U.S. ten-year treasury a year ago was around 4 percent, the dollar has declined relative to the Japanese currency by 9 percent in the same period.)

Losing the subsidy—in effect, the premium foreigners are willing to pay for the sake of holding the world's favorite currency—could be costly. For a rise in U.S. long-term interest rates to the levels recently predicted by the economist Paul Krugman (a ten-year bond rate of 7 percent, a mortgage rate of 8.5 percent) would have two devastating economic consequences. Not for big U.S. corporations—they are hedged (more than five eighths of all derivative contracts are based on interest rates). But a 3 percentage point jump in long-term rates would whack first the federal government and then U.S. homeowners with considerable force. For neither the U.S. treasury nor the average U.S. household is even a little bit hedged. The term structure of the federal debt is amazingly short: 35 percent of it has a maturity of less than one year, meaning, that higher rates would feed through almost instantly into debt service costs (and into the deficit). Meanwhile, even as rates have been nudging upward, the proportion of new American mortgages that are adjustable-rate rather than fixed has risen from around 12 percent in late 2002 to 32 percent.

The geopolitical implications of this are worth pondering. A rise in American interest rates has the potential not just to slow down the U.S. recovery, it could also cause the federal fiscal deficit to leap even higher. Under the circumstances, the pressure will increase to reduce discretionary spending, and that usually turns out to mean defense spending. It will get steadily harder to sell an expensive occupation of Iraq to a population groaning under rising debt service payments and alarmed by spiraling fiscal deficits. Meanwhile the Europeans will have added another string to their internationalist bow: not only will they be bigger contributors to aid and peace-keeping than the U.S., they will also be the supplier of the world's favorite money.

Such historical turning points are hard to identify. It is not clear when exactly the dollar usurped the pound. But once it did, the turnaround was rapid. If the euro has already nudged in front, it may not be long before oil producers club together to price their black gold in the European currency (an idea that must surely appeal to anti-American producers like Venezuela and Malaysia). World money does not mean world power: the EU is still very far from being able to match the U.S. when it comes to hard military power. But losing the position of number one currency would without question weaken the economic foundations of that hard power.

As the ghastly implications of the demise of the dollar sink in across the U.S., the specter of General De Gaulle will savor his belated vindication.

Benjamin J. Cohen and Paola Subacchi

A One-and-a-Half Currency System

Even before Europe's Economic and Monetary Union (EMU) came into existence nearly a decade ago, a brilliant future was predicted for the euro as an international currency At last, many argued, the European Union (EU) would have a monetary unit that could challenge the global dominance of the U.S. dollar. Typical was the confident assertion of two prominent European economists that "the most visible effect of EMU at the global level will be the emergence of a second global currency."[1] The conventional wisdom was clear. Leadership in monetary affairs would no longer be the privilege of the United States alone. The currency system would now rest on two pillars, not one.

Reality, however, has turned out to be quite different. There is no doubt that the system has changed. The euro has firmly established itself as an international currency, smoothly taking its place as successor to Germany's old deutsche mark (DM), which had already attained a rank second only to the dollar. The Eurozone has grown from eleven members to fifteen, with one more, Slovakia, due to enter in January 2009 and as many as a dozen or more set to join in the future. Yet the degree of change has been considerably smaller than expected. Euro enthusiasts assumed that once the tilt began, a new two-currency system would naturally emerge. But this was based on a fundamental misunderstanding of the nature of monetary power. In fact, the euro's success has been limited by structural constraints on Europe's ability to project power in monetary affairs. The Eurozone is largely a passive participant in global payments developments and remains a weak force in monetary diplomacy.

In this essay we argue that the euro is not yet ready for prime time and, at present, can play only a subordinate role in the global system as compared to the dollar. This can be described as a one-and-a-half currency system—certainly not a two-pillar world. We address two critical questions: First, how has the global system been changed by the arrival of the euro? We elaborate on what is meant by a one-and-a-half currency system and discuss why the euro is still not ready for prime time. Second, what can Europe do to overcome the euro's disadvantages and thus enhance the euro's role as the second pillar of the international monetary system? We argue that the main imperative is to improve the bloc's ability to project power effectively. Dual leadership at the global level is not out of reach, but will require determined reform of the EMU's governance structure.

One-and-a-half Currencies

Predictions about the euro's brilliant future were not misguided. From the start, the euro clearly enjoyed many of the attributes necessary for competitive success as an international currency. These include a large economic base, unquestioned political stability, and an enviably low rate of inflation, all backed by a joint monetary authority—the European Central Bank (ECB)—that was fully committed to preserving confidence in the currency's future value. Moreover, there was every reason to believe that sooner or later the global position of the dollar would weaken, owing to the United States' persistent payments deficits. Surely it was only a matter of time before the balance of monetary power across the Atlantic would tilt significantly in Europe's direction, naturally giving rise to a new two-currency system. But that belief was based on a fundamental misunderstanding of the nature of power in monetary affairs. In fact, capabilities in the broader currency system have changed much less than anticipated.

Monetary Power

Briefly summarizing an argument that has been developed at greater length elsewhere, we suggest that international monetary power is comprised of two critical dimensions: autonomy and influence.[2] More familiar is the dimension of influence, defined as the ability to shape events or outcomes. An actor, in this sense, is powerful to the extent that it can effectively pressure or coerce others—in short, to the extent that it can exercise leverage. As a dimension of power, influence is the *sine qua non* of systemic leadership. A clear example of the power influence dynamic can be found in the United States' ability to get its way in global monetary matters during the first decades after World War II.

The second dimension, autonomy, corresponds to the dictionary definition of power as a capacity for action. An actor is also powerful to the extent that it is able to exercise operational independence or to act freely, insulated from outside pressure. In this sense, power does not mean influencing others; rather, it means not allowing others to influence you. An example of this is provided by modern-day China, which successfully continues to resist foreign appeals for a major appreciation of its currency.

The distinction between the two dimensions of power is critical. Logically, power begins with autonomy. Influence is best understood as functionally derivative, inconceivable in practical terms without first attaining and sustaining a relatively high degree of operational independence. First and foremost, actors must be free to pursue their goals without outside constraint. Only then will an actor be in a position to exercise authority elsewhere. But influence does not automatically flow from autonomy. The actor must also be in a position to actualize its potential leverage—in practical terms, to translate passive autonomy into effective control. To aspire to a leadership role, an actor must have both the will and the ability to project its power onto others. Herein lies the problem for the euro: The EMU may have succeeded in augmenting Europe's autonomy in currency affairs, but it has yet to endow its members with enough direct influence to match the degree of leverage traditionally exercised by the United States.

Greater Autonomy . . .

That there has been an increase in autonomy is without question. With one joint money replacing a plethora of national currencies, the EMU's members need no longer fear the risk of exchange rate disturbances inside Europe. In the words of the European Commission, "The exchange rate realignments that periodically traumatised the European economies have become a thing of the past."[3] For a continent long plagued by currency instability, this is no small accomplishment. Moreover, with the now widespread acceptability of the euro, EMU countries have come to enjoy a much improved international liquidity position. Deficits that previously had required foreign exchange may now be financed with Europe's own money. Operational independence is now greater.

However, the gain should not be exaggerated. In some respects, considerable vulnerability remains, particularly in relation to the world outside Europe. The Eurozone is largely a passive participant in global payments developments, leaving members critically exposed to fluctuations of the euro's exchange rate vis-à-vis the dollar and other major currencies. Indeed, to date, the bloc has been something of a bystander, more reactive than active. For the ECB, the highest priority has been to establish its own credentials as a champion of monetary stability consistent with its narrowly drawn mandate under the Maastricht Treaty, the EMU's founding document. Policy has been targeted almost exclusively on the domestic price level. The balance of payments and exchange rates [have] been left largely to their own devices.

A near doubling of the euro's value since its lows in 2000 and 2001 has been a source of satisfaction to some, including the ECB, which initially had worried about the effect of the currency's early depreciation on the credibility of Europe's grand monetary experiment. Many Europeans have experienced a surge of pride as their currency has left the greenback in its wake. But there is also an obvious downside: the dampening effect that an increasingly expensive euro could have on economic growth. Particularly distressing to many Europeans is the knowledge that the euro's appreciation has more to do with dollar weakness than with euro strength. The euro has been favored by currency traders because of policy failures on the U.S. side, not because of relative productivity improvements or brighter growth prospects in Europe.

. . . Yet, except for one brief episode in the fall of 2000, the ECB has studiously avoided any manner of direct intervention in the foreign exchange market. The bank's management knows that any attempt to reverse the rise abroad, via sales of newly issued curds, would simply undermine the battle against inflation at home. In practice, the Eurozone can do little but remain passive witness to its currency's appreciation. Overall, the bloc's gain of autonomy, while undeniable, remains less substantial than many had hoped.

. . . But Not Greater Influence

However, this is not the heart of the problem. The issue is not the scale of the gains in autonomy, hut what the governments of Europe have been able to do with it. In fact, they have been able to do little. Slight or not, greater autonomy has not translated into more effective influence. Though freer now to pursue internal objectives without outside constraint, the Eurozone has yet to realize its potential for overt leverage over others.

In principle, currency unification should have been expected to enable Europe's governments to play a much larger role in monetary affairs. Joined together in the EMU, European states would surely have more bargaining power than if each had continued to act on its own. Europe's voice would be amplified on a wide range of issues from policy coordination or crisis management to reforming the international financial architecture. Power would be more effectively exercised in a purposeful manner.

In practice, however, Europe's voice has remained muted. A comparison with the United States is telling. Even without the participation of Britain and some other EU countries, the euro constitutes one of the largest economic units in the world—rivaling the United States in terms of output, population, and share of foreign trade. Yet despite the dollar's recent tribulations, Washington still speaks with a much louder voice in global forums such as the International Monetary Fund (IMF) or Group of Seven (G-7). As the European Commission unhappily acknowledges, Europe "still punches below its economic weight in international fora."[4] Europe has proved no match for the American heavyweight.

The reason for this lies in the governance structure of EMU, the constellation of rules and institutions that constitute the framework for Eurozone economic policy. Under the terms established by the Maastricht Treaty, no one knows who, precisely, speaks for the EMU. No single body is formally designated to represent the bloc in international discussions. As a result, Europe is at a permanent disadvantage in any effort to exert influence. The Eurozone, laments euro enthusiast Fred Bergsten, "still speaks with a multiplicity, even a cacophony, of voices . . . Hence it dissipates much of the potential for realizing a key international role."[5]

For example, the IMF bloc's fifteen present members are split up among no fewer than eight different constituencies. France and Germany each have a single chair on the Fund's twenty-four-member Executive Board. The other thirteen are all part of diverse constituencies that include non-EMU states as well as EMU members and in some cases are led by non-EMU governments. Collectively, the EMU's membership accounts for some 23 percent of total voting power at the IMF. But, because representation is so fragmented, it is difficult for Europe to exercise a commensurate influence on decision making or even to develop common policy positions.

Likewise, only the three biggest EMU countries—Germany, France, and Italy—are formally included in the influential G-7, which, with nearly half of all IMF voting power, plays a decisive role in IMF decision making. Each speaks only for itself. Other EMU governments have no direct voice at all.

The result is a lack of coherence that saps much of the authority that the Eurozone might otherwise be expected to exercise. Informally, efforts have been made to address the problem through tactical cooperation among the bloc's members on an ad hoc basis. However, in the absence of a strategic commitment to achieve and defend common positions backed by genuine political agreement, such actions are bound to lack impact. As one senior official of the European Commission, speaking anonymously, concedes. "We're a political dwarf and an economic giant." Without significant change, the Eurozone will remain condemned to lasting second-class status.

What Can Europe Do?

The problem for Europe lies in the fundamental mismatch between the domain of the EMU and the jurisdictions of its member governments. The euro is a currency without a country, the product of an interstate agreement. It is not, like the dollar, an expression of a single sovereign power. Hence the bloc's capacity to project power is structurally constrained. It is difficult to become a major player when speaking with many voices. The solution, therefore, lies in reform of the EMU's governance structure.

Building a Credible Currency

Addressing the structure of governance in this context is critical because of the institutional complexity of a monetary union established by a group of states that retain their sovereignty in most economic matters other than monetary policy. In the EMU, governance broadly covers four policy areas: monetary policy, fiscal policy, market structure, and exchange rates. All of these aspire to the same goals of promoting economic growth and employment. However, not all policy areas are addressed at all levels of policymaking. Monetary policy is a matter for the ECB, while fiscal policy and strategic exchange rate policy remain in the hands of EMU member states—the latter through the EU's Economic and Financial Affairs Council (Ecofin). The locus of responsibility for the external value of the euro is divided ambiguously.

The EMU's governance structure, not surprisingly, reflects issues that were embedded in the circumstances of the 1990s. In the process of building the EMU's institutional framework, the establishment of an independent central bank with a mandate over monetary policy for the currency union as a whole took priority. Using the DM as a template, the main concern was to ensure a smooth functioning of the single monetary area in order to create a strong and credible currency. It was correctly thought that confidence in the euro could only be established with the backing of a central bank firmly committed to price stability, on the model of the Deutsche Bundesbank, together with a set of rather stringent criteria to smooth the convergence process and ease adjustments to asymmetric shocks. The goal was to give credibility to the new currency by ensuring lasting macroeconomic stability across Europe's internal market. Besides appeasing German concerns about scrapping the DM, macroeconomic stability promised to protect the EMU's members from unnecessary volatility, to lower the cost of capital, and to encourage investment across Europe as a whole.

In short, the focus was placed single-mindedly on the EMU's internal conditions. The development of the euro as an international currency was not identified as an explicit policy goal. In the words of the ECB,

> From a policy perspective, the Eurosystem has adopted a neutral stance on the international use of its currency. It does not pursue the internationalisation of the euro as a policy goal. . . . The currency's use outside the euro area's borders is and should remain the outcome of economic and financial developments. . . . In any case, in a globalised world with deeply integrated and market-based financial systems, policymakers have limited scope to influence the internationalisation of a currency, even if they want to do so.[6]

Over the last ten years, the ECB has managed to build a solid reputation for independence by firmly sticking to its mandate of price stability. Even during the recent credit crisis, Jean-Claude Trichet, the ECB's president, maintained that price stability was the ECB's sole priority, reinforcing the bank's inflation-fighting credentials. The ECB, he declared, would not bow to political pressures to ease monetary policy in order to promote economic growth.[7] In other words, the ECB has played the "confidence game" well.[8] It has successfully established a track record of preserving market confidence in the value and usability of Europe's money.

After ten years, however, it is becoming clear that a single-minded focus on internal conditions is no longer enough if Europe is to be able to project power in monetary affairs to an extent commensurate with the growing international role of the euro.[9] While sound domestic policy and a credible central bank are integral to the successful exercise of monetary influence, they are not sufficient. Closer attention should also be paid both to the euro exchange rate and to the role of the Eurozone in international monetary forums.

The External Dimension of the Euro

A decade after the EMU's birth, the international role of the euro has grown well beyond the legacy of the eleven currencies that joined together at the outset. For example, the share of the euro in global central bank reserves is now some 26 percent—higher than the share of the sum of all its legacy currencies (including, most notably, the DM) at the end of 1998, which was about 18 percent.[10] The euro has also become the most popular currency in the world for international bond issues.[11]

During the same decade, the dynamics of the world economy have changed as well. Ten years ago, when Europe's EMU was established, the emergence of China was more a possibility than a reality, while the "Asian Tigers" were still coming to terms with a devastating financial crisis. Now the rise of the emerging market economies and the enlargement of the global economy's playing field pose significant challenges to the competitiveness of advanced economies such as Europe and the United States. These challenges particularly affect the labor market and the international division of labor, as well as income distribution, inflation, financial volatility, and the sustainability of current account imbalances. They also affect the way the Eurozone's adjustment process operates by altering both the typology of shocks and the available adjustment mechanisms.

The external dimension of a popular currency like the euro has two main components—one is its international use; the other, its external value. Though often conflated, the two components are not necessarily related. An international currency is the one that central banks and private-market actors are happy to use for transaction action purposes and to hold in their portfolios. On the other hand, the external value of a currency is related to a number of factors that surely include economic fundamentals and may also reflect transient trading conditions in foreign exchange markets. An international currency may not always have a stable or rising external value. A strong or appreciating currency may not be widely used for international purposes.

The distinction is important to any discussion of reform of the EMU's governance structure. Too often in the past, debate about the role of the euro in the global system has been muddled by issues related to the currency's exchange rate rather than to its international use. In fact, the two issues are institutionally and logically distinct and therefore need to be addressed separately.

Exchange Rates and EMU Member States

Given the strengthening of the euro's external value since 2001—coupled with the persistently weak performance of the Eurozone's real economy—it is hardly surprising that the exchange rate issue has, by now, become central to EMU policy discussions.[12] The question for policymakers is whether exchange rate management and coordinated currency interventions should play a more prominent role in the bloc's macro-policy tool kit.

Modern economic theory contends that a floating exchange rate is best understood as a forward-looking asset price determined at a level that induces market agents to willingly hold the outstanding stock of a currency. This contrasts with the older view—no longer endorsed by most economists—that the exchange rate is determined by the flow demand and supply of foreign exchange.[13] The exchange rate, accordingly, may be assumed to depend on expectations of future events rather than just on what is happening in the present or has happened in the past.[14] Given this theoretical framework, along with abundant empirical evidence, direct intervention in currency markets can be expected to have little scope and effect.[15] It may also risk sending wrong signals to the markets and setting unmanageable expectations. Central banks can still play a useful role, but mainly by helping market actors locate long-term equilibrium by signaling future changes in monetary policy and/or by changing the relative supplies of different assets.

In the case of the EMU, this suggests that the ECB should use its accumulated credibility to engage more proactively with the markets on the euro's exchange rate. In practice, this would mean focusing on the currency's long-term equilibrium rate as well as the short-term process of transition to equilibrium to counter the frequent tendency of market players to extrapolate recent exchange rate changes into long-term future trends. In doing so, the ECB must remain credible about the goal of internal price stability.

Effective exchange rate management will also require a concerted parallel effort by the EMU's member governments. Monetary policy alone cannot carry the load. Equally important is the role of fiscal policy as exercised by individual states, which can have a significant impact not only on the euro's external value but also on real rates of exchange within the EMU. Empirical evidence points to growing divergences of real exchange rates within the Eurozone.[16] At the root of these divergences are differences in national inflation rates. These are not only a function of cyclical positions, but are also determined by the shape of national institutions—above all, labor markets. Sound national policies aimed at strong productivity growth can help real exchange rate readjustment for converging economies with a fixed nominal exchange rate, and therefore improve competitiveness. Better coordination and surveillance of policies, in turn, would ensure that separate national targets and instruments are consistent with each other and are integrated into a non-conflicting framework in order to avoid negative spillovers. This is one of the three pillars of the European Commission's policy agenda.[17]

The function of coordination would be best undertaken by the Eurogroup, the Eurozone's informal committee of finance ministers, which, according to the European Commission, has become "a key body in the present EMU's system of economic governance."[18] The main strength of the Eurogroup is its relatively small size and cohesiveness, which enables it to debate issues thoroughly and with candor. Currently, it is charged with the surveillance of public finance and macroeconomic developments. Additionally, in recent years, it has increasingly discussed microeconomic issues relevant for a better functioning of the EMU. The Eurogroup can play a bigger role in overseeing structural reforms and policy linkages among its members.[19]

Speaking with One Voice?

Even with more effective exchange rate management, the Eurozone will remain a political dwarf on the global stage so long as it continues to speak as it currently does with a so-called cacophony of voices. The disadvantages of the EMU's lack of coherence are by now well understood. In a report marking the ECB's tenth anniversary, the European Commission explicitly identified the consolidation of the bloc's external representation as a policy target: "To be able to speak with a more coherent voice in global fora, the euro area needs to consolidate its external representation. . . . [T]he time is ripe for launching this process of consolidation."[20]

One possibility mooted by the Commission as a long-term objective would be the establishment of a single seat for all EMU members in relevant international bodies and forums such as the IMF and the G-7. Such a goal is easier to enunciate than to implement since those member states that now occupy individual seats are unlikely to relinquish their privileged positions without a struggle. Given the diffuse skepticism and increasing disillusionment toward the European project that seems rampant across Europe today—well demonstrated by the Irish public's rejection of the Lisbon Treaty in a referendum [in] June [2008]—there is little appetite in Brussels for any move now that might seem to threaten such a key element of national sovereignty. Consolidation of representation in a single seat for the Eurozone is simply not politically realistic under present circumstances.

More plausible is the possibility that a single EMU representative might be added to the EU's existing cast of characters to speak specifically for the Eurozone on matters of critical interest to its members. Who might provide that representative? One possible candidate is the ECB. As the Eurozone's only truly collective institution, the ECB seems to be the most natural candidate to speak for the EMU on global monetary issues. But that choice runs up against the tradition that, in most such settings, countries are usually represented not by central banks but by finance ministers with the political clout to speak for their respective governments. But the ECB cannot claim that kind of authority. Indeed, it is difficult to imagine the elected governments of Europe ever delegating such a fundamental power to an institution that was deliberately designed to he as free from political influence as possible.

The obvious alternative would be the Eurogroup, whose members have the necessary political clout. A start in this direction came in January 2005 when the position of Eurogroup president was created. Having improved the running of the Eurogroup's meetings, the president plays a key role in the economic governance of the EMU and is now expected to represent and articulate the views of finance ministers in the relevant international forums. The president participates on a regular basis in the G-7 finance ministers meetings, albeit with no specified responsibilities. Likewise, when issues relating to the euro are discussed at the IMF, the president is invited to make a statement on behalf of all EMU members.

Nevertheless, this is only a start and clearly falls short of what is needed to fully transform the EMU into a monetary heavyweight comparable to the United States. Because the Eurogroup remains an informal grouping within the EU, its president lacks any sort of formal mandate to negotiate on behalf of EMU members. Worse yet, the president's ability to speak authoritatively for the Eurozone emends only to issues on which the members are able to agree, which are usually the least controversial. The ruling principle within the Eurogroup is consensus, which effectively gives each member a potential veto. As a result, the president's voice can be easily muffled by policy differences among governments. Given the EMU's present governance structure, a single official cannot ignore or override the preferences of diverse sovereign states.

Can the voice of the president be strengthened? It would help if the role of the Eurogroup were to be formally institutionalized within the EU's complex governance structure. Likewise, the president's legitimacy and credibility could be enhanced by the grant of an official mandate to represent the EMU in all international organizations and forums. There would also be great benefit if the finance ministers of the Eurogroup could be persuaded to look more often at the bigger picture, reflecting a genuine sense of community and common identity.

However, herein lies a difficult balancing act between the interests of the euro area as whole and those of member states. The euro's external representation and governance must fit within a framework in which member states pursue their own goals without conflicting with the EMU's overall interests.[21]

Eventually some way must be found around the de facto veto currently available to EMU members. One possibility is to make the Eurogroup's decision-making procedures more transparent, in hopes of reducing temptations for opportunistic behavior. Another is to take the ECB's executive board as a model to create a small inner council of no more than six elected members authorized to decide on policies after consultations with all EMU members. A third possibility is to introduce weighted majority voting in the Eurogroup with appropriate safeguards for smaller states. With any of these options, there would be grounds for concern about a possible democratic deficit in the delegation of authority over potentially critical matters to such a small group of decision makers. Notwithstanding, such worries could be alleviated by suitable provisions for accountability For example, the Eurogroup president might be required to report regularly to the European Parliament, while finance ministers would continue to report as they do now to their respective national legislatures.

In the end, any step toward consolidation of Eurozone representation is bound to be accused of infringing on national sovereignty. Indeed, contestation over who speaks for the EMU is inevitable so long as the euro remains a currency without a country. The tradeoff is inherent in the inter-state agreement that underlies the EMU. Still, if Europe really wishes to punch its true weight on monetary matters, there is no choice. Without the reforms needed to project power more effectively, Europe will never be ready for prime time.

Conclusion

Throughout the decade since its birth, the euro has clearly established itself as the second most important international currency in the world. Nevertheless, contrary to expectations, the euro has not become a second pillar of the system on par with the U.S. dollar. Though an economic giant, the EMU remains a political dwarf, unable to punch its weight in monetary affairs. The outcome can best be described as a one-and-a-half currency system—certainly not the two-pillar world that many anticipated.

The problem lies in the governance of the EMU, which structurally constrains the role that the bloc can play in monetary governance. Therefore, the solution lies in a reform of the bloc's rules and institutions that would put greater emphasis on the euro's external dimension. On one hand, this calls for more proactive management of the currency's exchange rate by the ECB in conjunction with an explicit commitment by the Eurogroup to undertake effective coordination of national fiscal policies. On the other hand, it would mean designating a single representative of the EMU with real authority to speak on behalf of members in international councils. Unless the Eurozone can learn how to project power more successfully, dual leadership of monetary affairs at the global level will remain out of reach.

ENDNOTES

*   Some portions of this article have been published as part of the Chatam House Briefing Paper IEP BP 08/03 "Is the Euro Ready for 'Prime Time'?" by Benjamin J. Cohen and Paola Subacchi published by the Royal Institute of International Affairs in July 2008. Please see http://www.chathamhouse. org_uk/file/11792_bp0708euro.pdf for this version.

** The authors thank Stewart Fleming, Benedicta Marzinotto, and Jim Rollo for their valuable comments. An earlier draft was presented at the GARNET Conference "The EU in International Affairs" held in Brussels on 24–26 April 2008. Comments from conference participants are gratefully acknowledged. A shorter version appeared in Chatham House Briefing Papers Series, July 2008, which gave permission for the relevant excerpts to be reprinted here.

1. Daniel Cros and Niels Thygesen, *European Monetary Integration: From the European Monetary System to European Monetary Union* (London: Longman, 1998), 373.

2. Benjamin J. Cohen. "The Macrofoundations of Monetary Power." in *International Monetary Power*. ed. David M. Andrews (Ithaca, NY: Cornell University Press, 2006), 31–50.

3. "EMU @ 10: successes and challenges after 10 years of Economic and Monetary Union" (Brussels: European Commission. 2008), 4.

4. Ibid., 11.

5. C. Fred Bergsten, "The Euro and the Dollar: Toward a 'Finance G-2'?" *in The Euro at Five: Ready for a Global Role?* ed. Adam Posen (Washington, DC: Peterson Institute for International Economics, 2005), 33.

6. "The Euro's Impact on Trade and Capital Flows and its international Role," *Monthly Bulletin: 10th Anniversary of the ECB* (European Central Bank: Germany, May 2008), 96.

7. Jean-Claude Trichet. "Hearing at the Economic and Monetary Affairs Committee of the European Parliament" (speech. European Parliament, Brussels: 26 March 2008). This point Was echoed by the Bundesbank President and ECB Council member Axel Weber: "Given our mandate of price stability and the identified upside risks especially in the medium-term we have today re-iterated and emphasised our commitment to maintaining price stability as our primary objective in accordance with our mandate." Axel Weber, "Globalisation, Monetary Policy and the Euro" (speech. Norges Bank Conference on Monetary Policy, Jarle Bergo Colloquium: *Globalization and Monetary Policy*, Oslo, 7 March 2008).

8. Paul R. Krugman, "The confidence game," *New Republic*, (5 October 1998), 24.

9. Benjamin J. Cohen, "The Euro in a Global Context: Challenges and Capacities." in *The Euro at Ten: Europeanization, Power, and Convergence*, ed. Kenneth Dyson

(Oxford: Oxford University Press, 2008), 37–53. See also Paola Subacchi, Benedicta Marzinotto, and Vanessa Rossi, "Exploiting Europe's Strong Potential: Governance, Institutions and Policies" (briefing paper, *Chatham House*, January 2008) 1–6.

10. European Central Bank, 97.
11. Ibid.
12. "We believe the euro will not survive in the long run in the absence of some kind of political support. . . . Otherwise you'll see the euro at $1.80 and no action." Tony Barber, "Business chiefs warn of dangers to currency," *Financial Times*, (7 March 2008).
13. John Williamson, "Exchange Rate Economics" (Working Paper No. 2. Commission on Growth and Development, Washington, DC, 2008), 2–3.
14. Current account outcomes also depend on saving and investment, with income flows and exchange rates both determined simultaneously in a general equilibrium setting. For a discussion of exchange rate economies. see Williamson. 1–24.
15. For a contrary view see Williamson, 15–16.
16. Subacchi et al. (2008).
17. European Commission, 3.
18. Ibid., 287
19. "Germany's 3 percent value-added tax increase in January 2007 was, apparently, not discussed by the Eurogroup, even though such a move by so big a country was likely to have a spillover effect for its neighbours." Stuart Fleming, "Europe must shape debate on global issues." *European Voice*, 14, no. 8 (28 February 2008).
20. European Commission, 279.
21. Jean Pisani-Ferry et al., "Coming of Age: Report on the Euro Area," Bruegel Blueprint Series IV, (Bruegel. Brussels: 2008).

CHAPTER 10 CHINA MUST REVALUE TO CORRECT GLOBAL IMBALANCES *v.* CHINESE REVALUATION WILL NOT CORRECT GLOBAL IMBALANCES

China Must Revalue to Correct Global Imbalances

Advocate: C. Fred Bergsten

Source: "The Dollar and the Renminbi," Statement before the Hearing on U.S. Economic Relations with China: Strategies and Options on Exchange Rates and Market Access, Subcommittee on Security and International Trade and Finance, Committee on Banking, Housing and Urban Affairs, United States Senate, May 23, 2007.

Chinese Revaluation Will Not Correct Global Imbalances

Advocate: David D. Hale and Lyric Hughes Hale

Source: "Reconsidering Revaluation: The Wrong Approach to the U.S.-Chinese Trade Imbalance," *Foreign Affairs* 87 (January/February 2008): 57–66.

Should China revalue its currency, the renminbi (whose principal unit is the yuan), against the dollar? Officially, the Chinese government pegs the renminbi to a basket of currencies in a crawling peg regime. Unofficially, China continues to maintain the renminbi at a fairly stable exchange rate against the dollar. Many economists have argued that the renminbi is undervalued against the dollar and that China's exchange-rate policy intentionally maintains this undervaluation to promote exports. Such concerns prompted Congress to pressure first the Bush administration and now the Obama administration to urge the Chinese government to revalue the renminbi and to threaten to impose tariffs on imports from China if it doesn't.

Efforts to pressure China to revalue its currency come in the broader context of global current account imbalances. The United States has run current account deficits of unprecedented magnitude since 2000; in 2007, this deficit reached $731 billion, about 5% of U.S. income. For its part, China has run very large current account surpluses—about $231 billion or 10% of its gross domestic product (GDP) in 2007. Moreover, the United States runs its largest bilateral deficit with China: $289 billion in 2007. Many observers conclude from these facts that the U.S. current account deficit is largely a consequence of the bilateral deficit with China, and that the bilateral deficit in turn is a consequence of the exchange rate between the dollar and the renminbi.

CHINA MUST REVALUE TO CORRECT GLOBAL IMBALANCES

Advocates of renminbi revaluation assert that the imbalance in U.S.–China trade is a direct consequence of China's exchange-rate policy. Because China pegs its currency to the dollar at an undervalued rate, it reduces the price of Chinese-made products in the U.S. market and raises the price of American products in the Chinese market. Consequently, demand for Chinese goods rises while demand for American goods falls. Renminbi revaluation would reverse these relative prices, leading to greater demand for American goods, falling demand for Chinese goods, and an adjustment of the trade imbalance.

C. Fred Bergsten develops this argument in detail here. Bergsten argues that the global current account imbalances that are the consequence of Chinese exchange-rate policies pose a serious threat to global economic stability. Adjustment of these imbalances requires exchange-rate realignments wherein the renminbi is revalued by as much as 40% against the dollar. And although Bergsten calls for other changes in Chinese practices, he claims that "China's currency policy . . . is thus by far the single most important issue in U.S.–China economic relations."

CHINESE REVALUATION WILL NOT CORRECT GLOBAL IMBALANCES

Others are more skeptical about the need for a change in China's exchange-rate policy and the impact that any such change would have on the U.S. current account deficit. These observers analyze contemporary global imbalances through an economic model that emphasizes cross-national differences in savings and investment rates rather than exchange rates. Within this framework, the U.S. current account deficit is a consequence of a very low national savings rate relative to investment. For the past few years, the U.S. savings rate has been close to zero. In contrast, China's current account surplus is a consequence of a very high national savings rate relative to its investment. Indeed, China saved almost 50% of its national income in 2008. Adjustment of the imbalance will thus require changes in these national savings rates. Americans must consume less and save more and the Chinese must consume more and save less.

Such logic underpins the analysis of David Hale and Lyric Hughes Hale. They suggest that Congress has placed far too much emphasis on the bilateral relationship with China. What matters is the multilateral position. Moreover, focusing on the exchange rate is unwise because a revaluation will not only do little to correct the imbalance but will also create a backlash in China. Instead, they advocate a broader range of reforms designed to integrate China more firmly into the global economy. In addition, China must reform its tax system, restructure its corporate and banking sectors, and encourage consumption.

POINTS **TO PONDER**

1. What industries in China have an interest in an undervalued exchange rate? Does this valuation hurt any group in China?
2. What are the arguments for and against Bergsten's proposition that a revaluation of the renminbi will correct the bilateral trade imbalance?
3. What, if anything, could the U.S. Congress do to reduce the U.S. multilateral current account deficit?
4. How should the burden of adjustment be distributed between surplus and deficit countries?

C. Fred Bergsten

The Dollar and the Renminbi

The Central Role of China in the Global Imbalances

The U.S. global merchandise trade and current account deficits rose to $857 billion in 2006. This amounted to about 6.5 percent of our GDP [gross domestic product], twice the previous record of the middle 1980s and by far the largest deficit ever recorded by a single country.[1] The deficits have risen by an annual average of $100 billion over the past four years.

China's global current account surplus soared to about $250 billion in 2006, more than 9 percent of its GDP. Its trade surplus has doubled again in the first quarter of 2007, suggesting that its current account deficit will exceed $300 billion in 2007—the largest ever recorded by any country. China has become by far the largest surplus country in the world, recently passing Japan and far ahead of all others. Its foreign exchange reserves have also passed Japan's to become the largest in the world and now exceed $1 trillion, an enormous waste of resources for a country where most of the huge population remains very poor.

China's role in the global imbalances is even greater than these numbers might suggest. A substantial increase in the value of the Chinese currency is an essential component of reducing the imbalances, but China has blocked any significant rise in the RMB [renminbi] by intervening massively in the foreign exchange markets. It has been buying $15–$20 billion per month for several years to hold its currency down, and its level of intervention jumped to a monthly average of $45 billion in the first quarter of this year.

By keeping its own currency undervalued, China has also deterred a number of other Asian countries from letting their currencies rise very much (if at all) against the dollar for fear of losing competitive position against China. Hence, China's currency policy has taken much of Asia out of the international adjustment process. This is critical because Asia accounts for about half the global surpluses that are the counterparts of the U.S. current account deficit, has accumulated the great bulk of the increase in global reserves in recent years, and is essential to the needed correction of the exchange rate of the dollar because it makes up about 40 percent of the dollar's trade-weighted index. The most obvious Asian candidates for sizable currency appreciation in addition to China are Japan, whose currency is also substantially undervalued despite the absence of intervention for over three years, Taiwan, Hong Kong, Singapore, and Malaysia.

China has recently let the RMB rise marginally against the dollar. Since China continues to link its exchange rate to the dollar and the dollar has fallen against virtually all other currencies, however, the average exchange rate of the RMB is weaker now than in 2001 when China's current account surplus accounted for a modest 1 percent of its GDP. The world's most competitive economy has become even more competitive through a deliberate policy of currency undervaluation.

About one quarter of all of China's economic growth in the past two years has stemmed from the continued sharp rise in its trade surplus. China is thus overtly exporting unemployment to other countries and apparently sees its currency undervaluation as an off-budget export and job subsidy that, at least to date, has avoided effective international sanction.

The Risks for the U.S. and World Economies

These global imbalances are unsustainable for both international financial and U.S. domestic political reasons. On the international side, the United States must now attract about $8 billion of capital from the rest of the world every working day to finance our current account deficit and our own foreign investment outflows. Even a modest reduction of this inflow, let alone its cessation or a sell-off from the $14 trillion of dollar claims on the United States now held around the world, could initiate a precipitous decline in the dollar. Especially under the present circumstances of nearly full employment and full capacity utilization in the United States, this could in turn sharply increase U.S. inflation and interest rates, severely affecting the equity and housing markets and potentially triggering a recession. The global imbalances represent the single largest threat to the continued growth and stability of the U.S. and world economies.

The domestic political unsustainability derives from the historical reality that sizeable dollar overvaluation, and the huge and rising trade deficits that it produces, are the most accurate leading indicators of resistance to open trade policies in the United States. Such overvaluation and deficits alter the domestic politics of U.S. trade policy, adding to the number of industries seeking relief from imports and dampening the ability of exporters to mount effective countervailing pressures. Acute trade policy pressures of this type, threatening the basic thrust of U.S. trade policy and thus the openness of the global trading system, prompted drastic policy reversals by the Reagan Administration to drive the dollar down by more than 30 percent via the Plaza Agreement in the middle 1980s, and by the Nixon Administration to impose an import surcharge and take the dollar off gold to achieve a cumulative devaluation of more than 20 percent in the early 1970s.

The escalation of trade pressures against China at present, despite the strength of the U.S. economy and the low level of unemployment, is the latest evidence of this relationship between currency values and trade policies. With deep-seated anxieties over globalization already prevalent in our body politic, and the failure of the Doha Round to maintain the momentum of trade liberalization around the world, continued failure to correct the currency misalignments could have a devastating impact on the global trading system.

The Policy Implications

It is thus essential to reduce the U.S. and China imbalances by substantial amounts in as orderly a manner as possible. The goal of the global adjustment should be to cut the U.S. global current account deficit 1to 3–3½ percent of GDP, about half its present level, at which point the ratio of U.S. foreign debt to GDP would eventually stabilize and should be sustainable. China's goal, already accepted in principle by its political leadership but without any significant policy follow-up, should be to totally eliminate its global current account surplus and stop the buildup of foreign exchange reserves.

The United States should take the lead in addressing the imbalances by developing a credible program to convert its present, and especially foreseeable, budget deficits into modest surpluses like those that were achieved in 1998–2001. Such a shift, of perhaps 3–4 percent of our GDP, would have two crucial payoffs vis-à-vis our external economic position: It would reduce the excess of our domestic spending relative to domestic output, which can only be met by additional net imports, and it would reduce the shortfall of our domestic savings relative to domestic investment, thereby cutting our reliance on the foreign capital inflows that drive up the value of the dollar and undermine our trade competitiveness. Fiscal tightening is the only available policy instrument that will produce such adjustments. Hence I strongly recommend that the new Congress take effective and immediate steps in that direction.[2]

China needs to adopt policies to promote an opposite adjustment, reducing its uniquely high national saving rate by increasing domestic consumption. China can increase domestic spending directly through higher government expenditures on health care, pensions, and education. Such new government programs are needed for purely internal reasons because of the unrest in China that has resulted from the demise of state-owned enterprises that provided these benefits in previous times. They would also reduce the precautionary motive for household saving in China; this would boost private as well as government demand, contributing importantly to the needed international adjustment.[3] A number of important Chinese policy goals, such as increasing employment and curbing energy consumption, would also be served by such shifts in the composition of China's growth strategy.[4]

Large changes in exchange rates will also have to be a major component of the adjustment process. The dollar will need to fall, hopefully in a gradual and orderly manner over the next several years, by a trade-weighted average of about 20 percent. A change in China's currency policy, in both the short and longer runs, is thus by far the single most important issue in U.S.–China economic relations.[5]

An increase of at least 20 percent in the average value of the RMB against all other currencies, which would imply an appreciation of about 40 percent against the dollar,[6] and sizable appreciations against the dollar of other key Asian currencies, will be required to achieve an orderly correction of the global imbalances.[7] Such a change could be phased in over several years to ease the transitional impact on China.[8] It could be accomplished either by a series of step-level revaluations, like the 2.1-percent change of July 2005 against the dollar, but of much larger magnitudes and with a substantial initial "down payment" of at least 10–15 percent, or by a much more rapid upward managed float of the RMB than is underway at present. An increase of 40 percent in the RMB and other Asian currencies against the dollar would reduce the U.S. global current account deficit by about $150 billion per year, more than one third of the total adjustment that is required.

Over the longer run, China should adopt a more flexible exchange rate that will respond primarily to market forces. These forces would clearly have pushed the RMB to much higher levels by now in the absence of China's official intervention. There is some justification, however, for China's fears that an abrupt move to a freely floating exchange rate now, particularly if accompanied by abolition of its controls on financial outflows, could trigger capital flight and jeopardize its economy in view of the fragility of its banking system. Full-scale reform of China's exchange rate system will have to await completion of the reform of its banking system, which will take at least several more years. Hence the adoption of a flexible exchange rate regime in China, which is essential to avoid re-creation of the present imbalances in the future, can be only a second stage in the resolution of the currency problem, and the immediate need is for a substantial increase in the price of the RMB (especially against the dollar) through whatever technique is most feasible for the Chinese authorities.[9]

A U.S. Strategy for the Renminbi

It is obvious that China is extremely reluctant to make the needed changes in its currency policy. It is equally obvious that U.S. efforts on the issue over the past three years, whether the "quiet diplomacy" of the Administration or the threats of Congressional action, have borne little fruit to date. A new U.S. policy is clearly needed.

One cardinal requirement is for the Administration and Congress to adopt a unified, or at least consistent, position. To date, there has been something of "good cop" (Administration)–"bad cop" (Congress, e.g., the threat of the Schumer-Graham legislation) bifurcation between the two branches. China has exploited these differences, essentially counting on the Administration to protect it from the Congress—a bet that, to date, has paid off.

I would therefore suggest a new five-part strategy for US policy on the currency issue.

First, it is clear that China has aggressively blocked appreciation of the RMB through its massive intervention in the currency markets and that the Treasury Department has severely jeopardized its credibility on the issue by failing to carry out the requirements of current law to label China a "currency manipulator."[10] The Treasury report of May 2005 indicated that "if current trends continue *without substantial alteration* (italics added), China's policies will likely meet the statute's technical requirements for designation." The report of May 2006 sharply criticized China for its currency policies, clearly suggesting that there has been no "substantial alteration" in those practices, but inexplicably failed to draw the obvious conclusion of its own analysis.[11] The latest report, submitted last December, was much milder. Treasury has thus been reducing its criticism of China's currency practices even as the RMB has become increasingly undervalued and China's external surpluses have soared.

The Treasury policy needs to be changed sharply and quickly. The Administration should notify the Chinese that, if China fails to make a significant "down payment" appreciation of at least 10 percent prior to the release of Treasury's next semiannual report, it will be labeled a "manipulator." This would trigger an explicit U.S. negotiation with China on the currency issue.

Second, the Administration should notify its G-7 [Group of Seven] partners and the IMF [International Monetary Fund] that it plans to make such a designation in the absence of major preventive action by China. These other countries would prefer to avoid a U.S.–China confrontation on the issue and could be brought into a multilateral effort on the issue, reducing its confrontational bilateral character, if they were convinced that the United States was serious about pursuing it. The objective of that international effort, hopefully spearheaded by the IMF,[12] should be a "Plaza II" or "Asian Plaza" agreement that would work out the needed appreciation of all the major Asian currencies through which the impact on the individual countries involved (including China) would be tempered because they would not be moving very much vis-à-vis each other.[13] The Europeans have an especially large incentive to join the United States in such an initiative because their own currencies will rise much more sharply when the dollar experiences its next large decline if China and the other Asians continue to block their own adjustment (and perhaps to head off the incipient United States–China "G-2" implied by the Strategic Economic Dialogue).

Third, the Administration (with as many other countries as it can mobilize) should also take a new multilateral initiative on the trade side by filing a WTO [World Trade Organization] case against China's currency intervention as an export subsidy and/or as a violation of the provision in Article XV (4) that member countries "shall not, by exchange action, frustrate the intent of the provisions of the Agreement." As Chairman Ben Bernanke indicated in his highly publicized speech in Beijing in December 2006, in connection with the first Strategic Economic Dialogue, China's exchange rate intervention clearly represents an effective subsidy (to exports, as well as an import barrier) in economic terms. It should be addressed as such.[14]

Fourth, if the multilateral efforts fail, the United States will have to address the China currency issue unilaterally. Treasury can pursue the most effective unilateral approach by entering the currency markets itself. It is impossible to buy RMB directly, because of its inconvertibility on capital account, so Treasury would have to select the best available proxies in the financial markets. The message of U.S. policy intent would be crystal clear, however, and at a minimum there would be a further sharp increase in inflows into the RMB that would make it even more difficult for the Chinese authorities to resist their inflationary consequences and thus the resultant pressures to let the exchange rate appreciate. (All other undervalued Asian currencies, including the Japanese yen, could be purchased directly, with immediate impact on their exchange rates against the dollar.)[15]

The United States has of course conducted such currency intervention on many occasions in the past, most dramatically via the Plaza Agreement in 1985 and most recently when it bought yen to counter the excessive weakness of that currency in 1998 (when it approached 150:1, about the same level in real terms as its current rate of about 120:1). All those actions have been taken with the agreement of the counterpart currency country, however, and usually in cooperation with that country. This would be the essence of the proposed "Plaza II" or "Asian Plaza" agreement, as suggested above, and the multilateral approach would be preferable and should be pursued vigorously by the Administration. Failing such agreement, however, the unilateral option is available and might have to be adopted.

Fifth, the Administration should quietly notify the Chinese that it will be unable to oppose responsible Congressional initiatives to address the issue. Congress should then proceed, hopefully in cooperation with the Administration, to craft legislation that would effectively sanction the Chinese (and perhaps some other Asians) for their failure to observe their international currency obligations.

Such unilateral steps by the United States, although decidedly inferior to the multilateral alternatives proposed above and as long as they are compatible with the rules of the WTO, could hardly be labeled "protectionist" since they are designed to counter a massive distortion in the market (China's intervention) and indeed promote a market-oriented outcome. Nor could they be viewed as excessively intrusive in China's internal affairs, since they would be no more aggressive than current U.S. efforts on intellectual property rights and other trade policy issues (including the filing of subsidy and other cases on such issues with the WTO). Such steps should therefore be considered seriously if China continues to refuse to contribute constructively to the needed global adjustments and if the Treasury Department continues to whitewash the Chinese policies by failing to carry out the clear intent of the law fashioned by this Committee [U.S. Senate Subcommittee on Security and International Trade and Finance; Committee on Banking, Housing and Urban Affairs] almost two decades ago.

ENDNOTES

1. I note with pride that, based on the work of my colleague Catherine L. Mann, I predicted precisely such an outcome for 2006 in the third paragraph of my testimony before the full Committee on May 1, 2002.
2. See my testimonies on that topic to the House Budget Committee on January 23 and the Senate Budget Committee on February 1. I suggest there that the external imbalances are in fact the most likely source of a crisis that could force the United States into precipitous and thus unpalatable budget adjustments if pre-emptive action is not taken.
3. See Chapter 2 of *China: The Balance Sheet* and Nicholas Lardy, "China: Toward a Consumption-Driven Growth Path," Washington: Institute for International Economics, October 2006.
4. See Daniel H. Rosen and Trevor Houser, "What Drives China's Demand for Energy (and What It Means for the Rest of Us)," in C. Fred Bergsten, Nicholas Lardy, Bates Gill and Derek Mitchell, eds. *The China Balance Sheet in 2007 and Beyond*, Washington: Peter G. Peterson Institute for International Economics and Center for Strategic and International Studies, April 2007.
5. The short-term success of the new Strategic Economic Dialogue will be judged largely by whether it achieves effective resolution of this problem. The SED also has the long-term potential to foster a more constructive relationship between the two countries that will inevitably lead the world economy over the coming years and perhaps decades. It thus begins to implement the "G-2" concept proposed in my "A New Foreign Economic Policy for the United States" in C. Fred Bergsten and the Institute for International Economics, *The United States and the World Economy: Foreign Economic Policy for the Next Decade*, Washington: Institute for International Economics, 2005, pp. 53–4.
6. See William R. Cline, *The United States as a Debtor Nation*, Washington: Institute for International Economics, 2005, especially Table 6.2 on page 242.
7. I have studiously refrained from mentioning the very large Chinese bilateral trade surplus with the United States, which should not be a primary focus of policy because of the multilateral nature of international trade and payments. At present, however, the bilateral imbalance is a fairly accurate reflection of the global imbalances and is thus more relevant than usual.

8. See Morris Goldstein and Nicholas Lardy, "A New Way to Deal with the Renminbi," *Financial Times*, January 20, 2006.

9. This two-step approach was initially proposed by my colleagues Morris Goldstein and Nicholas Lardy, "Two-Stage Currency Reform for China," *Financial Times*, September 12, 2003.

10. See Morris Goldstein, "Paulson's First Challenge," *The International Economy*, Summer 2006.

11. Treasury (and the IMF) has justified their inaction on the grounds that there is insufficient evidence that China is manipulating its exchange rate with the "intent" of frustrating effective current account adjustment. This is of course ludicrous because it is highly unlikely that China (or any country) would admit such a motive and it is impossible to discern any other purpose for the policy. It might be desirable to amend U.S. law, however, by replacing the controversial (and pejorative) term "manipulation" with the unambiguous (and emotionally neutral) term "intervention."

12. Congress could direct Treasury to use the "voice and vote" of the United States to seek effective implementation by the IMF of its existing rules against competitive currency undervaluation.

13. See William R. Cline's "The Case for a New Plaza Agreement," Washington: Institute for International Economics, December 2005.

14. These ideas are analyzed in Gary Clyde Hufbauer, Yee Wong, and Ketki Sheth, *US-China Trade Disputes: Rising Tide, Rising Stakes*, Washington: Institute for International Economics, August 2006, pp. 16–24. Congress could require the Administration to bring such a case or cases, once a country was found to be violating its currency obligations, in any legislation that it passed on these issues.

15. Congress could write a requirement for such action, once a country was found to be violating its currency obligations, into legislation on these issues.

David D. Hale and Lyric Hughes Hale

Reconsidering Revaluation: The Wrong Approach to the U.S.-Chinese Trade Imbalance

China's economy has grown dramatically in the last decade: it is more than twice as large as it was ten years ago. This spectacular rise means that Beijing can influence the global economy today in ways that would have been unimaginable in the 1990s—a development that has led to widespread concerns in the United States. Many officials in Washington and small U.S. manufacturing companies allege that Beijing has deliberately undervalued its currency and manipulated markets in order to promote the growth of its exports.

Consequently, many U.S. politicians are clamoring for action to redress China's growing annual trade surplus with the United States, which currently stands at $250 billion. They assume that increasing the value of the yuan against the dollar will simultaneously decrease Chinese exports to the United States by making them more expensive and boost U.S. imports to China by making them cheaper. As the 2008 presidential election [approached], the U.S. Congress [was] actively discussing protectionist legislation and new tariffs that would punish China if its currency does not appreciate faster than the current rate of five percent.

But revaluation—no matter how vehemently it is advocated—is unlikely to achieve the desired result of reducing the U.S. trade imbalance with China. Taxation reform, the restructuring of the corporate and banking sectors, the gradual opening of capital accounts, and the encouragement of domestic consumer spending would each have a more measurable and lasting effect on China's current account surplus. There is also scant reason to believe that Beijing will accept the large-scale revaluation of 20 percent or more sought by certain members of the U.S. Congress. Such a policy could result in fewer exports, lost jobs, and capital flight to other emerging markets with cheaper labor costs, not to mention increased currency speculation and exchange-rate losses on hundreds of billions of dollars worth of U.S. Treasury debt now held by the Chinese government.

In addition, the trade imbalance that a revaluation of the yuan is supposed to fix is not the dire threat that many in Congress have made it out to be. The growing Chinese trade surplus has actually produced numerous benefits for the world economy and for U.S. corporations and consumers. It has handsomely rewarded U.S. companies, such as Wal-Mart, which have enjoyed record profitability as a result of low labor and production costs in China. Critics forget that China's central bank, the People's Bank of China, uses the surplus to buy U.S. debt, which benefits the U.S. economy, Furthermore, some 27 percent of China's exports are actually generated by U.S.-owned corporations, which pass on their savings to consumers back home.

Simply strengthening the yuan will not correct the U.S.-Chinese trade imbalance, much less bring China's dynamic economy into lasting equilibrium; at best, it is a flawed solution to an ancillary problem. The greater and far more critical challenge is to properly complete China's integration into the global economy. China is but one cog, and revaluation just one lever, in the complex machinery of international trade. Unfortunately, many U.S. politicians with little knowledge of economic theory, trade flows, or investment patterns have not grasped the intricacies of the Chinese economy and its place in the global marketplace. And so they seek a jingoistic, politically popular solution to a complex and multifaceted problem.

The Perils of Revaluation

This is not the first time Washington has sought to intervene in Beijing's monetary affairs. In the early 1930s, President Franklin Roosevelt's administration supported legislation to raise the price of silver in order to both garner support for the New Deal from western senators in silver-producing states and increase U.S. exports to China. But this proved to be a disaster for China, which was then on the silver standard rather than the gold standard. Unlike the rest of the world, China had experienced economic growth during the early years of the Great Depression due to low silver prices and rapid industrialization. The Silver Purchase Act of 1934 compelled China to revalue its currency, decreased its exports by almost 60 percent, and plunged the Chinese economy into chaos—while failing to increase U.S. exports to China. In the twenty-first-century world of highly mobile capital, information, talent, and technology, similar policies of economic containment, such as those currently circulating in Congress, are even more likely to fail.

Nevertheless, Washington remains obsessed with China's exchange-rate policy. Labor unions and second-tier U.S. manufacturing firms insist that China has kept its currency artificially undervalued in order to boost its international competitive position. They point out that China has a trade surplus with the United States equal to nearly two percent of its GDP [gross domestic product], compared with a peak of 1.2 percent for Japan in the 1980s, when the U.S. government last panicked about trade imbalances with Asia.

Washington has already taken punitive action. The U.S. Commerce Department shocked the financial markets on March 30, 2006, by announcing new trade measures against China's paper industry, potentially opening the door to many more attempts by U.S. companies to block Chinese imports. It introduced duties on Chinese paper imports because of allegations that the paper industry in China benefits from unfair subsidies, such as low tax rates and low-cost loans. This announcement broke with the 23-year-old U.S. policy of treating China as a nonmarket economy not subject to countervailing duties. Before this change, U.S. companies could only file antidumping cases against Chinese firms. The Bush administration's decision to pursue these sanctions reflects the new political mood inside the Beltway.

Washington may have forgotten how its silver policy affected China in the 1930s, but Chinese policymakers remember, and they do not want to undertake another massive revaluation that could produce domestic deflation and cripple exports, leading to massive job losses. Such caution is especially understandable given the experience of other Asian countries that heeded international advice. When China's neighbors followed the International Monetary Fund's prescription to liberalize their financial systems during the 1990s, they experienced a major crisis because of their large current account deficits and huge dollar debts. China was actually on the road to a freely floating exchange rate and full convertibility just prior to the East Asian financial crisis of 1998. But after the meltdown throughout the region, Beijing was convinced that in a world of hedge funds and rampant speculation, it was safer to protect one's currency.

In the aftermath of the Asian crash, there was a risk that China would devalue the yuan, leading to a cascade of other devaluations throughout Asia, which would have deepened the crisis. Instead, China took a long-term view. It exhibited regional leadership and left the yuan alone. After all, it did not really need to take the risk. In fact, due to forced devaluations elsewhere in the region, China's real exchange rate actually appreciated by 30 percent during the crisis. Nevertheless, its exports remained resilient due to high productivity growth. As late as 2002, Beijing continued to resist the temptation to devalue, even though doing so would have been to the country's immediate export advantage. China was unafraid to stand alone; its steadfastness proved to be its first act of global citizenship in the postwar period.

Traditionally, it has been China's banks that have opposed currency revaluation, out of fear that it might damage the financial sector. But today, resistance to a more flexible exchange rate is also coming from interest groups in China, such as industrialists and farmers, who fear losing their competitive edge in the export market. China depends on manufacturing employment for 109 million jobs—compared with the United States' 14 million manufacturing jobs—and the government is naturally concerned that a significant exchange-rate appreciation could reduce manufacturing employment in

China: export prices would rise, and markets for cheap Chinese products abroad could dry up. Some textile companies in the manufacturing hub of Guangdong Province are moving factories to Cambodia and Vietnam because of rapidly rising wages and uncertainty over Beijing's exchange-rate policy. Chinese farmers are also worried in the longer term about international competition now that World Trade Organization agreements have made the Chinese market more porous to imports. These farmers are a potentially powerful constituency given that two thirds of China's population resides in the countryside and increased imports would have a major impact on the developing rural economy.

China's Global Trade Deficit

Unlike many of their counterparts in Washington, officials in Beijing understand that U.S.-Chinese trade imbalances are a function of something much greater than exchange rates or even bilateral trade. Production has become so globally integrated today that very few manufactured goods are actually made in a single country from start to finish. Unlike Japan, for example, China does not have a vertically integrated domestic economy that can produce an entire product line from raw materials to finished goods. Instead, China is the last stop on the global assembly line. It imports components from other Asian countries, completes the manufacturing process, and then exports finished products to the United States. In 2003, intermediate goods produced by companies in Japan, Singapore, South Korea, and Taiwan accounted for 34 percent of all Chinese imports, compared with 18 percent in 1992—and the percentage is probably several points higher today. Also, because China serves essentially as a finishing shop, barely 20 percent of the value of the products it exports is actually captured by the Chinese economy. As a result, although China has a trade surplus with the United States, it has a trade deficit with the rest of Asia. In fact, China's trade deficit with East Asia grew more than threefold, from $39 billion to $130 billion, between 2000 and 2007, just as China's trade surplus with the United States increased nearly threefold, from $90 billion to over $250 billion, during the same period.

As these figures make clear, far too much emphasis has been placed on bilateral issues between the United States and China—rather than on trade imbalances as a global issue. For one thing, they suggest that being on the short end of a trade imbalance is not necessarily an economic liability. China supporters in the United States, including the Club for Growth and a number of academic and Wall Street economists, have warned against anti-China protectionism precisely on the grounds that the Chinese trade surplus is not necessarily such a bad thing for the United States. Ballooning corporate profits have given China a savings surplus, which it recycles into U.S. Treasury securities as part of its foreign exchange reserves. U.S. firms have also shared in this boom: their profits from business in China rose to over $4 billion this year—50 percent more than a year ago.

Furthermore, as a recent study by the Hong Kong Institute for Monetary Research ([HKIMR,] the think tank of Hong Kong's de facto central bank, the Hong Kong Monetary Authority) shows, the yuan's value is a function of China's overall trade balance, not simply of its surplus vis-à-vis the United States. In fact, the HKIMR researchers argue, currency appreciation would not have the expected effect of decreasing China's exports. It could actually have the opposite effect by decreasing the cost of the imports China needs in order to create finished goods for export to the United States and Europe.

Beyond Revaluation

The real challenge, as Beijing well understands, is helping China integrate its booming economy into the international system. As China's growth rate continues to rise, many in China, including Zhou Xiaochuan, the head of the People's Bank of China, have begun to worry about inflation, which is now at its highest level in 11 years. China's foreign exchange reserves now exceed $1.4 trillion—equal to approximately 50 percent of GDP. During the past two years, the Shanghai stock-market index has risen from 1,000 to 6,000. Last May, the trading volume on the stock markets in Shanghai and Shenzhen exceeded that on all the stock markets of the rest of Asia and Australia combined. Today, China accounts for five percent of all global stock-market activity.

So far, China's monetary policy alone has failed to curtail its very high growth rate, now over 11 percent. The People's Bank of China cannot use one common tool to restrain the stock market, regulating margin debt, which allows investors to use borrowed funds in order to buy stocks: such debt does not exist in China. It has instead responded by steadily increasing bank reserve requirements and nudging up interest rates. But if it raises interest rates sharply, it could attract capital inflows from foreign investors, which would bolster the currency. Higher interest rates could also keep even more Chinese money at home. Neither outcome would slow down the economy. Chinese policymakers will therefore need to look beyond monetary policy and focus instead on reforming tax laws, increasing consumer spending, encouraging capital outflows, and changing the regulations governing Chinese corporations.

China traditionally refunded to producers the 17 percent value-added tax (VAT) on production inputs that was paid on exports. But last June, it announced that it would phase out the VAT rebates on 25 percent of the products it exports. It has eliminated rebates on energy-intensive goods such as coal, refined copper, primary aluminum, crude steel, and activated carbon, all of which are produced in industries suffering from overinvestment. China will maintain the VAT rebates on higher-value-added products, such as machinery, because it regards them as the locomotive for growth in the future.

Due to its growing domestic market and the sheer scale of its manufacturing activities, China has managed to accrue corporate and government savings at an unprecedented rate. But the transition to capitalism has been rocky and imperfect. China's failure to pay corporate dividends has swollen corporate treasuries, leading to a cycle of overinvestment in capital equipment and to a form of corporate speculation on the stock market that is similar to the Japanese practice of using surplus capital for short-term, high-risk investing, known as zaitekku. A change in the regulations governing Chinese corporations that would force them to pay dividends to all shareholders would cure a major distortion.

Ultimately, China will also have to shift to a new policy that boosts domestic consumption and reduces the country's dependence on exports. Consumer spending has not kept pace with overall GDP growth: its share of GDP has slumped from 50 percent in the 1980s to 36 percent today. Consumption has been eclipsed by huge gains in capital spending and exports. The government has made some moves to increase consumer spending, such as introducing measures abolishing the taxation of farmers and increasing government spending on health care and education. Nevertheless, Chinese households still have the world's highest savings rate—between 23 and 25 percent. This is because the country's social safety net remains so inadequate that many people save more in order to pay for education, health care, and retirement. Ironically, to decrease the household savings rate and boost consumer spending, the government will have to reinstate some socialist policies that disappeared in the 1990s.

Beijing is also trying to slow the growth of its foreign exchange reserves by encouraging more capital outflows. Last May, Beijing changed the rules in this area, permitting Chinese special investment funds to invest in foreign equities and foreign firms to invest in Chinese equities. The change produced an immediate rally on the Hong Kong exchange, where Chinese institutions routinely buy "H" shares, shares of Chinese companies approved for listing in Hong Kong. (These sell at a significant discount compared with similar shares on the Shanghai exchange due to lower retail demand and a smaller market.) The Chinese government magnified the rally by announcing that it would give Chinese citizens more freedom to purchase Hong Kong equities and allow mutual funds to invest in a wider range of foreign markets. China hopes that this strategy of encouraging capital outflows will succeed in the same way that it did in Japan a few years ago—by reducing bloated foreign exchange reserves and bringing the economy into lasting equilibrium.

A Global Player

Despite Beijing's understandable reluctance to cave in to U.S. demands, the odds are good that China will eventually change tack and allow its exchange rate to appreciate more rapidly due to political pressure from Washington. But exchange-rate appreciation will have a far less significant impact on China's trade surplus than the economic policy changes China is already pursuing. For the past 30 years, China has been engaged in a complex process of integration into the world economy. No matter how many sensible economic reforms are implemented in Beijing, much of the burden for integrating China into the global economy will fall on the international community. And this process will require more than unilateral efforts by the United States to protect its own interests; it should instead be approached as a multilateral issue that will affect almost every nation on earth.

The time has come for a broad international effort to integrate China into the global economy. The United States should reform the traditional G-8 [Group of Eight] summits to include China as its ninth member. The G-7 ([Group of Seven,] the group of highly industrialized states) admitted Russia during the late 1990s, and China is a far more important economic player now than Russia was then. Indeed, there cannot be a serious discussion of global economic issues without the active participation of Beijing. The admission of China to the G-8 process would create a major global forum in which the leading industrialized countries could discuss the impact of China's export boom on other nations' economies and address the environmental impact of Beijing's growing demand for commodity imports and energy resources. In the end, only a skillful combination of structural reforms in China and coordinated multilateral efforts will create a more balanced economic relationship between Washington and Beijing.

PART IV

DEVELOPING COUNTRIES IN THE GLOBAL ECONOMY

Do developing societies benefit from participating in the global economy? Do they experience more rapid growth if they actively manage their participation in the global economy or if they simply open their borders and allow the global market to work? This basic question—is development best promoted by markets or by the state—has been at the center of the debate over development since at least 1950. The last twenty-five years have brought a dramatic shift in government orientations. The state played the central role and international markets a much smaller role in development strategies until the early 1980s. Today, the state's role is greatly reduced, and the role of markets is greatly enhanced. Has this change in the relative importance of the state and market been good for development, or would developing societies realize more rapid progress with a more active state role? Each chapter in this section looks at this question in a different specific context.

Chapter 11 takes a close look at the relationship between participation in the international trade system and economic growth. Since the mid-1980s, governments in developing societies have opted to integrate their economies into the global trade system. This strategy is quite distinct from the policy of the previous postwar period, when governments sought to develop by insulating themselves from the global trade system. The shift toward development strategies based on trade openness has generated a debate about the relationship between trade, economic development, and poverty reduction. David Dollar and Aart Kraay argue that trade boosts development and provides income gains that are distributed widely across society. In short, trade reduces poverty. Dani Rodrik argues that trade is not a "magic bullet" for development. There is little evidence, he argues, to support the claim that trade openness, by itself, is a recipe for sustained growth.

Chapter 12 considers the debate over the impact of foreign aid on the least developed societies. Policy-makers have long believed that development requires investment and that developing economies lack the savings required to finance the needed investment. Governments devised foreign-aid programs to provide the necessary financing. Yet, governments have been disappointed with the postwar foreign-aid record. The billions of dollars provided do not appear to have had much positive impact. David Dollar argues that foreign aid can be made to work more effectively by focusing on different objectives. Rather than focus on investment in physical capital, aid should target institutional development. William Easterly doubts that foreign aid can become more effective. He believes that aid fails because aid providers care more about keeping western governments happy than about achieving success in developing societies. Consequently, improvements in aid effectiveness will require fundamental reforms of how governments supply aid.

Chapter 13 concludes this section by examining whether developing economies are best served by opening themselves to or insulating themselves from the global financial system. Participation in the international financial system poses a trade-off. Societies gain access to foreign savings that enable them to invest more and thereby enjoy more rapid growth than otherwise possible. In exchange, developing societies expose themselves to the risk that financial markets will suddenly turn against them, precipitating a major economic crisis. Jagdish Bhagwati argues that this risk is too high. Financial markets, he argues, are highly volatile, and developing economies are very fragile. Consequently, developing economies are exposed to financial crises that they cannot easily withstand. Sebastian Edwards argues that the potential benefits far outweigh any risks. Edwards suggests that governments can minimize the risks by adopting and enforcing effective regulation to govern their domestic financial industry. For Edwards, therefore, developing societies are best served by opening to international finance and regulating at home.

CHAPTER 11

TRADE PROMOTES GROWTH v. TRADE DOES NOT PROMOTE GROWTH

Trade Promotes Growth

Advocate: David Dollar and Aart Kraay

Source: "Spreading the Wealth," *Foreign Affairs* 91 (January/February 2002): 120–133.

Trade Does Not Promote Growth

Advocate: Dani Rodrik

Source: "Trading in Illusions," *Foreign Policy* (March/April 2001): 55–62.

Active participation in the global economy, as well as pursuit of market-oriented economic policies, is a recent innovation for most developing countries. Until the mid-1980s, most developing countries pursued inward-looking development strategies called import substitution industrialization (ISI). ISI was a "statist" approach to development in which the state played the lead role in promoting industrialization. By using trade barriers to protect favored domestic producers, by subsidizing credit, and by sometimes creating and owning enterprises, policymakers used state power to transform largely agricultural societies into industrialized countries. Because this inward-looking strategy placed little emphasis on exports and depended on barriers to imports, developing countries participated little in the General Agreement on Tariffs and Trade (GATT) process.

This policy orientation changed dramatically in the mid-1980s. Facing internal problems with ISI, accumulating large foreign debts that they could not easily service, and confronting a deteriorating international climate, many governments were forced to turn to the International Monetary Fund (IMF) and the World Bank for financial assistance. Structural adjustment was the price of this assistance. Structural adjustment programs encouraged governments to scale back the state's role in the economy and increase the role of the market. Structural adjustment encouraged governments to shift from an inward-looking to an export-oriented development strategy. To that end, governments liberalized trade, deregulated the economy, and privatized state-owned industries. Most became active participants in the World Trade Organization.

TRADE PROMOTES GROWTH

By the late 1990s scholars and policymakers were beginning to evaluate the consequences of these reforms. Were the countries that had moved the furthest on the reform trajectory and had opened the most to global trade performing better than the countries that had reformed less and opened less to the global economy? Research conducted by economists working with and independent from the World Bank suggested that economic reform had delivered improved economic performance.

David Dollar and Aart Kraay, World Bank economists, summarize the result of perhaps the most comprehensive of these studies. They argue that the preponderance of evidence illustrates a positive relationship between trade openness and economic growth. Developing countries that liberalized trade and foreign investment have experienced more rapid growth than countries that remained relatively insulated from the global economy. For Dollar and Kraay, therefore, developing countries intent on reducing poverty should take further steps to integrate into the global economy.

TRADE DOES NOT PROMOTE GROWTH

Others argue that participation in the global economy is not causally related to better economic performance. Some of these critics accept the apparent correlation between trade openness and economic performance, but deny any causal relationship. Other critics are even skeptical about the existence of a relationship between trade openness and economic performance. Some suggest that causality runs in the other direction—growth spurts are followed by, rather than caused by, a growth of trade. The broader point such critics develop is that trade openness, although certainly not harmful, will not produce economic development. An important role remains for the state.

Dani Rodrik, a political economist at Harvard University, is perhaps the most prominent advocate of this alternative view. Rodrik is deeply skeptical about the claim that trade openness and economic performance are positively correlated. He argues that countries that opened most to the global economy during the 1980s and 1990s in fact grew more slowly than they grew during the 1960s and 1970s when they were more closed. He also claims that countries that have recently experienced long periods of rapid growth, such as China and India, liberalized trade gradually and only after growth had taken off. Hence, for Rodrik, trade openness is not the magic bullet of economic development.

POINTS **TO PONDER**

1. How would Dollar and Kraay respond to Rodrik's argument, and how would they evaluate the policies Rodrik recommends?

2. What countries do Dollar and Kraay point to as illustrations of the positive relationship between trade and growth? Does Rodrik agree with their interpretation of the reasons for rapid growth in these countries?

3. What complicates any attempt to evaluate the relationship between trade openness, broader market-friendly policy reform, and subsequent economic performance?

4. What is at stake in the debate about the relationship between trade and development? Do you think that there exists a single proper development strategy appropriate for all countries?

David Dollar and Aart Kraay
Spreading the Wealth

A Rising Tide

One of the main claims of the antiglobalization movement is that globalization is widening the gap between the haves and the have-nots. It benefits the rich and does little for the poor, perhaps even making their lot harder. As union leader Jay Mazur put it . . . , "globalization has dramatically increased inequality between and within nations" ("Labor's New Internationalism," [*Foreign Affairs,*] January/February 2000). The problem with this new conventional wisdom is that the best evidence available shows the exact opposite to be true. So far, the current wave of globalization, which started around 1980, has actually promoted economic equality and reduced poverty.

Global economic integration has complex effects on income, culture, society, and the environment. But in the debate over globalization's merits, its impact on poverty is particularly important. If international trade and investment primarily benefit the rich, many people will feel that restricting trade to protect jobs, culture, or the environment is worth the costs. But if restricting trade imposes further hardship on poor people in the developing world, many of the same people will think otherwise.

Three facts bear on this question. First, a long-term global trend toward greater inequality prevailed for at least 200 years; it peaked around 1975. But since then, it has stabilized and possibly even reversed. The chief reason for the change has been the accelerated growth of two large and initially poor countries: China and India.

Second, a strong correlation links increased participation in international trade and investment on the one hand and faster growth on the other. The developing world can be divided into a "globalizing" group of countries that have seen rapid increases in trade and foreign investment over the last two decades—well above the rates for rich countries—and a "nonglobalizing" group that trades even less of its income today than it did 20 years ago. The aggregate annual per capita growth rate of the globalizing group accelerated steadily from one percent in the 1960s to five percent in the 1990s. During that latter decade, in contrast, rich countries grew at two percent and nonglobalizers at only one percent. Economists are cautious about drawing conclusions concerning causality, but they largely agree that openness to foreign trade and investment (along with complementary reforms) explains the faster growth of the globalizers.

Third, and contrary to popular perception, globalization has not resulted in higher inequality within economies. Inequality has indeed gone up in some countries (such as China) and down in others (such as the Philippines). But those changes are not systematically linked to globalization measures such as trade and investment flows, tariff rates, and the presence of capital controls. Instead, shifts in inequality stem more from domestic education, taxes, and social policies. In general, higher growth rates in globalizing developing countries have translated into higher incomes for the poor. Even with its increased inequality, for example, China has seen the most spectacular reduction of poverty in world history—which was supported by opening its economy to foreign trade and investment.

Although globalization can be a powerful force for poverty reduction, its beneficial results are not inevitable. If policymakers hope to tap the full potential of economic integration and sustain its benefits, they must address three critical challenges. A growing protectionist movement in rich countries that aims to limit integration with poor ones must be stopped in its tracks. Developing countries need to acquire the kinds of institutions and policies that will allow them to prosper under globalization, both of which may be different from place to place. And more migration, both domestic and international, must be permitted when geography limits the potential for development.

The Great Divide

Over the past 200 years, different local economies around the world have become more integrated while the growth rate of the global economy has accelerated dramatically. Although it is impossible to prove causal linkage between the two developments—since there are no other world economies to be tested against—evidence suggests the arrows run in both directions. As Adam Smith argued, a larger market permits a finer division of labor, which in turn facilitates innovation and learning by doing. Some of that innovation involves transportation and communications technologies that lower costs and increase integration. So it is easy to see how integration and innovation can be mutually supportive.

Different locations have become more integrated because of increased flows of goods, capital, and knowledge. From 1820 to 1914, international trade increased faster than the global economy. Trade rose from about 2 percent of world income in 1820 to 18 percent in 1914. The globalization of trade took a step backward during the protectionist period of the Great Depression and World War II, and by 1950 trade (in relation to income) was lower than it had been in 1914. But thanks to a series of multilateral trade liberalizations under the General Agreement on Tariffs and Trade (GATT), trade dramatically expanded among industrialized countries between 1960 and 1980. Most developing countries remained largely isolated from this trade because of their own inward-focused policies, but the success of such notable exceptions as Taiwan and South Korea eventually helped encourage other developing economies to open themselves up to foreign trade and investment.

International capital flows, measured as foreign ownership of assets relative to world income, also grew during the first wave of globalization and declined during the Great Depression and World War II; they did not return to 1914 levels until 1980. But since then, such flows have increased markedly and changed their nature as well. One hundred years ago, foreign capital typically financed public infrastructure projects (such as canals and railroads) or direct investment related to natural resources. Today, in contrast, the bulk of capital flows to developing countries is direct investments tied to manufacturing and services.

The change in the nature of capital flows is clearly related to concurrent advances in economic integration, such as cheaper and faster transportation and revolutionary changes in telecommunications. Since 1920, seagoing freight charges have declined by about two-thirds and air travel costs by 84 percent; the cost of a three-minute call from New York City to London has dropped by 99 percent. Today, production in widely differing locations can be integrated in ways that simply were not possible before.

Another aspect of integration has been the movement of people. Yet here the trend is reversed: there is much more international travel than in the past but much less permanent migration. Between 1870 and 1910, about ten percent of the world's population relocated permanently from one country to another; over the past 25 years, only one to two percent have done so.

As economic integration has progressed, the annual growth rate of the world economy has accelerated, from 1 percent in the mid-nineteenth century to 3.5 percent in 1960–2000. Sustained over many years, such a jump in growth makes a huge difference in real living standards. It now takes only two to three years, for example, for the world economy to produce the same amount of goods and services that it did during the entire nineteenth century. Such a comparison is arguably a serious understatement of the true difference, since most of what is consumed today—airline travel, cars, televisions, synthetic fibers, life-extending drugs—did not exist 200 years ago. For any of these goods or services, therefore, the growth rate of output since 1820 is infinite. Human productivity has increased almost unimaginably.

All this tremendous growth in wealth was distributed very unequally up to about 1975, but since then growing equality has taken hold. One good measure of inequality among individuals worldwide is the mean log deviation—a measure of the gap between the income of any randomly selected person and a general average. It takes into account the fact that income distributions everywhere are skewed in favor of the rich, so that the typical person is poorer than the group average; the more skewed the distribution, the larger the gap. Per capita income in the world today, for example, is around $5,000, whereas a randomly selected person would most likely be living on close to $1,000—80 percent less. That gap translates into a mean log deviation of 0.8.

Taking this approach, an estimate of the world distribution of income among individuals shows rising inequality between 1820 and 1975. In that period, the gap between the typical person and world per capita income increased from about 40 percent to about 80 percent. Since changes in income inequality within countries were small, the increase in inequality was driven mostly by differences in growth rates across countries. Areas that were already relatively rich in 1820 (notably, Europe and the United States) grew faster than poor areas (notably, China and India). Global inequality peaked sometime in the 1970s, but it then stabilized and even began to decline, largely because growth in China and India began to accelerate.

Another way of looking at global inequality is to examine what is happening to the extreme poor—those people living on less than $1 per day. Although the percentage of the world's population living in poverty has declined over time, the absolute number rose fairly steadily until 1980. During the Great Depression and World War II, the number of poor increased particularly sharply, and it declined somewhat immediately thereafter. The world economy grew strongly between 1960 and 1980, but the number of poor rose because growth did not occur in the places where the worst-off live. But since then, the most rapid growth has occurred in poor locations. Consequently the number of poor has declined by 200 million since 1980. Again, this trend is explained primarily by the rapid income growth in China and India, which together in 1980 accounted for about one-third of the world's population and more than 60 percent of the world's extreme poor.

Upward Bound

The shift in the trend in global inequality coincides with the shift in the economic strategies of several large developing countries. Following World War II, most developing regions chose strategies that focused inward and discouraged integration with the global economy. But these approaches were not particularly successful, and throughout the 1960s and 1970s developing countries on the whole grew less rapidly than industrialized ones. The oil shocks and U.S. inflation of the 1970s created severe problems for them, contributing to negative growth, high inflation, and debt crises over the next several years. Faced with these disappointing results, several developing countries began to alter their strategies starting in the 1980s.

For example, China had an extremely closed economy until the mid-1970s. Although Beijing's initial economic reform focused on agriculture, a key part of its approach since the 1980s has involved opening up foreign trade and investment, including a drop in its tariff rates by two-thirds and its nontariff barriers by even more. These reforms have led to unprecedented economic growth in the country's coastal provinces and more moderate growth in the interior. From 1978 to 1994 the Chinese economy grew annually by 9 percent, while exports grew by 14 percent and imports by 13 percent. Of course, China and other globalizing developing countries have pursued a wide range of reforms, not just economic openness. Beijing has strengthened property rights through land reform and moved from a planned economy toward a market-oriented one, and these measures have contributed to its integration as well as to its growth.

Other developing countries have also opened up as a part of broader reform programs. During the 1990s, India liberalized foreign trade and investment with good results; its annual per capita income growth now tops four percent. It too has pursued a broad agenda of reform and has moved away from a highly regulated, planned system. Meanwhile, Uganda and Vietnam are the best examples of very low-income countries that have increased their participation in trade and investment and prospered as a result. And in the western hemisphere, Mexico is noteworthy both for signing its free-trade agreement with the United States and Canada in 1993 and for its rapid growth since then, especially in the northern regions near the U.S. border.

These cases illustrate how openness to foreign trade and investment, coupled with complementary reforms, typically leads to faster growth. India, China, Vietnam, Uganda, and Mexico are not isolated examples; in general, countries that have become more open have grown faster. The best way to illustrate this trend is to rank developing countries in order of their increases in trade relative to national income over the past 20 years. The top third of this list can be thought of as the "globalizing" camp, and the bottom two-thirds as the "nonglobalizing" camp. The globalizers have increased their trade relative to income by 104 percent over the past two decades, compared to 71 percent for rich countries. The nonglobalizers, meanwhile, actually trade less today than they did 20 years ago. The globalizers have also cut their import tariffs by 22 percentage points on average, compared to only 11 percentage points for the nonglobalizers.

How have the globalizers fared in terms of growth? Their average annual growth rates accelerated from 1 percent in the 1960s to 3 percent in the 1970s, 4 percent in the 1980s, and 5 percent in the 1990s. Rich countries' annual growth rates, by comparison, slowed to about 2 percent in the 1990s, and the nonglobalizers saw their growth rates decline from 3 percent in the 1970s to 1 percent in the 1980s and 1990s.

The same pattern can be observed on a local level. Within both China and India, the locations that are integrating with the global economy are growing much more rapidly than the disconnected regions. Indian states, for example, vary significantly in the quality of their investment climates as measured by government efficiency, corruption, and infrastructure. Those states with better investment climates have integrated themselves more closely with outside markets and have experienced more investment (domestic and foreign) than their less-integrated counterparts. Moreover, states that were initially poor and then created good investment climates had stronger poverty reduction in the 1990s than those not integrating with the global economy. Such internal comparisons are important because, by holding national trade and macroeconomic policies constant, they reveal how important it is to complement trade liberalization with institutional reform so that integration can actually occur.

The accelerated growth rates of globalizing countries such as China, India, and Vietnam are consistent with cross-country comparisons that find openness going hand in hand with faster growth. The most that these studies can establish is that more trade and investment is highly correlated with higher growth, so one needs to be careful about drawing conclusions about causality. Still, the overall evidence from individual cases and cross-country correlation is persuasive. As economists Peter Lindert and Jeffrey Williamson have written, "even though no one study can establish that openness to trade has unambiguously helped the representative Third World economy, the preponderance of evidence supports this conclusion." They go on to note that "there are no anti-global victories to report for the postwar Third World."

Contrary to the claims of the antiglobalization movement, therefore, greater openness to international trade and investment has in fact helped narrow the gap between rich and poor countries rather than widen it. During the 1990s, the economies of the globalizers, with a combined population of about 3 billion, grew more than twice as fast as the rich countries. The non-globalizers, in contrast, grew only half as fast and nowadays lag further and further behind. Much of the discussion of global inequality assumes that there is growing divergence between the developing world and the rich world, but this is simply not true. The most important development in global inequality in recent decades is the growing divergence within the developing world, and it is directly related to whether countries take advantage of the economic benefits that globalization can offer.

The Path Out of Poverty

The antiglobalization movement also claims that economic integration is worsening inequality within countries as well as between them. Until the mid-1980s, there was insufficient evidence to support strong conclusions on this important topic. But now more and more developing countries have begun to conduct household income and consumption surveys of reasonable quality. (In low-income countries, these surveys typically track what households actually consume because so much of their real income is self-produced and not part of the money economy.) Good surveys now exist for 137 countries, and many go back far enough to measure changes in inequality over time.

One way of looking at inequality within countries is to focus on what happens to the bottom 20 percent of households as globalization and growth proceed apace. Across all countries, incomes of the poor grow at around the same rate as GDP. Of course, there is a great deal of variation around that average relationship. In some countries, income distribution has shifted in favor of the poor; in others, against them. But these shifts cannot be explained by any globalization-related variable. So it simply cannot be said that inequality necessarily rises with more trade, more foreign investment, and lower tariffs. For many globalizers, the overall change in distribution was small, and in some cases (such as the Philippines and Malaysia) it was even in favor of the poor. What changes in inequality do reflect are country-specific policies on education, taxes, and social protection. It is important not to misunderstand this finding. China is an important example of a country that has had a large increase in inequality in the past decade, when the income of the bottom 20 percent has risen much less rapidly than per capita income. This trend may be related to greater openness, although domestic liberalization is a more likely cause. China started out in the 1970s with a highly equal distribution of income, and part of its reform has deliberately aimed at increasing the returns on education, which financially reward the better schooled. But the Chinese case is not typical; inequality has not increased in most of the developing countries that have opened up to foreign trade and investment. Furthermore, income distribution in China may have become more unequal, but the income of the poor in China has still risen rapidly. In fact, the country's progress in reducing poverty has been one of the most dramatic successes in history.

Because increased trade usually accompanies more rapid growth and does not systematically change household-income distribution, it generally is associated with improved well-being of the poor. Vietnam nicely illustrates this finding. As the nation has opened up, it has experienced a large increase in per capita income and no significant change in inequality. Thus the income of the poor has risen dramatically, and the number of Vietnamese living in absolute poverty dropped sharply from 75 percent of the population in 1988 to 37 percent in 1998. Of the poorest 5 percent of households in 1992, 98 percent were better off six years later. And the improved well-being is not just a matter of income. Child labor has declined, and school enrollment has increased. It should be no surprise that the vast majority of poor households in Vietnam benefited immediately from a more liberalized trading system, since the country's opening has resulted in exports of rice (produced by most of the poor farmers) and labor-intensive products such as footwear. But the experience of China and Vietnam is not unique. India and Uganda also enjoyed rapid poverty reduction as they grew along with their integration into the global economy.

The Open Societies

These findings have important implications for developing countries, for rich countries such as the United States, and for those who care about global poverty. All parties should recognize that the most recent wave of globalization has been a powerful force for equality and poverty reduction, and they should commit themselves to seeing that it continues despite the obstacles lying ahead.

It is not inevitable that globalization will proceed. In 1910, many believed globalization was unstoppable; they soon received a rude shock. History is not likely to repeat itself in the same way, but it is worth noting that antiglobalization sentiments are on the rise. A growing number of political leaders in the developing world realize that an open trading system is very much in their countries' interest. They would do well to heed Mexican President Vicente Fox, who said recently,

> We are convinced that globalization is good and it's good when you do your homework, . . . keep your fundamentals in line on the economy, build up high levels of education, respect the rule of law. . . . When you do your part, we are convinced that you get the benefit.

But today the narrow interests opposed to further integration—especially those in the rich countries—appear to be much more energetic than their opponents. In Quebec City last spring and in Genoa last summer, a group of democratically elected leaders gathered to discuss how to pursue economic integration and improve the lives of their peoples. Antiglobalization demonstrators were quite effective in disrupting the meetings and drawing media attention to themselves. Leaders in developed and developing countries alike must make the proglobalization case more directly and effectively or risk having their opponents dominate the discussion and stall the process.

In addition, industrialized countries still raise protectionist measures against agricultural and labor-intensive products. Reducing those barriers would help developing countries significantly. The poorer areas of the world would benefit from further openings of their own markets as well, since 70 percent of the tariff barriers that developing countries face are from other developing countries.

If globalization proceeds, its potential to be an equalizing force will depend on whether poor countries manage to integrate themselves into the global economic system. True integration requires not just trade liberalization but wide-ranging institutional reform. Many of the nonglobalizing developing countries, such as Myanmar, Nigeria, Ukraine, and Pakistan, offer an unattractive investment climate. Even if they decide to open themselves up to trade, not much is likely to happen unless other reforms are also pursued. It is not easy to predict the reform paths of these countries; some of the relative successes in recent years, such as China, India, Uganda, and Vietnam, have come as quite a surprise. But as long as a location has weak institutions and policies, people living there are going to fall further behind the rest of the world.

Through their trade policies, rich countries can make it easier for those developing countries that do choose to open up and join the global trading club. But in recent years, the rich countries have been doing just the opposite. GATT was originally built around agreements concerning trade practices. Now, institutional harmonization, such as agreement on policies toward intellectual property rights, is a requirement for joining the WTO [World Trade Organization]. Any sort of regulation of labor and environmental standards made under the threat of WTO sanctions would take this requirement for harmonization much further. Such measures would be neoprotectionist in effect, because they would thwart the integration of developing countries into the world economy and discourage trade between poor countries and rich ones.

The WTO meeting in Doha was an important step forward on trade integration. More forcefully than in Seattle, leaders of industrial countries were willing to make the case for further integration and put on the table issues of central concern to developing nations: access to pharmaceutical patents, use of antidumping measures against developing countries, and agricultural subsidies. The new round of trade negotiations launched at Doha has the potential to reverse the current trend, which makes it more difficult for poor countries to integrate with the world economy.

A final potential obstacle to successful and equitable globalization relates to geography. There is no inherent reason why coastal China should be poor; the same goes for southern India, northern Mexico, and Vietnam. All of these locations are near important markets or trade routes but were long held back by misguided policies. Now, with appropriate reforms, they are starting to grow rapidly and take their natural place in the world. But the same cannot be said for Mali, Chad, or other countries or regions cursed with "poor geography"—i.e., distance from markets, inherently high transport costs, and challenging health and agricultural problems. It would be naive to think that trade and investment alone can alleviate poverty in all locations. In fact, for those locations with poor geography, trade liberalization is less important than developing proper health care systems or providing basic infrastructure—or letting people move elsewhere.

Migration from poor locations is the missing factor in the current wave of globalization that could make a large contribution to reducing poverty. Each year, 83 million people are added to the world's population, 82 million of them in the developing world. In Europe and Japan, moreover, the population is aging and the labor force is set to shrink. Migration of relatively unskilled workers from South to North would thus offer clear economic benefits to both. Most migration from South to North is economically motivated, and it raises the living standard of the migrant while benefiting the sending country in three ways. First, it reduces the South's labor force and thus raises wages for those who remain behind. Second, migrants send remittances of hard currency back home. Finally, migration bolsters transnational trade and investment networks. In the case of Mexico, for example, ten percent of its citizens live and work in the United States, taking pressure off its own labor market and raising wages there. India gets six times as much in remittances from its workers overseas as it gets in foreign aid.

Unlike trade, however, migration remains highly restricted and controversial. Some critics perceive a disruptive impact on society and culture and fear downward pressure on wages and rising unemployment in the richer countries. Yet anti-immigration lobbies ignore the fact that geographical economic disparities are so strong that illegal immigration is growing rapidly anyway, despite restrictive policies. In a perverse irony, some of the worst abuses of globalization occur because there is not enough of it in key economic areas such as labor flows. Human traffic, for example, has become a highly lucrative, unregulated business in which illegal migrants are easy prey for exploitation.

Realistically, none of the industrialized countries is going to adopt open migration. But they should reconsider their migration policies. Some, for example, have a strong bias in their immigration rules toward highly skilled workers, which in fact spurs a "brain drain" from the developing world. Such policies do little to stop the flow of unskilled workers and instead push many of these people into the illegal category. If rich countries would legally accept more unskilled workers, they could address their own looming labor shortages, improve living standards in developing countries, and reduce illegal human traffic and its abuses. In sum, the integration of poor economies with richer ones over the past two decades has provided many opportunities for poor people to improve their lives. Examples of the beneficiaries of globalization can be found among Mexican migrants, Chinese factory workers, Vietnamese peasants, and Ugandan farmers. Many of the better-off in developing and rich countries alike also benefit. After all the rhetoric about globalization is stripped away, many of the policy questions come down to whether the rich world will make integrating with the world economy easy for those poor communities that want to do so. The world's poor have a large stake in how the rich countries answer.

Dani Rodrik
Trading in Illusions

Advocates of global economic integration hold out utopian visions of the prosperity that developing countries will reap if they open their borders to commerce and capital. This hollow promise diverts poor nations' attention and resources from the key domestic innovations needed to spur economic growth.

A senior U.S. Treasury official recently urged Mexico's government to work harder to reduce violent crime because "such high levels of crime and violence may drive away foreign investors." This admonition nicely illustrates how foreign trade and investment have become the ultimate yardstick for evaluating the social and economic policies of governments in developing countries. Forget the slum dwellers or *campesinos* who live amidst crime and poverty throughout the developing world. Just mention "investor sentiment" or "competitiveness in world markets" and policymakers will come to attention in a hurry.

Underlying this perversion of priorities is a remarkable consensus on the imperative of global economic integration. Openness to trade and investment flows is no longer viewed simply as a component of a country's development strategy; it has mutated into the most potent catalyst for economic growth known to humanity. Predictably, senior officials of the World Trade Organization (WTO), International Monetary Fund (IMF), and other international financial agencies incessantly repeat the openness mantra. In recent years, however, faith in integration has spread quickly to political leaders and policymakers around the world.

Joining the world economy is no longer a matter simply of dismantling barriers to trade and investment. Countries now must also comply with a long list of admission requirements, from new patent rules to more rigorous banking standards. The apostles of economic integration prescribe comprehensive institutional reforms that took today's advanced countries generations to accomplish, so that developing countries can, as the cliché goes, maximize the gains and minimize the risks of participation in the world economy. Global integration has become, for all practical purposes, a substitute for a development strategy.

This trend is bad news for the world's poor. The new agenda of global integration rests on shaky empirical ground and seriously distorts policymakers' priorities. By focusing on international integration, governments in poor nations divert human resources, administrative capabilities, and political capital away from more urgent development priorities such as education, public health, industrial capacity, and social cohesion. This emphasis also undermines nascent democratic institutions by removing the choice of development strategy from public debate.

World markets are a source of technology and capital; it would be silly for the developing world not to exploit these opportunities. But globalization is not a shortcut to development. Successful economic growth strategies have always required a judicious blend of imported practices with domestic institutional innovations. Policymakers need to forge a domestic growth strategy by relying on domestic investors and domestic institutions. The costliest downside of the integrationist faith is that it crowds out serious thinking and efforts along such lines.

Excuses, Excuses

Countries that have bought wholeheartedly into the integration orthodoxy are discovering that openness does not deliver on its promise. Despite sharply lowering their barriers to trade and investment since the 1980s, scores of countries in Latin America and Africa are stagnating or growing less rapidly than in the heyday of import substitution during the 1960s and 1970s. By contrast, the fastest growing countries are China, India, and others in East and Southeast Asia. Policymakers in these countries have also espoused trade and investment liberalization, but they have done so in an unorthodox manner—gradually, sequentially, and only after an initial period of high growth—and as part of a broader policy package with many unconventional features.

The disappointing outcomes with deep liberalization have been absorbed into the faith with remarkable aplomb. Those who view global integration as the prerequisite for economic development now simply add the caveat that opening borders is insufficient. Reaping the gains from openness, they argue, also requires a full complement of institutional reforms.

Consider trade liberalization. Asking any World Bank economist what a successful trade-liberalization program requires will likely elicit a laundry list of measures beyond the simple reduction of tariff and nontariff barriers: tax reform to make up for lost tariff revenues; social safety nets to compensate displaced workers; administrative reform to bring trade practices into compliance with WTO rules; labor market reform to enhance worker mobility across industries; technological assistance to upgrade firms hurt by import competition; and training programs to ensure that export-oriented firms and investors have access to skilled workers. As the promise of trade liberalization fails to materialize, the prerequisites keep expanding. For example, Clare Short, Great Britain's secretary of state for international development, recently added universal provision of health and education to the list.

In the financial arena, integrationists have pushed complementary reforms with even greater fanfare and urgency. The prevailing view in Washington and other Group of Seven (G-7) capitals is that weaknesses in banking systems, prudential regulation, and corporate governance were at the heart of the Asian financial crisis of the late 1990s. Hence the ambitious efforts by the G-7 to establish international codes and standards covering fiscal transparency, monetary and financial policy, banking supervision, data dissemination, corporate governance, and accounting standards. The Financial Stability Forum (FSF)—a G-7 organization with minimal representation from developing nations—has designated 12 of these standards as essential for creating sound financial systems in developing countries. The full FSF compendium includes an additional 59 standards the agency considers "relevant for sound financial systems," bringing the total number of codes to 71. To fend off speculative capital movements, the IMF and the G-7 also typically urge developing countries to accumulate foreign reserves and avoid exchange-rate regimes that differ from a "hard peg" (tying the value of one's currency to that of a more stable currency, such as the U.S. dollar) or a "pure float" (letting the market determine the appropriate exchange rate).

A cynic might wonder whether the point of all these prerequisites is merely to provide easy cover for eventual failure. Integrationists can conveniently blame disappointing growth performance or a financial crisis on "slippage" in the implementation of complementary reforms rather than on a poorly designed liberalization. So if Bangladesh's freer trade policy does not produce a large enough spurt in growth, the World Bank concludes that the problem must involve lagging reforms in public administration or continued "political uncertainty" (always a favorite). And if Argentina gets caught up in a confidence crisis despite significant trade and financial liberalization, the IMF reasons that structural reforms have been inadequate and must be deepened.

Free Trade-Offs

Most (but certainly not all) of the institutional reforms on the integrationist agenda are perfectly sensible, and in a world without financial, administrative, or political constraints, there would be little argument about the need to adopt them. But in the real world, governments face difficult choices over how to deploy their fiscal resources, administrative capabilities, and political capital. Setting institutional priorities to maximize integration into the global economy has real opportunity costs.

Consider some illustrative trade-offs. World Bank trade economist Michael Finger has estimated that a typical developing country must spend $150 million to implement requirements under just three WTO agreements (those on customs valuation, sanitary and phytosanitary measures, and trade-related intellectual property rights). As Finger notes, this sum equals a year's development budget for many least-developed countries. And while the budgetary burden of implementing financial codes and standards has never been fully estimated, it undoubtedly entails a substantial diversion of fiscal and human resources as well. Should governments in developing countries train more bank auditors and accountants, even if those investments mean fewer secondary-school teachers or reduced spending on primary education for girls?

In the area of legal reform, should governments focus their energies on "importing" legal codes and standards or on improving existing domestic legal institutions? In Turkey, a weak coalition government spent several months during 1999 gathering political support for a bill providing foreign investors the protection of international arbitration. But wouldn't a better long-run strategy have involved reforming the existing legal regime for the benefit of foreign and domestic investors alike?

In public health, should governments promote the reverse engineering of patented basic medicines and the importation of low-cost generic drugs from "unauthorized" suppliers, even if doing so means violating WTO rules against such practices? When South Africa passed legislation in 1997 allowing imports of patented AIDS drugs from cheaper sources, the country came under severe pressure from Western governments, which argued that the South African policy conflicted with WTO rules on intellectual property.

How much should politicians spend on social protection policies in view of the fiscal constraints imposed by market "discipline"? Peru's central bank holds foreign reserves equal to 15 months of imports as an insurance policy against the sudden capital outflows that financially open economies often experience. The opportunity cost of this policy amounts to almost 1 percent of gross domestic product annually—more than enough to fund a generous antipoverty program.

How should governments choose their exchange-rate regimes? During the last four decades, virtually every growth boom in the developing world has been accompanied by a controlled depreciation of the domestic currency. Yet financial openness makes it all but impossible to manage the exchange rate.

How should policymakers focus their anticorruption strategies? Should they target the high-level corruption that foreign investors often decry or the petty corruption that affects the poor the most? Perhaps, as the proponents of permanent normal trade relations with China argued in the recent U.S. debate, a government that is forced to protect the rights of foreign investors will become more inclined to protect the rights of its own citizens as well. But this is, at best, a trickledown strategy of institutional reform. Shouldn't reforms target the desired ends directly—whether those ends are the rule of law, improved observance of human rights, or reduced corruption?

The rules for admission into the world economy not only reflect little awareness of development priorities, they are often completely unrelated to sensible economic principles. For instance, WTO agreements on anti-dumping, subsidies and countervailing measures, agriculture, textiles, and trade-related intellectual property rights lack any economic rationale beyond the mercantilist interests of a narrow set of powerful groups in advanced industrial countries. Bilateral and regional trade agreements are typically far worse, as they impose even tighter prerequisites on developing countries in return for crumbs of enhanced "market access." For example, the African Growth and Opportunity Act signed by U.S. President Clinton in May 2000 provides increased access to the U.S. market only if African apparel manufacturers use U.S.-produced fabric and yarns. This restriction severely limits the potential economic spillovers in African countries.

There are similar questions about the appropriateness of financial codes and standards. These codes rely heavily on an Anglo-American style of corporate governance and an arm's-length model of financial development. They close off alternative paths to financial development of the sort that have been followed by many of today's rich countries (for example, Germany, Japan, or South Korea).

In each of these areas, a strategy of "globalization above all" crowds out alternatives that are potentially more development-friendly. Many of the institutional reforms needed for insertion into the world economy can be independently desirable or produce broader economic benefits. But these priorities do not necessarily coincide with the priorities of a comprehensive development agenda.

Asian Myths

Even if the institutional reforms needed to join the international economic community are expensive and preclude investments in other crucial areas, pro-globalization advocates argue that the vast increases in economic growth that invariably result from insertion into the global marketplace will more than compensate for those costs. Take the East Asian tigers or China, the advocates say. Where would they be without international trade and foreign capital flows?

That these countries reaped enormous benefits from their progressive integration into the world economy is undeniable. But look closely at what policies produced those results, and you will find little that resembles today's rule book.

Countries like South Korea and Taiwan had to abide by few international constraints and pay few of the modern costs of integration during their formative growth experience in the 1960s and 1970s. At that time, global trade rules were sparse and economies faced almost none of today's common pressures to open their borders to capital flows. So these countries combined their outward orientation with unorthodox policies: high levels of tariff and nontariff barriers, public ownership of large segments of banking and industry, export subsidies, domestic-content requirements, patent and copyright infringements, and restrictions on capital flows (including on foreign direct investment). Such policies are either precluded by today's trade rules or are highly frowned upon by organizations like the IMF and the World Bank.

China also followed a highly unorthodox two-track strategy, violating practically every rule in the guidebook (including, most notably, the requirement of private property rights). India, which significantly raised its economic growth rate in the early 1980s, remains one of the world's most highly protected economies.

All of these countries liberalized trade gradually, over a period of decades, not years. Significant import liberalization did not occur until after a transition to high economic growth had taken place. And far from wiping the institutional slate clean, all of these nations managed to eke growth out of their existing institutions, imperfect as they may have been. Indeed, when some of the more successful Asian economies gave in to Western pressure to liberalize capital flows rapidly, they were rewarded with the Asian financial crisis.

That is why these countries can hardly be considered poster children for today's global rules. South Korea, China, India, and the other Asian success cases had the freedom to do their own thing, and they used that freedom abundantly. Today's globalizers would be unable to replicate these experiences without running afoul of the IMF or the WTO. The Asian experience highlights a deeper point: A sound overall development strategy that produces high economic growth is far more effective in achieving integration with the world economy than a purely integrationist strategy that relies on openness to work its magic. In other words, the globalizers have it exactly backwards. Integration is the result, not the cause, of economic and social development. A relatively protected economy like Vietnam is integrating with the world economy much more rapidly than an open economy like Haiti because Vietnam, unlike Haiti, has a reasonably functional economy and polity.

Integration into the global economy, unlike tariff rates or capital-account regulations, is not something that policymakers control directly. Telling finance ministers in developing nations that they should increase their "participation in world trade" is as meaningful as telling them that they need to improve technological capabilities—and just as helpful. Policymakers need to know which strategies will produce these results, and whether the specific prescriptions that the current orthodoxy offers are up to the task.

Too Good to Be True

Do lower trade barriers spur greater economic progress? The available studies reveal no systematic relationship between a country's average level of tariff and nontariff barriers and its subsequent economic growth rate. If anything, the evidence for the 1990s indicates a positive relationship between import tariffs and economic growth. The only clear pattern is that countries dismantle their trade restrictions as they grow richer. This finding explains why today's rich countries, with few exceptions, embarked on modern economic growth behind protective barriers but now display low trade barriers.

The absence of a strong negative relationship between trade restrictions and economic growth may seem surprising in view of the ubiquitous claim that trade liberalization promotes higher growth. Indeed, the economics literature is replete with cross-national studies concluding that growth and economic dynamism are strongly linked to more open trade policies. A particularly influential study finds that economies that are "open," by the study's own definition, grew 2.45 percentage points faster annually than closed ones—an enormous difference.

Upon closer look, however, such studies turn out to be unreliable. In a detailed review of the empirical literature, University of Maryland economist Francisco Rodriguez and I have found a major gap between the results that economists have actually obtained and the policy conclusions they have typically drawn. For example, in many cases economists blame poor growth on the government's failure to liberalize trade policies, when the true culprits are ineffective institutions, geographic determinants (such as location in a tropical region), or inappropriate macroeconomic policies (such as an overvalued exchange rate). Once these misdiagnoses are corrected, any meaningful relationship across countries between the level of trade barriers and economic growth evaporates.

The evidence on the benefits of liberalizing capital flows is even weaker. In theory, the appeal of capital mobility seems obvious: If capital is free to enter (and leave) markets based on the potential return on investment, the result will be an efficient allocation of global resources. But in reality, financial markets are inherently unstable, subject to bubbles (rational or otherwise), panics, shortsightedness, and self-fulfilling prophecies. There is plenty of evidence that financial liberalization is often followed by financial crash—just ask Mexico, Thailand, or Turkey—while there is little convincing evidence to suggest that higher rates of economic growth follow capital-account liberalization.

Perhaps the most disingenuous argument in favor of liberalizing international financial flows is that the threat of massive and sudden capital movements serves to discipline policymakers in developing nations who might otherwise manage their economies irresponsibly. In other words, governments might be less inclined to squander their societies' resources if such actions would spook foreign lenders. In practice, however, the discipline argument falls apart. Behavior in international capital markets is dominated by mood swings unrelated to fundamentals. In good times, a government with a chronic fiscal deficit has an easier time financing its spending when it can borrow funds from investors abroad; witness Russia prior to 1998 or Argentina in the 1990s. And in bad times, governments may be forced to adopt inappropriate policies in order to conform to the biases of foreign investors; witness the excessively restrictive monetary and fiscal policies in much of East Asia in the immediate aftermath of the Asian financial crisis.

A key reason why Malaysia was able to recover so quickly after the imposition of capital controls in September 1998 was that Prime Minister Mahathir Mohamad resisted the high interest rates and tight fiscal policies that South Korea, Thailand, and Indonesia adopted at the behest of the International Monetary Fund.

Growth Begins at Home

Well-trained economists are justifiably proud of the textbook case in favor of free trade. For all the theory's simplicity, it is one of our profession's most significant achievements. However, in their zeal to promote the virtues of trade, the most ardent proponents are peddling a cartoon version of the argument, vastly overstating the effectiveness of economic openness as a tool for fostering development. Such claims only endanger broad public acceptance of the real article because they unleash unrealistic expectations about the benefits of free trade. Neither economic theory nor empirical evidence guarantees that deep trade liberalization will deliver higher economic growth. Economic openness and all its accouterments do not deserve the priority they typically receive in the development strategies pushed by leading multilateral organizations.

Countries that have achieved long-term economic growth have usually combined the opportunities offered by world markets with a growth strategy that mobilizes the capabilities of domestic institutions and investors. Designing such a growth strategy is both harder and easier than implementing typical integration policies. It is harder because the binding constraints on growth are usually country specific and do not respond well to standardized recipes. But it is easier because once those constraints are targeted, relatively simple policy changes can yield enormous economic payoffs and start a virtuous cycle of growth and additional reform.

Unorthodox innovations that depart from the integration rule book are typically part and parcel of such strategies. Public enterprises during the Meiji restoration in Japan; township and village enterprises in China; an export processing zone in Mauritius; generous tax incentives for priority investments in Taiwan; extensive credit subsidies in South Korea; infant-industry protection in Brazil during the 1960s and 1970s—these are some of the innovations that have been instrumental in kick-starting investment and growth in the past. None came out of a Washington economist's tool kit.

Few of these experiments have worked as well when transplanted to other settings, only underscoring the decisive importance of local conditions. To be effective, development strategies need to be tailored to prevailing domestic institutional strengths. There is simply no alternative to a home-grown business plan. Policymakers who look to Washington and financial markets for the answers are condemning themselves to mimicking the conventional wisdom du jour, and to eventual disillusionment.

CHAPTER 12

FOREIGN AID PROMOTES DEVELOPMENT *v.* FOREIGN AID IS INEFFECTIVE

Foreign Aid Promotes Development

Advocate: David Dollar

Source: "Eyes Wide Open: On the Targeted Use of Foreign Aid," *Harvard International Review* 25 (Spring 2003): 48–52.

Foreign Aid Is Ineffective

Advocate: William Easterly

Source: "The Cartel of Good Intentions," *Foreign Policy* (July/August 2002): 40–44.

In the last ten years, governments and multilateral lending agencies have made important changes in their thinking about foreign aid. For most of the postwar period, agencies based the rationale for foreign aid on an economic model called the "finance gap." According to this approach, poverty was a result of insufficient physical and human capital. Creating such capital by investing in manufacturing industries would thus generate growth and rising per capita incomes. Lending agencies encouraged governments to develop investment plans and then calculate the amount of local savings they had available. The difference between planned investment and available savings was the finance gap, which multilateral agencies filled with foreign aid.

Lenders became disenchanted with this aid model in the 1990s. Almost four decades of experience failed to produce compelling results. World Bank studies found little relationship between the amount of foreign aid a country received and its subsequent economic performance. Although foreign aid contributed to growth in some countries, there was little evidence that the postwar regime was successful overall. Growing disenchantment, in conjunction with the end of the Cold War, led governments to reduce their aid expenditures and rethink the underlying rationale for aid. As governments began to increase aid in the wake of the 9/11 terrorist attacks, multilateral agencies searched for a framework that would ensure that aid expenditures had a positive impact.

FOREIGN AID PROMOTES DEVELOPMENT

Most advocates of aid suggest that aid can work if it targets the right things. A key conclusion of the recent reevaluation was that aid had been directed toward the wrong goal. Rather than focus on the creation of physical and human capital, governments should use aid instead to build high-quality institutions. Rather than thinking of foreign aid as an input into manufacturing, as the finance gap model did, this new approach conceives of aid as an input into governance. By helping create effective institutions, aid helps to create the infrastructure within which individuals can make the investments that will drive economic development. Moreover, by providing aid to societies where governance is already strong, the chances that the aid is misdirected or consumed by corrupt officials are reduced substantially.

David Dollar, a World Bank official, develops this argument here. He argues that foreign aid must promote high-quality institutions. Institutions that enable the state to act effectively within society are of particular importance. Dollar argues that property rights need protection, that state bureaucracies must be able to provide essential public services.

FOREIGN AID IS INEFFECTIVE

Other participants argued that the problem lies not in what aid targets, but in the structure of the foreign aid regime itself. William Easterly, a professor of economics at New York University, is the most prominent advocate of this position. Easterly argues that a central limitation of aid's effectiveness lies in the multilateral organizations that manage aid provision. Focusing on what he calls the "foreign aid cartel," Easterly argues that the bureaucratic agencies responsible for delivering and administering aid are accountable solely to politicians in wealthy donor countries. They therefore concentrate on projects that please their constituents rather than on projects that would generate a higher return in developing societies. Making foreign aid more effective, Easterly argues, requires fundamental reform of the international organizations. These organizations must be made accountable to their clients in developing countries. He suggests that bringing market competition into the distribution of foreign aid could create such accountability.

POINTS TO PONDER

1. Dollar stresses the importance of high-quality institutions. What specific institutions does he have in mind? Why does aid have a greater impact on countries with high-quality institutions?

2. Does Dollar believe that traditional forms of aid conditionality can be used to promote high-quality institutions? What are the consequences of this for the distribution of aid across countries?

3. What does Easterly mean by the "foreign aid cartel" and why does he call it that? What impact does this cartel have on the projects that aid agencies fund?

4. What solutions does Easterly propose for the problems created by the aid cartel?

5. Which author do you believe offers the best strategy for making aid more effective?

David Dollar

Eyes Wide Open: On the Targeted Use of Foreign Aid

Conventional wisdom on international development holds that "the rich get richer while the poor get poorer." This saying does not capture exactly what has happened between the rich and poor regions of the world over the past century, but it comes pretty close. In general, poor areas of the world have not become poorer, but their per capita income has grown quite slowly. On the other hand, income in the club of rich countries (Western Europe, the United States, Canada, Japan, Australia, and New Zealand), has increased at a much more rapid pace. As a result, by 1980 an unprecedented level of worldwide inequality had developed. The richest fifth of the world's population—which essentially corresponds to the population of the rich countries—produced and consumed 70 percent of the world's goods and services, while the poorest fifth of the global population, in contrast, held only two percent.

There has been a modest decline in global inequality since 1980 because two large poor countries—China and India—have outperformed the rich countries economically. This shift represents an interesting change that has important lessons for development. However, if one ignores the performance of China and India, much of the rest of the developing world still languishes, and there continues to be an appalling gap between rich countries and poor countries.

Inequality within countries is an important issue as well, but it pales in comparison with inequality between countries across the world. A homeless person pan-handling for two US dollars a day on the streets of Boston would sit in the top half of the world income distribution. Without traveling through rural parts of the developing world, it is difficult to comprehend the magnitude of this gap, which is not just one of income. Life expectancy in the United States has risen to 77 years whereas in Zambia it has fallen to 38 years. Infant mortality is down to seven deaths per 1,000 live births in the United States, compared to 115 in Zambia. How can these gaps in living standards be understood? And, more importantly, what can be done about it?

Traditionally, one part of the answer to the latter question has been foreign aid. Since the end of the Cold War, aid has been in decline, both in terms of volume (down to about 0.2 percent of the gross national product of the rich countries) and popularity as an effective policy. However, since before September 11, 2001, aid has made something of a comeback, with a number of European countries, notably the United Kingdom, arguing for the importance of addressing global poverty by implementing reforms to make aid more effective. Since September 11, the US government has shown renewed interest as well.

What can come from this renewed interest in foreign aid? Foreign aid bureaucracies have a long history of mistaking symptoms for causes. If this trend continues uncorrected, then it is unlikely that greater volumes of aid will make much of a dent in global poverty and inequality. On the other hand there is much more evidence about what leads to successful development and how aid can assist in that process. Thus, the potential exists to make aid a much more important tool in the fight against poverty. My argument on this matter is comprised of four points.

First, countries are poor primarily because of weak underlying institutions and policies. Features such as lack of capital, poor education, or absence of modern industry are symptoms rather than causes of underdevelopment. Aid focused on these symptoms has not had much lasting impact.

Second, local institutions in developing countries are persistent, and foreign aid donors have little influence over them. Efforts to reform countries through conditionality of aid from the Bretton Woods organizations have generally failed to bring about lasting reform within developing country institutions. It is difficult to predict when serious movements will emerge, but the positive developments in global poverty in the past 20 years have been the result of home-grown reform movements in countries such as China, India, Uganda, and Vietnam.

Third, foreign aid has had a positive effect in these and other cases, and arguably its most useful role has been to support learning at the state and community level. Countries and communities can learn from each other, but there are no simple blueprints of institutional reform that can be transferred from one location to the next. Thus, helping countries analyze, implement, and evaluate options is useful, whereas promoting a "best-practice" approach to each issue through conditionality is not.

Fourth, the financial aspect of foreign aid is also important. In poor countries that have made significant steps toward improving their institutions and policies, financial aid accelerates growth and poverty reduction and helps cement popular support for reform. Hence, large-scale financial assistance needs to be "selective," targeting countries that can put aid to effective use building schools, roads, and other aspects of social infrastructure.

Institutions and Policies

Economists have long underestimated the importance of state institutions in explaining the differences in economic performance between countries. Recent work in economic history and development is beginning to rectify this oversight. In their 2001 study, "Colonial Origins of Comparative Development: An Empirical Investigation," Daron Acemoglu, Simon Johnson, and James Robinson find that much of the variation in per capita income across countries can be explained by differences in institutional quality. They look at a number of different institutional measures, which generally capture the extent to which the state effectively provides a framework in which property is secure and markets can operate. Thus, indicators of institutional quality try to measure people's confidence in their property rights and the government bureaucracy's ability to provide public services relatively free of interest group appropriation and corruption. All countries have some problems with appropriation and corruption, so the practical issue is the extent of these problems. While these differences are inherently hard to measure, some contrasts are obvious; there is, for example, no doubt that Singapore or Finland has a better environment of property rights and clean government than Mobutu's Zaire or many similar locations in the developing world.

Differences in institutional quality explain much of the variation in per capita income across countries, an empirical result that is very intuitive. In a poor institutional environment, households must focus on day-to-day subsistence. The state fails to provide the complementary infrastructure—such as roads and schools—necessary to encourage long-term investment, while the lack of confidence in property rights further discourages entrepreneurial activity. In this type of setting, any surplus accumulated by individuals is more likely to fund capital flight, investment abroad, or emigration than to be reinvested in the local economy.

In addition, there is evidence that access to markets is also important as well for economic growth. If a region is cut off from larger markets either because of its natural geography or because of man-made trade barriers, then the incentives for entrepreneurial activity and investment are again reduced. In 1999, Jeffrey Frankel and David Romer cautiously concluded that the converse holds as well: better trading opportunities do lead to faster growth. There is still some debate among economists about the relative importance of institutions and trade, but it seems likely that both are important and that in fact they complement each other. Several years ago, Kenneth Sokoloff found that rates of invention were extremely responsive to the expansion of markets during the early industrialization of the United States by examining how patenting activity varied over time and with the extension of navigable waterways. For example, as the construction of the Erie Canal progressed westward across the state of New York, patenting per capita rose sharply county-by-county. The United States had a good system of protecting these intellectual properties, and the development of transport links to broader markets stimulated individuals and firms to invest more in developing new technologies.

Indeed, looking back over the past century, locations with access to markets and good property rights have generally prospered, while locations disconnected from markets and with poor property rights have remained poor. Many of the features that we associate with underdevelopment are therefore results of these underlying weaknesses in institutions and policies. In such environments, there is little incentive to invest in equipment or education and develop modern industry.

But these symptoms have often been mistaken by aid donors as causes of underdevelopment. If low levels of investment are a problem, then give poor countries foreign aid to invest in capital. If a lack of education is a problem, finance broad expansion of schools. If modern industry is absent, erect infant-industry protection to allow firms to develop behind a protected wall. All of these approaches have been pushed by aid donors. In poor countries with weak underlying institutions, however, the results have not been impressive.

Over several decades, Zambia received an amount of foreign aid that would have made every Zambian rich had it achieved the kind of return that is normal in developed economies. If lack of capital was the key problem in Zambia, then that was certainly addressed by massive amounts of aid; but the result was virtually no increase in the country's per capita income. Similarly, large amounts of aid targeted at expanding education in Africa yielded little measurable improvement in achievement or skills. Donors financed power plants, steel mills, and even shoe factories behind high levels of protection, but again there was virtually no return on these investments.

The recent thinking in economic history and development suggests that these efforts failed because they were aimed at symptoms rather than at underlying causes. If a government is very corrupt or dominated by powerful special interests, then giving it money, or schools, or shoe factories will not promote lasting growth and development. These findings suggest that much of the frustration about foreign aid comes from the many failed efforts to develop social infrastructure in weak institutional environments where governments and communities cannot make effective use of these resources—not from the intrinsic inability of aid itself to generate positive results.

There are a number of important caveats about these findings on aid effectiveness. First, humanitarian or food aid is a different story. When there is a famine or humanitarian crisis, international donors have shown that they can bring in short-term relief effectively. Second, there are some health interventions that can be delivered in a weak institutional environment. In much of Africa, donors have collaborated to eradicate river blindness, a disease that can be controlled by taking a single pill each year. That intervention—and certain types of vaccinations—can be carried out in almost any environment. But many other social services require an effective institutional delivery system; other health projects in countries with weak institutions have tended to fail without producing any benefits.

Persistent Institutions

A second important finding from recent work in economic history is that institutions are persistent. Last year, Stanley Engerman and Sokoloff showed how differences in the natural endowments of South and North American colonies centuries ago led to the development of different institutions in the two environments. Furthermore, many of these institutional differences have persisted to this day. If institutions are important and if they typically change slowly over time, then it is easy to understand the pattern of rising global inequality over the past century. Locations with better institutions have consistently grown faster than ones with poor institutions, widening inequalities. Because it is relatively rare for a country to switch from poor institutions and policies to good ones, countries that began at a disadvantage only fell further behind in the years that followed.

The importance of good institutions and policies for development in general and for aid effectiveness in particular is something that donors have gradually realized through experience and research. International donors' first instincts were to make improved institutions and policies a condition of their assistance. In the 1980s in particular, donors loaded assistance packages with large numbers of conditions concerning specific institutional and policy reforms. Some World Bank loans, for example, had more than 100 specific reform conditions. However, the persistence of institutions and policies hints at the difficulty of changing them. There are always powerful interests who benefit from bad policies, and donor conditionality has proved largely ineffective at overcoming these interest groups. A 2000 study that I coauthored with Jakob Svensson examined a large sample of World Bank structural adjustment programs to find that the success or failure of reform can largely be predicted by underlying institutional features of the country, including whether or not the government is democratically elected and how long the executive has been in power. Governments are often willing to sign aid agreements with large amounts of conditionality, but in many low-income countries the government is either uninterested in implementing reform or politically blocked from doing so. "Aid and Reform in Africa," a set of case studies written by African scholars on 10 African states, reaches similar conclusions: institutional and policy reform is driven primarily by domestic movements and not by outside agents.

Prospects for Reform

The good news is that a number of important developing countries have accomplished considerable reforms in the past two decades. In 1980, about 60 percent of the world's extreme poor—those living on less than one U.S. dollar per day—lived in just two countries: China and India. At that time, neither country seemed a particularly likely candidate for reform. Both had rather poor property rights and government efficiency according to the measures used in cross-country studies, and both were extremely closed to the world market. Over the past two decades, however, China has introduced truly revolutionary reforms, restoring property rights over land, opening the economy to foreign trade and investment, and gradually making the legal and regulatory changes that have permitted the domestic private sector to become the main engine of growth. Reforms in India have not been quite as dramatic, but have still been very successful at reducing the government's heavy-handed management of the economy and dismantling the protectionist trade regime. Among low-income countries, there have been a number of other notable reformers as well; Uganda is a good example in Africa, and Vietnam in Southeast Asia.

The general point about all of these low-income reformers is that outside donors were not particularly important at the start of these reform efforts. These movements are home-grown and each has an interesting and distinct political-economy story behind it. Once these reforms began, however, foreign assistance played an important supporting role in each case. Institutional reform involves much social and political experimentation. The way that China has gradually strengthened private property rights is an excellent example, as is the way India reformed its energy sector. Foreign assistance can help governments and communities examine options, implement innovations, and evaluate them. To do this effectively, donor agencies need to have good technical staff, worldwide experience, and an open mind about what might work in different circumstances.

The World Bank is often criticized for giving the same advice everywhere, but this simply is not true. World Bank reports on different countries show that the World Bank typically makes quite different recommendations in different countries. The criticism that comes from government officials in the developing world is a different and more telling one: that the World Bank tends to make a single strong recommendation on each issue, instead of helping clients analyze the pros and cons of different options so that communities can make up their own minds about what to do. We do not know much about institutional change, so it is more useful to promote community learning than to push particular institutional models.

For example, the Education, Health, and Nutrition Program—known by its Spanish acronym, PROGRESA—is a successful program of cash transfers that encourages poor families to keep their children in school that was developed and evaluated in Mexico without any donor support. A number of donors now have helped communities in Central American countries to implement similar programs. In each case, communities need to tailor the program to their particular situation. Systematic re-evaluation is important because the same idea will not necessarily work everywhere. But this is a good example of how donors can promote learning across countries and support institutional change by presenting a variety of reform options for developing countries to follow.

Money Matters

While supporting country and community learning is probably the most useful role for aid, and the one that will have the largest impact, there is still a role for large-scale financial aid. Studies have shown that there is little relationship between aid amounts and growth rates in developing countries, but there is a rather strong relationship between growth and the interaction of aid and economic policies. This finding, as well as microeconomic evidence about individual projects, suggests that the growth effect of aid is greater in countries with reasonably good institutions and policies. The success of the Marshall Plan is a classic historical example. More recently, states such as Uganda show that the combination of substantial reform and large-scale aid goes together with rapid growth and poverty reduction. In a poor institutional environment, however, large-scale aid seems to have little lasting economic impact and may even make things worse by sustaining a bad government.

What follows from this is that aid is going to have more impact on poverty reduction if it is targeted to countries that are poor and have favorable institutions and policies. This philosophy underlies a number of new initiatives in foreign aid—European countries, including the United Kingdom and the Netherlands, have reformed and expanded their aid program along these lines. The new U.S. Millennium Challenge Account is based on these principles as well.

Using aid to support learning and being selective in the allocation of large-scale financial resources are linked. When donors tried to push large amounts of money into weak institutional environments, they naturally wanted to have large numbers of conditions dictating how institutions and policies would change. But this neither promoted effective learning nor led to good use of money. The new model argues for much less conditionality—encouraging countries and communities to figure out what works for them—but retaining some form of selectivity in the allocation of financial resources.

Keeping in mind the persistence of institutions and the difficulty of changing them, one should have modest hopes for what foreign aid can accomplish. But as long as there are countries and communities around the world struggling to change, the international community must support them. Afghanistan today is a good example. The country is trying to develop new institutions at the national and local levels, and the world has a big stake in helping it succeed. The international community does not know for sure what will work, but outsiders dictating a new set of institutions will almost certainly fail. On the other hand, donor agencies can help both national and local governments learn about options, implement policies, evaluate results, and re-design if necessary. As a sound institutional framework develops, there will be increasing scope for large-scale funding of roads, schools, and other social infrastructure. The effort may fail. No doubt the lack of good institutions in Afghanistan reflects extensive historical and political factors that will be hard to overcome. It is important to go in with eyes wide open; trying to reform aid based on what we know is preferable to giving up on aid and closing our eyes to the massive poverty that remains throughout the developing world.

William Easterly
The Cartel of Good Intentions

The world's richest governments have pledged to boost financial aid to the developing world. So why won't poor nations reap the benefits? Because in the way stands a bloated, unaccountable foreign aid bureaucracy out of touch with sound economics. The solution: Subject the foreign assistance business to the forces of market competition.

The mere mention of a "cartel" usually strikes fear in the hearts and wallets of consumers and regulators around the globe. Though the term normally evokes images of greedy oil producers or murderous drug lords, a new, more well-intentioned cartel has emerged on the global scene. Its members are the world's leading foreign aid organizations, which constitute a near monopoly relative to the powerless poor.

This state of affairs helps explain why the global foreign aid bureaucracy has run amok in recent years. Consider the steps that beleaguered government officials in low-income countries must take to receive foreign aid. Among other things, they must prepare a participatory Poverty Reduction Strategy Paper (PRSP)—a detailed plan for uplifting the destitute that the World Bank and International Monetary Fund (IMF) require before granting debt forgiveness and new loans. This document in turn must adhere to the World Bank's Comprehensive Development Framework, a 14-point checklist covering everything from lumber policy to labor practices. And the list goes on: Policymakers seeking aid dollars must also prepare a Financial Information Management System report, a Report on Observance of Standards and Codes, a Medium Term Expenditure Framework, and a Debt Sustainability Analysis for the Enhanced Heavily Indebted Poor Countries Initiative. Each document can run to hundreds of pages and consume months of preparation time. For example, Niger's recently completed PRSP is 187 pages long, took 15 months to prepare, and sets out spending for a 2002–05 poverty reduction plan with such detailed line items as $17,600 a year on "sensitizing population to traffic circulation."

Meanwhile, the U.N. International Conference on Financing for Development held in Monterrey, Mexico, in March 2002 produced a document— "the Monterrey Consensus"—that has a welcome emphasis on partnership between rich donor and poor recipient nations. But it's somewhat challenging for poor countries to carry out the 73 actions that the document recommends, including such ambitions as establishing democracy, equality between boys and girls, and peace on Earth.

Visitors to the World Bank Web site will find 31 major development topics listed there, each with multiple subtopics. For example, browsers can explore 13 subcategories under "Social Development," including indige-nous peoples, resettlement, and culture in sustainable development. This last item in turn includes the music industry in Africa, the preservation of cultural artifacts, a seven-point framework for action, and—well, you get the idea.

It's not that aid bureaucrats are bad; in fact, many smart, hardworking, dedicated professionals toil away in the world's top aid agencies. But the per-verse incentives they face explain the organizations' obtuse behavior. The international aid bureaucracy will never work properly under the conditions that make it operate like a cartel—the cartel of good intentions.

All Together Now

Cartels thrive when customers have little opportunity to complain or to find alternative suppliers. In its heyday during the 1970s, for example, the Organization of the Petroleum Exporting Countries (OPEC) could dictate severe terms to customers; it was only when more non-OPEC oil exporters emerged that the cartel's power weakened. In the foreign aid business, customers (i.e., poor citizens in developing countries) have few chances to express their needs, yet they cannot exit the system. Meanwhile, rich nations paying the aid bills are clueless about what those customers want. Nongovernmental organizations (NGOs) can hold aid institutions to task on only a few high-visibility issues, such as conspicuous environmental destruc-tion. Under these circumstances, even while foreign aid agencies make good-faith efforts to consult their clients, these agencies remain accountable mainly to themselves.

The typical aid agency forces governments seeking its money to work exclusively with that agency's own bureaucracy—its project appraisal and selection apparatus, its economic and social analysts, its procurement proce-dures, and its own interests and objectives. Each aid agency constitutes a mini-monopoly, and the collection of all such monopolies forms a cartel. The foreign aid community also resembles a cartel in that the IMF, World Bank, regional development banks, European Union, United Nations, and bilateral aid agencies all agree to "coordinate" their efforts. The customers therefore have even less opportunity to find alternative aid suppliers. And the entry of new suppliers into the foreign assistance business is difficult because large aid agencies must be sponsored either by an individual government (as in the case of national agencies, such as the U.S. Agency for International Development) or by an international agreement (as in the case of multilateral agencies, such as the World Bank). Most NGOs are too small to make much of a difference.

Of course, cartels always display fierce jostling for advantage and even mutual enmity among members. That explains why the aid community concludes that "to realize our increasingly reciprocal ambitions, a lot of hard work, compromises and true goodwill must come into play." Oops, wait, that's a quote from a recent OPEC meeting. The foreign aid community simply maintains that "better coordination among international financial institutions is needed." However, the difficulties of organizing parties with diverse objectives and interests and the inherent tensions in a cartel render such coordination forever elusive. Doomed attempts at coordination create the worst of all worlds—no central planner exists to tell each agency what to do, nor is there any market pressure from customers to reward successful agencies and discipline unsuccessful ones.

As a result, aid organizations mindlessly duplicate services for the world's poor. Some analysts see this duplication as a sign of competition to satisfy the customer—not so. True market competition should eliminate duplication: When you choose where to eat lunch, the restaurant next door usually doesn't force you to sit down for an extra meal. But things are different in the world of foreign aid, where a team from the U.S. Agency for International Development produced a report on corruption in Uganda in 2001, unaware that British analysts had produced a report on the same topic six months earlier. The Tanzanian government churns out more than 2,400 reports annually for its various donors, who send the poor country some 1,000 missions each year. (Borrowing terminology from missionaries who show the locals the one true path to heaven, "missions" are visits of aid agency staff to developing countries to discuss desirable government policy.) No wonder, then, that in the early 1990s, Tanzania was implementing 15 separate stand-alone health-sector projects funded by 15 different donors. Even small bilateral aid agencies plant their flags everywhere. Were the endless meetings and staff hours worth the effort for the Senegalese government to receive $38,957 from the Finnish Ministry for Foreign Affairs Development Cooperation in 2001?

By forming a united front and duplicating efforts, the aid cartel is also able to diffuse blame among its various members when economic conditions in recipient countries don't improve according to plan. Should observers blame the IMF for fiscal austerity that restricts funding for worthy programs, or should they fault the World Bank for failing to preserve high-return areas from public expenditure cuts? Are the IMF and World Bank too tough or too lax in enforcing conditions? Or are the regional development banks too inflexible (or too lenient) in their conditions for aid? Should bilateral aid agencies be criticized for succumbing to national and commercial interests, or should multilateral agencies be condemned for applying a "one size fits all" reform program to all countries? Like squabbling children, aid organizations find safety in numbers. Take Argentina. From 1980 to 2001, the Argentine government received 33 structural adjustment loans from the IMF and World Bank, all under the watchful eye of the U.S. Treasury. Ultimately, then, is

Argentina's ongoing implosion the fault of the World Bank, the IMF, or the Treasury Department? The buck stops nowhere in the world of development assistance. Each party can point fingers at the others, and bewildered observers don't know whom to blame—making each agency less accountable.

The $3,521 Quandary

Like any good monopoly, the cartel of good intentions seeks to maximize net revenues. Indeed, if any single objective has characterized the aid community since its inception, it is an obsession with increasing the total aid money mobilized. Traditionally, aid agencies justify this goal by identifying the aid "requirements" needed to achieve a target rate of economic growth, calculating the difference between existing aid and the requirements, and then advocating a commensurate aid increase. In 1951, the U.N. Group of Experts calculated exactly how much aid poor countries needed to achieve an annual growth rate of 2 percent per capita, coming up with an amount that would equal $20 billion in today's dollars. Similarly, the economist Walt Rostow calculated in 1960 the aid increase (roughly double the aid levels at the time) that would lift Asia, Africa, and Latin America into self-sustaining growth. ("Self-sustaining" meant that aid would no longer be necessary 10 to 15 years after the increase.) Despite the looming expiration of the 15-year aid window, then World Bank President Robert McNamara called for a doubling of aid in 1973. The call for doubling was repeated at the World Bank in its 1990 "World Development Report." Not to be outdone, current World Bank President James Wolfensohn is now advocating a doubling of aid.

The cartel's efforts have succeeded: Total assistance flows to developing countries have doubled several times since the early days of large-scale foreign aid. (Meanwhile, the World Bank's staff increased from 657 people in 1959–60 to some 10,000 today.) In fact, if all foreign aid given since 1950 had been invested in U.S. Treasury bills, the cumulative assets of poor countries by 2001 from foreign aid alone would have amounted to $2.3 trillion. This aid may have helped achieve such important accomplishments as lower infant mortality and rising literacy throughout the developing world. And high growth in aid-intensive countries like Botswana and Uganda is something to which aid agencies can (and do) point. The growth outcome in most aid recipients, however, has been extremely disappointing. For example, on average, aid-intensive African nations saw growth decline despite constant increases in aid as a percentage of their income.

Aid agencies always claim that their main goal is to reduce the number of poor people in the world, with poverty defined as an annual income below $365. To this end, the World Bank's 2002 aid accounting estimates that an extra $1 billion in overseas development assistance would lift more than 284,000 people out of poverty. (This claim has appeared prominently

in the press and has been repeated in other government reports on aid effectiveness.) If these figures are correct, however, then the additional annual
aid spending per person lifted out of poverty (whose annual income is less
than $365) comes to $3,521. Of course, aid agencies don't follow their own
logic to this absurd conclusion—common sense says that aid should help
everyone and not just target those who can stagger across the minimum
poverty threshold. Regrettably, this claim for aid's effect on poverty has
more to do with the aid bureaucracy's desperate need for good publicity
than with sound economics.

A Framework for Failure

To the extent that anyone monitors the performance of global aid agencies,
it is the politicians and the public in rich nations. Aid agencies therefore
strive to produce outputs (projects, loans, etc.) that these audiences can
easily observe, even if such outputs provide low economic returns for recipient nations. Conversely, aid bureaucrats don't try as hard to produce less
visible, high-return outputs. This emphasis on visibility results in shiny
showcase projects, countless international meetings and summits, glossy
reports for public consumption, and the proliferation of "frameworks" and
strategy papers. Few are concerned about whether the showcase projects
endure beyond the ribbon-cutting ceremony or if all those meetings,
frameworks, and strategies produce anything of value.

This quest for visibility explains why donors like to finance new, high-
profile capital investment projects yet seem reluctant to fund operating
expenses and maintenance after high-profile projects are completed. The
resulting problem is a recurrent theme in the World Bank's periodic reports
on Africa. In 1981, the bank's Africa study concluded that "vehicles and
equipment frequently lie idle for lack of spare parts, repairs, gasoline, or
other necessities. Schools lack operating funds for salaries and teaching
materials, and agricultural research stations have difficulty keeping up field
trials. Roads, public buildings, and processing facilities suffer from lack of
maintenance." Five years later, another study of Africa found that "road
maintenance crews lack fuel and bitumen . . . teachers lack books . . . [and]
health workers have no medicines to distribute." In 1986, the Word Bank
declared that in Africa, "schools are now short of books, clinics lack medicines, and infrastructure maintenance is avoided." Meanwhile, a recent study
for a number of different poor countries estimated that the return on spending on educational instructional materials was up to 14 times higher than the
return on spending on physical facilities.

And then there are the frameworks. In 1999, World Bank President
James Wolfensohn unveiled his Comprehensive Development Framework,
a checklist of 14 items, each with multiple subitems. The framework covers

clean government, property rights, finance, social safety nets, education, health, water, the environment, the spoken word and the arts, roads, cities, the countryside, microcredit, tax policy, and motherhood. (Somehow, macro-economic policy was omitted.) Perhaps this framework explains why the World Bank says management has simultaneously "refocused and broadened the development agenda." Yet even Wolfensohn seems relatively restrained compared with the framework being readied for the forthcoming U.N. World Summit on Sustainable Development in Johannesburg in late August 2002, where 185 "action recommendations"—covering everything from efficient use of cow dung to harmonized labeling of chemicals—await unsuspecting delegates.

Of course, the Millennium Development Goals (MDGs) are the real 800-pound gorilla of foreign aid frameworks. The representatives of planet Earth agreed on these goals at yet another U.N. conference in September 2000. The MDGs call for the simultaneous achievement of multiple targets by 2015, involving poverty, hunger, infant and maternal mortality, primary education, clean water, contraceptive use, HIV/AIDS, gender equality, the environment, and an ill-defined "partnership for development." These are all worthy causes, of course, yet would the real development customers necessarily choose to spend their scarce resources to attain these particular objectives under this particular timetable? Economic principles dictate that greater effort should be devoted to goals with low costs and high benefits, and less effort to goals where the costs are prohibitive relative to the benefits. But the "do everything" approach of the MDGs suggests that the aid bureaucracy feels above such trade-offs. As a result, government officials in recipient countries and the foreign aid agency's own frontline workers gradually go insane trying to keep up with pro-liferating objectives—each of which is deemed Priority Number One.

All Payin', No Gain

A 2002 World Bank technical study found that a doubling of aid flows is required for the world to meet the U.N. goals. The logic is somewhat circular, however, since a World Bank guidebook also stipulates that increasing aid is undoubtedly "a primary function of targets set by the international donor community such as the [Millennium] Development Goals." Thus increased aid becomes self-perpetuating—both cause and effect.

Foreign Aid and Abet

Pity the poor aid bureaucracy that must maintain support for foreign assistance while bad news is breaking out everywhere. Aid agencies have thus perfected the art of smoothing over unpleasant realities with diplomatic language. A war is deemed a "conflict-related reallocation of resources." Countries run by homicidal warlords like those in Liberia or Somalia are "low-income countries under stress." Nations where presidents loot the treasury experience "governance issues." The meaning of other aid community jargon, like "investment climate," remains elusive. The investment climate will be stormy in the morning, gradually clearing in the afternoon with scattered expropriations.

Another typical spin-control technique is to answer any criticism by acknowledging that, "Indeed, we aid agencies used to make that mistake, but now we have corrected it." This defense is hard to refute, since it is much more difficult to evaluate the present than the past. (One only doubts that the sinner has now found true religion from the knowledge of many previous conversions.) Recent conversions supposedly include improved coordination among donors, a special focus on poverty alleviation, and renewed economic reform efforts in African countries. And among the most popular concepts the aid community has recently discovered is "selectivity"—the principle that aid will only work in countries with good economic policies and efficient, squeaky-clean institutions. The moment of aid donors' conversion on this point supposedly came with the end of the Cold War, but in truth, selectivity (and other "new" ideas) has been a recurrent aid theme over the last 40 years.

Unfortunately, evidence of a true conversion on selectivity remains mixed. Take Kenya, where President Daniel arap Moi has mismanaged the economy since 1978. Moi has consistently failed to keep conditions on the 19 economic reform loans his government obtained from the World Bank and IMF (described by one NGO as "financing corruption and repression") since he took office. How might international aid organizations explain the selectivity guidelines that awarded President Moi yet another reform loan from the World Bank and another from the IMF in 2000, the same year prominent members of Moi's government appeared on a corruption "list of shame" issued by Kenya's parliament? Since then, Moi has again failed to deliver on his economic reform promises, and international rating agencies still rank the Kenyan government among the world's most corrupt and lawless. Ever delicate, a 2002 IMF report conceded that "efforts to bring the program back on track have been only partially successful" in Kenya. More systematically, however, a recent cross-country survey revealed no difference in government ratings on democracy, public service delivery, rule of law, and corruption between those countries that received IMF and World Bank reform loans in 2001 and those that did not. Perhaps the foreign aid community applies the selectivity principle a bit selectively.

Dismantling the Cartel

How can the cartel of good intentions be reformed so that foreign aid might actually reach and benefit the world's poor? Clearly, a good dose of humility is in order, considering all the bright ideas that have failed in the past.

Moreover, those of us in the aid industry should not be so arrogant to think we are the main determinants of whether low-income countries develop— poor nations must accomplish that mainly on their own.

Still, if aid is to have some positive effect, the aid community cannot remain stuck in the same old bureaucratic rut. Perhaps using market mechanisms for foreign aid is a better approach. While bureaucratic cartels supply too many goods for which there is little demand and too few goods for which there is much demand, markets are about matching supply and demand. Cartels are all about "coordination," whereas markets are about the decentralized matching of customers and suppliers.

One option is to break the link between aid money and the obligatory use of a particular agency's bureaucracy. Foreign assistance agencies could put part of their resources into a common pool devoted to helping countries with acceptably pro-development governments. Governments would compete for the "pro-development" seal of approval, but donors should compete, too. Recipient nations could take the funds and work with any agency they choose. This scenario would minimize duplication and foster competition among aid agencies.

Another market-oriented step would be for the common pool to issue vouchers to poor individuals or communities, who could exchange them for development services at any aid agency, NGO, or domestic government agency. These service providers would in turn redeem the vouchers for cash out of the common pool. Aid agencies would be forced to compete to attract aid vouchers (and thus money) for their budgets. The vouchers could also trade in a secondary market; how far their price is below par would reflect the inefficiency of this aid scheme and would require remedial action. Most important, vouchers would provide real market power to the impoverished customers to express their true needs and desires.

Intermediaries such as a new Washington-based company called Development Space could help assemble the vouchers into blocks and identify aid suppliers; the intermediaries could even compete with each other to attract funding and find projects that satisfy the customers, much as venture capital firms do. (Development Space is a private Web-based company established last year by former World Bank staff members—kind of an eBay for foreign aid.) Aid agencies could establish their own intermediation units to add to the competition. An information bank could facilitate transparency and communication, posting news on projects searching for funding, donors searching for projects, and the reputation of various intermediaries.

Bureaucratic cartels probably last longer than private cartels, but they need not last forever. President George W. Bush's proposed Millennium Challenge Account (under which, to use Bush's words, "countries that live by these three broad standards—ruling justly, investing in their people, and encouraging economic freedom—will receive more aid from America") and the accompanying increase in U.S. aid dollars will challenge the IMF and World Bank's near monopoly over reform-related lending. Development Space may be the first of many market-oriented endeavors to compete with aid agencies, but private philanthropists such as Bill Gates and George Soros have entered the industry as well. NGOs and independent academic economists are also more aggressively entering the market for advice on aid to poor countries. Globalization protesters are not well informed in all areas, but they seem largely on target when it comes to the failure of international financial institutions to foment "adjustment with growth" in many poor countries. Even within the World Bank itself, a recent board of directors paper suggested experimenting with "output-based aid" in which assistance would compensate service providers only when services are actually delivered to the poor—sadly, a novel concept. Here again, private firms, NGOs, and government agencies could compete to serve as providers.

Now that rich countries again seem interested in foreign aid, pressure is growing to reform a global aid bureaucracy that is increasingly out of touch with good economics. The high-income countries that finance aid and that genuinely want aid to reach the poor should subject the cartel of good intentions to the bracing wind of competition, markets, and accountability to the customers. Donors and recipients alike should not put up with $3,521 in aid to reduce the poverty head count by one, 185-point development frameworks, or an alphabet soup of bureaucratic fads. The poor deserve better.

CHAPTER 13

CLOSE CAPITAL ACCOUNTS v. LIBERALIZE CAPITAL FLOWS

Close Capital Accounts

Advocate: Jagdish Bhagwati

Source: "The Capital Myth: The Difference Between Trade in Widgets and Dollars," *Foreign Affairs* 77 (May/June 1998): 7–12.

Liberalize Capital Flows

Advocate: Sebastian Edwards

Source: "A Capital Idea," *Foreign Affairs* 78 (May/June 1999): 18–22.

In the 1990s, many governments removed restrictions on cross-border flows of financial capital. As they did, financial markets began funneling large quantities of short-term funds to these emerging market countries. In a very short period of time, countries that had previously found it difficult to attract any foreign investment found themselves inundated with more foreign capital than they could productively employ. The emergence of such capital flows provided new opportunities by making it possible to enjoy a higher rate of investment than would be possible otherwise.

These new opportunities also carried heightened risk. Country after country and region after region were hit by devastating financial crises between the late 1990s and 2001. Mexico fell first in 1994; the East Asian crisis of 1997 affected Indonesia, Thailand, South Korea, Hong Kong, Singapore, and the Philippines. Russia and Brazil experienced crises in 1998, Argentina in 1999 and 2000, and Turkey in 2000. In each case, enthusiasm by private investors about the opportunities in these emerging markets produced a tidal wave of capital inflows. In the absence of sound financial regulation and a lack of experience managing and investing this volume of funds, many countries developed precarious financial positions that were maintained only by continuous rolling over of short-term liabilities. When foreign lenders ceased rolling over these credits, countries found themselves facing severe financial and economic crises. Domestic financial systems collapsed, currencies lost value, and output fell sharply.

CLOSE CAPITAL ACCOUNTS

Although the last few years have brought greater financial stability to emerging market countries, the debate sparked by this experience continues to hold value. The basic question is how to balance the potential gains from capital inflows against the downside risk of crises. Some observers emphasize the downside risk and de-emphasize the potential gains. A common characteristic of people who stress the risk of participation in the global financial system is a belief that financial markets are inherently unstable—prone to irrational manias that drive bubbles and to panics that necessarily pop the bubbles. Participating in global financial markets, therefore, necessarily exposes emerging market countries to such cycles.

Jagdish Bhagwati, an enthusiastic supporter of trade liberalization, develops the argument against capital account liberalization. Financial markets, he argues, are prone to sudden changes in market sentiment. Investors can be wildly enthusiastic about an emerging-market country one day and equally pessimistic about the same country the next day. Because investor sentiments can change so sharply, capital flows tend to be volatile and the volatility is quite destructive. Bhagwati thus advocates that developing countries use capital controls to restrict cross-border flows.

LIBERALIZE CAPITAL FLOWS

Other scholars emphasize the potential gains and de-emphasize the downside risk. The key argument is that emerging-market financial crises are fully preventable. Governments can establish and enforce financial regulation that ensures domestic financial institutions borrow from abroad and lend at home in ways that minimize the risk of instability. Crises that do occur, therefore, merely reflect bad or inappropriate regulatory regimes.

Sebastian Edwards, a leading development economist based at the University of California, Los Angeles (UCLA), develops an argument along these lines. Edwards argues that the empirical evidence clearly indicates that capital controls are ineffective. Capital controls neither prevent countries from falling into crises nor promote more rapid recovery from crises. Edwards thus encourages governments in emerging markets to liberalize their capital accounts and adopt appropriate financial regulation.

POINTS **TO PONDER**

1. Why, according to Bhagwati, is free trade in financial capital different from free trade in goods? Would Edwards agree with Bhagwati?

2. What does Bhagwati point to as an explanation for the liberalization of finance in emerging markets? Do you find his explanation convincing? Why or why not?

3. What causes financial crises? Do you think the two authors share a common belief about these causes?

4. Explain why these two articles, now ten years old, remain relevant. How might Asian countries' current policy of foreign exchange reserve accumulation be related to these crises?

Jagdish Bhagwati

The Capital Myth: The Difference Between Trade in Widgets and Dollars

The Difference Between Trade in Widgets and Dollars

In the aftermath of the Asian financial crisis, the mainstream view that dominates policy circles, indeed the prevalent myth, is that despite the striking evidence of the inherently crisis-prone nature of freer capital movements, a world of full capital mobility continues to be inevitable and immensely desirable. Instead of maintaining careful restrictions, we are told, the only sensible course is to continue working toward unfettered capital flows; the favored solution is to turn the IMF [International Monetary Fund] even more firmly into an international lender of last resort that dispenses bailout funds to crisis-afflicted countries. The IMF took an important step in this direction at its annual meeting in Hong Kong last September, when the Interim Committee issued a statement virtually endorsing an eventual move to capital account convertibility—which means that you and I, nationals or foreigners, could take capital in and out freely, in any volume and at any time—for IMF members. The obligations originally listed in 1944 in the Articles of Agreement, on the other hand, included only "avoidance of restrictions on payments for current transactions" and did not embrace capital account convertibility as an obligation or even a goal.

This is a seductive idea: freeing up trade is good, why not also let capital move freely across borders? But the claims of enormous benefits from free capital mobility are not persuasive. Substantial gains have been asserted, not demonstrated, and most of the payoff can be obtained by direct equity investment. And even a richer IMF with attendant changes in its methods of operation will probably not rule out crises or reduce their costs significantly. The myth to the contrary has been created by what one might christen the Wall Street-Treasury complex, following in the footsteps of President Eisenhower, who had warned of the military-industrial complex.

Capital Mobility Ideology

Until the Asian crisis sensitized the public to the reality that capital movements could repeatedly generate crises, many assumed that free capital mobility among all nations was exactly like free trade in their goods and services, a mutual-gain phenomenon. Hence restricted capital mobility, just like protectionism, was seen to be harmful to economic performance in each country, whether rich or poor. That the gains might be problematic because of the cost of crises was not considered.

However, the Asian crisis cannot be separated from the excessive borrowings of foreign short-term capital as Asian economies loosened up their capital account controls and enabled their banks and firms to borrow abroad. In 1996, total private capital inflows to Indonesia, Malaysia, South Korea, Thailand, and the Philippines were $93 billion, up from $41 billion in 1994. In 1997, that suddenly changed to an outflow of $12 billion. Hence it has become apparent that crises attendant on capital mobility cannot be ignored.

Although it is conceded that this downside exists, many claim that it can be ameliorated, if not eliminated, and that free capital mobility's immense advantages can be enjoyed by all. Conservatives would do this by letting the markets rip, untended by the IMF, which could then be sidelined or even disbanded. Liberals would do it instead by turning the IMF into the world's lender of last resort, dispensing funds during crises with several sorts of conditions, and overseeing, buttressing, and managing the world of free capital mobility.

To understand why neither of these modifications is enough, it is necessary to understand why the original version of the myth, which has steadily propelled the IMF into its complacent and dangerous moves toward the goal of capital account convertibility, was just that. True, economists properly say that there is a correspondence between free trade in goods and services and free capital mobility: interfering with either will produce efficiency losses. But only an untutored economist will argue that, therefore, free trade in widgets and life insurance policies is the same as free capital mobility. Capital flows are characterized, as the economic historian Charles Kindleberger of the Massachusetts Institute of Technology has famously noted, by panics and manias.

Each time a crisis related to capital inflows hits a country, it typically goes through the wringer. The debt crisis of the 1980s cost South America a decade of growth. The Mexicans, who were vastly overexposed through short-term inflows, were devastated in 1994. The Asian economies of Thailand, Indonesia, and South Korea, all heavily burdened with short-term debt, went into a tailspin nearly a year ago, drastically lowering their growth rates. Sure enough, serious economic downturns and crises can arise even when governments are not particularly vulnerable due to short-term borrowing: macroeconomic mismanagement in Japan has restrained its growth rate for nearly seven years now, and Japan is still a net lender of capital. But it is a non sequitur to suggest, as the defenders of free capital mobility do, that this possibility somehow negates the fact that short-term borrowings under free capital mobility will be, and have been, a source of considerable economic difficulty.

Downsizing Gains

When a crisis hits, the downside of free capital mobility arises. To ensure that capital returns, the country must do everything it can to restore the confidence of those who have taken their money out. This typically means raising interest rates, as the IMF has required of Indonesia. Across Asia this has decimated firms with large amounts of debt. It also means having to sell domestic assets, which are greatly undervalued because of the credit crunch, in a fire sale to foreign buyers with better access to funds. (Economists have usually advised the exact opposite in such depressed circumstances: restricting foreign access to a country's assets when its credit, but not that of others, has dried up.) Thus, Thailand and South Korea have been forced to further open their capital markets, even though the short-term capital inflow played a principal role in their troubles in the first place.

Besides suffering these economic setbacks, these countries have lost the political independence to run their economic policies as they deem fit. That their independence is lost not directly to foreign nations but to an IMF increasingly extending its agenda, at the behest of the U.S. Congress, to invade domestic policies on matters of social policy—as with the 1994 Sanders-Frank Amendment, which seeks to attach labor standards conditions to any increase in bailout funds—is small consolation indeed.

Thus, any nation contemplating the embrace of free capital mobility must reckon with these costs and also consider the probability of running into a crisis. The gains from economic efficiency that would flow from free capital mobility, in a hypothetical crisis-free world, must be set against this loss if a wise decision is to be made.

None of the proponents of free capital mobility have estimated the size of the gains they expect to materialize, even leaving out the losses from crises that can ensue. For free trade, numerous studies have measured the costs of protection. The overwhelming majority of trade economists judge the gains from free trade to be significant, coming down somewhere between Paul Krugman's view that they are too small to be taken seriously and Jeffrey Sachs' view that they are huge and cannot be ignored. But all we have from the proponents of capital mobility is banner-waving, such as that of Bradford De Long, the Berkeley economist and former deputy assistant secretary for economic policy in the Clinton administration:

> So now we have all the benefits of free flows of international capital. These benefits are mammoth: the ability to borrow abroad kept the Reagan deficits from crushing U.S. growth like an egg, and the ability to borrow from abroad has enabled successful emerging market economies to double or triple the speed at which their productivity levels and living standards converge to the industrial core.

And of Roger C. Altman, the investment banker, who served in the Treasury Department under Presidents Clinton and Carter:

> The worldwide elimination of barriers to trade and capital . . . have created the global financial marketplace, which informed observers hailed for bringing private capital to the developing world, encouraging economic growth and democracy.[1]

These assertions assume that free capital mobility is enormously beneficial while simultaneously failing to evaluate its crisis-prone downside. But even a cursory glance at history suggests that these gains may be negligible. After all, China and Japan, different in politics and sociology as well as historical experience, have registered remarkable growth rates without capital account convertibility. Western Europe's return to prosperity was also achieved without capital account convertibility. Except for Switzerland, capital account liberalization was pretty slow at the outset and did not gain strength until the late 1980s, and some European countries, among them Portugal and Ireland, did not implement it until the early 1990s.

Besides, even if one believes that capital flows are greatly productive, there is still an important difference between embracing free portfolio capital mobility and having a policy of attracting direct equity investment. Maybe the amount of direct foreign investment that a country attracts will be reduced somewhat by not having freedom of portfolio capital flows, but there is little evidence for this assertion. Even then such a loss would be a small fraction of the gains from having a pro-foreign investment strategy.

A Wall Street–Treasury Complex

That brings us to the myth that crises under capital account convertibility can be eliminated. We have, of course, heard this assertion before as each crisis has been confronted, and then we have been hit by yet another one. Like cats, crises have many lives, and macroeconomists, never a tribe that enjoyed a great reputation for getting things right or for agreeing among themselves, have been kept busy adding to the taxonomy of crises and their explanations. None of the solutions currently propounded can really rid the system of free capital mobility of instability.

Thus, while no one can disagree with Secretary of the Treasury Robert Rubin's contention that reform of banking systems around the world will help, few should agree with him that it will eliminate the crises that unregulated capital flows inherently generate. Nor can the abolition of the IMF and its lender of last resort bailouts be the magic bullet: there were crises before the writer Walter Bagehot invented this function for domestic central banks in the nineteenth century. Nor can making the IMF more powerful kill the crises or give it the nonexistent macroeconomic wisdom to manage them at least cost when they arise.

In short, when we penetrate the fog of implausible assertions that surrounds the case for free capital mobility, we realize that the idea and the ideology of free trade and its benefits—and this extends to the continuing liberalization of trade in goods and financial and other services at the World Trade Organization—have, in effect, been hijacked by the proponents of capital mobility. They have been used to bamboozle us into celebrating the new world of trillions of dollars moving about daily in a borderless world, creating gigantic economic gains, rewarding virtue and punishing profligacy. The pretty face presented to us is, in fact, a mask that hides the warts and wrinkles underneath.

The question, then, is why the world has nonetheless been moving in this direction. The answer, as always, reflects ideology and interests— that is, lobbies. The ideology is clearly that of markets. The steady move away from central planning, overregulation, and general overreach in state intervention toward letting markets function has now reached across many sectors and countries. This is indeed all to the good and promises worldwide prosperity. But this wave has also lulled many economists and policymakers into complacency about the pitfalls that certain markets inherently pose even when they were understood in the classroom. Free capital mobility is just one example of this unwarranted attitude. Indeed, Stanley Fischer, the deputy managing director of the IMF, admitted in a February appearance on the Charlie Rose show on PBS that he had underestimated the probability of such crises arising in a world of capital mobility.

But interests have also played a central role. Wall Street's financial firms have obvious self-interest in a world of free capital mobility since it only enlarges the arena in which to make money. It is not surprising, therefore, that Wall Street has put its powerful oar into the turbulent waters of Washington political lobbying to steer in this direction. Thus, when testifying before the Senate Foreign Relations Committee on South Asia in March 1995, right after the Mexican peso crisis, I was witness to the grilling of Undersecretary of Commerce Jeffrey E. Garten on why India's financial system was not fully open to U.S. firms. To his credit, Garten said that this was not exactly a propitious time for the United States to pressure India in this direction.

Then again, Wall Street has exceptional clout with Washington for the simple reason that there is, in the sense of a power elite a la C. Wright Mills, a definite networking of like-minded luminaries among the powerful institutions—Wall Street, the Treasury Department, the State Department, the IMF, and the World Bank most prominent among them. Secretary

Rubin comes from Wall Street; Altman went from Wall Street to the Treasury and back; Nicholas Brady, President Bush's Secretary of the Treasury, is back in finance as well; Ernest Stern, who has served as acting president of the World Bank, is now managing director of J.P. Morgan; James Wolfensohn, an investment banker, is now president of the World Bank. One could go on.

This powerful network, which may aptly, if loosely, be called the Wall Street–Treasury complex, is unable to look much beyond the interest of Wall Street, which it equates with the good of the world. Thus the IMF has been relentlessly propelled toward embracing the goal of capital account convertibility. The Mexican bailout of 1994 was presented as necessary, which was true. But so too was the flip side, that the Wall Street investors had to be bailed out as well, which was not. Surely other policy instruments, such as a surcharge, could have been deployed simultaneously to punish Wall Street for its mistakes. Even in the current Asian crisis, particularly in South Korea, U.S. banks could all have been forced to the bargaining table, absorbing far larger losses than they did, but they were cushioned by the IMF acting virtually as a lender of first, rather than last, resort.

And despite the evidence of the inherent risks of free capital flows, the Wall Street–Treasury complex is currently proceeding on the self-serving assumption that the ideal world is indeed one of free capital flows, with the IMF and its bailouts at the apex in a role that guarantees its survival and enhances its status. But the weight of evidence and the force of logic point in the opposite direction, toward restraints on capital flows. It is time to shift the burden of proof from those who oppose to those who favor liberated capital.

ENDNOTE

1. Bradford DeLong, "What's Wrong with Our Bloody Economies?" January 11, 1998, from his World Wide Web page, http://econ 161.berkeley.edu/; Roger C. Altman, "The Nuke of the 90's," *The New York Times Magazine*, March 1, 1998, p. 34.

Sebastian Edwards

A Capital Idea?

Reconsidering a Financial Quick Fix

Massive capital flows have been at the heart of every major currency crisis in the 1990s. Whether Mexico in 1994, Thailand in 1997, Russia in 1998, or Brazil in 1999, the stories are depressingly similar. High domestic interest rates, perceived stability stemming from rigid exchange rates, and apparently rosy economic prospects all attracted foreign funds into these emerging markets, lifting stock prices and helping finance bloated current account deficits. When these funds eventually trickled to a halt or reversed direction, significant corrections in macroeconomic policies became necessary. But governments often watered down or delayed reform, which increased investor uncertainty and nervousness over risk. As a result, more and more capital poured out of the countries and foreign exchange reserves dropped to dangerously low levels. Eventually, the governments had no choice but to abandon their pegged exchange rates and float their currencies. In Brazil and Russia, runaway fiscal deficits made the situation even more explosive.

In the aftermath of these crises, a number of influential academics have argued that the wild capital movements wrought by globalization have gone too far. In the words of Paul Krugman, "sooner or later we will have to turn the clock at least part of the way back" to limit the free mobility of capital. Bolstered by the growing number of capital-controls advocates, proposals for a new international financial architecture have focused on two types of controls: restrictions on short-term capital inflows, similar to those implemented in Chile between 1991 and 1998; and controls on capital outflows, like those Malaysia imposed in 1998. Both schemes try to reduce the "irrational" volatility inherent in capital flows and foster longer-term forms of investment, such as direct foreign investment, including investment in equipment and machinery.

Despite their good intentions, these proposals share a common flaw: they ignore the discouraging empirical record of capital controls in developing countries. The blunt fact is that capital controls are not only ineffective in avoiding crises, but also breed corruption and inflate the costs of managing investment.

Don't Bank on it

Chile, which experimented with short-term capital controls during 1978–82 and 1991–98, has become a favorite test case for proponents of such measures. In both episodes, foreigners wishing to move short-term funds into

Chile were required to first deposit their money with Chile's central bank for a specified amount of time—at no interest. By stemming inflows, the policy aimed to mitigate capital volatility, prevent the currency from rising too quickly (a common result of accelerated capital inflows), and increase the central bank's control over domestic monetary policy. From 1978 to 1982, the controls were particularly stringent; foreign capital was virtually forbidden from entering the country for less than five and a half years. In this way, it was thought, the country would not be vulnerable to short-term speculation.

Proponents of controls cite all the above facts but miss the bigger picture. Indeed, their brand of wishful thinking misreads Chile's history and oversells the effectiveness of this policy. What you do not hear from them is that the draconian restrictions on capital inflows could not prevent Chile from going through a traumatic economic crisis from 1981 to 1982, which caused a peso depreciation of almost 90 percent and a systemic banking collapse. The problem lay with the largely unregulated banking sector, which used international loans to speculate on real estate and lend generously to bank owners, ultimately creating an asset-price bubble. When it burst, loans could not be repaid. Hence, many banks went under and had to be rescued by the government at a very high cost to taxpayers. A massive 1986 banking reform finally put an end to that by establishing strict guidelines on bank exposure and instituting rigorous on-site inspections. A healthy, strong, and efficient banking system emerged as a result, which to this day has helped Chile withstand the most recent global turmoil.

This historical episode underscores a key factor in evaluating restrictions on capital mobility: without effective prudential banking regulations, restrictions on capital inflows alone are unlikely to reduce a country's vulnerability. Moreover, capital controls may foster a false sense of security, encouraging complacent and careless behavior by policymakers and investors alike. South Korea's recent experience is a case in point. Until late 1997, international market players and local policymakers believed that Seoul's restrictions on capital mobility would inoculate the country from a currency crisis. Indeed, even after giving South Korea's central bank and private banks their next-to-lowest rating in early 1997, Goldman Sachs still argued that the nation's "relatively closed capital account" necessitated the exclusion of such gloomy data from its overall assessment of South Korea's financial vulnerability. Hence, Goldman Sachs played down the extent of the Korean won crisis throughout most of 1997. Had it correctly recognized that capital restrictions cannot truly protect an economy from financial turbulence, it would have accurately anticipated the South Korean debacle just as it forecast the Thai meltdown.

Brazil is another example that capital-control advocates should reconsider. Restrictions on short-term capital inflows in 1997 and 1998 lulled Brazilian policymakers into complacency. They repeatedly argued that their controls would preclude a Mexican-style currency crisis. As it turned out, they were wrong. Once the collapse of the Brazilian real became imminent in the autumn of 1998, domestic and foreign investors alike rushed to flee the country—just as in Mexico in 1994.

Control Freaks

Not surprisingly, most supporters of capital controls have focused only on Chile's experience during the 1990s, when 30 percent of all capital inflows had to be deposited for one year, at no interest, with the central bank, and direct foreign investment was required to stay in the country for at least one year. This policy was implemented in June 1991, when the newly elected democratic government of President Patricio Aylwin became concerned over the exchange rate and inflationary effects of the rapidly growing capital inflows. Aylwin sought the support of exporters, who resisted a strengthening of the currency, while taking a firm anti-inflationary stance. Accordingly, he turned to capital controls.

Despite positive media coverage and popularity with some academics, there is no firm evidence that this policy actually achieved its goals. First, Chile's short-term foreign-denominated debt was almost 50 percent of all debt from 1996 to 1998. Second, capital controls failed to slow the strengthening of Chile's currency. Throughout the 1990s, Chile's real exchange rate rose more than 30 percent despite capital controls. Finally, the argument that restrictions on inflows help increase central bank control over domestic monetary policy is tenuous at best. Tightening restrictions increases domestic interest rates only slightly and temporarily.

Chile's capital controls have also carried another price—by inflating the cost of capital. Large firms, with their easy access to international financial resources, can always find ways to circumvent the controls; smaller firms are not so fortunate. As a result, a prohibitively high cost of capital not only distorts the true cost of investment but discriminates against small- and medium-sized businesses. In fact, some analysts have calculated that investment costs for smaller firms exceeded 20 percent in dollar terms in 1996 and 1997; larger firms, on the other hand, could access the international market with dollar loans at a cost of only 7 or 8 percent per annum.

Go with the Flow

As their advocates would have it, temporary controls on capital outflows would allow stricken countries to lower interest rates and implement pro-growth policies without worrying about investors pulling out for fear of devaluation. Controlling capital outflows would also buy economies time to restructure their financial sector in an orderly fashion. Once the economy is back on its feet, so goes the argument, controls can be dismantled.

Again, the historical evidence flies in the face of this reasoning. According to two studies of 31 major currency crises in Latin America, countries that tightened controls after a major devaluation did not post better performances in economic growth, job creation, or inflation than those that did not. The Latin American debt crisis of the 1980s illustrates how ineffective these controls really were. Nations that imposed controls on capital outflows—Argentina, Brazil, Mexico, and Peru—muddled through but suffered rising inflation, worsening unemployment, and a long and painful decline in growth. Moreover, the stricter controls encouraged neither macroeconomic restructuring nor orderly reforms aimed at increasing efficiency and competitiveness. In fact, the opposite happened: politicians experimented with populist policies that ultimately deepened the crisis. Mexico nationalized the banking sector and confiscated dollar-denominated deposits. Argentina and Brazil launched new currencies while setting price controls and expanding public spending. In Peru, stricter controls on outflows allowed President Alan Garcia to whittle away the basis of a healthy and productive economy, squandering international reserves and pursuing a hyperinflationary policy. To make things even worse, in none of these countries did controls on capital outflows successfully stem capital flight.

Chile and Colombia, which did not tighten controls on capital outflows, provide an interesting contrast. These two states attempted to restructure their economies. Chile even implemented a modern bank supervisory system that greatly reduced domestic financial fragility. Accordingly, both countries emerged from the debt crisis significantly better off than the rest of the region. In fact, they were the only two large Latin American countries to experience positive growth in per capita gross domestic product and real wages during the "lost decade" of the 1980s.

Disciplinary Measures

The recent financial crises have dealt a severe blow to the International Monetary Fund's credibility. The IMF [International Monetary Fund] badly miscalculated the Mexican collapse of 1994, prescribed the wrong policies in East Asia in 1997, and offered vastly inadequate rescue packages to Russia and Brazil in 1998. This succession of embarrassments reflects the fact that the IMF's structure does not allow it to operate effectively in the modern world economy, where investor confidence and the frank, uncensored, and prompt dissemination of information are crucial. Sadly, international politics is likely to stand in the way of true IMF reform. After much talk about a new architecture, we will probably end up with a slightly embellished IMF that will continue to miss crises, throw good money after bad, and ultimately try to rationalize why currency crises persist.

Economists have long recognized that the issue of international capital movements is highly complicated. In the absence of strong financial and banking supervision in both lending and borrowing countries, unregulated capital flows may indeed be misallocated, generating major disruptions in the receiving nations. Many academics have rightly argued that relaxing controls on capital movement should therefore follow, not precede, market-oriented macroeconomic reform and the establishment of a reliable supervisory system for domestic financial markets. Governments should lift controls on capital movements carefully and gradually—but they should be lifted.

We must understand what capital controls can and cannot do. The historical record shows convincingly that, despite their new popularity, controls on capital outflows and inflows are ineffective. The best prescriptions to combat financial turmoil, now as then, are sound macroeconomic policies, sufficiently flexible exchange rates, and banking reforms that introduce effective prudential regulations and reduce moral hazard and corruption. Without a solid financial groundwork, emerging markets will remain as fragile as a house of cards, easily blown down by the first breezes of turbulence.

PART V

GLOBALIZATION AND GLOBAL GOVERNANCE

The growth of the global economy generates a lot of debate about governance structures. The key question running through all of this discussion is, does a global economy require global governance? If the answer is yes, then a number of subsidiary questions arise. Who should participate in making global rules—governments alone or governments and civil society? To what extent are common and highly specific regulatory standards required versus common agreement on broad principles? How much autonomy are governments likely to cede to international forums, and how does the continuation of sovereign national governments constrain the prospects for global governance? This section examines these questions in the context of the three central areas of the global economy that we have examined in this book: international trade, multinational corporations, and the international financial system.

Chapter 14 explores the debate about governance of the international trade system. Without question, international trade is the system in which governments have created the most fully elaborated set of rules. Thus, debates about governance of international trade focus less on whether such governance is needed and more on the structure of this governance. Two questions are central to the debate. First, who should have the right to participate in the creation of rules within the World Trade Organization (WTO)? Should participation be restricted to governments, as it is currently? Or should participation in the WTO process be opened to civil society? The second concerns the extent to which the WTO process focuses too narrowly on trade promotion at the expense of other desired social objectives such as human rights and environmental protection. Daniel Esty advocates substantial reform of the WTO. Participation must be expanded to include nongovernmental organizations (NGOs), and the WTO process must embed trade rules in a broader set of social concerns. David Henderson challenges both suggestions. He asserts that participation must remain restricted to national governments and claims that trade rules are already attentive to labor and environmental issues.

Chapter 15 looks at the prospects for creating global rules to govern the activities of multinational corporations (MNCs). If trade is the system with the most fully developed set of global rules, MNCs must be the area in which global rules are least developed. In fact, common global rules are largely absent in spite of almost continuous efforts over the last thirty years to establish some global framework. Current debate focuses on crafting codes of conduct that encourage or compel MNCs to promote human rights, treat their workers well, and not engage in practices that harm the environment. Although there is broad agreement on these objectives, less agreement exists about how to achieve them. Some argue that MNCs will take workers' rights and the environment into account only if they are forced to do so by global standards written and enforced by governments and governmental organizations like the United Nations (UN). Others argue that MNCs can be encouraged toward socially responsible behavior via public pressure and market mechanisms. Daniel Litvin argues the former point, suggesting that governments must build on and strengthen recent UN efforts to create enforceable codes of conduct. Gary Gereffi, Ronie Garcia-Johnson, and Erika Sasser argue that public pressure and market incentives might be sufficient to induce MNCs to engage in socially responsible practices.

Chapter 16 discusses the options for international financial regulation in the wake of the global financial crisis sparked by the collapse of the United States' real estate bubble. Most observers of this crisis agree that it highlights the need for more effective financial regulation. Moreover, most also agree that such regulation cannot be left solely in the hands of national governments, because uncoordinated national regulation could easily spark a regulatory race to the bottom. Much less agreement exists about what to do at the international level to craft more effective regulation. Should governments craft a single global regulatory regime that all governments must adopt? Is it sufficient to create a new process wherein governments regulate at home but turn to international authorities for a stamp of approval? Stijn Claessens argues for the development of a common global regulatory framework. Barry Eichengreen argues that common global rules are less necessary than a common process based on broad principles.

CHAPTER 14 THE WORLD TRADE ORGANIZATION LACKS LEGITIMACY v. THE WORLD TRADE ORGANIZATION IS LEGITIMATE

The World Trade Organization Lacks Legitimacy

Advocate: Daniel C. Esty

Source: "The World Trade Organization's Legitimacy Crisis," *World Trade Review* 1, no. 1 (2002): 7–22.

The World Trade Organization Is Legitimate

Advocate: David Henderson

Source: "WTO 2002: Imaginary Crisis, Real Problems," *World Trade Review* 1, no. 3 (2002): 277–296.

The World Trade Organization (WTO) has been controversial since its inception in 1995. Controversy arises in part from a widespread perception that global trade rules have broadened their reach substantially since the early 1990s. In addition, observers point to an equally common belief that governments create these seemingly ever-expanding rules through a process that seems to focus narrowly on the goal of trade liberalization and that excludes the interests and concerns of a large segment of society.

Global trade rules do reach further today than they did twenty years ago. For much of the postwar period, trade negotiations focused on tariff reductions. Although negotiations forayed on occasion into nontariff aspects of trade, including rules on government anti-dumping investigations, government procurement practices, and the use of product standards, most negotiations focused on selecting the industries in which and deciding the amount by which governments would reduce tariffs. The Uruguay Round extended global trade rules into new areas. Governments agreed to rules on the protection of intellectual property rights and to common practices regarding the use of trade restrictions to protect human, plant, and animal health and created a dispute settlement mechanism to enforce compliance with these rules.

As rules extend beyond tariffs, the likelihood that an international commitment will conflict with a domestic practice or regulation grows. Many of the more prominent recent disputes in the WTO, such as the shrimp-turtle dispute and disputes over genetically modified organisms and hormone-treated beef, illustrate how common rules regulating the use of trade restrictions complicate efforts to achieve other desired objectives.

THE WORLD TRADE ORGANIZATION LACKS LEGITIMACY

Some observers argue that the WTO's gradual encroachment on areas previously under exclusive domestic control warrants a widening of the actors authorized to participate in the WTO process. Whereas the "club model" of decision making, in which only national governments participate in the bargaining process, was acceptable when negotiations focused only on tariffs, it is not acceptable in this new world. Sticking with the club model as the trade rules extend ever deeper into domestic regulations concerning the environment, health and safety, and so on merely runs the risk of further undermining public support for the WTO process. Reinforcing the WTO's legitimacy requires the process be opened and more inclusive of actors other than national governments.

Daniel Esty develops this argument here. Esty asserts that the nontransparent and restrictive nature of WTO decision making is robbing the organization of legitimacy. The corrective is far-reaching reform of the process. He argues that a revitalized WTO must rest on a more representative form of decision making and a system of checks and balances. In addition, the system must pay greater attention to the broader social context in which trade is situated as well as to the importance of the impact of trade on poverty, the environment, and human rights.

THE WORLD TRADE ORGANIZATION IS LEGITIMATE

Other observers question the need for far-reaching reforms. Reform skeptics believe that the WTO's big challenges derive from the consequences of its success rather than from a loss of legitimacy in the public eye. Its success is reflected in its increased membership—currently 153 members. And as membership increases, governments find it increasingly difficult to achieve consensus. Adding additional participants to the process will only further reduce the organization's effectiveness. Moreover, although WTO rules reach deeper into the domestic realm than previously, governments have accepted these rules as part of a much broader set of agreements that together constitute the costs and benefits of participation in the WTO.

David Henderson develops this argument as a direct response to Daniel Esty. Henderson argues that the WTO's legitimacy rests on member governments' acceptance of and participation in the organization. Governments themselves are legitimate representatives of civil society in the countries they represent. He argues that allowing nongovernmental organizations (NGOs) to participate in the WTO will not enhance legitimacy, because NGOs are not legitimate representatives of any population. Moreover, he challenges Esty's assertion that the WTO process focuses on trade liberalization to the exclusion of all other objectives. On balance, Henderson concludes, the reforms Esty proposes would do more harm than good to the organization.

POINTS **TO PONDER**

1. What does Esty mean by political legitimacy? Does Henderson use the same definition? Which understanding do you think should be used in relation to the WTO?

2. On what grounds does Henderson criticize Esty's claim that the public interest NGO's should be given a more role in the WTO? How do you think Esty would respond? Do you think allowing NGOs to participate in the WTO provides more legitimacy to the organization?

3. Suppose you accept the force of Esty's critique and thus agree on the need for reform. Do you think the reforms that Esty proposes would enhance the WTO's legitimacy? How would you change these proposals? Do governments have incentives to adopt such reforms? Why or why not?

Daniel C. Esty
The World Trade Organization's Legitimacy Crisis

Turmoil surrounds the international trading system and especially the World Trade Organization (WTO). The 1999 WTO Ministerial Meeting in Seattle broke down in chaos. Other international gatherings to promote economic integration, including the European Union's 2000 Summit Meeting in Gothenburg and the 2001 Summit of the Americas in Quebec City, have triggered similar protests and violent clashes between demonstrators and the police. Undoubtedly, the anti-globalization backlash and the rioting in the streets has a number of causes (Blackurst 2001; Esty 2000). And, while some commentators have dismissed the demonstrations as mere "noise," I believe a "signal" can be extracted from the current difficulties of the trade regime. Simply put, the international trading system has not adapted to a rapidly changing global scene and now faces a serious legitimacy crisis (Keohane and Nye 2001). This article explores the origins and implications of this crisis.

I argue that the WTO stands at a watershed. The post-World War II international order centered on issue-based "decomposable hierarchies" has begun to break down (Simon 1996; Keohane and Nye 2001).[1] A new, more complex and fluid international system is beginning to emerge. But the new architecture has structural flaws. In particular, little attention has been paid to what is required to establish the legitimacy of international organizations in general and the WTO in particular (Bodansky 1999; Hurd 1999; Stephan 1999).

The WTO appears simultaneously to be at the leading edge of the economic integration process and yet curiously old-fashioned and out of step with some modern norms, particularly those involving good public decisionmaking. As recent events have demonstrated, coherently managing interdependence is of vital importance. This need makes the resolution of the legitimacy issues surrounding the WTO of even greater urgency.

Many of those who criticize the WTO and other elements of international economic structure have little foundation for the charges they make. Indeed, many of the attacks on the WTO are off-base and deeply confused. The suggestion, for instance, that freer trade leads to greater poverty disregards the enormous gains that have been made by hundreds of millions of people across the planet over the last several decades in countries that have opened themselves up to world markets (Bhagwati 1993; Anderson and Blackhurst 1992). Those chanting "no WTO" really do not want an international marketplace without structure or rules in which multinational corporations operate without constraints.

Legitimate Concerns

While much of the criticism of the WTO is analytically unfounded and some of it is positively upside down and backwards, there are a number of kernels of truth in the general angst about the future that is manifested in anti-globalization rhetoric. First, trade liberalization creates losers as well as winners. There can be no doubt, furthermore, that we live in a time of considerable turbulence. Fears about job insecurity and the prospect of wages being bid down in the globalized labor market have some foundation, even if the long-term broader economic trend is positive for most people.

Second, economic integration and the broader forces of globalization threaten some traditions and local cultures. But these changes—for example, the evolving rhythms of rural life in France, which Jose Bové decries—are not the product of some grand conspiracy but rather choices by everyday people about how they want to lead their lives (Jeffress and Mayanobe 2001). Similarly, the urbanization of countries across the world, the commercial prominence of global brands and multinational corporations, and the powerful presence of a worldwide media and entertainment culture are driven largely by public preferences. But the fear that an overemphasis on materialism and economic growth will result in policies that run roughshod over other values about which people care has an underlying logic. It may, for example, be more difficult to follow through on concerns about the environment or human rights within the context of an economic dynamic of global competition (Esty 1996; Esty and Geradin 2001).

Third, the benefits of trade liberalization and economic integration may not be fairly distributed. In many countries the general public benefits from access to a greater variety of goods at lower prices (Gilpin 1987). But in some nations, elite groups dominate both political processes and the economy, allowing them to claim a vastly disproportionate share of the "spoils" of freer trade and economic growth more generally (O'Rourke 2001). Thus, distributional questions cannot be ignored.

Too often the trade community leaders duck these concerns, arguing that economic transactions always result in some dislocation, that environmental harms are not related to trade, and that equity issues should be dealt with in other fora. But to disregard these issues damages the credibility of those pressing the trade liberalization agenda—and may mean that economic integration proceeds in ways that do not maximize social welfare (Esty 2001).

The Underlying Legitimacy Crisis

Beyond these broad sources of concern about trade liberalization lie a set of questions about the WTO specifically. In fact, the WTO's very legitimacy has been called into question (Weinstein and Charnovitz 2001; Stokes and

Choate 2001; Bodansky 1999). Public acceptance of the authority and decisions that emerge from the World Trade Organization can no longer be taken for granted in many countries.

Legitimacy is a complex concept in the context of governance. It can be derived through elections and a majority vote for representatives who reflect the political will of a community (in the spirit of Rousseau) (Franck 1990). Alternatively, a governing body may gain authority and public acceptance based on reason and the efficacy of the outcomes it generates (in the Kantian tradition) (Kahn 1989). Popular sovereignty and efficacy are to some extent fungible. Thus, some governments maintain their hold on power because they continue to win elections even though their results in office are not outstanding (consider the regimes in Argentina over the past century). In other cases, governments fall short of full democratic practices (think of Singapore), but maintain public support and acceptance by their effectiveness and their capacity to deliver on public expectations. As a general rule, people appear more willing to cede authority to "expert" decisionmaking in realms that are perceived to be technical or scientific (Kahn 1989; Weber 2000). The American public, for example, has seemed quite willing to leave monetary policy in the hands of the not-too-democratic Federal Reserve Board under the leadership of Alan Greenspan so long as the economy remained strong.[2]

Legitimacy also has a systemic dimension. The authority of a particular decisionmaking body depends not only on the electoral accountability of those making decisions or the perceived rationality of the choices that emerge but also on the popular sovereignty and efficacy of the broader system within which a decisionmaking entity is lodged (Breton 1996; Hurd 1999). Thus, for example, the US Supreme Court has a high degree of legitimacy although its justices are not elected and its decisions sometimes appear to fall short of full rationality. But the US Supreme Court is embedded in a broader structure of legislative, executive, and judicial decisionmaking bodies that provide a dense web of checks and balances (Strauss 1984; Eskridge and Ferejohn 1992). Taken as a whole, this system provides a reasonably strong connection between the American public and their political leadership and delivers generally good results over time (Ackerman 2000).

Historically, the trade regime has not been managed by elected officials accountable to a defined public. Instead, its legitimacy derived almost entirely from its perceived efficacy and value as part of the international economic management structured.[3] Indeed, the GATT [General Agreement on Tariffs and Trade]-WTO system may represent the high water mark of the twentieth-century commitment to technocratic decisionmaking (Charnovitz 1994; Howse 1999; Shaffer 2001) and belief in a governance model centered on bureaucratic rationality (Frug 1984; Weber 1994). Until recently, the trade regime benefited from a sense that international economics and trade policy making were highly technical realms best left in the hands of an elite cadre of qualified experts. To the extent that links to elected officials were required, the connection between appointed trade officials (both at the national level and in the international domain) and the elected governments to which they reported seemed sufficient.

But public perceptions about trade and trade policy making have changed. Trade is no longer considered to be an obscure policy domain best left to technical experts. Instead, trade issues and initiatives are now a major focus of public attention and discussion across the world. The trade regime can no longer function on the basis of technocratic rationality and quiet accomplishments. As I discuss in more detail below, with its efficacy-based claim to legitimacy under attack and lacking any undergirding in true popular sovereignty, the WTO needs a new foundation for its legitimacy. The organization needs to reestablish its reputation for efficacy and to build new connections to the publics around the world in whose name trade policy is advanced as well as to strengthen the broader institutional structure of checks and balances within which the WTO operates.

The "Club Model" Trade Regime

From its origins in the General Agreement on Tariffs and Trade (GATT), a cornerstone of the Bretton Woods system that undergirded the post-World War II international economic order (Ruggie 1983), the trade regime was long operated as a tight-knit "club" (Keohane and Nye 2001). This Club Model persisted because it was successful. In fact, the World Trade Organization (and the forerunner structure created under GATT auspices) generated an enviable record of accomplishment with regard to trade liberalization and successful settlement of international economic disputes. Through eight successive rounds of multilateral negotiations, the GATT provided a forum for coordinated commitment to significant tariff reductions and the creation of a system of rules to guide international commerce (Jackson 1996).

For a long period of time, the trade regime's clubbishness, low profile, and obscure workings were seen as a virtue. A clique of committed economists and diplomats and a small Secretariat in Geneva toiled quietly in pursuit of a vision of open markets and deeper economic integration as both a path to prosperity and a bulwark against the chaos and war that plagued the world through the first half of the twentieth century (Gilpin 1987; Jackson 1994). The closed and secretive nature of the regime isolated—and insulated—the trade policymaking process from day-to-day politics, keeping at bay the protectionist interests that are active in many countries (Schott 1996).

As a matter of theory, asymmetries of interest and commitment to political activity between the beneficiaries of liberalized trade (the broad public which often neither recognizes the benefits of free trade nor is willing to invest much political energy in defending the gains from open markets) and the losers from trade liberalization (special interests who face new competition and are highly motivated to intervene politically to protect their monopoly rents) create a powerful "public choice" logic for such a structure (Petersmann 1992). The international trade regime, as Robert Hudec has described it, serves as a mechanism by which governments can tie their hands to the mast and avoid protectionist siren calls (Hudec 1971). Under the Club Model, governments operating behind closed doors can cut deals to lower tariff barriers and to open markets for the benefit of the general public out of sight of rent seekers, protectionists, and other special interests (van Dijck and Faber 1996; Jackson 1996).

But the "insulation" advantages of the Club Model of trade policy making come at a price. Unable to gain any real appreciation for how the trade regime worked, the public sees the WTO as a "black box" where insiders take advantage of their access to the levers of power. Fears of special interest domination are now prevalent. And these worries are not limited to the public; many developing countries share the concern (Blackhurst 2001). The belief that the WTO is dominated by multinational corporations and other elite interests cannot be assuaged without a more transparent policymaking process (Goldman 1994). The Club Model no longer represents therefore a viable management structure for the international economic system. The days of major agreements being hammered out in Geneva hotels by a trade cognoscenti operating under the radar of public view are gone forever. Whatever the virtues of keeping special interests off balance and out of the way, the closed-door style of negotiations that lies at the heart of the Club Model is no longer workable. After years on the periphery of the global scene, trade policy now occupies center stage.

Indeed, for all their confusion (and there has been a great deal), the anti-globalization street protestors have one thing right: the WTO matters. The trade regime stands at the center of the emerging structure of global governance. While there have been many rounds of trade negotiations over the past 50 years, the central focus of the process has shifted from tit-for-tat reductions to the identification of rules and procedures to manage economic interdependence.

In important respects, the next round of negotiations will resemble a Global Constitutional Convention. The process of global constitutionalism—defining core principles, establishing international standards, and creating institutions to manage interdependence—is likely to involve decades or even centuries of discussions and refinements. Nevertheless, the WTO mission must be understood as fundamentally an exercise in global-scale regime building with profound effects for every person on the planet. Such an exercise inherently touches on big questions about how to structure the world in which we want to live and the mechanisms by which we will be governed. In this regard, we must find more robust modalities and substantive principles by which to square the economic gains of more efficient markets with other public priorities, such as poverty alleviation, environmental protection, or the promotion of human rights. The importance of the work of the WTO—including the goals defined, agenda pursued, rules of participation advanced, and the values and assumptions that underpin the discussions—cannot be gainsaid and must be undergirded by a strong foundation of legitimacy.

It is with good reason therefore that the whole world is now watching the WTO and asking questions about the organization's purpose, structure, representation, decision processes, and legitimacy (Bodansky 1999; Stephan 1999). Progress in opening markets is no longer justification enough for the organization's existence. Moreover, as I noted earlier, doubts are now being raised in many quarters about whether the WTO is delivering on its mission and promise of greater economic efficiency and prosperity. In the past, only the close-knit trade community—united by a common vision of a world of open markets, a commitment to a well-defined set of core principles (for example, non-discrimination), and common traditions of education (particularly a belief in the centrality of economics)—paid attention to the work of the WTO. Today, a broader community that does not share this cultural affinity and understanding stands in judgment on the organization. Different standards of efficacy are being applied. As a result, the WTO's marks are coming in much lower, eroding the organization's legitimacy. Fundamentally, the closed-door approach to decisionmaking that was a virtue under the Club Model has now emerged as an obstacle to popular understanding of and support for the WTO.

Simultaneously, the WTO's efficacy-based claim to legitimacy has been undermined by the trade system's ever-broader reach (Dunoff 1994; Esty 1998; Keohane and Nye 2001). The seeds of the WTO's current troubles were planted dialectically in the furrows of its success. Because the international trade regime is perceived to be effective, increasing numbers of people have come to see the WTO as a key decisionmaking body and an important point of policy leverage (Mearsheimer 1994/5). Environmentalists, for example, have focused on "greening the GATT" because there are no international environmental bodies or structures of comparable strength available for advancing pollution control and natural resource management initiatives (Esty 1994). Similarly, the relative vitality of the WTO's dispute resolution procedures has meant that a wide range of conflicts that involve trade (but other policy domains as well) have ended up being settled within the confines of the WTO (Wofford 2000). A number of these matters—involving, for instance, the protection of dolphins and sea turtles or the implementation of the reformulated gasoline provisions of the United States 1990 Clean Air Act—have forced the WTO to render judgments that go beyond the scope of its core competence. With its small trade-oriented staff, the WTO is not well positioned to make endangered species or air pollution policy decisions. As a result, there has been substantial unhappiness about the impacts of trade regime decisions in other arenas, such as the environment. Every time the WTO makes "trade and . . ." decisions, it is perceived as over-reaching and its claim to legitimacy based on 'reason' gets strained (Dunoff 1997).

Acceptance of a decisionmaking process based on bureaucratic rationality can only persist to the extent that the public is convinced that the decisions that are made are "technical" in nature and undergirded by "science." The WTO's impact has clearly moved beyond the narrow realm of trade economics; its decisions inescapably involve trade-offs with other policy goals, broadly affect other realms, and clearly require value judgments.[4] Under such circumstances, the presumption in favor of technocratic rationality cannot be sustained. And the problem is not merely one of perception. Insofar as the trade agenda intersects with other policy domains such as environmental protection, trade logic and principles cannot be counted upon to reconcile appropriately the competing policy pressures. In sum, while in some policy domains, there continues to be a push for more "science" as a way of reducing disputes and over-politicization, in trade policy making, the tide is flowing the other way. As the public learns more about the choices to be made, demands for open debate and more "politics" rise.

To the extent that legitimacy based on rationality erodes, the need for legitimacy based on democracy and links to the public whose interests are being affected mounts. But, here again, the former virtues of the Club Model WTO have become serious detriments. In particular, the WTO's "membership" policy has emerged as a source of strain. The old Club does not seem adequately representative. For example, the exclusion in Seattle of most developing country representatives from the "green rooms," where an inner circle of key countries did the real negotiating, raised hackles among many delegates (Blackhurst 2001). Similarly, the WTO'S long-standing exclusion of nongovernmental organizations (NGOs) from its decision processes has become a bone of contention. In addition to developing country negotiators and NGOs, a series of government officials, representing other issue areas (for example, Environment Ministers) were pushed to the fringes of the Seattle convocation. Their presence—and distress—at being marginalized provides further testament to the fissures in the old international regime and the strain on the traditional, issue-based hierarchical structures.

The trade regime's evolving mission has added to the legitimacy crisis. The central focus of trade negotiations is no longer tit-for-tat tariff reductions. Trade policy making now centers on creating a rules-based system to manage international economic interdependence. Moreover, as economic integration deepens, the trade agenda inevitably touches more often and more directly on other issue domains and values (Esty 2001). Thus, the WTO's recent trouble can, in part, be traced to the failure of many participants in the trade community to recognize the shift that has occurred in their goals over the last decade.

Many free traders argue that their ambition does not go beyond advancing a narrow trade-liberalizing agenda. But as the scope of GATT rules and the other elements of the trade regime have expanded—driven by a shift from a shallow integration model toward a much deeper integration program (Rodrik 1997; Lawrence et al. 1996)—the WTO's reach has extended into intellectual property, environment, competition rules, and health care policy. Some of these inter-connections are not only inevitable, they are desirable. For example, a failure to take account within the trade regime of the possibility of transboundary pollution spillovers would render the international economic system open to market failures resulting in diminished allocative efficiency, reduced gains from trade, and lost social welfare, not to mention environmental degradation. Other interactions have exposed the narrowness of the trade agenda. The clash between the trade system's intellectual property rules as applied to AIDS drugs and the need to treat a major public health crisis in Africa provides one such example (Harrelson 2001).

Deeper economic integration cannot be sustained without a concomitant deepening of political integration (Dua and Esty 1997). Some commentators recognize this economics-politics connection but believe there exists a degree of "useful inefficiency" in the trading system that reduces harmonization pressures and permits divergent domestic policy differences to persist (Cooper 1968), insulating politicians from the pressures of globalization (Garrett 1998; Keohane and Nye 2001). Clearly, there are some buffers which allow some elements of national policy autonomy. Borders do matter (Helliwell 1998). But those who highlight the ongoing vitality of national authorities do little to reconcile their vision of a trade policy buffer with the reality of growing "sensitivity" created by higher trade-to-GDP ratios and the fact of ever-diminishing inefficiency in international trade.

Economic integration and political integration are interactive and iterative. Progress depends on a deepening sense of community. For the public to be comfortable opening its markets to goods from other jurisdictions, they must believe that these other jurisdictions generally share their core values. And shared values define a community. As the scope and depth of common values expands, so does the sense of community, which makes the public more willing to accept further economic integration. As I explain in more detail below, what is lacking at the WTO is any recognition of the need for more politics—more dialogue and debate, and engagement with civil society—as a way of building the political foundation needed to support the economic structure that is being erected.

The "democratic deficit" of the WTO goes deeper (Stokes and Choate 2001). We live in a world where state power has been weakened, and powerful new actors have emerged (Talbott 1997; Keohane and Nye 2001). The theory that a small set of trade officials and representatives—even if appointed by legitimately elected national governments—can appropriately "represent" the diverse global public has come under strain. National governments simply cannot mediate all global-scale politics. Even duly elected national governments cannot fully represent all of the voices that should be heard in the global-scale policymaking process (Esty 1998). The diversity of views is simply too great. Moreover, some of the regimes of WTO members are not fully democratic. Even where elections are held, corruption and elite domination may result in less than fully representative leadership. Derivative legitimacy built on the popular sovereignty of unelected Trade Ministries in distant national governments is simply no longer adequate (Harms 2000).

Individual identity is also more textured and multi-layered than the traditional model of representation reflects, making geographic electoral constituencies an inadequate foundation for robust public decisionmaking. Many people identify with communities of interest defined by an issue focus (for example, animal lovers, human rights activists, trade union members) as much as they do with geographically defined communities (Esty 1996). Thus, to limit their participation in global politics to electing national representatives who will designate trade ministry officials to represent the nation in a narrowly confined intergovernmental dialogue produces a terribly thin reed of popular sovereignty on which to build the legitimacy of the WTO.

The distinction here is between representation and representativeness. While it is useful to legitimacy to have the public perceive that it chose (by voting) the decisionmaker, a more powerful sense of comfort with the decision process is generated when individuals feel that not only their votes but their views were taken seriously in the course of policy making. Thus, the process by which public decisions are made always matters (Fiss 1993). And given the constitutional implications of the current WTO agenda, procedural fairness and an open dialogue are of even greater importance (Fiss 2001).

The idea of global-scale participatory democracy is often dismissed as a Utopian dream (Keohane and Nye 2001). Clearly, with six billion people on the planet, international trade policy decisions cannot be made in a "town meeting" format. But the WTO policymaking process can be enriched by a shift toward more transparency and open debate that engages non-governmental interests and the spectrum of views from civil society more fully (Habermas 2001). This does not mean that NGOs will—or should—get to vote when the time comes to make a decision. But it is useful to have the governmental decisionmakers exposed to a range of views, questions, data, analyses, and options. Not only does such a full-scale dialogue provide a forum for intellectual "competition" that strengthens the ultimate outcome, the legitimacy of the choice will be enhanced to the extent that the process is perceived as more representative (Esty 1998).

Modern norms of good public decisionmaking furthermore demand transparency (Florini 2001; Hansen 1999). Public acceptance of governmental authority depends on having a clear view of who is making the decision and on what basis they are deciding. This entails administrative law and procedures that reveal the informational foundation for the decision (a public docket) and who has tried to shape the outcome (disclosure of lobbying) (Aman 2001; Shapiro 2001). The WTO has some distance to go in adopting such norms of modern policy making.

An Alternative Model of Legitimacy

Some commentators trace the legitimacy crisis at the WTO to a lack of political accountability. Keohane and Nye (2001, p. 280), for example, conclude that "politicians are needed who can link specific organizations and policies with a broader range of public issues through electoral accountability." I see a more granular world. Legitimacy is not simply a function of popular sovereignty and decisionmaking by majority vote. Institutions also win legitimacy and authority because of their capacity to deliver good results and from their systemic ties to other institutions (checks and balances) which provide an indirect link to those who have legitimacy derived through democratic elections. The WTO needs to move forward on all of these fronts.

Popular sovereignty

While global elections and thus directly accountable WTO "politicians" seem a long way off, the trade regime could dramatically improve the quality, authoritativeness, and representativeness of its decisionmaking and, in doing so, enhance its legitimacy. Lacking any global "demos," there will inescapably be limits to the accountability of WTO decisionmakers, but improved connections to the national (and sub-national) publics across the world can be established. In particular, non-governmental organizations (NGOs) can provide a degree of "connective tissue," linking distant citizens with the WTO (Esty 1998).[5] NGOs can pass information "down" from the WTO to their constituencies, ensuring better public understanding of the workings of the trade regime. A commitment to transparency and to greater involvement of civil society groups within the WTO would provide trade policymakers with access to fresh thinking, more diverse information sources, and a wide range of viewpoints coming "up" to Geneva from across the world. The presence of NGO-provided intellectual "competition" would produce a more vigorous

WTO policy dynamic and add to the trade regime's capacity to reflect popular will and to generate well-reasoned outcomes.

To improve its accountability and connection to those with electoral legitimacy, the WTO might also engage more directly with national-scale politicians. One idea would be for legislators from a diverse set of countries to hold joint "oversight hearings" on the WTO's performance. While the WTO cannot gain the full credibility that might be generated by having directly elected leaders, more outreach and more vigorous policy debates would go some distance towards enhanced legitimacy.

Reason

Trade policy making in its current form is not a technocratic science but rather a broad-gauged realm in which values inevitably play a role and through which the balancing of trade goals with other policy aims must be worked out. The Seattle fiasco marks the death knell of the WTO as a technocratic decisionmaking body operating out of sight. But the trade regime can reclaim a degree of legitimacy based on the rationality of its outputs if its capacity for generating "right" answers is restored.

As a critical first step, the WTO must trim its sails and reserve its strength for core trade liberalization activities. By retreating from its current role as dispute resolution mechanism to the world, perhaps the WTO can reestablish its reputation for authoritativeness, efficiency, and fairness. Whenever possible, the WTO should avoid making decisions that are viewed as extending beyond its scope of trade competence. The WTO's authoritativeness and legitimacy would be enhanced to the extent that "trade and environment" problems, for example, could be redirected to a functioning Global Environmental Organization (GEO).[6] Where decisions inescapably touch other policy domains, more effort should be made to draw in relevant expertise. A more virtual WTO that places itself within a web of global public policy networks would be more effective and durable (Reinecke 1997; Slaughter 1999).

Authoritativeness is also established by the breadth and depth of the debate that takes place when difficult decisions must be made. Especially where there are high degrees of uncertainty over issues, it is important to triangulate on the truth. To ensure the requisite spectrum of viewpoints, the WTO needs more robust, transparent and participatory decisionmaking processes (Weinstein and Charnovitz 2001). To the extent that the WTO makes decisions that reinforce a narrow set of values (for example, economic efficiency) and ignore other critical values (environmental protection, human rights, etc.), its credibility and authority suffer damage. The trade community today needs to bend over backwards to recognize the validity of the other policy goals and values that are impinged upon by the trading system.

The WTO's claim to reason-based legitimacy also depends on its perceived fairness and commitment to justice. Fairness has both procedural and substantive elements. A fundamental tenet of procedural fairness or "due process" is openness—identification of who is making decisions; disclosure of the assumptions on which the process turns; and an explanation of the values, influences, and information sources that are being brought to bear. Procedural fairness also requires appropriate opportunities for interested parties to contribute to the decision process as well as guarantees (enforced through a system of administrative law) that special interests will not be able to manipulate outcomes (Joerges and Dehousse 2002; Fiss 1993).

Substantive fairness is a function of consistency across circumstances and time as well as the generation of outcomes that comport a community's values and traditions (Fiss 2001). For the WTO there is a need to ensure that, in addition to getting the right answer from the trade perspective, the institution is capable of cross-issue balancing where other values (for example, environmental concerns) are at play.

Systemic reinforcement

WTO decisionmaking would also be strengthened to the extent it were embedded in a broader structure of "checks and balances."[7] As noted above, institutions draw strength from the broader systems of which they are a part. Multiple institutions occupying the same governance "space" can cross-check and reinforce each other. They can compete and cooperate in pursuit of optimal public decisionmaking (Esty 1998).

Such an architecture would entail a multi-tier system of international governance that provides a degree of "vertical" competition between international and national decisionmakers (Esty 1999; Esty and Geradin 2001). Simultaneously, the WTO would benefit from greater "horizontal" reinforcement from other international bodies that have policymaking authority and legitimacy. The presence of a Global Environment Organization would, for example, serve as a useful counterweight and counterbalance to the World Trade Organization. Similarly, a revitalized International Labor Organization (ILO) would help to broaden the institutional base of international economic management (Charnovitz 2000).

Conclusion

The WTO is capable of regaining broad public acceptance and legitimacy. But a restructuring of the trade regime's substantive rules and procedures will be required. Effective global institutions whose decisionmaking processes are understood and accepted are essential in a world of complex interdependence. While there may not be a coherent political community at the global scale nor any immediate prospect of accountability in international organizations provided by direct electoral processes, it is possible to envision more representative international decisionmaking bodies, including a revitalized World Trade Organization. Broadening the base of global governance and creating a system of checks and balances that spreads authority horizontally across international organizations as well as vertically across the global and national (and local) scales promises to deliver better results over time. Beyond strengthening its legitimacy through a commitment to more transparent procedures and to providing a forum for broader global-scale political dialogue, the WTO needs to rebuild its reputation for efficacy. To do this, the trade community must show that it recognizes the broader context of the choices made at the WTO and build sensitivity to the stresses of poverty, environmental concerns, human rights issues, and other matters into the trading system. Good governance almost always involves optimization across multiple criteria—and the WTO needs rules and procedures that better balances the (sometimes) competing goals of economic integration, trade, and investment liberalization, and economic efficiency on the one hand, with environmental protection, human rights, equity, and other virtues on the other.

Wistfulness about the disappearance of the Club Model trade regime, the old post-war economic order, and its implied shallow integration should be put aside. Such a vision is both dated and undesirable. Instead, the WTO must be seen as a crucial element of the emerging international governance system. We should acknowledge the challenge—whether we call it global constitutionalism or not—of defining the core principles, rules, and procedures for managing interdependence. Getting the structure of this new international regime right is an important challenge. As a number of commentators on globalization have observed, it is essential that "space" be reserved for separate domestic political processes (Keohane and Nye 2001), just as the U.S. Constitution reserves important elements of authority to the states. The trading regime must not over-reach and should maintain the "escape clauses" and other safety valves (Hudec 2001) which protect against too much domestic political pressure building up. But it would be a mistake to think that the future of the international economic regime would be on solid footings if we ignore the cry for reform or try to shift the focus of the trade debate to domestic fora. Revitalizing the WTO—and reestablishing its legitimacy—must be a high priority.

ENDNOTES

1. As Keohane and Nye explain, we are shifting from a mode of international relations in which people interact only through governments and where tightly controlled inter-governmental regimes facilitate international cooperation with regard to particular issues. This system can be seen as "decomposable" to the extent that

the specific regimes operate quite independently, with rules and traditions developed by a tight-knit "community" (that is, national government officials and a small number of officials serving as the staff to the relevant international organization) in the issue-area, making it hard for "outsiders" (NGOs, new state actors, etc.) to participate.

2. It will be interesting to see whether this acceptance of "expert" control over an important realm of policy continues with a faltering economy.

3. When I speak here of the trade "regime," I mean not only the small Secretariat that works within the World Trade Organization in Geneva but the entire set of trade ministry officials in all of the national capitals who contribute to the WTO policymaking process.

4. Courts similarly have their greatest legitimacy when they address issue-specific concerns raised by particularized parties and rule narrowly (on what might be considered a "negative" basis—that is, you cannot do . . .). Affirmative rulings that demand sweeping actions (for example, new laws or regulations) create much more stress and raise legitimate concerns.

5. Some critics of a more open WTO fear that a greater NGO presence within the WTO would expose the organization to greater special interest pressures and exacerbate the North-South imbalance because of the likely preponderance of Northern NGOs (Nichols 1996; Spiro 1996; Bhagwati and Srinivasan 1996). But, in fact, the logic runs the other way. Northern NGOs spend most of their time criticizing Northern governments, thereby ameliorating existing imbalances.

6. Of course, today we lack a functioning international environmental regime. For information on ongoing research into the possible structure of a GEO, see the Yale University Global Environmental Governance Web site (http://www.yale.edu/envirocenter/research).

7. The literature on the benefits of checks and balances runs deep (see, for example, Amar 1987; Strauss 1984; Webster and Bell 1997; Ackerman 2000).

REFERENCES

Ackerman, B. (2000), "The New Separation of Powers," *Harvard Law Review*, 113: 633.

Aman, A. C. (2001), "Globalization, Accountability, and the Future of Administrative Law: The Limits of Globalization and the Future of Administrative Law: From Government to Governance," *Indiana Journal of Global Legal Studies*, 8 (Spring): 379, 383–384, 396–401.

Amar, A. R. (1987), "Of Sovereignty and Federalism," *Yale Law Journal*, 96: 1492–1519.

Anderson, K. and R. Blackhurst (1992), *The Greening of World Trade Issues*, Ann Arbor, MI: University of Michigan Press.

Bhagwati, J. (1993), "The Case for Free Trade," *Scientific American*, 269 (November): 42.

Bhagwati, J. and T. N. Srinivasan (1996), "Trade and Environment," in J. Bhagwati and R. E. (eds.), *Fair Trade and Harmonization: Prerequisites for Free Trade*, Cambridge, MA: MIT Press.

Blackhurst, R. (2001), "Reforming WTO Decisionmaking: Lessons from Singapore and Seattle," in K. G. Deutsch and B. Speyer (eds.), *The World Trade Organization Millennium Round: Freer Trade in the Twenty-First Century*, London: Routledge.

Bodansky, D. (1999), "The Legitimacy of International Governance: A Coming Challenge for International Environmental Law," *American Journal of International Law*, 93 (July): 596.

Breton, A. (1996), *Competitive Governments: An Economic Theory of Politics and Public Finance*, Cambridge: Cambridge University Press.

Charnovitz, S. (1994), "The World Trade Organization and Social Issues," *Journal of World Trade*, 28 (October): 17.

Charnovitz, S. (2000), "The International Labour Organisation in Its Second Century," in J. A. Frowein and R. Wolfrum, *Max Planck Yearbook of United Nations Law—Volume IV*, The Hague: Kluwer Law International.

Cooper, R. M. (1968), *The Economics of Interdependence: Economic Policy in the Atlantic Community*, New York: McGraw-Hill.

Dua, A. and D. C. Esty (1997), *Sustaining the Asia Pacific Miracle*, Washington DC: Institute for International Economics, pp. 109–10, 120–127.

Dunoff, J. L. (1994), "Institutional Misfits: The GATT, the ICJ, and Trade-Environment Disputes," *Michigan Journal of International Law*, 15: 1043.

Dunoff, J. L. (1997), " 'Trade And': Recent Developments in Trade Policy and Scholarship—And Their Surprising Political Implications," *Northwestern Journal of International Law and Business*, 17 (Winter–Spring): 759.

Eskridge, Jr., William N. and John Ferejohn (1992), "The Article I, Section 7 Game," *Georgetown Law Journal*, 80: 523–64.

Esty, D. C. (1994), *Greening the GATT: Trade, Environment, and the Future*, Washington DC: Institute for International Economics.

Esty, D. C. (1996), "Revitalizing Environmental Federalism," *Michigan Law Review*, 95: 570.

Esty, D. C. (1998), "Nongovernmental Organizations at the World Trade Organization: Cooperation, Competition, or Exclusion," *Journal of International Economic Law*, 1: 123.

Esty, D. C. (1999), "Toward Optimal Environmental Governance," *New York University Law Review*, 74: 1495.

Esty, D. C. (2000), "An Environmental Perspective on Seattle," *Journal of International Economic Law*, 3: 176.

Esty, D. C. (2001), "Bridging the Trade-Environment Divide," *Journal of Economic Perspectives*, 15: 113.

Esty, D, C. and D. Geradin (2001), "Regulatory Co-opetition," in D. C. Esty and D. Geradin (eds.), *Regulatory Competition and Economic Integration: Comparative Perspectives*, Oxford: Oxford University Press.

Fiss, O. M. (2001), "The Autonomy of Law," *Yale Journal of International Law*, 26 (Summer): 517, 520, 525–526.

Fiss, O. M. (1993), "The Allure of Individualism," *Iowa Law Review*, 78: 970–971, 978–979.

Florini, A. (2001), "Decent Exposure," *World Link* (July/August): 12–13.

Franck, T. M. (1990), *The Power of Legitimacy Among Nations*, New York: Oxford University Press.

Frug, G. E. (1984), "The Ideology of Bureaucracy in American Law," *Harvard Law Review*, 97: 1276.

Garrett, G. (1998), *Partisan Politics in the Global Economy*, Cambridge: Cambridge University Press.

Goldman, P. (1994), "The Democratization of the Development of the United States Trade Policy," *Cornell International Law Journal*, 27: 631.

Gilpin, R. (1987), *The Political Economy of International Relations*, Princeton, NJ: Princeton University Press.

Habermas, J. (2001), *The Postnational Constellation*, Cambridge, MA: MIT Press.

Hansen, P. I. (1999), "Transparency, Standards of Review and the Use of Trade Measures to Protect the Global Environment," *Virginia Journal of International Law*, 39 (Summer): 1017, 1021, 1061–1068.

Harms, B. C. (2000), "Holding Public Officials Accountable in the International Realm: A New Multi-Layered Strategy to Combat Corruption," *Cornell International Law Journal*, 33: 159, 180–181.

Harrelson, J. A. (2001), "TRIPS, Pharmaceutical Patents and the HIV/AIDS Crisis: Finding the Proper Balance Between Intellectual Property Rights and Compassion," *Widener Law Symposium Journal*, 7 (Spring): 175.

Helliwell, J. (1998), *How Much Do National Borders Matter?* Washington DC: Brookings Institution Press.

Howse, R. (1999), "The House That Jackson Built: Restructuring the GATT System," *Michigan Law Review*, 20: 107.

Hudec, R. E. (1971), "GATT or GABB? The Future Design of the General Agreement on Tariffs and Trade," *Yale Law Journal*, 80: 1299.

Hudec, R. E. (2001), "Covenent," in Roger Porter et al. (eds.), *Efficiency, Equity and Legitimacy: The Multilateral Trading System at the Millennium*, Washington DC: Brookings Institution Press, pp. 295–300.

Hurd, I. (1999), "Legitimacy and Authority in International Politics," *International Organization*, 53 (Spring): 379.

Jackson J. (1994), *World Trade and the Law of GATT*, New York: Bobbs-Merrill.

Jackson J. (1996), "Reflections on Constitutional Challenges to the Global Trading System," *Chicago Kent Law Review*, 72: 511, 519–521.

Jeffress, L. and J.-P. Mayanobe (2001), "A World Struggle is Underway: An Interview with Jose Bove," *Z Magazine*, June.

Joerges, C. and R. Dehousse (eds.) (2002), "Good Governance in an Integrated Market," *The Collected Courses of the Academy of European Law*, Vol. XI, Book 2.

Kahn, P. (1989), "Reason and Will in the Origins of American Constitutionalism," *Yale Law Journal*, 98: 449.

Keohane, R. O. and J. S. Nye, Jr. (2001), "The Club Model of Multilateral Cooperation and Problems of Democratic Legitimacy," in Roger Porter et al. (eds.), *Efficiency, Equity and Legitimacy: The Multilateral Trading System at the Millennium*, Washington DC: Brookings Institution Press.

Kobrin, S. (1998), "Back to the Future: Neomedievalism and the Postmodern Digital World Economy," *Journal of International Affairs*, 51: 362–386.

Ku, C. (2001), "Global Governance and the Changing Face of International Law," *ACUNS Reports and Papers* 2: 1–4.

Lawrence, R. et al. (1996), *A Vision of the World Economy: Openness, Diversity, and Cohesion.* Washington DC: Brookings Institution Press.

Mearsheimer, J. (1994/5), "The False Promise of International Institutions," *International Security,* 19 (Winter): 3.

Nichols, P. M. (1996), "Realism, Liberalism, Values, and the World Trade Organization," *Pennsylvania Journal of International Economic Law,* 17: 851, 856–860.

O'Rourke, K. H. (2001), "Globalization and Inequality: Historical Trends," National Bureau of Economic Research, Working Paper 8339.

Petersmann, E.-U. (1992), "National Constitutions, Foreign Trade Policy, and European Community Law," *European Journal of International Law,* 3: 15.

Reinecke, W. (1997), *Global Public Policy,* Washington DC: Brookings Institution Press.

Rodrik, D. (1997), *Has Globalization Gone Too Far?* Washington DC: Institute for International Economics.

Ruggie, J. V. (1983), "International Regimes, Transactions, and Change: Embedded Liberalism in the Post-War Economic Order," in Stephen D. Krasner (ed.), *International Regimes,* Ithaca: Cornell University Press.

Shaffer, G. C. (2001), "The World Trade Organization Under Challenge: Democracy and the Law and Politics of the WTO's Treatment of Trade and Environment Matters," *Harvard Environmental Law Review,* 25: 1.

Schott, J. J. (ed.) (1996), *The World Trading System: Challenges Ahead,* Washington DC: Institute for International Economics.

Shapiro, M. (2001), "Administrative Law Unbounded: Reflections on Government and Governance," *Indiana Journal of Global Legal Studies,* 8: 369.

Simon, H. A. (1996), *The Sciences of the Artificial,* 3rd ed., Cambridge, MA: MIT Press.

Slaughter, A.-M. (1999), "The Long Arm of the Law," *Foreign Policy,* 114 (Spring): 34.

Spiro, P. J. (1996), "New Global Potentates: Nongovernmental Organizations and the 'Unregulated' Marketplace," *Cardozo Law Review,* 19: 957.

Stephan, P. B. (1999), "Part IV Relationship of the United States to International Institutions: The New International Law—Legitimacy, Accountability, Authority and Freedom in the New Global Order," *University of Colorado Law Review,* 70 (Fall): 1555.

Stokes, B. and P. Choate. (2001), *Democratizing US Trade Policy,* New York: Council on Foreign Relations.

Strauss, P. (1984), "The Place of Agencies in Government: Separation of Powers and the Fourth Branch," *Columbia Law Review,* 84: 573.

Talbott, S. (1997), "Globalization and Diplomacy: A Practitioner's Perspective," *Foreign Policy,* 108 (Fall): 69.

van Dijck, P. and G. F. Faber (1996), *Challenges to the New World Trade Organization (Legal Aspects of International Organization,* 28), The Hague: Kluwer Law International.

Weber, M. (1994), "The Profession and Vocation of Politics," in P. Lassman and R. Speirs (eds.), *Political Writings,* Cambridge: Cambridge University Press.

Weber, S. (2000), "International Organizations and the Pursuit of Justice in the World Economy," *Ethics and International Affairs,* 4.

Webster, D. and D. Bell (1997), "First Principles of Constitutional Revision," *Nova Law Review*, 22: 391.

Weinstein, M. M. and S. Charnovitz (2001), "The Greening of the WTO," *Foreign Affairs*, 80: 147.

Wilson, J. Q. (1989), *Bureaucracy: What Government Agencies Do and Why They Do It*, United States: Basic Books.

Wofford, C. (2000), "A Greener Future at the WTO: The Refinement of WTO Jurisprudence on Environmental Exceptions to the GATT," *Harvard Environmental Law Review*, 24: 563.

David Henderson

WTO 2002: Imaginary Crisis, Real Problems

Introduction

In his challenging article in the inaugural issue of *World Trade Review*, Daniel Esty takes the position that the international trading system, and with it the World Trade Organization, face "a serious legitimacy crisis." He argues that the world has changed profoundly, in ways that put in question the present status, objectives, and procedures of the WTO: hence the Organization now "stands at a watershed." He puts forward some radical proposals for reforming it.

While I agree with Esty that the trading system and the WTO currently face serious problems, I see the nature and origins of these problems in different terms from his. I believe that both his diagnosis and his prescription are wide of the mark.

Esty's thesis has three main interrelated elements.

The first of these concerns the issue of legitimacy which features in his title. The argument here runs as follows. The WTO's justification and effectiveness depend on its recovering, through far-reaching measures of reform, a legitimacy which it no longer possesses. The twin foundations of legitimacy for international agencies are "popular sovereignty" and "efficacy," and it is in relation to the former in particular that the present crisis has arisen, the WTO, like the GATT before it, is run by officials who are not elected, and whose allegiance is to member governments. Such official ties to governments provide only an indirect link with popular sovereignty; and given the now extended responsibilities of the Organization, and the increase in public concern about what it does, the time has come to establish a formal and direct connection. Efficacy alone is no longer enough to furnish legitimacy, and in any case, the efficacy of the Organization has now itself been put in question by its critics in 'civil society.' Hence the WTO should now make "a commitment to transparency and to greater involvement of civil society groups" (p. 17) so as to establish the foundation of popular sovereignty which it can no longer do without and regain the legitimacy that it has lost.

A second element concerns the objectives of the Organization. Here Esty argues (p. 7) that "the trade regime needs to pursue its economic goals in a fashion that shows sensitivity to other goals and values, such as poverty alleviation, environmental protection, and the promotion of public health." This is a strange form of words, since poverty alleviation is unmistakably an economic goal, and the same is true of both environmental protection and public health in so far as, under both headings, monetary values can be attributed to alternative states of affairs and outcomes. But the underlying idea can be expressed in a different way. Essentially, what Esty proposes is that in relation to trade rules and trade policies the WTO should explicitly weigh and take into account what could be their full effects, both economic and non-economic, and in particular their possible impact on the state of the environment and the distribution of income within and between countries. It should not treat trade liberalization as its sole purpose and concern.

A third element relates to global governance. Like many other observers, Esty takes the view that globalization has brought with it a need for new forms and mechanisms of international collective action: "Effective global institutions . . . are essential in a world of complex interdependence" (p. 19), and (p. 12) "the trade regime stands at the center of the emerging structure of global governance." In this new structure, "more representative international decision-making bodies, including a revitalized World Trade Organization," would play a larger role. In the case of the WTO, it is the two proposed changes in its functioning—the greater involvement of "civil society," and the conscious adoption of broader objectives—that would provide the necessary "revitalization." By embracing wider aims and ensuring closer ties with popular sovereignty, the Organization would gain acceptance and support, improve its efficacy, and enlarge its capacity to contribute to the stronger global governance that the world now stands in need of. The different elements of radical reform are thus presented as mutually reinforcing.

In what follows I focus mainly on Esty's thesis, but refer also to some related lines of thought. I begin by examining the issue of legitimacy in relation to international agencies in general and the WTO in particular.

International Agencies, Governments and "Popular Sovereignty"

Since Esty is so much concerned with the legitimacy of organizations, it is worth asking how this term is to be interpreted. His treatment of the issue has a missing dimension. Although he rightly notes (p. 9) that legitimacy "is a complex concept in the context of governance," he considers only one aspect of it. Both in his text and in an article that he draws on by Keohane and Nye (2001), the legitimacy of an institution is implicitly defined in terms of its acceptability to public opinion in a democratic society and the attributes that make for acceptability. But this is not the only possible interpretation; one can also think of the concept in more straight-forward formal terms. The Oxford English Dictionary provides a form of words that gives expression to this alternative—or additional—interpretation. It offers, as one meaning of legitimacy, "the condition of being in accord with law or principle" (1989, Vol. VIII, p. 811).[1] Admittedly, it can be argued that, at any rate in relation to political institutions, such an interpretation captures only a part of what is involved. But formal legitimacy, even if no more than a starting point, is neither irrelevant nor unimportant for international agencies as for other institutions of governance. In this restricted but pertinent sense of the term, the legitimacy of an organization such as the WTO does not derive from, nor depend on, public acceptability or support. It comes from governments alone.

This direct link with governments rather than peoples is inherent in the nature of institutions such as the WTO. It was the governments of national states that created the Organization, as they had created the GATT before it. In the same way, it is governments that have established an array of international organizations including the International Monetary Fund (IMF), the World Bank (IBRD), the regional development banks, the International Labour Organisation (ILO), the Organisation for Economic Cooperation and Development (OECD), and the various agencies that directly make up the United Nations (UN) system. All such organizations are, and can only be, the creatures of sovereign nation-states. It is their member governments that bring them into existence, lay down their initial roles and terms of reference, decide their future membership, finance their current activities (whether directly or indirectly), and exercise continuing control over what they do and how they do it. Admittedly there is no set pattern of relationships and procedures, and different agencies may acquire, or be granted, different degrees of initiative and autonomy. But whatever pattern may evolve, and whatever the differences between the agencies which are indeed substantial, it is the member governments that determine these matters and have the sole right to change them. Except by winding up an agency, a course of action which only they can decide on, its governments cannot escape these responsibilities. So long as an international agency continues to be maintained and financed by member governments, its right to exist, and to carry out the functions which those members have collectively assigned to it, is clear. To this extent, and in this sense, its legitimacy derives from governments alone. Questions of public acceptability and "direct links with popular sovereignty" do not enter in.

What is more, the formal legitimacy of an agency does not necessarily depend on its having the "indirect links with popular sovereignty" which are made possible by democratic processes within member states. Most existing international agencies include among their members governments which are far from democratic, and this is neither an oversight nor an anomaly. Now, as in the past, it is unusual for the observance of democratic forms to be made a condition of eligibility; generally speaking, the right of a member state to join an agency, and to participate in its affairs, does not depend on whether or how far the government of that state is democratically elected, accountable to its citizens, and concerned to safeguard civil and political rights.[2] This is most obviously the case with the United Nations, where Article 3 of the Charter specifies that membership is open "to all peace-loving states which accept the obligations contained in the present Charter and, in the judgement of the Organization, are able and willing to carry out these obligations." The reason for this is clear: insistence on the observance of democratic forms as a condition of membership would not only have created from the start huge and divisive problems of interpretation, but also put in question the principle of universality which is widely viewed as essential to the legitimacy of the UN system.

Forms of government were likewise not taken into account in defining eligibility for membership of the GATT, and this continues to be the case in the WTO. Thus—to take a recent leading instance—China was not barred from consideration for membership of the Organization on the grounds that its political system does not provide for free elections or protect basic liberties. As in other applications for membership, and in accordance with the WTO Articles of Agreement, the pre-conditions were more technical and specific to the Organization. Most people, including some though not all of today's critics of the WTO in "civil society," would take the view that the legitimacy of the WTO was not undermined by the accession of China. As to the future, extending the criteria for accession, so as to include within them the observance of democratic forms, would strengthen the Organization's claim to formal legitimacy only if it were agreed by the existing member governments. It is for them to determine the basis of eligibility.

Esty notes (p. 15) that "some of the regimes of WTO members are not fully democratic." Although he views this as one of the reasons why the Organization now lacks legitimacy in his sense of the term, he does not argue for a tightening of the conditions for WTO membership. He simply by-passes the aspect of formal legitimacy, to argue that those of the Organization's member governments that are democratic should now take effective steps to strengthen its claims to public acceptability, through new or stronger links to "popular sovereignty."

Whether such direct links would in fact make the WTO more legitimate is open to question. The notion that they make the democratic process within nations more legitimate has been questioned by Robert Hudec in the context of the history of trade policy in the United States. Hudec makes the point that the notorious Smoot-Hawley tariff of 1930 was a product of "direct democracy:" "Seldom has so much of the US electorate had so much direct impact on so many details of a major US statute" (Hudec 1999, p. 217). He argues (p. 220) that such episodes, as also the handling of present-day issues of sanitary and phyto-sanitary standards, cast doubt on what he terms "the simplistic notion that democratic participation is a one-dimensional phenomenon measured by the distance between the voter and the decision-maker."

In Esty's treatment of the issues, this "simplistic notion" goes unquestioned; legitimacy and "popular sovereignty" march together. Moreover, it is not sufficient for democratic participation to be achieved by actions taken, and procedures followed, within the boundaries of member states; the "diverse global public" has to be effectively brought into the processes of the WTO. Hence (he argues) the official machinery of trade policy must give more scope, in the WTO as well as at national level, to non-governmental organizations which directly represent the people of a country, and in some cases, arguably, the people of the world.

The Status and Claims of Non-Governmental Organizations

Esty's proposals for the WTO can be set against a wider background of institutions and events. In sketching out this background, I use the lower-case term "non-governmental organizations" in a broad sense, so that it covers unofficial associations of all kinds, national and international. Among non-governmental organizations thus broadly defined, two groups are especially relevant in relation to the constitution and working of international agencies. One comprises representatives of the "social partners"—that is, the organizations that represent businesses and trade unions. The second is the "public interest" groups which have grown in number and influence in recent years. Following general current practice, I refer to these latter as the (upper-case) NGOs. They stand for particular causes, rather than sectional or professional interests. They include consumer associations, conservation and environmental groups, societies concerned with economic development in poor countries, human rights groups, movements for social justice, humanitarian societies, organizations representing indigenous peoples, and church groups from all denominations. They are often classed together under the label of "civil society"; but this is a misuse of language, since the term should be, and historically has been, given a much broader meaning. It would appear that, in referring to "civil society," it is the NGOs that Esty has in mind.

The principle of non-official involvement in the proceedings of international agencies is neither new nor controversial. Right from the start, the UN system assigned a role to non-governmental organizations. Article 71 of the Charter authorized the Economic and Social Council "to make suitable arrangements for consultation with non-governmental organizations which are concerned with matters within its competence," and a recent text notes that there are now over 1,500 such organizations that are recognized as having consultative status within ECOSOC (Archer 2001, pp. 26–27). Well before the UN Charter was drafted, a much closer involvement of particular non-governmental organizations, going beyond consultation, had already been established by its member governments within the ILO, which was set up after the First World War. The ILO is now, and always has been, an agency in which "the trade union and employers' representatives . . . have an equal voice [with member governments] in formulating its policies" (ILO, 2002, opening page of text). In the OECD as in its predecessor agency, labor and business organizations have throughout been formally represented by advisory committees which have offices and staff in Paris. The committees function as channels for information, consultation, and exchange of views.

More recently, the NGOs, as distinct from business organizations and trade unions whose participation has a much longer history, have acquired a more prominent role in the working of many international agencies. In the main UN system, some notable steps towards involving them more closely were taken in the context of the 1992 UN Conference on Environment and Development (the 'Rio Summit'). Since then they have continued to grow in numbers, influence and (thanks largely to the Internet) in the ability to act in concert; and all the main international agencies, at varying stages and in different ways and degrees, and with the approval or acquiescence of their member governments, have made provision for enlarged NGO participation in their proceedings. The WTO is among these.

The question now is how much further, and in what ways, the involvement of non-governmental organizations should be taken; and though this aspect is rarely mentioned, and is not explicitly referred to by Esty, it applies not only to "public interest" NGOs but also to representatives of business and labor organizations. I begin with some general observations, and then turn to aspects that are more specific to the WTO.

Participation: the general aspect

It is possible to distinguish broadly between two forms of participation, both of which can be provided for within national states as well as—or possibly, rather than—within international agencies. Under the first, governments can involve non-governmental organizations more closely by making non-sensitive information widely and promptly available to them and by establishing, and treating seriously, procedures for consulting them. In such a process, the distinction between insiders and outsiders—the official participants and the non-governmental organizations—is fully maintained, though the outsiders are given more time, attention and opportunities to be heard. A second form of participation goes further, and brings closer interaction between the two worlds. It can cover active involvement of non-governmental organizations in intergovernmental meetings, substantive discussions, negotiations and decisions, and also in operations where—as with the IMF, the IBRD and the European Commission—an agency has major operational responsibilities.

The first form of participation is relatively straightforward and uncontroversial, at intergovernmental as well as national level. As noted above, governments have been taking this path in the WTO and elsewhere, with NGOs especially in mind. The Guidelines established in 1996 by the General Council of the WTO "mention the need to make documents more readily available than in the past, require the Secretariat to engage actively with NGOs, and rec-ommend the development of new mechanisms for fruitful engagement, includ-ing symposia on WTO-related issues" (Loy 2001, p. 122); and since then, recent Directors-General have made clear their commitment to act on these lines. Gary Sampson has noted (Sampson 2001, p. 12) that "In the run-up to the [1999] Seattle meeting, all negotiating proposals were posted on the WTO website with no apparent ill effects. This would have been considered unthink-able to many delegations even in the recent past." In the OECD, the 1999 ministerial communiqué said that "Ministers . . . looked to the Organisation to assist governments in the important task of improving communication and consultation with civil society."

Since making agencies more open and consultation processes fuller and more intensive gives rise to costs as well as benefits, there will always be ques-tions as to how far to go. Again, there may be problems in judging the claims to recognition of NGOs in particular, and in deciding which of them are to be brought into formal consultations; the issues of credentials and "modali-ties" are not to be seen as trivial. But the general principles of transparency and closer consultation are widely accepted, with good reason, and accepting them does not change or obscure the boundaries between insiders and outsiders. "Popular sovereignty" is not given serious expression.

For Esty and those who share his views, this does not meet the main problem, which is that even democratic governments and those who work for them are insufficiently representative of their peoples. The remedy is (to use Esty's wording, p. 19) "to establish more representative international decisionmaking bodies." Non-governmental organizations would then have a recognized place of their own, alongside ministers and officials, in the sub-stantive work and the decisions of an agency such as the WTO. This would supposedly ensure popular sovereignty and the legitimacy that depends on it.

I believe that this conception of legitimacy is at fault.[3] The whole notion of a 'civil society' which has claims of its own to speak for the people of a country has no basis when that country has a democratically elected and responsible government: persons who are not elected, and who are not accountable to a duly elected and broadly representative legislature, can have no such representative status. This is not to argue that democracy is only a matter of elections, nor that the notion of 'civil society' is without meaning or value, despite the questionable use that is now often made of it. The issue is one of defining admissible roles and claims, and here the main point is con-tained in the view that Gary Sampson attributes to WTO member states, that "the WTO is an intergovernmental organization and governments should represent the collectivity of their constituents" (Sampson 2000, p. 1114).

The above argument applies to all non-governmental organizations. It is sometimes argued, or simply assumed, that the NGOs have a special claim to represent society as a whole, which is not possessed by business or professional groups, because they speak for the "public interest." This is doubly mistaken. For one thing, the contrast is overdrawn. The involvement of groups representing special interests, including business organizations, may serve to promote better informed and more satisfactory outcomes. At the same time, the distinction between "sectional" and "public interest" groups is blurred in practice; there is no reason to presume that all NGOs, particularly those with large organizations and budgets, are free from self-regarding motives. Second, it may be that arguments typically advanced by NGOs are open to question, and that their recommendations for action, if taken seriously, would be contrary to the interests of people in general. (Esty himself notes [p. 8] that "Many of those who criticize the WTO and other elements of international economic structure have little foundation for the charges they make.") Fundamentally, though, what is in question is not the motives or wisdom of non-governmental organizations, including NGOs, but their status as bodies that are neither elected nor politically accountable.

This does not mean that involvement of these organizations cannot properly or usefully go beyond consultation—as witness the very different cases of the ILO, with its long-established tripartite structure, and the IBRD where, with the consent of member governments, NGOs are now closely keyed into operational work. But two principles should bear on such involvement. First, its nature and extent is for governments to decide, case by case. Second, no non-governmental organization, whether speaking for businesses, trade unions, professional groups, "public interest" concerns or any other constituency, has a valid claim to active participation in its own right in proceedings where the responsibility for outcomes rests, and has to rest, with the governments of member states, and is therefore exercised by political leaders and the officials who are authorized, qualified and paid to act on their behalf and in support of their role.[4]

The qualifying phrase, "in its own right," needs to be underlined. My contention is that "civil society" has no claim, on grounds of democratic legitimacy alone, to have a governing voice in international agencies, or even to close involvement in their substantive work. But the member governments are free to choose: it is for them to decide whether and how far to go down such a path. While they cannot shed their status or responsibilities, they can, if they so wish, assign to representatives of non-governmental organizations roles and tasks within the agencies alongside, or even in place of, official participants. I turn now to consider the case for moving in this direction within the WTO.

Participation: the WTO today

Up to now, member governments of the WTO have drawn a fairly clear line between the two forms of participation described above. While the Organization has made itself more accessible and open to the non-official world, through informing and consulting non-governmental organizations more fully, governments have not been prepared to sanction more active outside involvement. It is true that a few governments sometimes include representatives of non-governmental organizations in their delegations to biennial WTO Ministerial Conferences, but to the best of my knowledge none are directly involved in the day-to-day operations of the Organization. To quote Sampson (2000, p. 11) again, "Unlike a number of other international organizations, the WTO permits only representatives of governments and selected intergovernmental organizations to participate in or observe the processes of its regular activities."

There are sound reasons for retaining these restrictions on outside participation in the activities of the Organization.

One reason, and arguably the most decisive, concerns the Organization's agenda, As Sampson notes (p. 11 again), "WTO members justify their reluctance on the grounds that the WTO is both a legally binding instrument and a forum for negotiations." The latter aspect is especially telling. More than any other international agency, the work of the WTO is linked to intergovernmental negotiations, with the national delegates chiefly acting as actual or potential negotiators and the Secretariat assisting them in that capacity. Few governments, if any, would welcome the active and regular participation of outsiders in negotiating processes, and there are valid reasons for this. An essential part of the GATT/WTO's raison d'etre is that governments can negotiate the exchange of market-opening concessions in order to overcome the opposition of protectionist interests at home. It would hardly make sense to bring such outsiders inside the negotiating tent. The same argument applies to negotiations relating to revising existing rules or making new ones, where "protectionist capture" is an ever-present threat.

Second, many if not most of the NGOs which aspire to greater influence in the WTO either do not share or actually reject the objectives of the Organization. They are opposed to freedom of cross-border trade and capital flows, suspicious of further moves in that direction, and preoccupied with what they see as the damaging effects of globalization. These attitudes typically go with a generalized hostility to capitalism, multinational enterprises, and the idea of a market economy.[5]

Third, the issue is a divisive one. The support for closer NGO involvement has largely come from some of the OECD member countries, while it is firmly opposed by the governments of most developing countries.

For all these reasons, the active formal involvement in the substantive work of the WTO of non-governmental organizations in general, and NGOs in particular, would make it a less effective institution for achieving the objectives that its member governments have assigned to it. Esty's proposals for constitutional change, however, go together with the view that these objectives should now be broadened. I therefore turn to this second element of his thesis.

Objectives, Agenda, and the Ensemble of Policies

Esty believes that trade officials, national and international, need to change their ways, and hence the ways of the WTO. They should recognize that "The WTO's impact has clearly moved beyond the narrow realm of trade economics; its decisions inescapably involve trade-offs with other policy goals, broadly affect other realms, and clearly involve value judgements" (p. 13). This recognition should go together with an administrative reorientation. They should no longer work within the now outdated "club model" of international cooperation, under which groups of like-minded specialists conduct negotiations behind closed doors, and arrive at agreements largely in isolation from government policies in general, within what Robert Keohane and Joseph Nye (who invented the concept of the club model) refer to as "decomposable issue areas" (Keohane and Nye 2001, p. 291).

It is true that trade officials, like other specialists, live much of the time in a world of their own. Up to a point, however, such things are inevitable, and serve a useful purpose: one might expect that the same situation would soon prevail, in large part for valid reasons, in the new Global Environment Organization which Esty would like to see established. In any case, isolation is not the whole story: in most areas, including that of trade policies, the working environment is far from wholly closed. Governments remain responsible for the "ensemble of policies," in economic affairs as elsewhere, and in reviewing and deciding the economic ensemble they typically try to take account of a broad range of objectives and concerns including those that Esty lists. The fact that in a particular area of policy ministers and officials engage with limited and specific issues does not mean that they are required, expected or allowed to do so in isolation or without regard to wider aspects.

Esty gives an oversimplified picture of the work of trade officials, and of the WTO and the GATT before it. He portrays those involved as single-mindedly pursuing the cause of freer trade, with "economic efficiency" alone as their guiding principle. But the trade policies of member governments have never conformed to such a pattern. In a brilliant dissection of the draft Havana Charter of 1947, Jacob Viner showed that the International Trade Organisation (ITO) then proposed was a complex compromise reflecting the prevailing political realities of the time: it certainly was not a blueprint for free trade (Viner 1947). The GATT, which then emerged as a pared-down version of the ITO, was likewise a delicate political balancing act: rules were established to liberalize trade in goods, but these were circumscribed by other rules which allowed contracting parties wide leeway to continue existing protectionist measures and even to adopt new ones.

This balancing act was maintained throughout the history of the GATT, and has now been transferred to the WTO. Trade liberalization in the GATT/WTO process has throughout been gradual, patchy and laborious, sometimes reluctant, and always subject to limitations, reservations, and even on occasion reversals. With one surprising exception, which brought with it no tangible result, no WTO member has formally endorsed free trade.[6] Over the 55 years since the GATT came into existence, even those of its member governments that have participated fully in the various "trade rounds," and brought down their tariff rates accordingly, have pursued policies only of heavily qualified liberalism. This is hardly surprising, since in all of them trade policies have been, and continue to be, strongly influenced by considerations other than "efficiency," such as concern for particular interests and groups, and conceptions of national interest which can be viewed as justifying protectionist measures. The picture of trade ministers and officials as unconditional and narrowly focused proponents of trade liberalization, allowed by governments to do their will in obscurity, is a caricature.

Admittedly, to recognize these facts does not dispose of the case for a broadening of the objectives of the WTO—nor, more generally, for discarding the "club model." The main aims and concerns that governments assigned to the GATT, and which they have carried over into the WTO, are indeed restricted in scope: they relate specifically to the conduct of trade policies, where they give expression to liberal principles of quota abolition, tariff reduction, and non-discrimination. While the Organization is instructed, in its Articles of Agreement, to have regard to broader objectives, which now include "sustainable development" and ensuring that developing countries participate fully in the benefits of economic growth, these objectives form a background for officials and Secretariat, rather than serving directly as a basis for action. They do not meet the need that Esty perceives in the WTO of today, for "rules and procedures that better balance the (sometimes) competing goals of economic integration, trade, and investment liberalization, and economic efficiency on the one hand, with environmental protection, human rights, equity and other virtues on the other" (p. 19).

It is understandable that Esty's concerns relate specifically to the WTO of today rather than the GATT of old. As a result of the Uruguay Round agreements, the WTO provides market access rules for the bulk of international trade, not just trade in (some) industrial goods; it deals more extensively with non-tariff barriers, going deeper into domestic regulations that increasingly bear upon trade flows, it covers intellectual property (substantially) and trade-related investment measures (partially); nearly all agreements now form part of a "single undertaking," by which the obligations entered into by countries in different areas are linked; and these obligations have been made enforceable through a much stronger dispute settlement procedure. "New issues," such as labor and environmental standards, and rules governing competition and foreign direct investment, have swirled around the Organization for the last few years. With the exception of labor standards, all these form part of the agenda for the new WTO round launched at the Doha Ministerial Conference last year. Finally, the WTO membership has greatly increased, with the accession of many developing and transitional countries.

Overall, the WTO in 2002 is more politicized and legalized than the diplomacy-oriented GATT. It is politicized in the sense that it is in the spotlight of public heat and controversy, to a far greater extent than was ever the case with the GATT, It is legalized through what is in effect a quasi-automatic dispute settlement mechanism charged with interpreting and enforcing increasingly complicated legal agreements. The combination has manifestly put the squeeze on traditional GATT-style diplomacy. The WTO thus operates in a changed environment. Internally, it has wider though still limited scope; and partly in consequence, it faces strong and growing external pressures.

Even granting the differences between the GATT then and the WTO now, however, it does not follow that Esty's program of change should be adopted. For one thing, it is far from clear what form his new "rules and procedures" (or alternatively, as on p. 19, "new modalities and substantive principles") might take. In this connection, his two specific proposals for the Organization fit uneasily with the idea of broadening its concerns. On the one hand, he suggests (p. 17) that "As a critical first step, the WTO must trim its sails and reserve its strength for core liberalization activities," which would involve "retreating from its current role as dispute resolution mechanism to the world." At the same time, he wishes to involve the NGOs more closely in the Organization's work, even though the great majority of these are concerned with particular issues and causes rather than the ensemble of policies. More fundamentally, the whole notion of broadening the goals and concerns of the Organization is open to question.

In my view, it would be unwise for the WTO to be charged, in all its proceedings, with the duty of taking explicit account of a wide range of other objectives that governments have endorsed, but which are not directly related to the goal of a more liberal trade system. As David Robertson has noted, the fact that environment and development objectives have now been incorporated in the Organization's terms of reference does not mean that its distinctive role and purposes have to be redefined. Now as in the GATT, "the means specified in the WTO for achieving these objectives are limited to reciprocal and mutually advantageous reductions in tariffs and other barriers to trade, and the elimination of discriminatory treatment in trade relations" (Robertson 2000, p. 1119). The reason for retaining this focused agenda for the Organization is simply that (to quote Martin Wolf) "experience suggests that the opening of trade . . . flows enriches most citizens in the short run and virtually all citizens in the long run" (Wolf 2001a, p. 182). If anything, the WTO needs to re-emphasize, not redefine, the GATT's raison d'etre, albeit with a wider agenda of trade liberalization—in agriculture and services as well as industrial goods—and of rule-strengthening, especially in relation to anti-dumping measures and subsidies.

More broadly, and in relation to economic policies as a whole, it is going well beyond the evidence to argue that globalization has rendered obsolete the notion of "decomposable issue areas," with its corresponding division of labor between different specialists and different international agencies. Coordination problems are present today, as always, but they have not built up in a way that requires a jettisoning of the "club model" as a basis for international economic cooperation. There is no compelling reason to redraw the boundaries of the leading international agencies, and much to be said for the view that "at present the world does best by constructing regimes designed to achieve specific and limited ends" (Wolf 2001b, pp. 201–202).

This however raises the more general issue of "global governance," and leads onto the third element in Esty's thesis.

"Global Governance" and the Role of the WTO

Two closely related arguments are now brought to bear, by Esty and many others, to support the view that the world now requires, and is in course of developing, a stronger system of global governance in which international agencies, including the WTO, would play a leading part. Both arguments relate to the supposed effects of globalization, and both are without foundation.

Argument Number One, in its most basic form, is that the huge size and rapid growth of international trade and capital flows establishes in itself the case for more effective global governance: such flows, it is presumed, cannot be left unmanaged. For some commentators, globalization has brought the dawn of a new era. One of these international dawnists is the present Secretary-General of the UN: "Today, networks of production and trade have broken free from national borders and become truly global. But they have left the rest of the system far behind" (Annan 2001, p. 27).

A similarly melodramatic view is taken . . . by Peter Sutherland, John Sewell, and David Weiner: "It is obvious to many observers that the development of the world economy is out-pacing the capacity to govern it, at both the national and international level . . . The impact of globalization has made the 'logic' of the post-war period obsolete" (Sutherland et al. 2001, pp. 102, 103).

Argument Number Two is that (to quote Esty, p. 15) "We live in a world where state power has been weakened, and powerful new actors have emerged." It is now widely held, and endlessly reiterated on all sides, that globalization has deprived national governments of their ability to control events. This is often joined with a belief that the powers thus lost have passed in large part to multinational enterprises (MNEs), and indeed the MNEs may be among the "powerful new actors" that Esty refers to.

A presumption that globalization has had these effects often leads on to the thesis that increasingly there will be, and should be, greater involvement of NGOs and international businesses in shouldering the now heavier burdens of global governance. For example, the World Economic Forum, in a document issued after its annual meeting for 2002, advances the view that "Transparent multi-stakeholder networks will likely emerge as the most legitimate form of global problem solving in the 21st century. Governments must join with business, international organizations and the emerging transnational civil society to form coalitions around critical challenges on the global agenda and collaborate in flexible frameworks to resolve them" (World Economic Forum 2002). Other business spokespersons and organizations have voiced the same idea.

These twin arguments, or assumptions, take no account of the fact that closer international economic integration, both in recent years and farther back—for it is by no means a new phenomenon—has in large part resulted from decisions voluntarily taken by national governments. Generally speaking, governments have made their economies more open not because they were forced to but because, with good reason, they considered such actions to be in the interests of their citizens. In taking this course, they accepted specific constraints on their freedom of action; and in some cases, most notably the members and would-be members of the European Union, they have even ceded the right to determine their own trade policies. But they have done these things of their own accord. More than technological advance, national policies and institutions have determined the pace and depth of globalization, and governments remain free to decide how much further to go towards fuller economic integration with the rest of the world.

Aside from such constraints on external economic policies as they have freely accepted and wish to maintain, national states today remain almost as free to act and decide today as they were 10, 20 or 30 years ago.[7] Even small states, provided they have stable governments, retain in full the power to run their affairs in relation to such matters as defense, foreign policy, constitutional arrangements, the electoral system and voting rights, residence, citizenship, the legal system, public provision for health, pensions and welfare, and the status of the national language or languages. Even in relation to the choice of taxation rates, the evidence clearly shows that there remains substantial freedom of choice. The notion that today's more economically integrated world is one of "post-sovereign governance" has no basis.[8] As to the dreaded MNEs, the freeing of cross-border trade and investment flows tends to weaken such economic power as they may possess, because it widens the scope for competition.

For some commentators, globalization enhances the role of international agencies; thus Miles Kahler writes that "Growing international integration points to greater delegation" to the agencies (Kahler 2001, p. 104), while Keohane and Nye (2001, p. 265) begin a sentence with the words "As these institutions become more important . . ." There is in fact no such general tendency for the power of the agencies to increase. Both the IMF and the IBRD are less influential than they were 20 or 30 years ago, the Fund because its lending operations are now limited in practice to developing countries, and the Bank because of the growth of private lending to an increasing range of its borrowing countries. All the agencies, now as before, are the servants and instruments of their member governments. There is little or no evidence of any wish or tendency to delegate powers to them.

The WTO and Global Governance

It is true that the WTO can be portrayed as an exception to this generalization. At the time when the Organization was set up, John Jackson observed that its establishment marked "a watershed in the international economic system," resulting from "the mere fact of creating a definitive international arrangement, combined with the extraordinary expanse of the Uruguay Round negotiations." As noted above, the formal establishment of the WTO as an international agency (as distinct from a mere agreement), the extension of its concerns to a range of new areas, the notion of a "single undertaking," and, most notably, the enormous strengthening of the dispute settlement mechanism, have between them created a new political-legal situation for the agency and its members.

However, there is another side to the picture. It is also possible to take the view that, to quote from a recent book by Douglas Irwin, "The World Trade Organization is something more, but not much more, than the GATT . . ." (Irwin 2002, p. 186) and that both agencies should be seen as closely restricted in their capacity to act independently and to influence events. Four aspects of the WTO's inherited limitations are worth noting.

First, like the GATT, the Organization has a notably small Secretariat with a strictly limited role. Its complement of 575 permanent staff, plus some 200 persons on short term contracts, compares with a figure of over 2,800 for the IMF (counting "contractual employees" as well as regular staff), and some 11,000 staff names listed in the IBRD's current directory. The difference reflects the fact that both the Fund and the Bank, and especially the latter, have large operational responsibilities. By contrast, the primary role of the WTO Secretariat is to service national delegations. In this it resembles the OECD, where however Secretariat numbers are much larger, both absolutely and—still more—in relation to the numbers of national officials in permanent delegations, and where the scope for the Secretariat to do independent work is greater than in the WTO.

Second, the WTO like the GATT is an organization where decisions are made by consensus. The limits that this tends to impose are reinforced by a third factor, which is that, like most international agencies but unlike the Fund and the Bank, the Organization is financed by direct contributions from member governments which are subject each year to prolonged, detailed and often contentious scrutiny. Agreement on the budget is subject to consensus.

The last and most fundamental factor is that those who make up the Organization, whether in the Secretariat or the permanent delegations, have virtually no power to act independently. Generally speaking, though exceptions can occur, national delegations to the WTO are under close and continuous control from their capital cities. They are not independent actors, but persons under instruction.

Despite its enlarged scope and capacity to act, therefore, the Organization is not a powerful instrument of global governance, nor is it in course of becoming so, because this is not what its members wish or require of it. Here as elsewhere, national governments remain in charge, and show little tendency to cede or delegate authority.

Twin Illusions of Globalization

In so far as the WTO is required by its members to act in ways that constrain or put in question their conduct, the need for this does not mainly arise from globalization. To the contrary, the main activities of the Organization, and most of the debates and disputes that take place within it, arise from the fact that member governments have not fully liberalized their trade. Their failure and reluctance to do so gives rise to the rich and varied array of exceptions, qualifications, derogations, reservations and outright departures which go along with the rules, the handling of which accounts for a substantial part of the Organization's proceedings. If and in so far as member countries were prepared to liberalize unilaterally, as many of them have in fact done in the past, this would both increase the extent of globalization and reduce the WTO's present restricted role in global governance.

The notion that closer international economic integration demands new forms of collective action rests on a misconception, a distorted picture of what such integration involves.[9] In this picture, the growth of cross-border trade and capital flows, in response to liberalization, appears as an anarchic melee or tidal wave, which puts hapless people and governments at the mercy of events and forces which they cannot control. Alternatively, or even simultaneously, it is depicted as a means through which human lives are made subject to dictation by impersonal and uncaring markets.

A recent and striking instance of this second line of thinking is to be found in a document issued by the European Commission; "Existing international economic and social rules and structures are unbalanced at the global level. Global market governance has developed more quickly than global social governance" (European Commission 2001, p. 3, italics added).[10] More justly seen, the freeing of trade and capital flows is a source of neither disorder nor constraints. It is first and foremost a means by which people and enterprises, and even governments themselves as purchasers of goods and services, are enabled to realize more fully their legitimate goals and desires. Everywhere, it widens opportunities and enlarges the domain of individual freedom. There is no reason to treat it as a generalized threat, nor to suppose that it is inherently a subject for new forms or extensions of official regulation through mechanisms of "global governance."

Conclusions: The Challenges Facing the WTO

Historians often treat events with reference to two contrasting but ever-present elements, continuity and change. In the case of the WTO today, as compared with the GATT, both elements are very much in evidence. Like many commentators, Esty gives too much weight to the element of change; and in particular, he overstates the extent to which the external environment of the Organization has been transformed. Now as in the past, international agencies derive their legitimacy from their member governments; and in the case of the WTO, the fact that it is today more subject to attack, by NGOs especially, does not establish the existence of a genuine "legitimacy crisis." Now as in the past, WTO members are committed to freer trade only with many and substantial reservations: they are not subject to a narrow preoccupation with an "efficiency" criterion which has outlived its usefulness. Now as in the past, national governments possess substantial powers of action and decision. Globalization has not deprived them of these powers, and it does not render necessary, or even advisable, the creation of new modes of "global governance" in which they hand over responsibilities to international agencies. All three related elements of Esty's case for radical reform have little or no foundation of fact.

All the same, substantial changes have taken place in the role and status of the WTO, as compared with the GATT before it, and it is clear that these have brought with them problems as well as opportunities, The main problems that have emerged are summarized by David Robertson (p. 1131) as follows; "Extension of the GATT rules to services, government procurement and intellectual property has already stretched the system dangerously . . . With the dispute settlement process generating new rules which also extend the scope of the WTO into new areas, the cohesion of the membership is weakening." In addition, two recent developments have given rise to procedural problems. One is the large influx of new members. A second is the growing desire on the part of many members to participate more actively in WTO business as the Organization's agenda expands to include new and often potentially divisive subjects. As a result, changes in internal structure may well be needed in order to improve the conduct of business. One possibility, which has been proposed by Richard Blackhurst, is the creation of a formally constituted Consultative Board (Blackhurst 2001).

Last but not least among the problems that the Organization now faces is the growth in numbers, activity and influence of anti-liberal NGOs. This too is a relatively recent development, though it is linked, not with globalization as such, but with mistaken notions as to its meaning and effects.

I believe that the main threat today to the WTO, and still more to the purposes for which it and its predecessor were created by member governments, does not come from an erosion of democratic legitimacy. It arises from several sources, some old and some new. As ever, there is the combined influence of protectionist ideas and pressures, which remain strong almost everywhere, and the inherent and continuing sensitivity of trade policy questions. Alongside and reinforcing these are some newer interrelated elements. Internally, there are the problems that now arise from the combination of the Organization's expanded agenda and membership. More disturbing are external factors: the hostility of many NGOs to its aims and even its continued existence, the disposition of many member governments, as also of large and growing numbers of multinational enterprises, to fail to contest, or to make substantial concessions to, the dubious or unfounded arguments and claims of these organizations;[11] and the tendency of some member countries, including the US and the EU, to lend support to notions of "global governance" through which common international norms and standards could be defined and imposed without due regard for differing local circumstances, so that they became elements of disintegration in the world economy.

On this diagnosis, the way ahead for the Organization is not that prescribed by Esty—involving the NGOs in its substantive discussions and decisions, broadening its objectives and concerns, and extending its powers in the name of global governance. Rather, its future usefulness depends on the member governments consulting effectively with non-governmental organizations in general, especially though not only within their own borders, devising better ways of conducting the internal business of the WTO; using the now enlarged scope of the Organization in ways that are not unduly ambitious or divisive; and above all, being ready to defend the idea of trade liberalization against its many opponents and to give expression to it in their actions.

ENDNOTES

1. Oxford's main American rival, *Webster's Dictionary*, offers a similar though more explicit wording: "possession of title or status as a result of acquisition by means that are held to be in accordance with law or custom" (1961, p. 1291).
2. There are of course exceptions. Thus in the case of the OECD today, it is clear that new candidates for accession would have to establish democratic credentials as well as meeting other tests. (The fact that the criteria for OECD membership are notably more restrictive than the UN agencies is sometimes viewed, mistakenly, as weakening the Organization's claims to legitimacy.) In the case of the European Union, achieving membership is formally dependent on demonstrating "stability of institutions guaranteeing democracy"; but the EU is not an international agency, though the European Commission is.
3. The argument here draws on Henderson (1999, pp. 57–60).
4. As noted above, Esty appears uneasy about the fact that national and international civil servants are not elected persons. But any notion that they should be elected would be absurd.
5. In this connection, David Robertson has reported (Robertson 2000, p. 1132) his experience that "A search of NGOs' websites that claim to be part of 'civil society' does not reveal any that support liberal trade." The anti-liberal role of the NGOs in connection with the ill-fated Multilateral Agreement on Investment is reviewed in Henderson (1999).
6. In a White Paper issued in November 1996, the then (Conservative) British government formally endorsed the goal of global free trade by 2020. However, a different government came into office soon afterwards, and in any case the external trade regime of the UK has long been, aside from a few residual elements, that of the European Union as a whole. The White Paper appears to have left no trace on thinking or events.
7. Arguments and evidence in support of this statement are set out in Wolf (2001), in Chapter 5 of Henderson (2001), and in the final chapter of Sally (1998).
8. Such an assertion is to be found in a journal article on the WTO (Schoulte et al. 1999), where it is also stated that "Recent intensified globalization has broken the Westphalian mould of politics." All of this is pure fantasy.
9. Of course, today's argument for stronger global governance rests in part on the need to deal with external effects that are global rather than local, and in particular, to handle problems that could arise in connection with climate change. It is widely believed that greenhouse gas emissions should be substantially curbed, and the argument that this would require some form of binding international agreement is hard to question. But greenhouse gas emissions are not a product of closer international economic integration: they are generated in closed as well as open economies.
10. The Commission goes on to say that "global social governance" should take effect mainly through "the universal application of core labour standards."
11. The readiness of many MNEs to engage in appeasement of their critics and enemies has been treated in an incisive essay by Robert Halfon (1998), and in Henderson (2001) which further argues (1) that endorsement as well as appeasement may be involved, and (2) that generally speaking the contribution

of the international business world to public debate on leading current issues of economic policy has been inadequate or worse.

REFERENCES

Annan, K. (2001), "Laying the Foundations of a Fair and Free World Trade System," in Sampson (ed.), *The Role of the World Trade Organization in Global Governance*, Chapter 1.

Archer, C. (2001), *International Organizations*, Third Edition, London and New York: Routledge.

Blackhurst, R. (2001), "Reforming WTO Decision Making: Lessons from Singapore and Seattle," in K. G. Deutsch and B. Speyer (eds.), *The World Trade Organization Millennium Round: Freer Trade in the Twenty-first Century*, London and New York: Routledge.

Commission of the European Communities (2001), "Promoting Core Labour Standards and Improving Social Governance in the Context of Globalisation," a Communication from the Commission to the Council, the European Parliament, and the Economic and Social Committee, Brussels.

Esty, D. C. (2002), "The World Trade Organization's Legitimacy Crisis," *World Trade Review*, I (March): 7–22.

Halfon, R. (1998), *Corporate Irresponsibility: Is Business Appeasing Anti-business Activists?*, London: Social Affairs Unit.

Henderson, D. (1998), "International Agencies and Cross-Border Liberalization: The WTO in Context," in A. Krueger (ed.), *The WTO as an International Organization*, Chapter 3, Chicago: University of Chicago Press.

Henderson, D. (1999), *The MAI Affair: A Story and Its Lessons*, London: Royal Institute of International Affairs.

Henderson, D. (2001), *Misguided Virtue: False Notions of Corporate Social Responsibility*, London: Institute of Economic Affairs.

Hudec, R. E. (1999), *Essays on the Nature of International Trade Law*, London: Cameron and May.

International Labour Organisation (2002), *The ILO at Work: Factpack*, London: ILO.

Irwin, D. A. (2002), *Free Trade under Fire*, Princeton: Princeton University Press.

Jackson, J. (1995), "The World Trade Organization: Watershed Innovation or Cautious Small Step Forward?" *The World Economy*.

Kahler, M. (2001), *Leadership in the Major Multilaterals*, Washington, DC: Institute of International Economics.

Keohane, R. O. and J. S. Nye (2001), "The Club Model of Multilateral Cooperation and Problems of Democratic Legitimacy," in R. Porter et al. (eds.), *Efficiency, Equity and Legitimacy: The Multilateral Trading System at the Millennium*, Chapter 12, Washington, DC: Brookings Institution Press.

Letwin, W. A. (1989), "American Economic Policy, 1865–1939," in P. Mathias and S. Pollard (eds.), *The Cambridge Economic History of Europe*, Chapter IX, Vol. VIII, Cambridge: Cambridge University Press.

Loy, F. (2001), "Public Participation in the World Trade Organization," in Sampson (ed.), *The Role of the World Trade Organization in Global Governance*, Chapter 6.

Oxford English Dictionary (1989), Second Edition, Oxford: Clarendon Press.

Robertson, D. (2000), "Civil Society and the WTO," *The World Economy* 23 (September): 1119–1134.

Sally, R. (1998), *Classical Liberalism and International Economic Order: Studies in Theory and Intellectual History*, London and New York: Routledge.

Sampson, G. P. (2000), "The World Trade Organization after Seattle," *The World Economy* 23 (September): 1097–1117.

Sampson, G. P. (ed.) (2001), *The Role of the World Trade Organization in Global Governance*, Tokyo: United Nations University Press.

Schoulte, J. A., with R. O'Brien and M. Williams (1999), "The WTO and Civil Society," *Journal of World Trade* 33(1): 107–123.

Sutherland, P., J. Sewell and D. Weiner (2001), "Challenges Facing the WTO and Policies to Address Global Governance," in Sampson (ed.), *The Role of the World Trade Organization in Global Governance*, Chapter 5.

United Kingdom Government, Foreign and Commonwealth Office and Department of Trade and Industry (1996), *Free Trade and Foreign Policy: A Global Vision*, London: Her Majesty's Stationery Office.

Viner, J. (1947), "Conflicts of principle in drafting a trade charter," *Foreign Affairs*, XXV (July).

Webster's Third New International Dictionary (1961), Springfield: G. and C. Merriam.

Wolf, M. (2001a), "Will the Nation-State Survive Globalization?" *Foreign Affairs*, 80 (January–February): 178–190.

Wolf, M. (2001b), "What the World Needs from the Multilateral Trading System," in Sampson (ed.), *The Role of the World Trade Organization in Global Governance*, Chapter 9.

World Economic Forum (2002), *Annual Meeting 2002*, Cologny-Geneva: World Economic Forum.

CHAPTER 15

GOVERNMENTS MUST REGULATE MULTINATIONAL CORPORATIONS *v.* MULTINATIONAL CORPORATIONS CAN REGULATE THEMSELVES

Governments Must Regulate Multinational Corporations

Advocate: Daniel Litvin

Source: "Needed: A Global Business Code of Conduct," *Foreign Policy* 139 (November/December 2003): 68–72.

Multinational Corporations Can Be Encouraged to Regulate Themselves

Advocate: Gerri Gereffi, Ronie Garcia-Johnson, and Erika Sasser

Source: "The NGO-Industrial Complex," *Foreign Policy* 125 (July/August 2001): 56–65.

As multinational corporation (MNC) activity has increased, calls for global regulation of MNCs have also increased. Indeed, a central issue in the debate over globalization has been whether foreign direct investment and MNCs should be subject to international regulation and, if so, what this regulation should look like. Recent calls for effective regulation suggest that the issue is new; yet, for more than thirty years governments have been debating and negotiating common rules for MNCs with the United Nations, the General Agreement on Tariffs and Trade (GATT)/World Trade Organization (WTO), and the Organisation for Economic Co-operation and Development. Perhaps it is telling that they have not yet managed to agree on a comprehensive regulatory framework.

Such negotiations have moved along parallel tracks. On one track governments sought to craft international rules that limit governments' ability to restrict the activities of MNCs. On the other track, governments sought to establish rules that restrict the activities of MNCs. The goal of the first track, pushed hardest by western governments, is to make it easier for MNCs to operate in the global economy. The goal of the second track, pushed most forcefully by developing-country governments and by nongovernmental organizations, has been to create rules that compel MNCs to operate in a socially responsible fashion. The first track has been all but abandoned since the mid-1990s. The second track has received the most attention, and a central question in this regulatory discussion is whether governments must take the lead in crafting the required regulations or whether MNCs have incentive to police themselves.

GOVERNMENTS MUST REGULATE MULTINATIONAL CORPORATIONS

Advocates of government-crafted regulations governing MNC behavior desire ambitious rules establishing enforceable obligations for MNCs. NGOs active in this movement advocate international standards pertaining to the treatment of workers in developing countries, environmental practices, and human rights more generally. As Father Sergio Cobo, a member of the Catholic Agency for Overseas Development wrote, "We cannot be too idealistic in what we press for, but [MNCs] should be providing at least a minimum of basic human rights in the workplace. The obligations of the companies should include respect for the dignity of the person and acknowledgement of their social, economic, and cultural rights."[1]

Daniel Litvin pursues this line of argument. He calls for a strengthening of the codes of conduct developed by governments within the United Nations. These codes focus on human rights and other practices. Currently, adherence to these codes by MNCs is strictly voluntary. MNCs can elect to adhere to them, and MNCs are the sole enforcer of adherence to these codes. Litvin argues that governments, civil society, and businesses must work together to transform such codes into stricter and enforceable standards.

MULTINATIONAL CORPORATIONS CAN BE ENCOURAGED TO REGULATE THEMSELVES

Opponents of government-led efforts to regulate MNCs argue that such rules are potentially detrimental and possibly unnecessary. The strongest argument against such rules is that they can harm those they are most intended to protect. Relying on logic similar to that advanced by Paul Krugman in his argument in favor of sweatshops, opponents of MNC regulations suggest that tight standards could lead to less investment in developing countries. Less investment could in turn mean fewer jobs, and thus a larger number of people living in poverty. Moreover, some argue that government-imposed regulations may be unnecessary because MNCs can be encouraged to regulate themselves. As the public becomes more concerned about the labor and environmental practices of MNCs in developing societies, they will support companies with good practices

---

[1] Katherine Astill, *The Rough Guide to Multinational Corporations: A CAFOD Briefing* (London: Rough Guides Ltd, n.d.).

and boycott those with bad practices. Hence, market incentives—the desire to avoid being boycotted—may induce firms to regulate themselves.

Gary Gereffi, Ronie Garcia-Johnson, and Erika Sasser develop a variant of this argument here. They trace the development of these self-regulatory practices. They show how MNCs have written codes of conduct in response to public pressure and NGO campaigns. While highlighting the potential for self-regulation, the authors also highlight its limitations. They conclude by noting the apparent dilemma inherent in MNC regulations. It is clear that the traditional progressive solution, top-down regulation based on state intervention, is unlikely; consequently, NGOs typically skeptical about markets must rely more heavily on markets to achieve their objectives.

POINTS **TO PONDER**

1. In what specific ways is Litvin critical of the United Nations' "Global Compact" and "Norms"? What standards does he advocate in their place?

2. What are the strengths and weaknesses of third-party certification schemes?

3. What is the correct balance between market-based or voluntary standards and government-negotiated and -enforceable standards?

4. Do you agree that a compelling need for international regulation of MNC activity exists? Why or why not? If we assume a need does exist, should rules be created by governments or should MNCs and NGOs be left to work out standards that satisfy them both?

Daniel Litvin

Needed: A Global Business Code of Conduct

Memorandum:
To: U.N. Secretary-General Kofi Annan
From: Daniel Litvin
Re: Raising Human Rights Standards in the Private Sector

Ensuring that companies respect human rights is an important and controversial challenge, one in which the United Nations has a unique role to play. As you, Mr. Secretary-General, have recognized, maintaining broad political consensus in favor of globalization and increased flows of foreign investment is crucial to raising living standards in the developing world. In addition to being inexcusable, human rights transgressions by multinational corporations threaten this consensus by giving ammunition to the many groups opposed to further global integration.

This memorandum argues that the United Nations must develop new standards concerning the relationship between corporations and human rights. It recommends drafting a set of principles that is tough on multinationals and backed by an enforcement mechanism but that also recognizes the difficulties companies face. The two most recent U.N. initiatives in this area, the so-called "Global Compact" and the Human Rights Norms for Businesses (the "Norms," as they are now known), both lack this balanced approach.

The failure of these initiatives to set reasonable and well-defined limits on the human rights responsibilities of companies helps explain the current hostility of business lobbies to any effort to create an enforceable code of conduct. A more realistic and fair approach can resolve this problem and win the support of both businesses and nongovernmental organizations (NGOs).

What follows is a detailed look at the problem of human rights and multinationals; at the failure of U.N. efforts to address the problem; a proposed solution; and suggestions for that solution's implementation.

The Problem

Multinationals confer many benefits, but they also can cause or exacerbate a range of problems in the places they invest, particularly developing countries. At worst, these problems may include civil conflict, repression of minorities, abuse of workers' rights, and the perpetuation of abusive regimes (which obviously draw sustenance from foreign investment).

Only a tiny proportion of the world's 50,000-plus multinationals explicitly include respect for human rights in their codes of conduct, and among those that do, not many can claim to have honored this commitment in every aspect of their operations. Fully implementing a policy of social responsibility in a large, globally dispersed organization presents a genuine management challenge.

Even if multinationals were able to guarantee complete adherence to such a policy, how they would go about upholding human rights in practice is unclear, for the boundaries of their responsibility—where it begins and where it ends—are often undefined. This ambiguity is the nub of the problem.

Take the issue of labor exploitation. Most of the Western multinationals that have been accused in recent years of abusing workers (by employing underage children, for instance) did not actually commit violations themselves; rather, the guilty party was a supplier, or a supplier of a supplier. Multinationals certainly have some duty to try to prevent these abuses, but how far down the supply chain do their obligations extend?

Many human rights controversies involving multinationals can be attributed to the lack of a clear dividing line between the responsibilities of a company and a host government. No one disputes that companies ought to do everything they can to uphold the rights of their employees and of local communities and to generally be a force for good wherever they operate. But what that means in practice is unclear.

Should a company investing in a country where union organization is restricted—China, for example—contravene the law by hosting unauthorized unions in its factories? Is a company operating in a politically repressive state such as Burma, where a number of Western firms still have investments, obliged to petition the government on behalf of jailed dissidents?

Companies cannot simply ignore these issues, but limits to their responsibilities need to be set. At the root of these problems is the failure of states to protect adequately the rights of citizens. Profit-making enterprises have neither the expertise nor the capacity to supplant the role of government in this regard. Moreover, if a multinational were to intervene heavily in the internal affairs of a country, it would rightly be accused of neocolonialism.

Inadequate Solutions

The United Nations has made two recent attempts to establish a set of human rights and broader ethical standards for multinationals: the "Global Compact," which you unveiled at Davos in 1999 and which has now been embraced by over 1,000 companies; and the "Norms," adopted in August 2003 by the U.N. Sub-Commission on the Promotion and Protection of Human Rights. The first has been attacked for being too soft on business, the latter for being too tough, and unfortunately, these criticisms are well founded.

The "Global Compact" has had various successes. For example, it has encouraged many fruitful local partnerships on development issues among companies, labor organizations, and other groups. But the objection raised by NGOs—that the compact is toothless and allows multinationals to "blue-wash" themselves (that is, to gain favorable publicity by associating themselves with the United Nations without actually improving their behavior)—has merit, too.

Companies wishing to participate in this voluntary initiative face a relatively low set of hurdles: Their CEOs must write you a letter expressing support for the nine principles enunciated in the compact. The corporations must then "set in motion changes to business operations so that the Global Compact and its principles become part of strategy, culture, and day-to-day operations." But enforcement, such as it currently is, consists of a require-ment that firms describe in their annual reports the ways in which they are fulfilling their commitments.

Moreover, the two human rights provisions do little to define bound-aries for companies in this area, merely declaring that firms should support human rights "within their sphere of influence" and not be "complicit" in abuses. The supporting literature on the compact's Web site offers some sug-gestions for "possible actions" by companies in this respect—for example, that they undertake a "human rights assessment" of the situation in countries where they intend to do business. But obligations are not defined in any concrete fashion.

As for the "Norms," their weakness lies not so much in failing to define companies' responsibilities but in defining them too expansively. While declaring that governments have the "primary responsibility" for upholding human rights, the "Norms" list an array of rights that companies themselves must protect. However, little is said about how firms should behave when fulfillment of these obligations would force them to violate local laws or to demand changes in host government policy.

For instance, the "Norms" say that firms should not directly or indirectly benefit from abuses and that they should "contribute" to the realization of, among other things, "freedom of thought, conscience, and religion, and freedom of opinion and expression." This goal sounds admirable, but what does it actually mean? As a practical matter, how far is General Motors supposed to go in trying to support human rights in China? Should it break the law? Should it permit, for example, Falun Gong meetings at its Shanghai plant?

Furthermore, the "Norms" recommend that companies be subject to peri-odic monitoring by the United Nations and other national and international bodies and provide "reparation" should they fail to meet their responsibilities.

The long list of obligations, coupled with the threat of sanctions, suggests that even ethical firms could be held financially liable for myriad human rights abuses in countries in which they invest. Put another way, the "Norms" potentially could deter responsible firms from investing in precisely those developing countries where governance and human rights problems are most acute—a perverse result, given that these countries are also most likely to be in urgent need of foreign capital and of integration with the global economy.

The "Norms" approach has not been received warmly by business lobbies and is likely to encounter even stronger resistance when put before the full U.N. Commission on Human Rights. It confirms the corporate sector's worst fears: that multinationals will be held accountable for problems over which they have little, if any, influence.

A Better Solution

Corporations are generally averse to regulation and to proposals for binding international rules governing human rights. On the other hand, most CEOs are intelligent people; they understand that the issue of social responsibility is not going to disappear. They also recognize that without a more detailed code of conduct and some means of enforcement, charges leveled against companies will be adjudicated in the court of public opinion, where mitigating details count for little, where boundaries of corporate responsibility are defined by NGOs and other critics, and where firms are easily cast as ogres.

High-profile multinationals such as Shell and McDonald's have been vilified in recent years. Surely, it is a source of consternation to them that they are sometimes blamed for problems that are really the responsibilities of a host government and that they have been made symbols of corporate greed and callousness while less familiar firms often get away with worse sins.

In short, large, prominent firms have a strong incentive to create a global set of rules by which all multinationals should play—a set of rules that is fair, realistic, and, above all, clear. And obviously, corporate backing for any such initiative is essential if it is to work.

It is possible for the United Nations to develop a set of principles that is strict as well as enforceable and that commands the support of both NGOs and the business community. The details would need to be discussed carefully and hammered out partly through a process of consultation with the various lobbies and interests concerned. But the obligations and boundaries that might be placed on firms can be envisaged in general terms.

With regard to labor rights and supply chains, for example, companies above a certain size could be expected to demand appropriate standards of their immediate suppliers and to put in place basic monitoring systems to help guarantee these standards are being met. But they would have no obligation under these principles to ensure similar adherence from their suppliers' suppliers.

It would also be reasonable to expect companies to report to the United Nations substantial abuses perpetrated by host governments against local communities and to state publicly their opposition to such practices—but that should be the extent of their overt political involvement. With this issue and other equally knotty ones, the key will be to define obligations in such a way that they are politically and economically realistic but do not absolve multinationals of their responsibilities.

Making It Happen

The need for the United Nations to develop a balanced set of principles that elicit more than just a public relations response from multinationals is obvious. The question is how you, as secretary-general, can help the organization accomplish this task.

I would suggest you begin by establishing a timetable—by declaring that within, say, five years, you want the United Nations to have completed work on a new body of human rights commitments for multinationals and to have also conceived a means of enforcement to ensure compliance. You will need to mention enforcement to signal the seriousness of this endeavor but should not discuss the form it might take. (For the foreseeable future, the only politically practical enforcement mechanism may be a modest one—a U.N. rapporteur, for instance, to assess the behavior of a select number of firms each year.)

Drafting the new principles should be entrusted to a small, carefully selected group of experts from the business community, the NGO sector, the labor movement, and the United Nations itself. The participants should be equally drawn from the North and the South.

Once new standards have been agreed upon, the United Nations will need to secure the backing of the many multinationals and NGOs that have not participated in the drafting process. Assuming that the principles adequately address their interests and worries, it should be possible to get both sides to support the new rules. Governments will follow—although some developing countries may need reassurance that the code of conduct is not a rich world conspiracy to exclude them from Western markets but rather a means of ensuring the capital inflows they need.

If a way is found to bridge business and human rights concerns, the United Nations will have taken a big step toward building public trust in globalization and tempering some of its ill effects. And you, Mr. Secretary-General, will have secured a large part of your legacy.

Gary Gereffi, Ronie Garcia-Johnson, and Erika Sasser
The NGO-Industrial Complex

In April 2000, Starbucks Corporation announced it would buy coffee beans from importers who pay above market prices to small farmers (so-called fair trade beans) and sell them in more than 2,000 of its shops across the United States. In August of the same year, the McDonald's Corporation sent a letter to the producers of the nearly 2 billion eggs it buys annually, ordering them to comply with strict guidelines for the humane treatment of hens or risk losing the company's business. And in 1998, De Beers Consolidated Mines, the company that controls two-thirds of the world trade in uncut diamonds, began investing heavily in Canada to distance itself from the controversy surrounding "blood diamonds"—gems sold to finance warring rebel factions in Africa.

Are these episodes sudden attacks of conscience on the part of the world's top CEOs? Not quite. Under increasing pressure from environmental and labor activists, multilateral organizations, and regulatory agencies in their home countries, multinational firms are implementing "certification" arrangements—codes of conduct, production guidelines, and monitoring standards that govern and attest to not only the corporations' behavior but also to that of their suppliers around the world. Champions of these new mechanisms include United Nations Secretary-General Kofi Annan, who in January 1999 exhorted world business leaders to "embrace and enact" the U.N. Global Compact, whose nine principles covering human rights, labor, and the environment "unite the powers of markets with the authority of universal ideals."

Certification has appeared in almost every major industry targeted by environmentalists, including the chemical, coffee, forest products, oil, mining, nuclear power, and transportation sectors. Certification is also prevalent in the apparel, diamond, footwear, and toy industries, to name a few. A recent inventory by the Organisation for Economic Co-operation and Development (OECD) listed 246 codes of corporate conduct, while the Global Reporting Initiative, an organization dedicated to standardizing corporate sustainability reporting, estimates that more than 2,000 companies voluntarily report their social, environmental, and economic practice and performance.

Supporters believe that certification efforts embody a new model for global corporate governance—no mean feat when national governments appear unable to constrain powerful multinational corporations. Nevertheless, even while early signs suggest that certification arrangements may indeed improve working conditions and promote more environmentally friendly production, certification remains a blunt and imperfect tool for augmenting the accountability of global firms. Proliferating certification arrangements compete for legitimacy with non-governmental organizations (NGOs) and consumers, as well as for adoption by multinationals. And there is no guarantee that the most effective standards—in environmental or labor terms—will win these battles. Some observers even fear that certification driven by activists and corporations will preempt or supplant altogether the role of states and international organizations in addressing corporate accountability as free trade expands around the globe.

Manufacturing Shame

Certification institutions have two key components: a set of rules, principles, or guidelines (usually in the form of a code of conduct) and a reporting or monitoring mechanism (often a corporate environmental report, or a "social audit"). Certification can be broken down into four broad categories, according to who produces the guidelines and conducts the monitoring:

First-party certification is the most common variety, whereby a single firm develops its own rules and reports on compliance. For instance, the Johnson & Johnson company credo that General Robert Wood Johnson wrote in 1943, which bolstered the company during the Tylenol® crises of the 1980s, now includes environmental and social concerns. The company published its first Social Contributions Report in 1992 and its first Environmental, Health & Safety Report in 1993.

Second-party certification involves an industry or trade association fashioning a code of conduct and implementing reporting mechanisms. The chemical industry's global Responsible Care® program provides an apt example. During the initiative's early years in the United States, the Chemical Manufacturers Association (now known as the American Chemistry Council) developed environmental, health, and safety principles and codes, required participating firms to submit implementation reports, and reported aggregate industry progress.

Third-party certification involves an external group, often an NGO, imposing its rules and compliance methods onto a particular firm or industry. The Council on Economic Priorities (CEP), the pioneering New York–based NGO, has collected data on corporate activities since its creation in 1969 and publishes reports on corporate behavior. The CEP (recently renamed the Center for Responsibility in Business) created an accreditation agency that designed auditable standards and an independent use accreditation process for the protection of workers' rights, dubbed Social Accountability 8000 (SA8000). As of April 2001, the group certified 66 manufacturing facilities around the world that mainly make toys and apparel as SA8000-compliant.

Fourth-party certification involves government or multilateral agencies. The United Nations' Global Compact, for instance, lists environmental, labor, and human rights principles for companies to follow; participating corporations must submit online updates of their progress for NGOs to scrutinize.

The earliest efforts to set and monitor voluntary standards in the United States were prompted, quite literally, by accident; they were responses to industrial mishaps in the environmental arena. After the Three Mile Island incident in 1979, the U.S. nuclear power industry created the Institute of Nuclear Power Operations, an organization that privately evaluates the industry through the provision of standards and inspections. Similarly, the 1986 Chernobyl accident prompted a handful of nuclear power associations from the United States and Europe to create the World Association of Nuclear Operators. And the chemical industry's Responsible Care initiative emerged in Canada and then the United States after the 1984 disaster that killed some 2,500 people and injured many more at a Union Carbide subsidiary in Bhopal, India. By April 2001, chemical industry associations in 46 countries had adopted the initiative, which promotes improvement in environment, health, and safety performance for the industry.

Over time, however, certification arrangements became more proactive and preemptive, with NGOs no longer waiting for accidents but rather seeking out ongoing corporate wrongdoing. Labor-based certification in particular emerged in response to exposés against top brand-name companies that use international contractors and sub-contractors, such as Wal-Mart Stores in Honduras and Bangladesh, the Walt Disney Company in Haiti, Mattel in China, Nike in Indonesia, J.C. Penney Company and Kmart Corporation in Nicaragua, and Liz Claiborne Inc. and Gap Inc. in El Salvador. The most typical abuses included abysmally low wages, use of child labor, mistreatment of female workers, and the suppression of labor unions. Levi Strauss & Co. issued a code of conduct in 1991, and other apparel industry giants such as Liz Claiborne, Nike, Reebok, and Gap Inc. soon followed. These codes included prohibitions on child labor and forced labor, guarantees of nondiscrimination in the workplace, respect for prevailing national legislation, and "decent" remuneration at or above the local minimum wage. Industry associations and other groups developed similar policies: For instance, the International Federation of Football Association (FIFA) created a licensing program in 1996 to prevent members from using soccer balls made with child labor.

While this history shows that most certification institutions began as creations of advanced industrial countries—particularly the United States, where direct government intervention is universally maligned and corporate accountability movements are increasingly powerful—it should come as no surprise that businesses and NGOs alike are taking their U.S.-based certification solutions global. As activist networks expand and social and environmental concern spreads in country after country, major multinationals hope to reassure their customers at home while surpassing the expectations of overseas governments that have weak or unenforced laws. Creating or participating in voluntary certification initiatives may allow entire industries to preempt the development of international labor and environmental laws directed at multinational companies, and to avoid a nightmarish scenario of stringent and often contradictory regulations in country after country.

It's Not Easy Being Green

Do certification arrangements really affect corporate behavior? The answer depends on the particular industry, the ability of NGOs to mobilize effectively, and the unique interests of the groups involved. Although still relatively recent phenomena, the certification experiences of the forest products and apparel industries reveal how certification can compel companies to rethink their practices.

Forest Certification

As the extent of global forest destruction became more apparent during the 1970s and 1980s, so did concerns over the environmental impacts of deforestation, clear-cutting, loss of bio-diversity, and the effluent from pulp and paper mills. However, well-organized, developed-country NGOs that focused on protecting tropical forests in developing economies found it difficult to identify which firms operating in endangered forests were actually inflicting damage. Forest certification emerged in response to this need.

The race to certify began in 1993, when powerful NGOs such as the World Wildlife Fund and Greenpeace created the Forest Stewardship Council (FSC). The FSC accepts no funding from industry and has developed a set of core principles guiding on-the-ground timber management and harvesting operations, including restrictions on pesticide use and requirements for bio-diversity protection and erosion control. Firms seeking FSC approval must undergo an audit by one of a few accredited "certifiers"— private firms such as SmartWood and Scientific Certification Systems in the United States and the Silva Forest Foundation in Canada—which can verify compliance with FSC requirements. The FSC also offers "chain-of-custody" certification, which traces the amount of certified wood in a product from the forest floor to the consumer shelf. (Chain-of-custody accounting is particularly difficult for products, such as paper, made from multiple sources.) Corporations meeting the chain-of-custody requirements are allowed to display the FSC logo on their products.

Arguing that the FSC guidelines are onerous and unwieldy, the timber industries in the United States, Canada, and Europe quickly countered with their own templates for appropriate forestry practices. Today, more than 40 certification programs exist worldwide, most of them at the national level. Timber companies often establish umbrella certification programs through their national industry associations rather than develop firm-specific certification programs because they face a "shared reputation" problem: Consumers don't necessarily distinguish between wood harvested by Georgia-Pacific and International Paper, for instance, so individual action does little to solidify a green reputation.

The contrast between industry-led certification and the NGO variety is stark. Consider the differences between the FSC and the Sustainable Forestry Initiative (SFI) program, established by the industry's American Forest and Paper Association in 1994. As originally conceptualized, the SFI program required firms only to develop internal mechanisms to meet the SFI program's broad, overarching objectives of ensuring long-term forest productivity and conservation of forest resources. Firms themselves conducted monitoring and enforcement. And because the original SFI program standards mandated few particular forest-management techniques, firms enjoyed tremendous freedom to set their own management specifications. This leeway led to significant differences in the environmental standards established by different firms. Furthermore, the SFI program has not conducted chain-of-custody monitoring and has only recently revealed plans to introduce a labeling system for products. Since the firms supply compliance reports privately to the industry association, accountability to consumers and the public remains minimal.

However, under heavy criticism from environmental groups, the industry has gradually encompassed more stringent standards and encouraged independent monitoring. The firms that felt the pressure most keenly were not timber extractors such as Georgia-Pacific, Weyerhaeuser, and International Paper, but retailers, specifically the big do-it-yourself centers such as The Home Depot and Lowe's Home Improvement Warehouse stores. The Rainforest Action Network, Greenpeace, Natural Resources Defense Council, and other NGOs launched major grass-roots campaigns against these retail giants in the late 1990s. Ultimately, both Home Depot (August 1999) and Lowe's (August 2000) declared their preference for FSC-certified products, a blow to the industry groups who hoped for the adoption of the SFI program. With the credibility of their certification program at stake, the industry had little choice but to push standards toward FSC levels.

Apparel Certification

Aggressive campaigns by labor groups, NGOs, and student activists have compelled apparel corporations to adopt stringent codes of conduct and establish independent monitoring as well. The revelation in 1995 of the virtual enslavement of Thai workers in a garment factory in El Monte, California, prompted the Clinton administration to form a task force called the Apparel Industry Partnership (AIP). Made up of manufacturers, NGOs, unions, and U.S. Department of Labor representatives, the AIP forged a code of conduct for apparel firms, stipulating that companies pay the local minimum or prevailing wage, that workers be at least 14 years old, and that employees work no more than 60 hours per week (although they could work unlimited voluntary hours). In November 1998, the AIP created the Fair Labor Association (FLA) to implement and monitor this code of conduct.

Controversy arose when several unions and NGOs withdrew from the AIP, claiming that its provisions were too weak (they relied on voluntary enforcement and set no standard for a living wage) and that its monitoring was neither independent nor transparent (its external-inspection system gave manufacturers too much control over which factories were investigated and by whom, and its monitoring reports did not have to be released to the public). The industry-backed FLA has attempted to address the concerns of the student antisweatshop movement that gained momentum through demonstrations at several U.S. universities such as Duke, Georgetown, Notre Dame, and Wisconsin in 1997 and 1998. The FLA, which plans to begin certifying manufacturers by the end of 2001, calls for internal monitoring as well as external surveillance from an FLA-approved list of monitors, who will conduct announced and unannounced factory visits.

Some student activists sided with the criticisms of the unions and NGOs, leading the United Students Against Sweatshops (in collaboration with university administrators and labor-rights experts) to establish the Worker Rights Consortium (WRC) in 2000 as a more radical alternative. With support from the AFL-CIO and the Union of Needleworkers, Industrial, and Textile Employees (UNITE), the WRC advocates a living wage for garment workers, independent unions, unannounced factory investigations, and full disclosure of factory conditions. The WRC has support from more than 80 universities, compared with the 155 universities that have signed on with the FLA.

Notwithstanding the infighting among competing certification groups, codes of conduct and effective independent monitoring have led global apparel firms to change their behavior. Take the case of Gap Inc., which acquires a portion of its clothing in Central America. In 1995, one of Gap Inc.'s apparel contractors in El Salvador, Mandarin International, fired 350 workers when they formed a union to protest working conditions. This dismissal, plus numerous other abuses exposed in the factory, violated Gap Inc.'s well-publicized code of conduct. Instead of simply rescinding its contract with Mandarin, which would have left the garment workers without jobs, Gap Inc.—under considerable pressure from NGOs such as the National Labor Committee, a union-backed worker advocacy group that organized a U.S. speaking tour for several of the fired female Salvadoran workers—became the first retailer to agree to independent monitoring of a foreign contractor. This agreement was considered a major breakthrough in apparel certification. While the monitoring agency (called the Independent Monitoring Group of El Salvador) has improved working conditions in the Mandarin factory in El Salvador, Gap Inc.

has so far allowed independent monitoring of its codes of conduct in only a handful of the 55 countries where it does business (other sites are monitored in Honduras and Guatemala).

The WRC recently adopted a similar interventionist approach with Nike in Mexico. In January 2001, a large number of the 850 workers at the Korean-owned-and-operated Kukdong International factory in Puebla, Mexico—which produces Nike and Reebok sweat shirts for the $2.5 billion annual collegiate market—staged a work stoppage to protest the firing of five workers who opposed poor labor conditions. Operations in the Kukdong apparel factory violated a number of provisions in Nike's code of conduct, including freedom of association, harassment and abuse, and health and safety conditions. By early February, the independent monitoring organization, Verité, an Amherst, Massachusetts, nonprofit, sent a five-person team to Kukdong to examine the factory's workplace practices. The Verité factory evaluation report was completed and made public in a matter of weeks, and on March 14, 2001, Nike released its plan outlining the corrective actions and a timetable for Kukdong to comply with Nike's code of conduct. Just one week after the strike, nearly two thirds of the factory workers were back on the job.

Of course, companies do not always deal with factory abuses so readily. In February 2001, the Global Alliance for Workers and Communities released a 106-page, Nike-funded report on the labor conditions at nine Nike contract factories in Indonesia. The report detailed a variety of labor problems, including low wages, denial of the right to unionize, verbal and physical abuse by supervisors, sexual harassment, and forced overtime. The contents of the report are not surprising; similar findings were asserted throughout the 1990s. What is new about this report is that Nike paid for it, released it—and can't deny it. Nike's response to these problems will set new benchmarks that other apparel and footwear companies must match or else risk incurring relentless scrutiny by industry critics.

Although definitive conclusions may be premature, the forestry and apparel experiences underscore the growing power of NGOs to compel corporations to adopt new environmental and labor standards. In particular, NGOs have become highly sophisticated in using market-campaigning techniques to gain leverage over recalcitrant firms. Market campaigning, which focuses protests against highly visible branded retailers, is only about 10 years old, but in the words of one Greenpeace activist, "it was like discovering gunpowder for environmentalists." By targeting firms such as Gap Inc. or Home Depot—firms at the retail end of the supply chain with direct links to customers—NGOs are able to wield the power and vulnerability of corporate brand names to their advantage. Where resource-extractive firms like timber giant Georgia-Pacific may be isolated from consumers and thus insulated from negative press, companies such as Staples Inc. (a current Rainforest Action Network target) are much more vulnerable. By using tactics such as boycotts, banner hangings, leafleting, and other direct action, NGOs force retailers to take proactive labor and environmental stances.

The Certification Solution

The strength and influence of certification programs seem to be increasing. Third-party certification and monitoring may soon become the norm in many global industries. The battles over forest-product certification show that consumers and NGOs can quickly delegitimize weak standards and inadequate enforcement mechanisms, and they can also mobilize effectively for more stringent codes of conduct and more reliable monitoring. Corporations in the apparel industry are making concessions that would have been unthinkable just a few years ago as they too advocate third-party arrangements. Even the chemical industry's Responsible Care initiative is considering third-party verification.

Yet, watchdog activists cannot press for change in every industry and at all times. In the absence of their efforts, market forces and the drive toward standardization may lead firms to accept lowest-common-denominator certification, particularly when industry moves first and establishes a certification arrangement with widespread global membership. While competition can foster higher industry standards, less pressure will leave companies room to dictate their own terms of compliance. And even the most stringent certification initiatives may fail to address fundamental questions about industry structures, such as the international subcontracting system that allows brand-name companies, such as Nike or Gap Inc., to control their suppliers through large orders without the legal responsibilities that go with factory ownership.

More fundamentally, the rise of certification institutions poses profound dilemmas for the progressive notion popular during the 20th century that the remedy for social and environmental problems was a stronger and more interventionist state. When the state proved unable to meet all the demands placed upon it, particularly as firms and business transactions moved outside national territorial boundaries, alternative solutions were sought. Trends in the past decade suggest a new response in the 21st century: the certification solution. Whether certification programs are developed by business associations or pushed by activist NGOs, the development of voluntary governance mechanisms is transforming traditional power relationships in the global arena. Linking together diverse and often antagonistic actors from the local, national, and international levels, certification institutions have arisen to govern firm behavior in a global space that has eluded the control of states and international organizations.

While certification will never replace the state, it is quickly becoming a powerful tool for promoting worker rights and protecting the environment in an era of free trade. These new mechanisms of transnational private governance exist alongside and within national and international regimes like the North American Free Trade Agreement, complementing and, in some cases, bolstering their efforts. In countries with stringent, rigorously enforced labor and environmental laws, certification provides a private layer of governance that moves beyond state borders to shape global supply chains. In countries with nascent or ineffective labor and environmental legislation, certification can draw attention to uneven standards and help mitigate these disparities. The challenge is for states to accept certification not as a threat but as an opportunity to reinforce labor and environmental goals within their sovereign territory and beyond.

CHAPTER 16

COMMON *v.* NEW REGULATIONS FOR INTERNATIONAL FINANCE

We Need Common Regulations for International Finance

Advocate: Stijn Claessens

Source: "The New International Financial Architecture Requires Better Governance," in *What G20 Leaders Must Do to Stabilise Our Economy and Fix the Financial System*, ed. Barry Eichengreen and Richard Baldwin, 29–32 (Brussels: VoxEU.org, 2008).

We Need a New Process for Regulating Financial Institutions

Advocate: Barry Eichengreen

Source: "Not a New Bretton Woods but a New Bretton Woods Process," in *What G20 Leaders Must Do to Stabilise Our Economy and Fix the Financial System*, ed. Barry Eichengreen and Richard Baldwin, 25–27 (Brussels: VoxEU.org, 2008).

Every crisis of major proportions to strike the international financial and monetary systems is followed by calls for new and more effective international regulation. The 1997 Asian crisis provoked a long discussion about creating a new international financial architecture. The Latin American debt crisis provoked efforts to create common capital standards for commercial banks. The collapse of the Bretton Woods system in the early 1970s generated efforts to create a new international monetary system. And the Bretton Woods system itself was a reaction to interwar financial and monetary instability. The most recent crisis, that stemming from the collapse of the real estate bubble in the United States in 2007 and 2008 is thus only the most recent instance of a recurring dynamic.

In each case, including the current case, policy-makers and scholars alike conclude that the current financial crisis is evidence of a regulatory failure. In the current crisis, policy-makers focus on weaknesses in government regulations of the mortgage-backed securities and credit default swaps that have been the financial instruments most directly associated with the crisis. The case for regulation rests on the belief that, had regulators devised rules that more effectively required private financial institutions to minimize the risks they accepted as buyers and sellers of these instruments, the crisis could have been avoided. Current debate really revolves not so much around whether more effective regulation is required, but the specific form it should take.

WE NEED COMMON REGULATIONS FOR INTERNATIONAL FINANCE

Some observers argue that, in a world of global finance but national governance, financial institutions must be subject to common regulatory standards. In the absence of common regulation, financial institutions will engage in regulatory arbitrage by moving their operations to the lowest-regulation jurisdiction. Such arbitrage will provoke a race to the bottom. Avoiding such outcomes requires governments agree to and then enforce a common regulatory framework.

Stijn Claessens develops the case for a common regulatory framework. Noting that the current crisis merely makes obvious the need for better regulation, he proceeds to argue that providing such better regulation will require new ideas. He emphasizes the need for a common regulatory standard rather coordinated national standards. He also argues that the system needs an expanded lender of last resort.

WE NEED A NEW PROCESS FOR REGULATING FINANCIAL INSTITUTIONS

Other observers have placed greater emphasis on the need for new organizations and processes than new common rules. So long as governments retain sovereignty, they are unlikely to transfer their right to regulate national financial institutions. Consequently, even if a single international regulatory regime would be optimal, it lacks political feasibility. In its place governments should create an effective regulatory process that would promote adherence to general principles such as best practices for accounting and risk management, transparency of assets and liabilities, and so forth. Individual governments would be allowed to translate these broad principles into specific regulations as they best see fit.

Barry Eichengreen develops this perspective. Calling for the creation of a "World Financial Organization" (WFO), he argues that what is most needed is information sharing and discussion. A WFO could promote this by requiring governments to join the organization before their national banks can participate in global markets. The WFO could then function as an "independent body of experts" to evaluate and communicate the soundness of the regulatory practices in each country. Eichengreen argues that governments would join the system because it would enable them to maintain full regulatory autonomy but also provide valuable information about financial stability in other countries.

POINTS TO PONDER

1. How much difference in regulatory outcomes do you think there would be between a system based on Claessen's common standard approach and one based on Eichengreen's common process approach?

2. Eichengreen argues that a WFO is more feasible politically than the adoption of a single global regulatory regime. Do you agree or disagree? Why?

3. Both authors agree that better financial regulation will make financial crises less likely. Do you agree or disagree? What might Jagdish Bhagwati say (see chapter 13)?

Stijn Claessens

The New International Financial Architecture Requires Better Governance

New rules and institutions are needed to reduce systemic risks, improve financial intermediation, and properly adjust the perimeter of regulation and supervision. This could mean an 'International Bank Charter' for the world's largest, most international banks with accompanying regulation and supervision, liquidity support, and remedial actions as well as post-insolvency recapitalization funds in case things go wrong. The starting point, however, has to be a change in the governance of the international financial system.

As Heads of State gather in Washington, DC on November 15th to discuss the new international financial architecture, four questions should be on the agenda:

1. How can we improve financial regulation, as the systemic nature of the crisis shows that current approaches lag behind events?
2. How can we improve regulatory practices and information, as current approaches differ too much across countries and information gaps have been widening?
3. How can we design better liquidity mechanisms at a global scale to prevent spillovers from becoming solvency issues?
4. How can we ensure greater coordination and burden sharing, especially when financial institutions fail?

No doubt, leaders will conclude that this agenda will have to be addressed in phases and more background work and meetings will be necessary. And the ongoing economic and financial crises may force them into some emergency policy making.

But, perhaps they can at least agree on the most important starting point—reforming the governance of the international financial system. Better governance is needed for various reasons—it comes back under each question—and any new architecture needs broad legitimacy. Maybe the governance reform can start at this G20 Summit, in part since more than the usual number of countries will be present.

Better Regulation was Needed Long Ago; The Crisis Makes it Obvious

Financial innovation and integration have increased the speed and extent to which shocks are being transmitted across asset classes and countries. Innovation and integration have blurred boundaries, including between systemic and non-systemic institutions.

New rules and institutions are needed to reduce systemic risks, improve financial intermediation, and properly adjust the perimeter of regulation and supervision—all this without imposing unnecessary burdens. Accomplishing this task will require much new thinking. Designing counter-cyclical, macro-prudential rules and reducing systemic risk are particularly difficult. Designing such rules involves important governance issues. What processes will be followed for the development of the rules, standards and best practices? Will it again be done in small groupings of policymakers from advanced countries, with much private sector influence, or will it be more balanced this time, representing broader interests?

Regulatory convergence is not enough, common practices are needed

Broad participation in rulemaking will help as it increases legitimacy and eases the enforcement of rules. But it will not suffice; assessments of practices are still needed. The market can do some of this, but the crisis has again confirmed the need for public sector involvement. Here governance issues must be addressed: What form should this monitoring of regulators and regulation take? Who should do it, how should it be governed, and how should flags be raised when rules are not followed or practices fall behind?

More information and enhanced liquidity provisions

The crisis has highlighted the size of information gaps we face, both nationally and internationally. More and better information is needed if markets and authorities are to better assess the build-up of systemic risk. Addressing this requires a review of rules on transparency, disclosure and reporting. Information requirements will also need to cover a much larger set of institutions ranging from insurance companies to hedge funds, and off-balance sheet entities. More information will not emerge by itself. Moreover, the temptation will be to hoard new information, so proper governance structures are needed to ensure sufficient information is available to those who need it.

The current crisis has shown that in times of turmoil, even among developed countries, liquidity provision for financial institutions is not efficient, leading to confusion and higher costs. For emerging markets and developing countries, a temporary shortage of liquidity can be even worse. Again today, as has happened before, foreign investors are rapidly reducing their exposures and many countries, even those with otherwise good fundamentals, are greatly suffering from "sudden stops". These liquidity strains easily become solvency crises if not dealt with swiftly and effectively.

The Lack of a Sufficiently Large, Global Liquidity Provider

The IMF's resources are too small in today's world. Advanced countries' central banks swap lines are to date only available for some emerging countries. While regional pools of reserves, such as in Asia, provide a backstop, they can be too small. These approaches could be broadened and expanded: the Fund can get more money; greater coordination on swaps can be pursued; and larger pools of central bank money can be created. Fixing this again entails governance since what is crucial in the end is who gets to decide on liquidity provision. The fact that bilateral and regional approaches dominate so far suggests that truly multilateral solutions, with attendant risk-sharing and pooling benefits, are still viewed with some skepticism. Again better governance arrangements can make for improved outcomes.

In the end, many international financial architecture questions relate to burden-sharing. Consider the issue of international financial institutions. The crisis has clearly underscored the tension with regard to both risk prevention and crisis management between nationally bounded supervisors and large financial institutions that transcend national borders, have extensive operations across a large swathe of countries, and can be major transmitters of shocks. The tension is most evident in the resolution of global banks headquartered in relatively small countries that have balance sheets exceeding their home-country's GDP [gross domestic product]. Few single countries can deal with such institutions on their own, yet they affect many markets. Clearly, in this crisis, and even more so going forward as they will keep getting larger, a better method has to be found to handle these institutions.

A New Regime for Large, International Banks

One internally consistent approach, perhaps the only one, is to establish a separate regime for large, internationally active financial institutions. This could mean an "International Bank Charter" with accompanying regulation and supervision, liquidity support, remedial actions, as well as post-insolvency recapitalization fund in case things go wrong.

The idea is that a separate international college of supervisors, with professionals recruited internationally, would regulate, license and supervise these institutions. The arsenal of remedial actions available to supervisors would include: limits on operations, risk-taking, and capital as well as cease-and-desist orders. These actions should be as rule-bound as possible. The recapitalization fund could be fed by a fee paid by these banks themselves. Like a deposit insurance agency, the fund would need callable capital from its shareholders, the governments sponsoring the concept, with contributions based on, say, on GDP (since the ultimate gains relate to the real economy). In exchange for subjecting themselves to this regime, these banks could operate around the world without any further permission (except for country-specific requirements, such as macro-prudential requirements to mitigate booms or systemic risks).

This approach would differ from the ones tried and tested, but which have often failed in past (e.g. the messy constellation of home and host supervision in various Basel agreements). It would get around the problem that coordination is hard to agree on ex-ante, especially of actions aimed at containing and resolving a crisis. In the current crisis, as in the past, actions regarding large institutions were largely determined ex-post, and aimed only at (near) insolvent institutions, rather than being pre-emptive. While eventually there were more concerted and coordinated interventions, these happened only under great financial duress, were sometimes undone, and created unexpected repercussions in other markets.

A common and well resourced regulator is a much better solution; coordination is assured, and if intervention is necessary the regulator's powers are backed by sufficient resources to make it credible.

Author's note: The views expressed in this paper are those of the author and do not necessarily represent those of the IMF or IMF policy.

Barry Eichengreen

Not a New Bretton Woods but a New Bretton Woods Process

The November 15th meeting should explore the idea of a new "World Financial Organization" that, like the WTO [World Trade Organization], would blend national sovereignty with globally agreed rules on obligations for supervision and regulation. It should agree to immediately boost the IMF [International Monetary Fund]'s lending capacity, with nations like China contributing in exchange for a revamping of the old G7/8 group into a new G7 (US, EU [European Union], Japan, China, Saudi Arabia, South Africa and Brazil) that would provide a proper global steering committee.

Now that the quashing of excessive expectations is complete, it is time to ask what can realistically be accomplished by heads of state meeting in Washington on November 15th.

Basic orientations should be obvious.

1. Leaders should focus on financial stability.
2. They should commit to a series of meetings.
3. They should strive for a process rather than a quick, hollow agreement.
4. They should acknowledge that consensus, like Rome, is not built in a day.

Central Challenge: Consistent Supervision and Regulation with Comprehensive Coverage

Their central challenge is how to ensure comprehensive and consistent supervision and regulation of all systemically significant financial institutions, and cross-border financial institutions in particular. The crisis is a reminder that inadequate supervision at the national level can have global repercussions. Addressing this problem is the single most important step they can take to make the world a safer financial place.

There will be calls for a global regulator, echoing proposals for a World Financial Authority by John Eatwell and Lance Taylor a decade ago. But it is unrealistic to imagine that the US and for that matter any country will turn over the conduct of national financial regulation to an international body. (The US has already signaled its position on this question.) Regulation of financial markets is a valued national prerogative. Not even EU member states have been willing to agree to a single regulator. In any case there is the particularity of national financial structures, which places effective oversight beyond the grasp of any global body.

Create a "World Financial Organization" in the Image of the WTO

The European proposal for squaring this circle by creating a College of Regulators is weak soup. We need more than information sharing and discussions. Better would be to strive to create a World Financial Organization analogous to the World Trade Organization. Countries seeking access to foreign markets for financial institutions they charter would have to become members of the WFO. They would have to meet the obligations for supervision and regulation set out in its charter and supplementary agreements. But how they do so would be up to them. This would permit regulation to be tailored to the structure of individual financial markets.

An independent body of experts, not unlike the WTO's Dispute Settlement panels, would then decide whether countries have met their obligations. A finding of lax implementation would have consequences. Specifically, other countries could prohibit banks chartered in countries found to be in violation from operating in their markets. This would protect them from the destructive spillovers of poor regulation.

It would also foster a political economy of compliance. Governments seeking to secure market access for their banks would have an incentive to upgrade supervisory practice. Resident financial institutions desirous of operating abroad would be among those lobbying for the requisite reforms.

Would the US Accept a WFO?

Skeptics will question whether countries like the United States would ever accept having an independent panel of experts declaring the US regulatory regime to be inadequate and authorizing sanctions. But this is just what the WTO's independent dispute settlement panel does in the case of the trade regime. Why should finance be different?

Creation of a WFO is not a be-all and end-all. Trading in derivative securities should be moved onto an organized exchange to limit counterparty risk. Basel II should be urgently reformed to raise accepted measures of capital adequacy, reduce reliance on commercial credit ratings and banks' models of value at risk, and add a simple leverage ratio. These steps can and should be taken relatively quickly. But commencing negotiations on a World Financial Authority would be the most important single step.

Why a New International Organisation?

It would be preferable to create the WFO as a new entity rather than building it on the platform of an existing institution—like the IMF or the Financial Stability Forum. The Financial Stability Forum is dominated by the

G7 and the various international organizations with only Hong Kong and Singapore as token "emerging-market members." The IMF has the advantage of universal membership, but its past capital-market surveillance has not exactly covered it in glory. The Fund continues to be regarded with suspicion in Asia and Latin America. Countries there would be reluctant to sign up to a World Financial Authority that was a wholly owned and operated subsidiary of the IMF. This reality is also evident in the reluctance of governments like China's to deploy their reserves in support of other countries by channeling them through the Fund.

The Other Key Challenge: Boost the IMF's Lending Capacity

This brings us to the other key challenge that must be met to make the world a safer financial place: mobilizing the resources, both financial and political, of emerging markets. The IMF desperately needs additional funding to aid crisis economies, and governments like China's are the logical contributors. The question is what to give them in return.

We cannot afford another inconclusive multi-year negotiation of new IMF quotas. More effective would be for the US, Europe and Japan to agree to abandon the G7/8, which is no longer a suitable steering committee for the world economy, in favor of a new G7 composed of the US, the EU, Japan, China, Saudi Arabia, South Africa and Brazil. This would not require negotiations among hundreds of countries stretching over a period of years—time which is not available given the urgency of the task. It would give China and the others a seat at a table that really matters. It would give them ownership and the sense that they have a stake in the stability of the global economy. This would not exactly be a club of democracies, but then it was the 'talk-to-who-matters' man and not the 'club-of-democracies' man who won the US election.

In addition, Europe could agree to a single executive director on the IMF board, freeing up directorships for emerging markets. And who better than a far-sighted European leader like Dominique Strauss-Kahn to announce that leadership of the Fund should be thrown open to the most qualified candidate regardless of nationality? But while all this would be helpful, creating a new G7 would be the most important single step.

Starting on November 15th, everyone will roll out their pet ideas, from a substantial revaluation of the renminbi to a global system of target zones to a single world currency. (You know who you are!) But it is important to avoid non-starters and superfluous initiatives. Creating a new G7 now and committing to establish a World Financial Organization soon are the ways forward.

CREDITS